RSF: The Russell Sage Foundation Journal of the Social Sciences

The Elementary and Secondary Education Act at Fifty and Beyond

VOLUME 1 • NUMBER 3 • DECEMBER 2015

RSF: The Russell Sage Foundation Journal of the Social Sciences   ISSN 2377-8261

The Russell Sage Foundation

The Russell Sage Foundation, one of the oldest of America's general purpose foundations, was established in 1907 by Mrs. Margaret Olivia Sage for "the improvement of social and living conditions in the United States." The foundation seeks to fulfill this mandate by fostering the development and dissemination of knowledge about the country's political, social, and economic problems. While the foundation endeavors to assure the accuracy and objectivity of each book it publishes, the conclusions and interpretations in Russell Sage Foundation publications are those of the authors and not of the foundation, its trustees, or its staff. Publication by Russell Sage, therefore, does not imply foundation endorsement.

Board of Trustees

Sara S. McLanahan, *Chair*
Larry M. Bartels
Karen S. Cook
W. Bowman Cutter III
Sheldon H. Danziger
Kathryn Edin
Lawrence F. Katz
David Laibson
Nicholas Lemann
Peter R. Orszag
Claude M. Steele
Shelley E. Taylor
Richard H. Thaler
Hirokazu Yoshikawa

Mission Statement

RSF: The Russell Sage Foundation Journal of the Social Sciences is a peer-reviewed, open-access journal of original empirical research articles by both established and emerging scholars. It is designed to promote cross-disciplinary collaborations on timely issues of interest to academics, policymakers, and the public at large. Each issue is thematic in nature and focuses on a specific research question or area of interest. The introduction to each issue will include an accessible, broad, and synthetic overview of the research question under consideration and the current thinking from the various social sciences.

RSF Journal Editorial Board

Annette Bernhardt, University of California, Berkeley
Marianne Bertrand, University of Chicago
Karen S. Cook, Stanford University
Sheldon H. Danziger, Russell Sage Foundation
Nancy Folbre, University of Massachusetts
Janet C. Gornick, The CUNY Graduate Center
John A. Ferejohn, Stanford University
Larry V. Hedges, Northwestern University
Jennifer Hochschild, Harvard University
Rucker C. Johnson, University of California, Berkeley
Douglas S. Massey, Princeton University
James Sidanius, Harvard University
Mary C. Waters, Harvard University
Bruce Western, Harvard University

Copyright © 2015 by Russell Sage Foundation. All rights reserved. Printed in the United States of America. No part of this publication may be reproduced, stored in a retrieval system, or transmitted in any form or by any means, electronic, mechanical, photocopying, recording, or otherwise, without the prior written permission of the publisher. Reproduction by the United States Government in whole or in part is permitted for any purpose.

Opinions expressed in this journal are not necessarily those of the editors, editorial board, trustees, or the Russell Sage Foundation.

We invite scholars to submit proposals for potential issues through the *RSF* application portal: https://rsfjournal.onlineapplicationportal.com/. Submissions should be addressed to Suzanne Nichols, Director of Publications.

To view the complete text and additional features online please go to **www.rsfjournal.org**.

Russell Sage Foundation
112 East 64th Street
New York, NY 10065

ISSN (print):   2377-8253
ISSN (electronic): 2377-8261
ISBN: 978-0-87154-673-9

The Elementary and Secondary Education Act at Fifty and Beyond

ISSUE EDITORS
David A. Gamson, Kathryn A. McDermott, and Douglas S. Reed

CONTENTS

The Elementary and Secondary Education Act at Fifty: Aspirations, Effects, and Limitations **1**
David A. Gamson, Kathryn A. McDermott, and Douglas S. Reed

Part I. Consequences of the Elementary and Secondary Education Act

ESEA and the Civil Rights Act: An Interbranch Approach to Furthering Desegregation **32**
Erica Frankenberg and Kendra Taylor

Follow the Money: School Spending from Title I to Adult Earnings **50**
Rucker C. Johnson

Schooling the State: ESEA and the Evolution of the U.S. Department of Education **77**
Patrick McGuinn

Part II. Limitations and Proposals for Change

Getting to Sesame Street? Fifty Years of Federal Compensatory Education **96**
Gloria Ladson-Billings

Charting the Relationship of English Learners and the ESEA: One Step Forward, Two Steps Back **112**
Patricia Gándara

The Quest for a Targeted and Effective Title I ESEA: Challenges in Designing and Implementing Fiscal Compliance Rules **129**
Nora Gordon and Sarah Reber

The Shift from Adequacy to Equity in Federal Education Policymaking: A Proposal for How ESEA Could Reshape the State Role in Education Finance **148**
Eric A. Houck and Elizabeth DeBray

Part III. ESEA Policy Instruments and Their Future

Stability and Change in Title I Testing Policy **170**
Lorraine M. McDonnell

The State of Title I: Developing the Capability to Support Instructional Improvement **187**
Susan L. Moffitt and David K. Cohen

The Elementary and Secondary Education Act at Fifty: Aspirations, Effects, and Limitations

DAVID A. GAMSON, KATHRYN A. MCDERMOTT, AND DOUGLAS S. REED

The most important piece of education legislation in U.S. history, which had its fiftieth anniversary on April 11, 2015, is a law most people have never heard of. Parents do not discuss it on the sidelines of children's sports events. Teachers do not hear about it in professional development sessions. Only a few highly specialized education policy bloggers ever mention it. Despite this relative obscurity, the Elementary and Secondary Education Act (ESEA) of 1965 has—over the course of its fifty years—changed the course of U.S. public education.

ESEA's low profile stems, in part, from the contemporary fashion of giving legislation catchy titles. Indeed, when ESEA came due for reauthorization in 2001, Congress renamed it the No Child Left Behind Act (NCLB)—a legislative title that has far greater brand recognition.[1] The recent rebranding of ESEA, however, could only address name recognition; it did little to advance public understanding of how the legislation works or its effects. That is, in part, the goal of this issue of *RSF*.

The challenge for scholars and policy officials seeking to explain ESEA is the law's place in the complex mix of federal, state, and local authority over U.S. public schools. In many ways, the Elementary and Secondary Education Act is like the framing inside the walls of a house. This framing gives the structure its overall shape and footprint, but the original design and materials are obscured because so

---

David A. Gamson is associate professor of education in the Department of Education Policy Studies at the Pennsylvania State University. **Kathryn A. McDermott** is professor of education and public policy at the University of Massachusetts, Amherst. **Douglas S. Reed** is associate professor of government and director of the Program in Education, Inquiry and Justice at Georgetown University.

We wish to dedicate this issue of *RSF* to Carl F. Kaestle. It was through the Advanced Studies Fellowship (ASF) at Brown University, a program created and directed by Carl (and funded by the Spencer Foundation), that the three of us undertook our own work on the federal role in education, along with seven other scholars selected for ASF (some of whom are also included in this issue). Carl represents a model of mentorship, collaboration, and fine scholarship. Our continued intellectual cooperation is a testament to the strength of his guidance and influence. We also wish to thank the Russell Sage Foundation, and its excellent staff, for providing us the opportunity to pursue our investigation of the ESEA via a conference and this issue of *RSF*. All three authors contributed equally to the writing of this article. Direct correspondence to: David A. Gamson, dag17@psu.edu, Pennsylvania State University, Department of Education Policy Studies, University Park, PA 16802; Kathryn A. McDermott, mcdermott@educ.umass.edu, University of Massachusetts, Amherst, Rm. 429, Hills House North, Amherst, MA 01003; Douglas S. Reed, reedd@georgetown.edu, Georgetown University, 37th St., N.W., O St., N.W., Washington, D.C. 20057.

1. Section 1 of Public Law 107-110 declares that the law's title is the No Child Left Behind Act of 2001. However, it did not become a law until President George W. Bush signed it on January 8, 2002. Throughout this issue of *RSF*, we use 2001 when citing the law and 2002 when referring to the signing date.

much has been built around it. The framing suddenly becomes important, however, when the walls need repair, or when we need to identify the load-bearing sections in order to put on an addition or reconfigure existing spaces.

Lately we have been in a bit of a building spree, putting on several new additions: the current NCLB reflects federal education priorities that have grown much broader since ESEA was first passed in 1965. While Title I still governs, as it did fifty years ago, programs focused on "improving the education of the disadvantaged," it now also requires students to meet performance expectations on standardized tests. Title II now seeks to improve instruction by authorizing programs related to recruiting, preparing, and training "high quality" teachers and principals. In the 2001 reauthorization, Title III absorbed the Bilingual Education Act of 1968, and imposed new requirements on English language learner programs, deemphasizing bilingual instruction and promoting more rapid English language acquisition. At the same time, section 9527 of Title IX of ESEA prevents the federal government from mandating any particular "curriculum or program of instruction" to any state, local district or school. The list of expanded requirements and new mandates could go on, but the point is clear: ESEA's structural framing of educational institutions is extensive and has changed significantly over time.

This expansion of federal educational ambitions means that NCLB is doing things inconceivable under the original ESEA. NCLB requires states to have educational content standards, to test students on those standards, and to hold schools and districts accountable for their students' test scores. But just because the federal government demands these things does not mean that the implementation is uniform. What these policies look like on the ground depends on state government—and local district—decisions. Because federal money flows to districts and schools through their state governments, the origins of policies can be obscured. From the perspective of teachers and school and district administrators, it is often unclear whether a particular mandate comes from federal law, state law, or local interpretations of federal and state requirements. In other words, it is not always clear whether the framing that supports the walls of our educational edifice is the work of federal, state, or local carpenters.

In this introductory essay, we provide an overview of the various ideals and contending assumptions about education and government that have shaped the ESEA over the past fifty years. ESEA, particularly its largest program, Title I, has expanded from targeted interventions for low-income students to become a platform for leveraging a larger federal role and reconstruction of federal, state, and local relations in education governance. The idea of the federal government playing a role in education was once extremely controversial, and although that controversy continues, a significant federal presence in K–12 education has become an increasingly entrenched and accepted part of intergovernmental relations. Initially, the federal government focused on using education to alleviate poverty. This, in turn, meant that the federal government was not terribly focused on how schools and school districts taught students, only that poor students were receiving additional inputs under the new federal law. This hands-off approach was reinforced by ESEA's language that the federal government could not dictate curricula of schools or any particular subject matter, a stipulation that continues to this day.

When Congress reshaped ESEA in an attempt to reform teaching and learning, beginning in the 1990s, the limitations of federal framing became apparent. This introduction to this issue of *RSF* also surveys ESEA's effects since 1965 and some potential future directions of federal educational policy. The political challenge confronting ESEA is that federal spending authority under the law currently has lapsed due to a congressional reauthorization stalemate that began at the end of President George W. Bush's second term. As a result, federal educational spending must be extended every year, ensnaring it in political fights over the continuing resolutions by which Congress has, in recent years, paid its bills. In the hope that this stalemate over ESEA may be coming to an end, we conclude with recommendations for ESEA and federal education policy, drawn from the articles included in this issue.

FOUNDING IDEALS AND CONTENDING ASSUMPTIONS

Since 1965, the largest financial component of ESEA has been Title I, concerning "compensatory education" for "disadvantaged students." Initially, the appropriation for Title I was three times larger than the combined appropriation for the other four Titles (Cascio and Reber 2013, 68). Currently, Title I remains the largest single such program, although the number of federal K–12 education programs has grown since 1965. Figure 1 breaks down federal K–12 education spending by program for fiscal year 2011, the most recent year available.

The original ESEA also funded other parts of the education system. Title II made federal funds available to improve schools' libraries, and to buy textbooks and instructional materials. Title III funded Supplemental Education Centers and educational innovation. Title IV supported educational research and development. Title V provided federal funds to improve the capacity of state education agencies, which would face new administrative tasks related to distributing federal funds. Title I is by far the most important part of ESEA (see table 1).

Federal policymakers have transformed their expectations for Title I from a program that would help individual low-income children to a program that provides leverage for improving all of the nation's public schools.

ESEA's Origins and Intent

The original ESEA was passed at a time of great optimism about the ability of government to improve the lives of the poor. When he signed ESEA into law in 1965, President Johnson asserted that the legislation would "bridge the gap between helplessness and hope for more than 5 million educationally deprived children." The nation, he said, had made "a new commitment to quality and to equality in the education of our young people" (Johnson 1965). Three years later, after Congress had passed the 1967 amendments to ESEA, Johnson rattled off the initiatives that were now supported by ESEA and that broadened the scope of the federal government's involvement in education even further: dropout prevention, funding for children with disabilities, bilingual education programs, the addition of 3,600 new school libraries and 2,200 new education projects outside the classroom, and regional laboratories for basic educational research. Johnson believed that such innovations would be the most important legacy of the Great Society programs.

In that sense, ESEA should be seen as part of a grand experiment, one so large in scope and aspiration that it seems naïve today, living as we do in a more chastened age, one more familiar with incrementalism than large-scale design. The ESEA of 1965 was passed in the same year as the Voting Rights Act and just one year after the Economic Opportunity Act and the Civil Rights Act. Taken together, the legislative victories of the Great Society demonstrated an enormous faith in the power of the

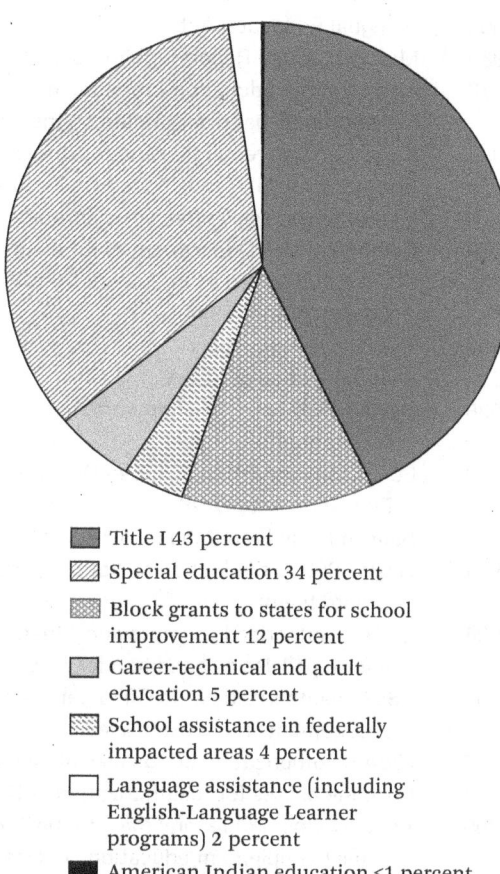

Figure 1. Federal Spending on K–12 Education, Fiscal Year 2011

- Title I 43 percent
- Special education 34 percent
- Block grants to states for school improvement 12 percent
- Career-technical and adult education 5 percent
- School assistance in federally impacted areas 4 percent
- Language assistance (including English-Language Learner programs) 2 percent
- American Indian education <1 percent

Source: Snyder and Dillow 2013, table 424.

Table 1. Timeline of ESEA and Related Events

1965	Original enactment of law
1968	Bilingual Education Act
1969	Martin-McClure Report highlights misuse of ESEA funds
1972	Title IX of the Education Amendments of 1972 forbids federal funding of educational institutions that discriminate on the basis of gender
1973	*Keyes* decision requires compensatory programs in desegregated schools
1975	Education for All Handicapped Children Act (P.L. 94-142) requires that students with disabilities receive free and appropriate public education
1979	Creation of U.S. Department of Education (ED)
1981	ESEA reauthorized as Education Consolidation and Improvement Act Title I becomes Chapter 1 until 1994
1983	*A Nation at Risk* report
1984	Reauthorization of ESEA
1988	Hawkins-Stafford Amendments to ESEA expand options for whole-school rather than pull-out programs
1990	Education for All Handicapped Children Act reauthorized as Individuals with Disabilities Education Act (IDEA)
1994	Safe and Gun Free Schools Act
1994	Goals 2000 Act (adoption of National Education Goals and funding for programs that work toward them)
1994	ESEA reauthorized as Improving America's Schools Act (IASA) Requires standards-based reform policies as condition for receiving Title I funds
2002	ESEA reauthorized as No Child Left Behind Act (NCLB) Makes standards-based reform requirements more extensive
2004	IDEA reauthorization brings law into alignment with NCLB
2007	Deadline passes for reauthorization of NCLB/ESEA
2009	Announcement of federal Race to the Top grant competition—states could win funds for plans to implement education policies favored by the Obama administration
2011	Obama administration begins granting NCLB waivers for states that met conditions similar to the Race to the Top criteria

Source: Authors' compilation.

federal government to enhance the lives of American citizens. Alongside the other Great Society programs, ESEA tested the proposition that the federal government has the capacity to alleviate poverty and other social ills. More specifically, ESEA assumed that education is a lever powerful enough to dramatically affect the lives of poor children. A standard narrative of American history, one voiced by President Reagan in 1987, is that "in the sixties we waged a war on poverty, and poverty won." Plenty of evidence questions this narrative (some of which is contained in the articles in this issue), but the debate is hardly settled. Big questions about the role of the federal government remain.

One of our motives for holding the 2014 conference on ESEA at the Russell Sage Foundation was to provide more scholarship on the history, legacy, and outcomes of ESEA. Despite its importance, there is still not as much research on ESEA as there should be. Talk to most scholars in education, and one is likely to get a standard (but somewhat foggy) story about ESEA and Title I emerging from the War on Poverty. Revisiting the origins of ESEA reveals a surprising number of perspectives on its genesis, both in the historical accounts and in the primary source material. In fact, the murky stories of ESEA's origins are themselves products of competing visions about how the legislation was crafted and about what the legislation should do. One looks in vain for a single historical account that captures all dimensions of the background to ESEA.

With that in mind, we see the multiple origin stories of ESEA as more reliable than a single master narrative that ultimately becomes marred by internal inconsistencies on closer examination. Understanding the underlying tensions among these origin stories fosters a more comprehensive understanding of the law and its outcomes. Perhaps this is not surprising after all. As with any piece of omnibus legislation, the successful passage of the bill was due in part to the fact that the law was designed to satisfy different constituencies. But these origin stories also frame our views of the law's impact: whether one sees ESEA, especially Title I, as a success depends in part on which origin story you believe.

These origin stories, however, need to be first situated within three historical developments that are crucial to understanding the passage of ESEA: the shifting perceptions of the appropriate federal role in education, Americans' changing understandings of poverty, and the significance of the civil rights movement taking place before, during, and after ESEA.

A key to comprehending ESEA is to recognize the growing acceptance of a federal role in education in the decade and a half before 1965. Since the days of the common schools, in no period in American history have the public schools been completely free from criticism, but because education had always been a local affair, critiques rarely resonated beyond towns, counties, or states. However, as education became more and more a national affair, educators and lay people alike began to speak of an American "school system." These sentiments first emerged in the 1890s and early 1900s as muckrakers and others lambasted what they saw as the inhumane practices of urban schools. The progressive education movement was the response of American educational reformers to turn-of-the-century educational problems, sparking a movement that lasted until the 1940s, one that affected virtually every school and educator in the country.

In the years following World War II, observers of American education once again began to raise doubts about the quality of the nation's schools. By the late 1940s, critics began issuing monographs claiming that the public schools were undermining academic quality; collectively they pointed their finger, whether warranted or not, at progressive education reforms. Such critiques were perhaps most vigorously expressed by scholar Arthur Bestor, a historian who launched an attack on the public schools in his 1953 book *Educational Wastelands*. Bestor and others like him charged the schools with dethroning intellectual values and debasing the aims of education. Bestor placed the blame at the feet of pre–World War II educational progressives; his solution was to return to a more traditional liberal arts education that would offer more rigorous standards (1953, 7). The Soviet Union's launch of *Sputnik* into space in October 1957, well ahead of any comparable American effort, seemed to confirm critics' complaints about education: the United States was falling behind its international rivals.

The following year, *Life* magazine ran a series of articles charging just that. There was a "Crisis in Education," a cover story claimed: "There is no general agreement on what the schools should teach. A quarter century has been wasted with the squabbling over whether to make a child well adjusted or to teach him something." The editors ended their list of educational deficiencies with a clincher sure to rattle its readers: "Most appalling, the standards of education are shockingly low" (1958, 25). *Life* included a story comparing the lives of two public school teenagers—the hardworking Moscow pupil and his frivolous peer from the Chicago suburbs—designed to make American education look shoddy in comparison. Once couched in the language of international competition, especially within the context of the Cold War, a federal government response to national educational problems suddenly seemed sensible.

The result of this national turmoil was the passage of the National Defense Education Act of 1958 (NDEA), which offered federal assistance for several purposes: to improve the teaching of math, science, and foreign language; to strengthen counseling and testing in the high schools; to promote research and experimentation with educational technology; and to provide college loans and National Defense fellowships in higher education. Beyond the specific provisions of the law, NDEA set an important precedent: that substantial reform of education had to occur at the national level and be funded by the federal government.

At the same time, the civil rights movement, bolstered by the 1954 *Brown* decision, began to pick up momentum. Indeed, an often-overlooked fact is that the NAACP pushed to integrate Little Rock High School at exactly the same time that the Soviets launched *Sputnik*. A number of key civil rights events surrounded the discussions of antipoverty programs and federal education legislation. In 1963 alone, recalled one observer, Birmingham residents staged a campaign of civil disobedience against segregation and hiring discrimination, civil rights leaders led the March on Washington in August, and a series of church bombings hit the headlines. Although participants in White House discussions later disagreed about the relative role played by race, as opposed to class, in educational legislation, that these events were a potent political backdrop cannot be denied (Katz 2013, 107).

Aside from issues of race and socioeconomic status, another tension that emerged in the early 1960s was the conceptual conflict between two core questions in education: should reformers push for academic excellence, as NDEA tended to do, or should they insist on equal educational opportunity, a goal that had been a tenet of American schooling since the common school reform era? Again, the common assumption of both questions was the notion that the federal government should do *something*.

In 1961, John W. Gardner—president of the Carnegie Corporation and, from 1965 to 1968, secretary of the Department of Health, Education, and Welfare (HEW)—published *Excellence: Can We Be Equal and Excellent Too?* in part to resolve the seeming conflict between these two ideas. Yet even as he sought to calm the waters, he revealed an assumption common among many American elites: that schools should provide differentiated offerings to students of different abilities. "The sorting out of individuals according to ability," he said, "is very nearly the most delicate and difficult process our society has to face" (1961, 71).

"Differences in educational opportunity will never be eradicated," Gardner contended. "They must be reduced in scope and significance. But it would be wrong to leave the impression that stratification of educational opportunity is still a dominant feature of our system. It is not. The vestiges of stratification still exist, but the great drama of American education has been the democratization of educational opportunity over the past century" (1961, 41). According to Gardner, youngsters might be given multiple chances in our egalitarian culture, but it was up to each student to demonstrate her or his individual worth. This emphasis on individual accomplishment both buoyed those who believed in the American Dream and became a governing assumption of the compensatory education approach that Title I used to deliver services to poor children.

As of 1961, many middle-class Americans could remain comfortable with the notion that poor children need only apply themselves should they wish to escape poverty; indeed, an idea that has run throughout American history is that some poor people are undeserving of help because they brought poverty on themselves (Katz 2013). That complacency was shattered the following year with the publication of Michael Harrington's *The Other America: Poverty in the United States*. Harrington's book was a sensation, selling more than a million copies. In 1962, intellectuals, politicians, and educators, if not the general public, were forced to rediscover poverty and to recognize that it was not self-inflicted. "The real explanation of why the poor are where they are," Harrington wrote, "is that they made the mistake of being born to the wrong parent, in the wrong section of the country, in the wrong industry, or in the wrong racial or ethnic group. Once that mistake has been made," Harrington said, preparing to overturn the standard logic of smugness, "they could have been paragons of will and morality, but most of them would never even have had a chance to get out of the other America" (1962, 13–14). Harrington intended to shame his American readers. Indeed, he hoped his descriptions would be a call to action; otherwise, he said, "the other America will continue to exist, a monstrous example of needless suffering in the most advanced society in the world" (191).

The early 1960s focus on poverty once again drew attention to the role the federal government might play in ensuring that all Americans were offered equal educational opportunity. The decentralized nature of American education, and the reliance of schools on local property taxes for their funding, had long contributed to the disparities in education. Through the 1920s, states paid only a small share of the total funds for education. That began to change with the Great Depression as nationally prominent educators pushed states to boost their spending to offset major disparities across their districts, one of the major equity initiatives of the era.

Still, by 1940, states contributed only roughly 30 percent of the average educational costs. By 1964, that figure had increased to 40 percent, but as Stephen Bailey and Edith Mosher point out, the quality of education varied in direct proportion to the availability of local tax revenues. The increase in state spending had little effect on the "glaring" financial and educational inequities. "Grim differences in school-district revenues continued to exist," they explain, and urban districts in particular were habitually underfunded, "a morbid manifestation of mal-apportioned and rurally dominated state legislatures" (1968, 13). As evidence of the mid-decade disparities, the authors point to the examples of two states. In 1966, for example, New York State spent $912 per pupil and Mississippi $315 (14).[2] Grim though these differences may have been for 1966, we might wish to compare these figures with expenses today. Recent data shows that in 2011 New York State spent $18,167 per pupil, whereas Mississippi spent $8,104 and Utah $6,452 (Cornman 2013). Then, as today, American leaders struggled to provide fiscal equity.

As the late Michael Katz pointed out, histories of the War on Poverty disagree about the relative influence of ideas, bureaucratic politics, and political strategy. ESEA has its own prismatic history. We suggest that three stories underlie the origins of ESEA, each with its own guiding logic.

First is the view that ESEA was hatched in the White House as a way to alleviate poverty, principally through providing funds that would give poor children an educational leg up, allowing them to boost themselves out of desperate conditions. This story tends to stress the significance of individuals, emphasizing both the leaders who fomented change and the individual child as the target of policy intervention. Second, ESEA can also be seen as a way for Congress to direct funding to areas most affected by poverty. Here the emphasis falls on the work of groups in spreading ideas, coming to compromise, and viewing poverty as a social curse that had broad roots. The third way of understanding the origins of ESEA, a view that is less common, is to see it as part of early- to mid-1960s efforts to reenvision education, primarily emphasizing the need for innovation, experimentation, and research. These three depictions of ESEA are not necessarily mutually exclusive, nor are they completely irreconcilable. However, we highlight these perspectives because they help illustrate tensions within American political and educational culture, both then and now. Moreover, we see them as prismatic perspectives that allow us to develop a fuller account of federal education policy.

Story I: The President, Francis Keppel, and the U.S. Office of Education

On becoming president in November 1963 after the assassination of President Kennedy, Lyndon Johnson inherited a variety of proposals that had been in the works under the Kennedy administration. Among these were broad plans for an attack on poverty, something Johnson enthusiastically embraced as a foundation for his own presidency and, ultimately, for the Great Society. One key component of the War on Poverty that quickly gained Johnson's attention was public education.

Legislation proposing large-scale federal funding did not enjoy much success during Kennedy's administration. In early 1961, Kennedy proposed a large, but ultimately unsuc-

---

2. Figures are in 1966 dollars.

cessful, education package totaling grants of $2.3 billion to be spent by states over three years for the construction of school buildings and for increasing teachers' salaries. Throughout 1962 and 1963, the Kennedy administration developed a variety of proposals, including provisions to assist with school construction and teacher salaries, but the U.S. Office of Education (USOE) also worked on a series of programs that identified the basic requirements for upgrading the educational system. Such efforts sought to build off NDEA.

The National Education Association (NEA) had long supported the idea of more federal educational spending but federal spending faced three main obstacles. First, southerners were worried that federal aid to schools would contain requirements for forced integration of African Americans and whites. Second, many local-control stalwarts resisted any aid that could lead to federal control of American schools or school curricula. Third, was the opposition of influential religious organizations—especially the National Catholic Welfare Conference (NCWC), an organization of American bishops, and the National Catholic Education Association (NCEA)—which took the position that they would support no federal aid to education, general or categorical, unless it also provided some kind of educational aid to parochial school children.

At this point in the story the role of one individual becomes supremely important: U.S. Commissioner of Education Francis Keppel. Keppel had been elevated to the position of dean of the Harvard Graduate School of Education at the age of thirty-two by Harvard President James B. Conant. Keppel spent a successful fourteen years as dean before he became the U.S. commissioner of education, serving from 1962 to 1965. Many scholars, including Julie Roy Jeffrey, tend to attribute much of the successful formulation of ESEA to Keppel's political and intellectual acumen.

According to one of his colleagues, Keppel shrewdly developed a solution to the parochial school funding problem. His reasoning went something like this: "'Suppose,' [Keppel] said, 'that a Federal-aid program could be put together in which the money would go to the public schools but the services it purchased would be available to all pupils, no matter where they went to school, whether in public institutions or nonpublic. The benefit would be to the pupil, not to the school'" (quoted in Jeffrey 1978, 74).

Once a funding compromise had been worked out, leaders at USOE were fairly certain that money would immediately help. As one Senate committee report put it,

> School superintendents, educational leaders, and research scholars have provided evidence that there is no lack of techniques, equipment, and materials which can be used or developed to meet this problem, but that the school districts which need them most are least able to provide the necessary financial support. There was virtually unanimous agreement among those testifying that aid to the educationally deprived child represented the basic approach to widespread improvement in the country. (Quoted in Jennings 2001, 8)

This confidence that the schools already had solutions to educating children in poverty provided the conceptual foundation for Title I.

The task of distributing the $1 billion in new funds became the responsibility of the USOE. According to John F. Hughes, the first administrator of Title I funds at the USOE, struggles both within the federal agency and between USOE and the state departments of education led to other challenges. The chief state school officers tended to be traditionalists, in favor of general aid not categorical aid. The USOE Title I staff knew that to make their program successful they needed allies within each state department (Hughes and Hughes 1972). Therefore, the USOE team "created" a new state-level "position" to which they began to direct federal correspondence: the state "Title I Coordinator."

The USOE Title I group also believed that to make Title I a substantive categorical program it needed a glamor name—like Head Start—that would symbolize its primary mission. Title I's original legislative heading was Financial Assistance to Local Educational Agencies for the Education of Children of Low-Income Families, not a phrase that falls trippingly off the tongue. Therefore, USOE staff adopted a phrase for the program that only recently had entered into academic usage: *compensatory education*. If the new understanding of Title I's purpose was as compensatory education, the shift was more than a simple rhetorical one. It may have added glamor to the title, but it also established a theoretical, if not ideological, foundation that would become the justification for the kinds of programs that Title I was to financially support.

Story II: Broad-Based Consensus to Focus on Concentrated Areas of Poverty

Helping the individual child was one way of looking at the purpose of education proposals of the 1960s, but other contemporaries were influenced by work that emphasized the broad social challenges that faced children growing up in poverty.

Since the early 1940s, Congress had provided federal impact aid to local school districts that lost property tax revenue due to the presence, within district boundaries, of military bases or tax-exempt federal property. At times, additional funding was provided when a federal project or activity caused an influx of people into a community, resulting in an increased number of children needing an education.

One influential group of educators and scholars looking into federal educational support (organized by the Bank Street School of Education) had previously recommended that the federal government provide aid to what they called "educational disaster areas." The Bank Street report explained that "on the basis of suitable criteria, including a standard test of literacy and achievement, educational disaster areas should be designated. Federal funds sufficient to achieve presently attainable national educational standards should be made available to school systems in these areas" (Kearney 1967, 186).

The notion that poverty went beyond the individual child had been advanced, by Harrington, and it was now becoming accepted knowledge among Washington politicians. As Senator Carl Perkins explained it, "all studies show that educational deficiencies are nowhere more marked than in the poverty of the schools that serve the children of the poor—this is true in the heart of our great cities and throughout many rural communities in America" (quoted in Jennings 2001, 6).

Such a view soon spread through Congress. As one Senate report explained it matter-of-factly, "The heart of the problem lies in our elementary and secondary school systems where there are concentrations of American children of poverty.... It has been apparent for some time that there is a close relationship between conditions of poverty and lack of educational development and poor academic performance.... Under Title I of this legislation the schools will become a vital factor in breaking the poverty cycle by providing full educational opportunity to every child regardless of economic background" (quoted in Jennings 2001, 6).

Indeed, when Senator Wayne Morse, the manager of the bill in the Senate, explained the origins of the law, he used similar terms:

> Last year my subcommittee had a brainstorm. We were working on impacted areas legislation. I felt that we needed a new section to this impacted area legislation to provide Federal funds for another types of impact—namely the impact of poverty and deprivation upon youngsters in the low-standard school districts of the country and in rural and urban slums. We talked about it for quite a while as an amendment to the impacted area legislation. Finally we introduced a separate bill.
>
> We didn't think we had a chance of getting it passed last year, but we felt we could get some hearings. That's how the Morse Bill of last year came into being. Unless you understand this bill and its history, you can't possibly understand Title I of the Perkins-Morse bill (P.L. 89–10). (Quoted in Bailey and Mosher 1968, 27)

Despite Morse's rhetoric, it was not only the Senate that inserted such ideas into public discussion.

Story III: Federal Stimulus to Educational Innovation

Richard I. Miller, who chaired a team charged by Congress to complete an evaluation of ESEA's Title III—issued in a 1967 report titled

Catalyst for Change—argued that the Task Force President Johnson established in 1964 to propose broad ideas for the reform of American education had originally conceived a plan that was much closer to Title III than to Title I. Johnson's original charge to the committee was to rethink urgent problems in education and to recommend possible solutions to these problems, a goal that was reputedly influential in composing the first draft of ESEA. In particular, Miller noted that early versions of ESEA reflected two core concepts hatched by the presidential task force. Notably, because the task force held private meetings and its report was never made public, most accounts of its proceedings and recommendations are based on review of the report in the Johnson archives or on interviews with participants after the fact.[3] Its first stance emphasized its members' belief that American educational improvement required dispensing with the practice of offering piecemeal support for small-scale individual projects; instead, the task force wanted to focus federal support squarely on assistance for large-scale model programs and institutions. According to this view, the American educational problem was not as much a shortage of new ideas as the absence of solid means for converting these ideas into usable forms in the classroom (Miller 1967, 15–16).

Second, the task force wanted to avoid providing general aid to schools and districts and instead wanted to fund outside institutions, such as museums, libraries, private nonprofit groups, or local community centers. Because school systems were concerned primarily with meeting the exigencies of day-to-day operations, the task force logic went, schools and districts often stifled efforts at introducing new ideas or new kinds of services. Thus emerged, as Miller explained it, the task force brainchild of creating "supplementary educational centers that would be financed by the Federal Government and staffed by artists, museum directors, novelists, journalists and the like—designed to bring about change and to provide new services from the outside in" (1967, 16). Some scholars, such as Hugh Davis Graham, have seen the supplementary education center plan as the Task Force's "most original creation." Graham describes the idea as the "subversive favorite" of William Cannon—chief of the Bureau of the Budget's Division of Education, Manpower, and Sciences—because such centers could offer a "massive lever for change" and would not be "hostage to local educational establishments." And, as many commentators have pointed out, the individuals who most favored the supplementary education center idea also tended to be rather cynical about American educators and deeply skeptical about the ability of the public schools to reform themselves (Graham 1984, 67, 63).

By all accounts, neither of the two original task force proposals fared well as their recommendations became diluted into the kind of legislative provisions that had political viability. Why? To have model institutions officially sponsored by the federal government, for example, smacked too much of federal control, and grants made to private nonprofit groups raised worries that religious schools could potentially be direct recipients of Title III funding. The model institutions idea was therefore downgraded to a relatively minor role in the legislation—a strategic move designed to mollify both congressional critics and groups that had been traditionally resistant to certain kinds of educational funding, such as the National Education Association. "Thus ESEA Title I was born," Miller recounted, "although the idea was never really mentioned in the Task Force." Title I "became the major title and Title III, which was formed from the core of the Task Force recommendations, slipped into the background" (1967, 16).

Together these three origin stories provide a fuller, if somewhat conflicted, account of how ESEA came into being. Once ESEA was enacted, however, the divergent rationales for its creation influenced the divergent ways ESEA was put to use, particularly in the mid-1960s to mid-1970s, as the effects of the civil rights movement radiated throughout U.S. politics and policymaking.

---

3. Miller's view of the Task Force differs markedly from that offered by Julie Roy Jeffrey, who saw the task force primarily as a "legitimizing device" (1978, 75).

Expanding Aspirations for ESEA

The multiple authors of ESEA may have had modest aspirations for using federal power to change U.S. educational practices, but other actors at the federal level were at the time seeking more fundamental transformations in the racial organization of schooling. Thus, although ESEA's origin stories provide some evidence of a federal transformative educational agenda, the story of desegregation and integration and the effects of the civil rights movement on the growing federal education agenda paints a much more ambitious picture, though that ambition was at first judicial rather than executive or legislative. Eventually, however, those ambitions were fused when federal officials used ESEA to promote desegregation.

ESEA and Civil Rights in Education
Over the course of the 1960s, the federal effort both to desegregate schools and to improve educational practices often reinforced one another. In some instances, Congress took its cue from federal court decisions and extended the civil rights agenda, creating more opportunities for previously excluded groups, such as special needs students and English learners. In other instances, Congress adapted carrot and stick strategies initially developed to promote desegregation to induce local districts and states to undertake education reforms they would not have otherwise tackled.

ESEA as Leverage for Desegregation Despite the Supreme Court's unanimous ruling in *Brown v. Board of Education* in 1954 requiring southern schools to desegregate, few complied with the court's order. The limited compliance that took place was in border states where African American populations were comparatively small. In the Deep South, as massive resistance to integration roared in the late 1950s, only a federal military presence, which President Eisenhower reluctantly ordered, produced token desegregation of Little Rock's Central High. Other states required equally forceful efforts to produce equally token results. Even as late as the 1962–1963 school year, less than half of 1 percent of African American children in the South attended school with whites. Omitting Texas and Tennessee, the percentage drops to less than a fifth of 1 percent (0.17 percent) (Rosenberg 1991, 50).

As the civil rights movement pursued a strategy of direct action and civil disobedience, media images of police dogs lunging at children and fire hoses blasting away at peaceful protesters were splashed across the nation's television screens, galvanizing northern public opinion against southern segregationists. Congress, in turn, responded with the landmark 1964 Civil Rights Act. Among its many elements, the Civil Rights Act included Title VI, which barred the spending of federal money in any program that discriminated on the basis of race, including public schools.

The restructuring of southern schools was not a direct aim of ESEA, but in conjunction with Title VI of the Civil Rights Act, ESEA's commitment to spend federal funds was a forceful lever to induce compliance with the federal government's nondiscrimination policies, a lever possibly more powerful than federal district court rulings. As Erica Frankenberg and Kendra Taylor write in this issue, the massive influence of ESEA dollars induced southern states to comply much more rapidly with *Brown v. Board of Education* than they otherwise would have.

Although federal educational funds were limited when the Civil Rights Act was enacted in 1964, the issue became much more pressing the next year as the enactment of ESEA opened a significant flow of federal money to districts and states. To be eligible for federal funds, school districts had one of three options: declare that they did not racially segregate students, demonstrate compliance with a court order to desegregate, or submit a voluntary desegregation plan. In many states, the draw of federal dollars outweighed the commitment to racially segregated schooling. As federal dollars began to flow, the number of African American children attending previously all-white schools jumped dramatically: from the 1965–1966 to the 1966–1967 school year, the percentage of African American students in the South who attended school with whites increased from roughly 6 percent to nearly 17 percent. Two years after that, the figure stood at 32 percent (Rosenberg 1991, 50).

As Frankenberg and Taylor explain, the federal legislative and executive branches continued the momentum that the courts began, even though this willingness to act depended entirely on political pressure. Desegregation of northern schools posed a different set of challenges. In the South, plaintiffs were challenging districts that had followed state laws that required racial segregation. In contrast, northern racial segregation typically resulted from the racially biased operation of laws and policies that were race-neutral on their face (see, generally, Douglas 2005). For example, a school district might build new neighborhood schools in locations where their students would be mainly white or black because of residential segregation. In Congress, northern representatives and senators who were willing to require integration in the South were also willing to fight forced busing and other remedies for segregation in their region.

The Department of Health, Education, and Welfare, which had responsibility for enforcing the law, was often more concerned with maintaining relationships with local educational officials than ensuring compliance with Title VI of the 1964 Civil Rights Act. The NAACP at one point undertook a massive lawsuit against HEW seeking to compel HEW's compliance with Title VI and shut off the flow of federal money to local school districts—more than forty were named in the lawsuit—that were not making any progress toward desegregation. Eventually, NAACP prevailed in that case, *Adams v. Richardson* (351 F. Supp 636, 1972), forcing HEW to start the process of shutting down the flow of federal money to districts in violation of the Civil Rights Act. The increasing pressure quickly forced compliance with Title VI.

Today, fifty years after ESEA, the federal position on racial integration has effectively reversed. Federal courts now interpret the Constitution not as requiring racially balanced schools, but as forbidding any racial classification of students. In its 2007 *Parents Involved in Community Schools* decision (551 U.S. 701), the U.S. Supreme Court ruled that under most circumstances local school districts may not use individual students' race as the decisive factor in assigning them to schools, except to remedy past overt, official discrimination. As a result, local school districts that want to make diversity a priority have to step carefully to avoid running afoul of federal courts. In addition, local political will to promote racial integration has diminished significantly in the United States. In 2011, the U.S. Department of Education (ED) and Department of Justice jointly issued guidance on diversity, but by this point many school districts had already eliminated race-conscious student assignment policies (Sokol 2014; McDermott et al. 2014).

The Bilingual Education Act and English-Language Learner Education The hard-fought victories of the civil rights movement also inspired other groups to pursue greater educational justice through both courts and Congress. The claims of English learners emerged, in significant part, from the events of the 1960s that radicalized a generation of Mexican American activists and students. In California, and to a lesser extent Texas, these activists demanded changes to classroom language practices that had isolated and denigrated Mexican American students and their culture. Their demands for basic respect for Mexican American students led to calls for bicultural and bilingual programs that granted full recognition of the equal status of Mexican American students within schools. In addition, the 1965 immigration reform led to a new wave of immigration that has given the U.S. public school student population its highest proportion of immigrant students—many of whom are classified as English-language learners—since the early twentieth-century wave of European immigration.

Texas Senator Ralph Yarborough, a former rural educator himself, led the charge to enact the 1968 Bilingual Education Act, also known as Title VII of ESEA. The bill, the first federal effort to ensure that language minority students received some assistance in their first language, imposed no obligations on states or school districts and simply offered modest grants to schools seeking to build such programs. Moreover, the act did not address a perennial tension in programs for English learners: should federal policies seek to promote the learning and use of English or should federal assistance maintain or even develop first language skills alongside English?

Although many have long contended that English is a necessary prerequisite for both academic and economic success in the United States, and that federal policies should promote the rapid development of English-language skills, some activists within the Mexican American community saw the creation of English-language learner (ELL) programs not as an effort to acculturate or assist students, but as a way to extinguish their Mexican American heritage. Within a context of deep discrimination against Mexican Americans, activists contended that the push to develop English skills would necessarily erode first language skills and, ultimately, diminish the political presence of Spanish-language students and their families. They argued instead for dual bilingual and bicultural programs that, at a minimum, preserved first language skills and reinforced the cultural (that is, Mexican American) heritage of students.

The limited funding available under the Bilingual Education Act meant that this debate was not a primary concern for most school districts, which chose not to pursue federal grants for bilingual programs. The question of how to meet the needs of students who spoke no English really only became a much larger issue when the federal courts imposed, for the first time, an affirmative duty on local school districts to meet the educational needs of students who spoke no English. In 1974 in *Lau v. Nichols*, the U.S. Supreme Court ruled that San Francisco violated the civil rights of nearly two thousand students who spoke only Chinese when it provided them with only English-language instruction and services. Declaring that San Francisco violated Title VI of the 1964 when it failed to meet the linguistic needs of its students, the Court declared, "there is no equality of treatment merely by providing students with the same facilities textbooks, teachers and curriculum; for students who do not understand English are effectively foreclosed from any meaningful education" (*Lau v. Nichols*, 414 U.S. 563).

The Supreme Court did not provide any specific relief, but simply demanded that the school district "apply its expertise" to the problem, rather than ignore it. Later, the Office of Civil Rights at HEW promulgated a series of steps, known as *Lau* Remedies, that would enable all school districts to meet their statutory obligation to provide equal education to English learners under Title VI of the Civil Rights Act. Again, it was the combination of the ESEA and Title VI that enabled activists to extend localist demands for change in educational practices for English learners into a federal structure that managed these educational changes. Between 1975 and 1980, the *Lau* remedies provided the basis for the federal government's consent decrees with nearly five hundred school districts that had failed to provide sufficient language resources for their students (Reed 2014, 166). Without ESEA providing assistance to school districts, the leverage of the federal government would be much more attenuated.

As Patricia Gándara describes in greater detail in this issue, the relationship between ESEA and English learners is a complex and fraught one. On the one hand, NCLB's new Title III delivers significant resources to English learners. On the other, both NCLB and ESEA's framing of the educational issues confronting English learners assumes that speaking another language is a deficit of students, rather than an intellectual resource that is in short supply in the United States. ESEA's institutional development—informed by both an ambition to restructure public education and a civil rights agenda—has not yet adequately addressed the complexity of English learners' educational needs.

ESEA, IDEA, and Efforts to Address Special Needs Another major federal educational policy that intersects with ESEA, particularly NCLB's assessment and accountability provisions, is the Individuals with Disabilities Education Act (IDEA). Originally enacted in 1975 as the Education for All Handicapped Children Act, the law emerged from a disability-rights movement inspired by the African American civil rights movement. In 1972, two federal court decisions, *Pennsylvania Association of Retarded Citizens (PARC) v. Commonwealth of Pennsylvania* (343 F. Supp. 279, E.D. Pa. 1972) and *Mills v. D.C. Board of Education* (348 F. Supp.

866 D.D.C. 1972), established that an absolute deprivation of education to students with special needs violated their due process rights under the Fourteenth Amendment (see Melnick 1994). As a result of *PARC*'s consent decree, Pennsylvania agreed to provide special needs students free and appropriate education, place them within a regular classroom whenever possible, and develop an individualized plan to set out goals of academic progress. Although an earlier federal law in 1970 had expanded programs for special needs children, the federal government had not directly mandated states or districts to provide particular services. Combined, *PARC* and *Mills* did just that. In 1975, Congress effectively codified *PARC* and *Mills* in the Education for All Handicapped Children Act (EAHCA), more popularly known as P.L. 94–142.

With EAHCA, Congress undertook a major redefinition of the federal role in special education—in large part because the federal court decisions had articulated a specific set of rights that special education students must be granted. Indeed, the EAHCA borrowed directly from both the *PARC* and *Mills* decisions, particularly in its requirements that states and districts provide "free and appropriate public education," ensure due process protections for special education students, develop an individual education plan (IEP) for each special education student, and (preferably) "mainstream" children with special needs. As the chief sponsor of the EAHCA, Senator Harrison Williams, stated during the 1975 debate, "Certainly the courts have helped us define the right to an education in the last few years. That is what we are trying to find, the means to carry out the fundamental law of the land" (Reed 2014, 140).

In EAHCA, Congress also reserved for the courts a key role in the regulation and oversight of school districts' delivery of special education. Parents who were dissatisfied with the special education offered to their special needs children could take advantage of formal grievance procedures. They also possessed the right to appeal decisions about their children's education to federal district courts. Special education thus became further legalized, with federal entities—judges—playing a central role in the implementation of a major initiative designed to expand educational equality. Congress left the key elements of the measure undefined (for instance, not defining an appropriate education) and at the same time assigned the task of defining the substantive meaning of its own language to the courts. Despite the efforts of the Supreme Court in the early 1970s to withdraw from the field of educational regulation, Congress's use of EAHCA to reach into local educational practices for special needs children effectively relied on courts to serve as enforcement agents. According to the political scientist Shep Melnick, "the procedures [Congress] created [in the EAHCA] not only made proceedings within the schools more adversarial and courtlike but made it easy for federal judges to play an active role in policymaking under the act. . . . Just as the Supreme Court was pulling the federal judiciary away from educational policy-making, Congress was pushing it back in" (1994, 142). The result was further widening of the federal role in education and the ambitions of education reformers.

This expansion took on a larger importance when No Child Left Behind specifically included special needs students as one of the demographic groups that schools and school districts had to demonstrate were making progress toward proficiency to make adequate yearly progress (AYP). Before NCLB, schools and districts were required under law to make provision for special needs students, and to construct personalized learning goals through an IEP. After NCLB the stakes for the learning outcomes of special needs students were felt school and district wide: failure of a school to meet its proficiency targets under NCLB for special needs students for two or more years in succession meant that the entire school underwent federally mandated restructuring. By tying the fates of schools to the academic performance of special needs students, NCLB reformers sought to ensure that they would receive more attention from school officials.

At the same time, however, both state-level standards and the assessments used to determine mastery of those standards were not always appropriate for special needs students, particularly those with severe cognitive impairments. In addition, the anxiety that standardized assessments, rather than alternative strategies, generate may exacerbate behavorial issues of some students and contribute to their underperformance. Either way, critics of NCLB have singled out the assessment of special needs students in the NCLB era as one of its biggest flaws.

The Evolution of Title I from Pull-Outs to Reform Leverage

Beyond English learners and special needs students are numerous examples of how ESEA's implementation has not always been adequate to the needs of the learners it was seeking to aid. In particular, Title I's approach to compensatory education and lax spending oversight meant that, in the early years, districts often spent their Title I money on educationally dubious activities or on instructional practices inadequate to the challenges of Title I students. Efforts to improve the administration of Title I programs evolved over the 1970s and 1980s were initially undertaken to ensure that federal programs led to real gains in student learning. Later these reform efforts became mechanisms by which the federal government sought to generate systemic reforms in U.S. education.

Changing Title I Administration In 1969, the Martin-McClure report detailed ways in which school districts had inappropriately spent Title I funds on purchases such as band uniforms and swimming pools. In response, federal oversight became more stringent. Beyond misspent money, other early evaluations of Title I indicated that federal spending had not dramatically boosted the educational performance of students in poverty. Although these studies were not the most methodologically rigorous, more substantial evidence existed that many districts were diverting federal money away from the true educational needs of children in poverty (and special needs and English learners). In turn, the federal government tightened up the fiscal reporting requirements on districts for their Title I money. This, as several articles in this issue show, led to a series of pedagogical practices (instructional pull-outs of children eligible for Title I, in particular) that may have produced a more accurate accounting of federal money, but also diminished the instructional effectiveness of federally funded interventions.

Moreover, many of the early evaluations of Title I could not directly compare which kind of intervention worked better than another, often because very few Title I evaluations examined student achievement data. A summary of the early efforts to evaluate Title I concluded that "the few early federal efforts to gauge the educational effectiveness of the program on a national scale were complete failures because sufficient and uniform local achievement data were lacking" (Borman and D'Agostino 2001, 28). In response to the concerns of misapplication of Title I funds and a need for a better assessment of Title I effects on achievement, Congress required that "objective criteria be used in the evaluation of all [Title I] programs . . . producing data which are comparable on a statewide and nationwide basis" (Borman and D'Agostino 2001, 27). This effort led in 1979 to the development of the Title I Evaluation Reporting System (TIERS), which could finally, some fifteen years after ESEA's enactment, provide some meaningful assessments of particular programs.

Title I as Reform Leverage and the Evolution of ESEA The development in TIERS of comparable data on Title I program performance came at a key moment in U.S. educational history. The 1983 "A Nation at Risk" report gave national visibility and urgency to reformers' calls for higher standards in U.S. public education. Its depiction of a "rising tide of mediocrity" overrunning U.S. schools spurred states not only to raise educational standards, but also to implement systems of accountability that imposed sanctions on students, teachers, or schools if they failed to meet the benchmark goals established by state-level educational officials. Over the course of the 1980s and 1990s, the fusion of standards, assessments, and accountability into the predominant focus of education reform emerged as both states, and later the federal government, sought to add "rigor" to schools and change the incentive structures for personnel within schools. By enabling the federal government to accelerate and focus those trends, ESEA (and congressional changes to the law) played a pivotal role in nationalizing the standards and accountability movements.

The idea of using standards as leverage for school improvement has several roots, including the Effective Schools research, which identified common characteristics of schools that were successfully educating low-income students. Standards were also at the heart of *systemic reform*, a term popularized by Marshall Smith and Jennifer O'Day. Smith and O'Day argue that piecemeal reforms in educational practices do not radiate throughout an educational system unless the incentives of multiple actors in that system align to advance the goals of reform (Smith and O'Day 1990; see also McDermott 2011). State-level curricular frameworks and educational standards, they argue, combined with more robust state governance, would focus reform efforts and provide coherence to strategies to improve schooling outcomes. At a time when many states were becoming more assertive in challenging prevailing patterns of local control in public education, the ideas of systemic reform gained traction among educational researchers and policymakers alike.

At the federal level, the 1988 Hawkins-Stafford amendments to ESEA made it easier for school districts to use Chapter 1 funds schoolwide, with the goals of using the federal funds as leverage for improving entire schools, and of reducing fragmentation of the curriculum (Cohen and Moffitt 2009, 119). In 1994, Congress passed the Goals 2000: Educate America Act, which identified key education outcomes to be achieved nationally by the year 2000 and funded grants to states based on those goals.

Also at this time, Congress began using ESEA as leverage for standards-based reform. The 1994 ESEA reauthorization aligned Title I with the standards-based reforms that many states had enacted beginning in the 1980s. As a condition for receiving Title I funds, states had to set challenging standards in math and English, require all students to take tests based on those standards at three points in their schooling, and hold schools and districts accountable for students' performance. Requiring Title I students and non–Title I students to take the same tests on the same standards was a departure from past practice, which allowed schools to assess the progress of Title I students with "basic skills" tests.

Under the Improving America's Schools Act of 1994 (IASA), "federal involvement in K–12 education began to touch the core functions of the nation's schools" for the first time, and once again set a new precedent for federal mandates (Manna 2006, 100). IASA's changes required all states to develop educational standards and to assess students at least once at the elementary level, once in middle school, and once again in high school. It further demanded that schools not meeting performance standards devise a school improvement plan that would ensure schools had the capacity to meet the new standards. These changes marked the first time that the federal government began requiring schools to hit performance benchmarks to receive Title I money. By "borrowing strength," the federal government expanded its educational ambitions under Title I, moving from addressing the educational disadvantages of children in poverty to creating a regulatory structure that sought to incentivize systemic reform throughout state educational systems (Manna 2006).

The 2001 reauthorization, better known as NCLB, required states to test students annually in grades three through eight and to define adequate yearly progress in terms of those annual test scores, with the goal of moving toward 100 percent proficiency for all students by 2014. Finally, NCLB required schools to disaggregate the results of state-level tests by student demographic groups. Failure to make progress within one subgroup meant that the entire school would not make AYP. Not making AYP exposed schools to a series of increasingly demanding reforms and restructuring if the benchmark was not hit in subsequent years. Although the ostensible goal was to ensure that all groups moved toward the nationwide goal in math and reading by 2014, in reality the law imposed increasingly draconian reforms on schools that enrolled predominantly poor and minority students. Moreover, NCLB's testing requirements for English-language learners effectively eliminated bilingual education for many students (Reed 2014). As Patricia Gándara and Gloria Ladson-Billings report elsewhere in this issue, these efforts to improve the education of students in poverty have, in some circumstances, resulted in the creation of incentives to neglect the needs of minority students and English learners.

ESEA and Intergovernmental Relations

At the height of federal support for desegregation and bilingual education, the federal government limited local autonomy in order to protect the educational rights of students of color and students who spoke languages other than English at home. Since IASA and NCLB, the priority of federal education policy has shifted from ensuring that funds were spent only on the appropriate students for the intended purposes to pushing states to adopt particular kinds of education reform. These changes, combined with federal civil rights enforcement and support for education reforms, have created a far more complex governing arrangement for public education. This new intergovernmental system is marked by endemic conflict. In many instances, no party to the educational task feels it has sufficient control or influence over any particular outcome. The federal push for standards and accountability has focused attention of reformers at the school level. At the same time, it has placed school districts in the challenging and awkward task of managing schools for local constituents, but in some ways contrary to the desires of local constituents, or without any mechanism to obtain and register their input. Recent federal actions have also encouraged the growth of alternatives to school districts as they have historically existed, such as charter schools and education management organizations.

State-Federal Tensions

A few states have sought to resist NCLB and Race to the Top (RTT) restrictions on state educational practices and policies. Connecticut's lawsuit against NCLB alleged that the federal law was an unfunded mandate and impermissibly intruded on the traditional state role in education. The federal judiciary was not impressed by Connecticut's argument, however, and in a pair of rulings in 2006 and 2008 rejected it (*Connecticut v. Spellings*, 453 F. Supp. 2d 459 (2006); *Connecticut v. Spellings*, 549 F. Supp. 2d 161 (2008)).[4] Another case, filed by Governor Bobby Jindal of Louisiana, contends that the Obama administration's scoring for Race to the Top competition coerced states into adopting the Common Core State Standards, intruding on traditional state Tenth Amendment rights and violating the federal government's own ban on instituting a national curriculum. Others have urged Oklahoma Governor Mary Fallin, whose state lost its NCLB waiver when it repealed the Common Core State Standards, to challenge the denial of the waiver on the grounds that the administration's use of the waiver process is violating the intent of Congress. This argument contends that, although Congress created a waiver process, it did not authorize the executive branch to pursue policy objectives that Congress had either rejected or not authorized—or were contrary to existing federal law. To date, no such lawsuit has been filed.

The current complexity of intergovernmental relations in education policy can be seen in prominent Republicans' differences of opinion. In contrast to Governor Jindal, former Florida governor Jeb Bush wants to keep intact federal standards-based reforms, including incentives for states to adopt the Common Core State Standards. Bush's support for the Common Core separates him from other Republican conservatives, who characterize it as a federal mandate despite its origins as a project of the National Governors Association and the Council of Chief State School Officers.

In short, the old assumptions about the nature of political cleavages within education policy no longer hold. Although the original ESEA was controversial, NCLB received remarkable bipartisan support. Despite this support, the National Education Association, the

---

4. The district court's rulings were upheld by the 2nd Circuit Court of Appeals in *Connecticut v. Duncan*, 612 F.3d 107 (2010). The Supreme Court declined to accept the case.

largest labor union representing educators, challenged NCLB's testing requirements as an infringement on states' rights. More recently, Democrats have chafed at the Obama administration's support for charter schools, private "turnaround partners" for low-performing public schools, and teacher evaluations based partly on student test scores. These tensions have challenged the policy expectation that federal intervention in education is always an imposition of progressive priorities on recalcitrant state and local governments.

Alternatives to Traditional District Governance
The Obama administration's education policies have increasingly sought to unsettle the existing practices of localism in U.S. schools. Both NCLB and the Obama administration's Race to the Top have created a policy opening for schools that are organized quite differently from the traditional, neighborhood, or geographically based local school. Since No Child Left Behind, federal policy under ESEA has indirectly promoted the development of public charter schools by deeming them legitimate elements of the restructuring plans required of schools that fail to meet AYP for successive years. Although some contend that NCLB has, in effect, served as a stalking horse for the privatization of U.S. schooling (Kohn 2004), others argue that the persistent failure of schools to meet even the basic academic needs of students indicates a gross educational malpractice that merits their closure. Either way, the NCLB-dominated policy environment of standards, assessment, and accountability has hastened the quest for alternative governance structures for schooling in the United States. In short, the post-1994 ESEA amendments have persistently challenged long-standing assumptions of localism in U.S. schooling and effectively weakened them.

In some states, the legal environment for charter schools is far more restrictive than in other states, slowing the transformation of traditional neighborhood schools to charters. In response, the Obama administration has encouraged the spread of charters through its Race to the Top competition. Not part of ESEA, but enacted as part of the American Recovery and Reinvestment Act of 2009 (also known as the Stimulus Bill), RTT offered states a chance to compete for $4.35 billion in educational spending precisely when state coffers were hit hard by declining tax revenues of the Great Recession. Structured as a competition designed to induce states to adopt numerous education reforms, RTT's "grading rubric" included the expansion of longitudinal data systems for student assessments, the adoption of "college and career-ready" standards such as the Common Core State Standards, and the development and use of data to evaluate teacher and principal performance. Also included among RTT's point allocation was a liberalization of a state's public charter school licensing procedures and the removal of caps on the number of charter school seats within a state. As a result, RTT further encouraged states to devise alternative governance arrangements for schools. Again, though not part of ESEA, RTT advanced the fragmentation of local governance structures in education as an effort to both standardize educational goals, but also to work around local obstacles to reform efforts.

STRUCTURAL LIMITATIONS OF THE EXPANDED FEDERAL ROLE

Our metaphor of ESEA as the framing structure of the U.S. educational system captures the challenges and limitations of the institutional contexts in which ESEA operates, as well as the distinctive quality of the U.S. system of schooling. Just as the streets in many American towns do not look much like European streets, so too our educational system does not look much like European ones. Similarly, the U.S. education governance system looks quite different from those of other industrialized countries. Instead of a strong central ministry of education that has devolved some authority to regional and local authorities, the United States has a federal department of education younger than any of the state and local education authorities that is often seen as usurping power from states and school districts. Built around ESEA funding as its internal framework, the shape of the expanded federal role is a response to available resources and broader contexts.

Like wood-frame structures, the contemporary federal role in education also does not perform some functions well. Buildings that need to support great weight, such as factories and skyscrapers, cannot be made of wood. As the federal government has tried to take on more of the burden of supporting instructional improvement, its structural limitations have similarly become clear. The U.S. public education system lacks a strong administrative infrastructure for leading educational improvement. Recall that ESEA itself specifically prohibits the use of federal funds to require or promote particular curricula or instructional practices. State education departments may have the constitutional authority to direct public education, but often lack the staffing and funding to translate this authority into action.

Both when ESEA's goal was to provide "compensatory" programs for low-income students and now, when federal policy uses ESEA as a lever to induce systemic educational change, success depends on millions of teachers' effectiveness in their classrooms. To enhance teachers' effectiveness, the education system as a whole—including federal and state departments of education—needs to have adequate instructional capacity: relevant resources and knowledge, organized in ways that help students—of all types—learn.

Cohen and Moffitt's book *The Ordeal of Equality* explains that at ESEA's birth in 1965, the knowledge of how teaching and learning worked was weak, and our national understanding of how to improve schools was similarly limited (2009, 27). Julie Roy Jeffrey notes in her history of ESEA that "little thought had gone into the whole problem of how education, formal or informal, related to the goals of the poverty program. . . . Policy-makers and Congressmen just never looked at the evidence of what schools did" (1978, 51). According to Jeffrey, HEW Secretary Robert Finch said in 1969, "Many curriculum developers are not aware of the best methods of meeting the educational needs of poverty children. Schools and school districts differ greatly in their capacity to provide quality educational programs for disadvantaged children" (Jeffrey 1978, 131). This befuddled reality stood in stark contrast to the confident assurances of educational leaders in the pre-ESEA congressional hearings.

School districts had little expertise or organizational capacity to respond to the changing expectations of the federal government. Research into what, exactly, school districts did under Title I programs to provide compensatory education reveals a kind of grasping at straws as school districts came to terms with the concerns of students they had systematically neglected for decades. From a twenty-first-century vantage point, early efforts to engage in compensatory education seem paternalistic, condescending, and indeed naïve about the educational needs of poor children. One approach was to remove Title I–eligible children from their regular classrooms for pull-out services that focused on basic skills. Another was to expose low-income children to middle-class experiences like field trips to art museums and concert halls. In her article in this issue, Gloria Ladson-Billings criticizes these approaches for focusing on perceived deficits rather than strengths and cultural resources of Title I–eligible children.

The federal and state governments themselves had little experience with educational improvement (Cohen and Moffitt 2009). The USOE initially faced an enormous challenge just getting money to the right places, to say nothing of leading instructional improvement. Donald McLaughlin's 1977 synthesis of studies of ESEA's effects notes that "in 1965, Congress was apparently not aware of the immensity of the problem of developing and implementing a program to deal successfully with educational disadvantage on a national scope" (4). State governments were, at this time, even less well prepared for these new assignments.

According to Education Commissioner Francis Keppel, members of the original ESEA Task Force opposed giving support to state departments of education, because they believed state educational officials to be incompetent and intransigent (for discussion of the Gardner Task Force, see Graham 1984, 76). Although ESEA Title V provided funding to increase the capacity of state departments of education, their ability to lead educational improvement remained weak. When state legislatures enacted new education reforms in the 1980s and 1990s, their departments of education often struggled to implement the ambitious new laws (Manna 2006). NCLB led to increased attention on the problem of "state capacity" and reform (Minnici and Hill 2007), but states' ability to lead districts and schools in educational improvement remains uneven. David Cohen and Susan Moffitt's article in this issue considers the challenges that government institutions face in building instructional capacity.

HOW WELL HAVE ESEA'S ASPIRATIONS BEEN ACHIEVED?

Despite these structural limitations, ESEA has inspired and induced many changes in the U.S. educational system. Scholarly accounts of these changes, however, reveal a mixed record when it comes to ESEA's achieving its objectives. ESEA's effects in educational finance, educational outcomes, reductions in poverty and educational innovation, though important, have been varied. Moreover, the recent policy stalemate over ESEA's reauthorization means that the ability of federal education policy to respond quickly to changing educational circumstances is increasingly limited.

Education Finance

In 1965, targeted federal grants to state and local governments were a relatively new policy idea. The authors of ESEA and other federal grant programs assumed that legislative and regulatory requirements could ensure that federal funds would supplement rather than replace state and local funds, as Nora Gordon and Sarah Reber discuss elsewhere in this issue. Fifty years later, research on public finance has shown that intergovernmental grants, unlike flypaper, do not necessarily "stick where they hit." Despite this limitation, ESEA has mostly had its intended effects on education finance.

Most obviously, ESEA has produced a dramatic increase in federal spending on K–12 education. It more than doubled (1965 dollars), from $923,337,000 in the 1963–1964 school year to $1,996,954,000 in the 1965–1966 school year. As a proportion of total K–12 education spending, the federal share rose from 4.4 percent in 1963–1964 to 7.9 percent in 1965–1966 (Snyder and Hoffman 1991).[5]

As figure 2 shows, after ESEA the federal share of K–12 education revenue has typically fluctuated between about 8 percent and just under 10 percent. It is important to bear in mind that this is the share of the entire nation's education revenue, and that individual states may get more of their education funds from federal sources. For example, at the end of the 1960s, Title I funds constituted 17.2 percent of education revenue in the southern states (Cascio and Reber 2013, 68).

The majority of U.S. school districts receive funds through ESEA Title I. Spreading Title I funds broadly, rather than concentrating them in the neediest districts, creates a strong incentive for members of Congress to support the program. However, because the funds are broadly distributed, they do not make up a large proportion of local school districts' budgets. Even in the 10 percent of districts that rely most heavily on Title I, it generally provides between 5 percent and 10 percent of total spending (Gordon 2004).

Rucker Johnson's article in this issue finds that increased Title I funding to school districts does indeed lead to increased per-pupil spending. As Gordon and Reber show, school districts take the federal requirements for maintenance of effort, supplement not supplant, and comparability of spending seriously, because of the threat of negative audit findings. However, analyses of how Title I funds affect local education spending show that when Title I aid to a district increases, its per-pupil spending increases by less than the amount of the federal increase (Gordon 2004; for a brief explanation of why grants like Title I do not lead to dollar-for-dollar increases in spending at lower levels of government, see Gordon and Reber in this issue).

As Eric Houck and Elizabeth DeBray describe in their article, federal funding has not been a major force for increased financial equality within or between states. Changes in how states fund public education have had far

---

5. Both spending amounts are in 1965 dollars, adjusted with the U.S. Bureau of Labor Statistics Inflation Calculator. Available at: http://www.bls.gov/data/inflation_calculator.htm (accessed July 22, 2015).

Figure 2. Local, State, and Federal Sources as Percentage of K–12 Education Revenue, 1961–2010

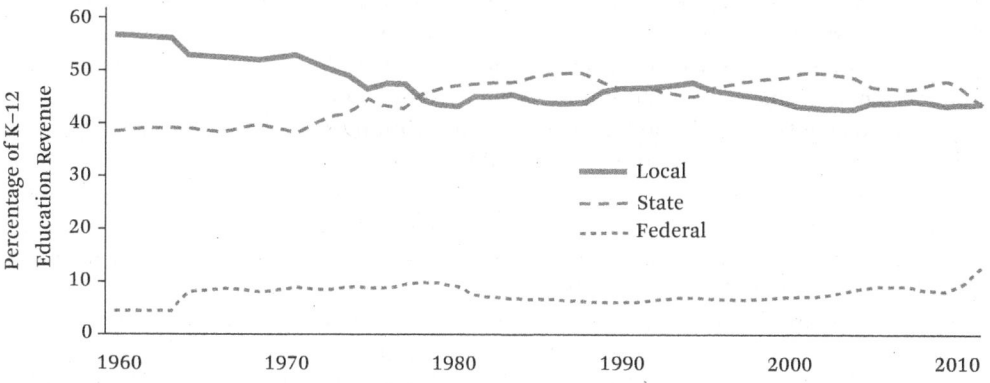

Sources: Snyder and Hoffman 1993, table 156; Snyder and Dillow 2013, table 202.

larger effects on equity than have increases in federal spending. Since the 1970s, lawsuits challenging unequal local school spending have led to both an increased funding role for most states and an increasing state share of public education revenue. In 1900, states provided only 16.5 percent of funds for public K–12 education and localities made up the rest. Just before enactment of ESEA in 1965, the state share was 39.3 percent. As figure 2 shows, the state share continued to increase to nearly 50 percent in 2000–2001, and remained in the upper 40 percent range until the Great Recession. An increasing state share of funds has helped make public school funding more equal across districts (Cascio, Gordon, and Reber 2013, 130). At the same time, this trend has meant that comparatively low levels of federal funding have kept school funding unequal across states.

Educational Outcomes

ESEA's effect on educational outcomes has on balance been positive, though not revolutionary. The American labor force is, on the whole, better educated than it was in 1965, though much of this growth had already happened before ESEA. Goldin and Katz report "substantial" growth in the average years of schooling completed by United States natives born between 1876 and 1951, a plateau for the 1952 through 1965 birth cohorts, and only modest growth in educational attainment for those born after 1965 (Goldin and Katz 2008).

Although the 1966 Coleman report, which the federal government commissioned, was not a study of Title I, its general conclusion that student characteristics affected their school performance more than their schools' per pupil spending, or other school-related factors, undermined optimism that ESEA could make a difference. Pessimism increased when initial evaluations of Title I found weak academic results (McLaughlin 1977).

Recent analyses have reached different conclusions about Title I's academic effects—specifically, its effect on students' total years of schooling and their likelihood of completing high school. Elizabeth Cascio and Reber found that Title I spending narrowed gaps in educational attainment, though not necessarily because Title I–eligible students did better (2013). Similarly, Cascio, Gordon, and Reber found that, in the South in the 1960s, Title I funds contributed to, but do not fully explain, declining dropout rates (2013, 154). In his article in this issue, Rucker Johnson finds that higher Title I spending in school districts between 1965 and 1980 is associated with increased likelihood of high school graduation, and that the effect for low-income students is stronger than for others. He also finds that students in districts with higher Title I spending were less likely to repeat grades and to be suspended or expelled from school.

Effects on Poverty

In addition to being a time of optimism about government's ability to improve social conditions, the middle of the twentieth century was also a period of exceptional wage equality (Piketty 2014, 24–25). It was easy to believe that modest improvements in low-income children's educational attainment would enable them to get well-paid jobs as adults and to raise their own children under better conditions than those in which they had grown up. Fifty years after ESEA was enacted, U.S. wage inequality is at or above its pre–World War II peak. Claudia Goldin and Lawrence Katz attribute rising U.S. economic inequality since 1980 to an increased relative demand for highly educated and skilled workers, globalization, slowing U.S. educational attainment, and changes in labor market institutions like declining rates of unionization and eroding value of the minimum wage (2008, 52–53).

Because of population growth and women's move into paid employment, the U.S. workforce has grown from about eighty-eight million people in 1966 (the data series did not include 1965) to about 158 million in 2013 (DeNavas-Walt and Proctor 2014, table A-4). According to the U.S. Bureau of Labor Statistics (BLS), in 1965, about thirteen million Americans had production or nonsupervisory jobs in manufacturing. Employment in these jobs dropped after 1980, then again in the 2000s. In August 2014, the most recent month available, 8.6 million Americans worked in production and nonsupervisory manufacturing jobs. Put differently, production and nonsupervisory manufacturing workers went from 14.7 percent of the U.S. workforce in 1965 to 5.4 percent in 2014 (BLS 2014). The largest job categories in the contemporary U.S. economy tend to be poorly paid. According to an April 2014 BLS news release, the ten largest U.S. occupations in 2013 accounted for 21 percent of total employment, and only one of these occupations (registered nurses) had an average wage higher than that for all U.S. occupations. The other largest occupations include retail salespersons and cashiers, food preparation and service, office clerks, waiters and waitresses, and customer service representatives (BLS 2014). These changes matter for economic inequality because fewer manufacturing jobs means fewer opportunities for workers with fewer educational credentials to move into, or remain in, the middle class.[6]

In addition to the challenges posed by overall shifts in the jobs available to U.S. workers, employment discrimination has persisted longer than seemed likely in 1965. Political pressure for race and gender equity lessened in the 1980s, and legal attacks on affirmative action took away the strongest tools for making workplaces more diverse (Stainback and Tomaskovic-Devey 2012). The mechanisms for discrimination have shifted over time, and evidence of continued racial and ethnic bias in hiring is strong (Pager and Shepherd 2008). Another set of limits on education's ability to reduce poverty for black and Latino Americans comes from the criminal justice system. During the war on drugs of the 1980s and 1990s, states and the federal government enacted mandatory minimum sentences that have had a far greater impact on black people than others. Contemporary stop-and-frisk policing practices also make young people of color likelier than their white counterparts to have criminal records. Zero-tolerance school discipline, which often includes referral to the criminal justice system, is more prevalent in schools attended by black youth. Criminal records make it hard for young people to get jobs and housing, and thus constitute another set of obstacles to opportunity that are likelier to affect urban youth of color than their suburban, white contemporaries (Alexander 2010).

Educational Innovation

ESEA Title I seemed to assume that local school districts would be able to provide effective programs for disadvantaged students once they had more money to do so. ESEA's original Title III funded educational innovations, suggesting some awareness that new ideas were needed. (Title III of the 1965 ESEA was notably a completely different program from the current Title III of NCLB, which establishes re-

---

6. The overall manufacturing-employment numbers probably understate the problem, given that the manufacturing jobs that remain in the United States are likely to require more education than the ones that have moved overseas or been automated.

quirements for programs that serve English-language learner students.) Innovation funding under the old Title III demonstrates some of the key tensions inherent in using the federal government as an agent of instructional change.

As we highlighted in our account of ESEA's origin stories, the original Title III's core purpose was to inject innovation into the American educational system. Before ESEA was enacted, President Johnson had appointed a task force to advise him on what shape federal education aid should take. The task force's concept of what ailed U.S. education was not as much a shortage of new ideas as the few ways to convert the ideas into usable forms in the classroom, hence its call for providing funding to outside institutions such as museums, libraries, private nonprofit groups, or local community centers (Goldin and Katz 2008, 19, 15–16). It also called for creating "supplementary educational centers that would be financed by the Federal Government and staffed by artists, museum directors, novelists, journalists and the like—designed to bring about change and to provide new services from the outside in" (Subcommittee on Education 1967, 16).

Considering Congress's tendency to spread federal funds widely among states and congressional districts, it is not surprising that ESEA emphasized aid to school districts rather than creation of new centers for innovation. Even Title III designated local public school districts as the only legal recipients of its funding. However, it also stated that districts could be eligible for funding "only if there is satisfactory assurance that in the planning of that program there has been, and in the establishing and carrying out of that program there will be, participation of persons broadly representative of the cultural and educational resources of the area to be served" (Title III, 1965, Sec. 304). Title III thus contained vestiges of the task force's vision, and it echoed the language of the Community Action Program established as part of the Economic Opportunity Act of 1964.

Title III's model of innovation was based on a set of assumptions, most prominently that innovative ideas were out there just waiting to break free, whether in schools or community agencies. In addition, Title III authors assumed that schools, students, teachers, and parents could learn to work seamlessly with community agencies in ways that would enhance student achievement. Finally, the program assumed that ambitious educators or community-based reformers could quickly organize and submit proposals that met the stipulations of the application process, and then embark on a major new project—often within a matter of weeks or months.

Many federal officials lauded Title III as a success, citing statistics showing that local school districts had answered the federal call to action by submitting more than 2,700 proposals, requesting a total of $250 million by July 1966. The USOE reported that by 1967 some 1,700 projects had been funded and were underway, impacting either directly or indirectly an estimated six thousand districts and eight to ten million children (Graham 1984). As it turned out, some of the harshest critiques of Title III came not from those who opposed federal funding, or who sought to shift control of Title III to the states, but from those who had the highest hopes for it. Blaine Worthen, an Ohio State researcher who edited a special issue of the journal *Theory into Practice* devoted to Title III, complained that too many projects focused on "expanding and improving extant services such as educational TV, audio-visual materials, counseling programs, etc. . . . One is left with the definite impression," he concluded, "that the majority of these proposals are mere attempts to procure additional funding and thus reduce strain on the internal budget" (Worthen 1967, 107).

Over time, the federal government became less enamored with the innovative aspirations of Title III. Indeed, by the time NCLB was enacted, ESEA requirements had moved away from the idea that federal funding should unleash new ideas. Instead, the law's more than one hundred requirements that federal funds be used only for instructional practices grounded in "scientifically based research" reflected a different belief: that scientifically proven solutions to common educational problems already exist, and educators need to be required to use them. The U.S. Department of Education's (ED's) Office of Educational Research and Improvement was reorganized into the Institute of Education Sciences, which sponsored the What Works Clearinghouse to help educators find appropriately scientific methods.

The Department of Education continues trying to support educational innovation, though not through the ESEA. The most recent chapter of this history is the Investing in Innovation Fund (i3) initiative that began in 2009, as part of the federal stimulus bill. According to federal officials, the purpose of i3 is to provide competitive grants that will "expand the implementation of, and investment in, innovative and evidence-based practices, programs and strategies," with a special emphasis on initiatives that significantly improve K–12 achievement and close achievement gaps, decrease dropout rates, increase graduation rates, or improve teacher and school leader effectiveness ("i3 at a Glance"). However, the first round of successful i3 applicants were not necessarily seen as innovative or new. As some commentators put it after the awards were announced, it seemed as if the federal government was simply funding "the usual suspects" (McNeil 2011). They included Success for All ($49 million), Teach for America ($50 million), the KIPP Foundation ($50 million), and Reading Recovery/Ohio State University ($45 million). Another way of thinking of the awards is that ED was continuing its efforts to see that What Works (according to its standards of scientific research) would be put into practice.

FUTURE DIRECTIONS FOR ESEA AND THE FEDERAL ROLE

Between 1965 and 2001, Congress reauthorized ESEA at regular intervals. ESEA has been due for reauthorization since 2007, but Congress has to date failed to pass a new version. Even before the reauthorization deadlines, some of NCLB's central provisions seeemed ripe for revision, such as the 2014 deadline for all subgroups of students in all schools to score proficient on state tests, the 100 percent proficiency target for students with disabilities, and the AYP targets that identified steadily increasing numbers of schools and districts for sanctions and potential state intervention. During George W. Bush's second term in office, ED granted waivers that allowed states to experiment with adding academic growth models to their accountability systems, set different standards for the small number of students with "persistent academic disabilities" such as cognitive impairments, and implement "supplemental educational services" for students before rather than after granting them the right to transfer out of underperforming schools (Olson 2005; Hoff 2005).

In the absence of a reauthorization, the Obama administration has issued NCLB waivers to forty-three states. In contrast to the more limited Bush administration waivers, the Obama administration's waivers require states to enact new policies not included in NCLB, such as adopting the Common Core State Standards or similar college- and career-readiness standards, including student performance in teacher evaluations, and removing obstacles to charter school expansion. ED revoked the state of Washington's waiver in April 2014 when the state's legislature voted to let districts decide whether to use student test scores in teacher evaluations (Rich 2014). A few months later, Oklahoma lost its waiver when it dropped the Common Core State Standards (Camera 2014), but it was later reinstated. Some Republicans have attacked the Obama administration for advancing its own policy agenda without congressional action, thus violating the constitutional separation of powers, and Louisiana Governor Bobby Jindal filed a federal lawsuit over the Common Core. Skepticism about the waivers is not confined to national Republican leaders; Douglas Reed points out that ED "has utilized waivers from a law that is impossible to comply with in order to extract further education reforms from states" (2014, 221). In this concluding section, we hazard some predictions and recommendations for ESEA's possible futures.

Will the Reauthorization Stalemate Continue?

Whenever Congress has debated NCLB reauthorization, serious substantive disagreements have arisen. The Obama administration's 2010 reauthorization blueprint included many ideas also found in Race to the Top and the later NCLB waiver criteria. Both of the national teachers' unions and many members of Congress disagreed with these ideas. In 2011, the Senate Committee on Health, Education, Labor, and Pensions approved a reauthorization bill, but the Obama administration did not believe its provisions were strong enough and it never came up for a vote in the full Senate. In 2013, the Senate committee again approved a reauthorization bill with provisions that closely resembled the NCLB waiver requirements, but only Democrats voted for it. The House of Representatives passed a completely different bill that would have greatly reduced the federal government's role in school accountability. As in the past, conservative Republicans object in principle to a large federal presence in K–12 education. How much to spend on ESEA has also been an area of disagreement; in general, Democrats have wanted to increase funding and Republicans have wanted to decrease it. The promise of increased spending helped overcome objections to parts of NCLB during congressional deliberations in 2001, and without this promise, it has been even harder than it would otherwise have been to work through disagreements.

As of this writing, both the Senate and the House have passed versions of the ESEA reauthorization bill. The differences will need to be ironed out in conference committees and center on the nature of Title I funding—particularly funding portability—as well as the nature of federally-mandated reforms for underperforming schools. Without a conference agreement, no reauthorization bill will be forthcoming in the near future. Across policy areas, Congress is increasingly polarized, to the point of being unable or unwilling (or both) to pass new legislation and to perform routine tasks like oversight of executive-branch agencies and reauthorization of existing laws (Ravitch 2013; Mann and Ornstein 2006; Mettler 2014, 35). Other important programs, such as Temporary Assistance for Needy Families (Falk 2014), and the federal highway bill, are also overdue for reauthorization.

Even if one or the other party were to win both the presidency and control of both houses of Congress in 2016, gridlock could well continue if the Senate majority party has fewer than sixty senators. A Democratic sweep in 2016 is highly unlikely because the current House districts disadvantage Democratic candidates (McDonnell and Weatherford 2011). The Republican party is currently split over education issues, particularly the Common Core (Giroux 2013). Even with a Republican sweep in 2016, a reauthorization could be elusive, and the new president might follow the Obama administration's precedent and continue to use executive agency power to shape education policy.

A Department of Education able to sustain its policy agenda under a president of either party (and is not eliminated by conservatives) would imply a power shift from the generalist Congress to the specialist executive agency. In theory, this could mean a more expertise-driven federal policy. On the other hand, a greater role for the ED could also simply empower the few political appointees at the head of the agency to enact presidential priorities without reliance on the traditional mechanisms for policy legitimation—or without even consulting actors outside the inner circle.

If Congress does not reauthorize ESEA and the executive branch continues to shape policy unilaterally, one possible result would be more litigation, such as Louisiana Governor Bobby Jindal's suit over the Common Core State Standards, or a suit challenging the ability of the Department of Education to seek policy advances without explicit authorization from Congress to pursue them. These suits—no matter what the outcome—would further complicate the education policy landscape by placing into jeopardy the continuing relevance of ESEA. Because NCLB is currently unworkable as policy, if Congress remains unable to devise an alternative, a judicial ruling that denied the Department of Education the ability to grant waivers would throw federal educational policy into turmoil, and reinforce the status of states and localities as the primary locus of educational policymaking.

Other lawsuits, such as the *Vergara* suit in California—which ruled that California's tenure system violated poor students' right to a quality education—further highlight the multiplicity of actors within the educational arena and the sometimes limited ability of the federal government to play a meaningful role. As in the state-level school finance equalization lawsuits, the *Vergara* case saw a state-level constitutional requirement for equal educational opportunity used to contest a central element of state educational law. Although earlier cases focused on the financing of schools, the *Vergara* case challenged the teacher tenure and employment provisions of the California code, which the plaintiffs allege disproportionately denied low-income and minority students access to a quality education. The state judge's agreement with the plaintiff's position is a harbinger of major reforms in California's system of teacher tenuring and dismissal—all without direct federal involvement. The U.S. practice of layering new educational authority on top of—or adjacent to—existing educational authority creates a complex and, at times, contradictory educational policy environment. As a result, educational changes and institutional reforms may occur in venues far from Washington and outside federal control. At the same time, federal lawmakers and policy makers play a key role in establishing the contexts of educational change.

Recommendations for a Future ESEA

The nine articles in this issue analyze different facets of ESEA but converge around a few key challenges to the federal government's ability to increase educational equality. One set of challenges comes from the complex relationships among the federal, state, and local governments, and the federal government's limited ability to influence education. Within the intergovernmental system as it currently exists, ED's leverage over states and school districts comes from the conditions that Congress includes in grant programs like Title I and the fiscal rules that govern how states and districts use the money. Based on his analysis of ED's history, Patrick McGuinn argues for an overall increase in the agency's statutory authority and administrative capacity. Nora Gordon and Sarah Reber advocate making ED's guidance on Title I fiscal rules clearer and more concise and disseminating these directions across the states and local school districts, thereby allowing school administrators to be more confident about using the flexibility already allowed by federal law. Although a reauthorized ESEA (should there be one) may be more flexible in its requirements for state testing, Lorraine McDonnell identifies the mandates on states to disaggregate test scores by demographic subgroups and to participate in the NAEP as two positive elements of the current system that should continue.

Several articles in this issue identify persistent inequity of educational resources as a major obstacle to achieving greater educational and social equality. Over ESEA's fifty-year history, the federal government has not had much effect on finance equity because it has provided 10 percent or less of total educational revenue. Because states have the constitutional authority over public education, the federal government cannot directly compel states to change how they fund schooling. However, it might be able to use the funding it controls more strategically. For example, Rucker Johnson argues that Title I could be refined so that it rewards rather than crowds out local funding effort, boosts spending in low-wealth school districts, and narrows spending inequality. Eric Houck and Elizabeth DeBray propose an expansion of ESEA to include competitive grants that would reward states for addressing inequalities in finance and ultimately reduce interstate variations in school spending.

Since 1965, policymakers' aspirations for ESEA have grown from simply providing funds for education to supporting improvement in teaching and learning. As David Cohen and Susan Moffitt explain in their article, these expanded aspirations have not been paired with practices that offer direct paths for improving the quality of instruction. Based on their research, Cohen and Moffitt call for the federal government to engage with nongovernmental organizations, following the model of the Comprehensive School Reform Demonstration Project, to build a stronger system within the limits on federal power. According to both Patricia Gándara and Gloria Ladson-Billings, federal policy also needs to shift away from a deficit framing of low-income students, students of color, and students in ELL programs. Ladson-Billings calls for culturally responsive pedagogy to be a priority. Gándara argues, on the basis of research that highlights the advantages of bilingualism, that federal policy should reverse its post-NCLB emphasis on English-language acquisition, and instead focus on developing true academic bilingualism.

Finally, the articles in this issue also call attention to the need for change in other policies that create the context in which ESEA operates. Erica Frankenberg and Kendra Taylor call attention to ESEA's power as a lever for school integration, arguing for increased federal attention to new forms of racial segregation and inequality. Federal officials could make clear that diversity and equality are still priorities, and federal spending programs like ESEA and grants to magnet and charter schools could all align around the goal of maintaining diversity. Public schooling is only one part of low-income students' overall life experiences. Several authors note that to make U.S. society more egalitarian, policy also needs to address disparities in nutrition, health, housing, and exposure to violence.

CONCLUSION

When President Johnson signed ESEA in 1965, his remarks looked forward to a time when compensatory education for low-income students would help them overcome the limitations imposed by poverty. Indeed, Johnson and his political allies believed that the Great Society programs, including ESEA, would lead to a future in which poverty no longer threatened Americans. Federal funding coupled with judicial and executive action clearly provided leverage for desegregation of southern public schools. Although economic analyses suggest that ESEA did have some modest positive effects on students' educational attainment and employment prospects, it is clear in retrospect that a relatively small federal contribution to K–12 education spending, deployed in supplemental programs for a subpopulation of students, could not have lived up to Johnson's larger promises.

Fifty years later, policymakers still have audacious goals for ESEA as the centerpiece of an expanded federal presence in K–12 education. The ESEA reauthorization passed during Bill Clinton's presidency used federal funding for "improving America's schools" by pushing states toward standards-based education reform. President George W. Bush's version of ESEA promised that no child would be "left behind" and called on public schools to educate all of their students to a common level of proficiency within twelve years. President Barack Obama has organized his administration's education policy around "college and career readiness" for all high school graduates. On one hand, these goals are more modest than LBJ's: they do not place public education at the center of a strategy for eradicating poverty. On the other hand, they are in fact more ambitious than the goals of 1965, because they attempt to use a federal program not just as leverage on state and local policies, but also as a way to make teaching and learning more effective at the classroom level. The nine articles in this issue of *RSF* analyze how these shifts took place, where they have succeeded and fallen short, and where ESEA might go in the future.

REFERENCES

Alexander, Michelle. 2010. *The New Jim Crow: Mass Incarceration in the Age of Colorblindness.* New York: The New Press.

Bailey, Stephen Kemp, and Edith K. Mosher. 1968. *ESEA: The Office of Education Administers a Law.* Syracuse, N.Y.: Syracuse University Press.

Bestor, Arthur Eugene. 1953. *Educational Wastelands: The Retreat from Learning in Our Public Schools.* Urbana: University of Illinois Press.

Borman, Geoffrey D., and Jerome V. D'Agostino. 2001. "Title I and Student Achievement: A Quantitative Synthesis." In *Title I: Compensatory Education at the Crossroads*, edited by Geoffrey D. Borman, Samuel C. Stringfield and Robert E. Slavin. New York: Routledge.

Camera, Lauren. 2014. "Oklahoma, Louisiana Center Stage in Common-Core Fight." *Education Week*, September 10, 2014, p. 21.

Cascio, Elizabeth U., and Sarah Reber. 2013. "The K–12 Education Battle." In *Legacies of the War on Poverty*, edited by Sheldon Danziger. New York: Russell Sage Foundation.

Cascio, Elizabeth U., Nora Gordon, and Sarah Reber. 2013. "Local Responses to Federal Grants: Evidence from the Introduction of Title I in the South." *American Economic Journal* 5(3): 126–59.

Cohen, David K., and Susan L. Moffitt. 2009. *The*

Ordeal of Equality: Did Federal Regulation Fix the Schools? Cambridge, Mass.: Harvard University Press.

Cornman, Stephen Q. 2013. "Revenues and Expenditures for Public Elementary and Secondary Education: School Year 2010–11 (Fiscal Year 2011)." NCES no. 2013-342. Washington: National Center for Education Statistics.

"Crisis in Education." *Life*, March 24, 1958, 25–37.

DeNavas-Walt, Carmen, and Bernadette D. Proctor. 2014. "Income and Poverty in the United States: 2013." Current Population Reports, series P60, no. 249. Washington: Government Printing Office for U.S. Bureau of the Census. Available at: http://www.census.gov/content/dam/Census/library/publications/2014/demo/p60-249.pdf (accessed August 24, 2015).

Douglas, Davison M. 2005. *Jim Crow Moves North: The Battle over Northern School Segregation, 1865–1954*. New York: Cambridge University Press.

Falk, Gene. 2014. *The Temporary Assistance for Needy Families (TANF) Block Grant: Responses to Frequently Asked Questions*. CRS Report. Washington: Congressional Research Service.

Gardner, John W. 1961. *Excellence: Can We Be Equal and Excellent Too?* New York: Harper.

Giroux, Greg. 2013. "Republicans Win Congress as Democrats Get Most Votes." *Bloomberg News*, March 18. Available at: http://www.bloomberg.com/news/2013-03-19/republicans-win-congress-as-democrats-get-most-votes.html (accessed July 10, 2015).

Goldin, Claudia Dale, and Lawrence F. Katz. 2008. *The Race Between Education and Technology*. Cambridge, Mass.: Belknap Press of Harvard University Press.

Gordon, Nora. 2004. "Do Federal Grants Boost School Spending?: Evidence from Title I." *Journal of Public Economics* 88(9/10): 1771–92. doi: 10.1016/j.jpubeco.2003.09.002.

Graham, Hugh Davis. 1984. *The Uncertain Triumph: Federal Education Policy in the Kennedy and Johnson Years*. Chapel Hill: University of North Carolina Press.

Harrington, Michael. 1962. *The Other America: Poverty in the United States*. New York: Macmillan.

Hoff, David J. 2005. "States to Get New Options on NCLB Law." *Education Week*, April 13, 2005, p. 1.

Hughes, John F., and Anne O. Hughes. 1972. *Equal Education: A New National Strategy*. Bloomington: Indiana University Press.

Jeffrey, Julie Roy. 1978. *Education for Children of the Poor: A Study of the Origins and Implementation of the Elementary and Secondary Education Act of 1965*. Columbus: Ohio State University Press.

Jennings, John F. 2001. "Title I: Its Legislative History and Its Promise." In *Title I: Compensatory Education at the Crossroads*, edited by Geoffrey D. Borman, Samuel C. Stringfield and Robert E. Slavin. Mahwah, N.J.: Lawrence Erlbaum.

Johnson, Lyndon Baines. 1965. "Johnson's Remarks on Signing the Elementary and Secondary Education Act." LBJ Presidential Library. Available at: http://www.lbjlibrary.org/lyndon-baines-johnson/timeline/johnsons-remarks-on-signing-the-elementary-and-secondary-education-act (accessed August 24, 2015).

Katz, Michael B. 2013. *The Undeserving Poor: America's Enduring Confrontation with Poverty*, 2nd ed. New York: Oxford University Press.

Kearney, Charles Philip. 1967. "The 1964 Presidential Task Force on Education and the Elementary and Secondary Education Act of 1965." Ph.D. diss., Department of Education, University of Chicago.

Kohn, Alfie. 2004. "NCLB and the Effort to Privatize Public Education." In *Many Children Left Behind*, edited by Deborah Meier and George Wood. Boston: Beacon Press.

Mann, Thomas E., and Norman J. Ornstein. 2006. *The Broken Branch: How Congress Is Failing America and How to Get It Back on Track*. New York: Oxford University Press.

Manna, Paul. 2006. *School's In: Federalism and the National Educational Agenda*. Washington, D.C.: Georgetown University Press.

McDermott, Kathryn A. 2011. *High-Stakes Reform: The Politics of Educational Accountability*. Washington, D.C.: Georgetown University Press.

McDermott, Kathryn A., Elizabeth H. DeBray, Erica Frankenberg, Anna Fung-Morley, and Anne Elizabeth Blankenship. 2014. "Good Intentions, Limited Impact: The Technical Assistance for Student Assignment Plans Program." Working paper. Amherst: University of Massachusetts. Available at: http://school-diversity.org/pdf/Good_Intentions_Limited_Impact.pdf (accessed July 10, 2015).

McDonnell, Lorraine M., and M. Stephen Weatherford. 2011. "Crafting an Education Reform Agenda Through Economic Stimulus Policy." *Peabody Journal of Education* 86(3): 304–18. doi: 10.1080/0161956X.2011.579001.

McLaughlin, Donald H. 1977. *Title I, 1965–1975: A Synthesis of the Findings of Federal Studies*. Palo Alto, Calif.: American Institutes for Research.

McNeil, Michele. 2011. "Study Gives First Round of 'i3' Mixed Grades." *Education Week*, August 9, 2011. Available at: http://www.edweek.org/ew/articles/2011/08/10/37i3-2.h30.html (accessed August 24, 2015).

Melnick, R. Shep. 1994. *Between the Lines: Interpreting Welfare Rights*. Washington, D.C.: Brookings Institution Press.

Mettler, Suzanne. 2014. *Degrees of Inequality: How the Politics of Higher Education Sabotaged the American Dream*. New York: Basic Books.

Miller, Richard I. 1967. *Catalyst for Change: A National Study of ESEA, Title III (PACE)*. Washington: U.S. Government. Printing Office.

Minnici, Angela, and Deanna Hill. 2007. *Educational Architects: Do State Education Agencies Have the Tools Necessary to Implement NCLB?* Washington, D.C.: Center on Education Policy.

Olson, Lynn. 2005. "NCLB Waiver Let's Virginia Offer Tutoring Before Choice." *Education Week*, September 7, 2005, p. 26.

Pager, Devah, and Hana Shepherd. 2008. "The Sociology of Discrimination: Racial Discrimination in Employment, Housing, Credit, and Consumer Markets." *Annual Review of Sociology* 34: 181–209.

Piketty, Thomas. 2014. *Capital in the Twenty-First Century*, trans. Arthur Goldhammer. Cambridge, Mass.: The Belknap Press of Harvard University Press.

Ravitch, Diane. 2013. *Reign of Error: The Hoax of the Privatization Movement and the Danger to America's Public Schools*. New York: Knopf.

Reed, Douglas S. 2014. *Building the Federal Schoolhouse: Localism and the American Education State*. New York: Oxford University Press.

Rich, Motoko. 2014. "In Washington State, Political Stance Puts Schools in a Bind." *New York Times*, October 5, 2014, p. A21.

Rosenberg, Gerald. 1991. *The Hollow Hope*. Chicago: University of Chicago Press.

Smith, Marshall S., and Jennifer O'Day. 1990. "Systemic School Reform." *Journal of Education Policy* 5(5): 233–67. doi: 10.1080/02680939008549074.

Snyder, Thomas D., and Sally A. Dillow. 2013. *Digest of Education Statistics 2012*. Washington: National Center for Education Statistics, Institute of Education Sciences, U.S. Department of Education. Available at: http://nces.ed.gov/pubs2014/2014015.pdf (accessed August 11, 2015).

Snyder, Thomas D., and Charlene M. Hoffman. 1991. *Digest of Education Statistics 1990*. Washington: National Center for Education Statistics, U.S. Department of Education. Available at: http://nces.ed.gov/pubs91/91660.pdf (accessed August 12, 2015).

———. 1993. *Digest of Education Statistics 1993*. Washington: National Center for Education Statistics, U.S. Department of Education. Available at: http://nces.ed.gov/pubs93/93292.pdf (accessed August 12, 2015).

Sokol, Jason. 2014. *All Eyes Are Upon Us: Race and Politics from Boston to Brooklyn*. New York: Basic Books.

Stainback, Kevin, and Donald Tomoskovic-Devey. 2012. *Documenting Desegregation: Racial and Gender Segregation in Private Sector Employment Since the Civil Rights Act*. New York: Russell Sage Foundation.

Subcommittee on Education, Committee on Labor and Public Welfare. 1967. *Notes and Working Papers Concerning the Administration of Programs Authorized Under Title III of P.L. 89-10, the Elementary and Secondary Education Act of 1965, as Amended by P.L. 89-750*. 90th Congress, 1st session committee print. Washington: U.S. Government Printing Office (April).

U.S. Bureau of Labor Statistics (BLS). 2014. "Manufacturing: NAICS 31-33." *Industries at a Glance*. Washington: U.S. Department of Labor. Available at: http://www.bls.gov/iag/tgs/iag31-33.htm (accessed July 22, 2015).

Worthen, Blaine R. 1967. "The Evolution of Title III: A Study in Change." *Theory into Practice* 6(3): 104–11.

PART I
Consequences of the Elementary and Secondary Education Act

ESEA and the Civil Rights Act: An Interbranch Approach to Furthering Desegregation

ERICA FRANKENBERG AND KENDRA TAYLOR

To understand the impact of the Elementary and Secondary Education Act (ESEA) and the Civil Rights Act in contributing to school desegregation, it is necessary to take an interbranch perspective that accounts for the ways in which interplay among the branches of the federal government occurred to further a policy agenda that would have been improbable had one branch acted alone. This paper examines the passage and implementation of the ESEA and the Civil Rights Act during the Johnson and Nixon years, considering how the legislative, judicial, and executive branches collaborated with each other to strengthen the impact of this legislation beyond what was initially conceived. Despite complex desegregation issues left unresolved, this period marks the only time when all branches of government employed their unique powers to implement and enforce desegregation, offering important insights into the ways in which the federal government can effectively accomplish progress in changing local practice on contentious civil rights issues.

Keywords: ESEA, Civil Rights Act, desegregation, interbranch, enforcement

The passage of the Elementary and Secondary Education Act (ESEA) in 1965 occurred shortly after the Civil Rights Act of 1964 became law. Together these laws responded to local intransigence and expanded desegregation across the South in ways that had not occurred prior to 1964. ESEA provided federal funds in such quantities to schools that Title VI of the Civil Rights Act, which had been viewed as inconsequential in congressional debates prior to its passage, became a critical tool in desegregating schools in the South. Without the Civil Rights Act, ESEA would have been unable to withhold funds from segregated districts, and conversely, Title VI of the Civil Rights Act would have been less effective without ESEA funds with which to threaten districts. However, the Civil Rights Act (together with ESEA) is limited in furthering school desegregation because of the law's provisions and enforcement. These constraints were particularly visible in the years following the laws' passage when federal officials lacked the resources and expertise to fully carry out enforcement. Though the tools to desegregate schools may be available, their use is dependent on those in power, illustrating barriers limiting past, and likely future, efforts to furthering the rights of minorities through popularly elected officials.

The passage of the Civil Rights Act and ESEA in 1964 and 1965, respectively, in comparison with the failures of prior weaker bills, demonstrates the importance of the unique historical conditions that allowed for their pas-

Erica Frankenberg is associate professor at the Pennsylvania State University. **Kendra Taylor** is a doctoral student at the Pennsylvania State University.

The authors gratefully acknowledge the assistance of Penn State reference librarians Ellysa Cahoy Stern and Andrew J. Tig Wartluft. Direct correspondence to: Erica Frankenberg, euf10@psu.edu, Pennsylvania State University, College of Education, 207B Rackley Bldg., University Park, PA 16802; Kendra Taylor, kat5123@psu.edu, Pennsylvania State University, College of Education, 200 Rackley Bldg., University Park, PA 16802.

sage. The Civil Rights Act of 1964 emerged from a social movement against racial discrimination, which rose to a level of national consciousness demanding legislative action following the Birmingham crisis in 1963. ESEA passed as part of Johnson's legislative agenda bringing attention to the economic disparities in the country and the plight of the poor. Passing federal aid to education bills had been difficult prior to 1965 in part because of race, while enacting a strong civil rights bill had faced barriers due to a lack of public and political support and a southern filibuster. Key elements of the success of the legislative approach were the social and political context that allowed for expanding federal involvement and the foresight of those who crafted the acts in order to maintain their viability to affect local change well after the conditions that were favorable to their passage had disappeared.

Considering ESEA and the Civil Rights Act together demonstrates the possibilities and limitations of executive, legislative and judicial branch interplay at the federal level to further school desegregation. In American policymaking, it is not the edict of one branch alone that creates policy; rather it emerges from the interactions among all three branches of the federal government (Miller and Barnes 2004). We consider the ESEA and Civil Rights Act from an interbranch perspective in the context of the Johnson administration, when the acts were passed, and the Nixon administration, the start of conservative domination of the executive branch that limited school desegregation efforts. Under both administrations, desegregation advanced markedly from the decade following *Brown* when little progress was made. Ten years after *Brown*, just 2.3 percent of black students in the South attended a majority white school. By 1968, amid implementation of the Civil Rights Act and ESEA, that figure grew to 23.4 percent (Orfield 1978). We discuss conditions allowing for this progress, but also examine how enforcement efforts were thwarted by a lack of resources and, later on, by a lack of political will. Interplay between the three branches of government shifted depending on those in power following the passage of ESEA and the Civil Rights Act.

Once implementation of this legislation began, attacks that would substantially alter them were not able to pass through the change-adverse wheels of the federal system, but executive enforcement was more variable.

The coalition that passed the Civil Rights Act in 1964 coalesced around the need for federal intervention into the harsh state-sponsored segregation (for example, de Jure) in the South. The consensus disappeared, however, in the following years when the debate moved outside the South. The idea of federal intervention in nonsouthern regions—where the history of discriminatory policies left a legacy of residential, and thus school, segregation that was harder to prove under existing legal theories—was unpalatable to many. Despite the language of Title VI that allowed agencies such as the U.S. Department of Health, Education, and Welfare (HEW) to adopt a broad definition of discrimination to include de facto segregation, this issue was instead left unresolved—with long-lasting ramifications for contemporary segregation. Today, urban, and increasingly suburban, districts are still contested sites of desegregation. We trace the unraveling of the consensus that successfully dismantled de jure segregation in the mid-1960s, explain the conditions that contributed to the failure to address de facto segregation, and consider implications for future federal desegregation efforts.

CONTEXT AND PASSAGE OF THE CIVIL RIGHTS ACT AND ESEA

A decade of sluggish judicial progress in furthering desegregation after *Brown* suggested that segregation would not be eradicated solely through the judiciary. Yet, concerns about the proper federal role in desegregation prevented action for nearly a decade. A rapidly changing context allowed for two pieces of legislation that, when examined in tandem, affected school desegregation. The passage of the Civil Rights Act of 1964, by prohibiting federal funds from going to recipients that discriminate, removed a major impediment to passing ESEA that had doomed prior educational funding bills. Additionally, the civil rights movement more generally showed the need for the Civil Rights Act and raised awareness about inequality that provided an important rationale for targeting aid for disadvantaged students.

The Civil Rights Act of 1964

A decade after the *Brown* decision, little progress had been made in eradicating the segregated schools in many southern states. Because *Brown II* in 1955 remaded segregation cases back to district courts to devise the remedy, progress towards desegregation was halting; the Court did not again issue desegregation guidance until 1968. Instead of broad desegregation guidelines, it required private resources and plaintiffs in each district to legally challenge segregation. Under the Kennedy administration, the attorney general tried to bring in the federal government by filing several desegregation suits in districts receiving federal funding but the courts did not permit them to intervene without congressional authorization. In early 1964, fewer than 20 percent of districts in the South had begun to desegregate (Orfield 1969). A U.S. Justice Department official feared that the intransigence from many states was causing the federal system to fail because it required an "endless" chain of litigation on a "case by case" approach (Marshall 1962, 6).

In early 1963, desegregation action from other branches did not appear likely, but that quickly changed illustrating how popularly elected branches are more susceptible to public opinion and events, which is a benefit of involving all branches in the desegregation effort. In April 1963, President Kennedy dismissed a suggestion that federal funds to a project be cut off because funding was being distributed in a discriminatory manner. In the same month, the House summarily defeated two such amendments to educational funding bills (Orfield 1969). In May 1963, however, nonviolent civil rights demonstrations in Birmingham, Alabama, and the vicious police response to it were broadcast via television and newspapers around the country and beyond. Seeing images of the brutality of local control in Birmingham helped the country understand the dangers of unchecked localism and the need for federal action on racial discrimination at this point in time. In public opinion polls shortly after Birmingham, a majority of respondents reported that civil rights was the most pressing item on the national agenda, which was a dramatic increase from only months earlier (Klarman 2005). Dozens of bills were introduced in Congress, many of them calling for funding only desegregated districts. The Kennedy administration, sensing the policy window open for federal intervention, sent a strengthened civil rights bill with a range of proposals to demonstrate a comprehensive response to address the continued racial discrimination African Americans faced. In his June 1963 speech announcing the bill, Kennedy noted the importance of Birmingham: "The events in Birmingham and elsewhere have so increased the desires for equality that no city or state or legislative body can prudently choose to ignore them. The fires of frustration and discord are burning in every city, North and South, where legal remedies are not at hand." With public support firmly behind civil rights, Congress was ready to show their support for civil rights and many members advocated for a bill stronger than the president's (Orfield 1969).

Despite the initial support in the aftermath of Birmingham, southern congressional resistance to the proposed bill was fierce, and the debate and filibuster were lengthy. It was finally enacted on July 2, 1964. Segregation, of course, was prevalent in many aspects of public life and the Civil Rights Act of 1964 applied to areas such as voting and employment. Titles IV and VI bear directly on the desegregation of schools.[1] Title IV specifically pertained to schools—it commissioned the Coleman report on educational opportunity and provided for technical assistance grants and training for desegregating schools. It also allowed the U.S. attorney general to initiate lawsuits to compel desegregation in local districts, which was the Kennedy administration's school desegregation priority in drafting the legislation. Although architects of Title IV intended for it to be applicable in both de jure and de facto segregated schools, language was added to obtain cloture on the Civil Rights Act that limited its

---

1. Title VII, focusing on employment, did relate to teacher desegregation efforts.

applicability in de facto segregated schools (House of Representatives Subcommittee 1963; Bolner and Shanley 1974). Title VI permits, but does not require, cutting off funds from agencies that are found to discriminate on the basis of race, color and national origin.

Title VI originated from the oft-proposed Powell Amendment, first suggested in a 1947 presidential report on civil rights. The amendment was aimed at using the force of the federal government to bring about desegregation by cutting off federal funds to any institution that was not in compliance with *Brown*. Representative Powell and the NAACP believed in the necessity of a legislative solution as there was "no other alternative to endless litigation" after *Brown* (Orfield 1969, 26). Originally, drafters of the bill added Title VI at the suggestion of some members of Congress; the administration was prepared to compromise on this title in order to gain the passage of other parts of the bill (Orfield 1969). Far from being eliminated, Title VI was strengthened, although it received little attention during congressional debate. Because little federal money was available for education in 1964, Title VI was expected to have relatively little impact. The way in which it was drafted allowed federal officials to cut off funds, but such action was at their discretion—not required. The Justice Department emphasized during Congressional debate that federal agencies likely already possessed such authority to withhold funds, and this was not conferring any additional federal authority. Indeed, a Justice Department official testified that it would not be used to establish federal desegregation standards because that would require, in his estimation, military intervention. In response to concerns in the House, judicial review or administrative hearings prior to fund termination were included as a safeguard against arbitrary fund termination.

The origins of Title VI indicate that it was seen as affecting practices beyond what was prohibited by the Constitution alone (Abernathy 1981). Yet it was ambiguous enough such that actors could have different interpretations of how it should be applied. Foreshadowing future debate, after testimony from a HEW secretary suggesting an expansive interpretation of *discrimination* to include racial imbalance, Congress amended Title VI to allow federal agencies to determine what constituted discrimination. It removed language from Title IV that referenced action against racial imbalance (for example, de facto segregation more common outside the South), which the secretary had linked to his definition of discrimination referred to in Title VI (Bolner and Shanley 1974; Orfield 1969). *Racial imbalance* became a politicized term that, to its critics, came to mean achieving certain quotas of racial groups in schools regardless of the impacts such social planning had. To proponents of remedying racial imbalance, it came to mean equating racial imbalance with segregation (Bolner and Shanley 1974). The congressional compromise in wording acknowledged that as judicial interpretation of what was required by the Constitution changed, so too might the requirements of Title VI, and administrative agencies might even demand more than the Constitution. As an example, HEW had been clear in debates about the bill that they saw correcting racial imbalance as a goal of Title VI, which went beyond judicial interpretation at the time. Almost immediately after the Civil Rights Act was passed, Title VI was bolstered dramatically by the increasingly comprehensive understanding of what was required to protect the rights of black students and the passage of ESEA. Nevertheless, HEW did not fully exploit the ambiguity of Title VI to adopt an expansive understanding of discrimination as encompassing de facto segregation.

The Elementary and Secondary Education Act of 1965

The ESEA was a significant expansion in the role of the federal government in funding K–12 education, which had been the purview of state and local governments. Unlike education bills of the preceding decade that had failed to pass, this bill had several advantages. President Johnson had been elected in a landslide in late 1964, bringing with him a more liberal Congress. With the Civil Rights Act now law, the 1965 bill did not get conflated with racial politics that had made passage of previous education bills impossible (Meranto 1967, 132). A judicial review of ESEA's legislative history noted that "It is a fair assumption that Congress would not have taken this step [passing ESEA] had Title VI not established the principle that schools receiving federal assistance must meet uniform national standards for desegregation" (*U.S. v. Jefferson Co. Bd. of Ed.*, 372 F.836 (5th Cir. 1966), 851).

ESEA was part of Johnson's broader Great Society. The Great Society, with an ambitious goal to cure and prevent poverty, contained a variety of legislative initiatives to improve the education, health, and job skills for low-income individuals. President Johnson believed that issues of educational inequality were intimately linked to race and poverty, and that blacks and Latinos were disadvantaged in the public school system as it existed (Orfield 2015). The rediscovery of the existence of poverty in America was part of a larger policy shift allowing for the passage of federal aid to education. Education was seen as key to breaking the vicious cycle of poverty and improving the lives of "the culturally deprived student" and "the socially impoverished student" (Meranto 1967, 18). ESEA can also be viewed as an indirect response to the civil rights movement by improving aid to black children, many of whom were also economically disadvantaged, without actually being race conscious (Meranto 1967). Just as the civil rights movement created an impetus for the Civil Rights Act by displaying the harsh nature of segregation, it helped create awareness about the inequalities for black students. With the erosion of segregation, white schools and administrators were now faced with the task of educating large numbers of poor African American students (Reed 2014; McGuinn and Hess 2005). For these schools, the challenges of desegregation were related to the challenges of educating students in poverty, and thus the incentive for complying with the HEW standards to continue to receive ESEA funds cannot be understated.

ESEA was signed into law in April 1965 and was almost identical to the bill Johnson proposed in his State of the Union address in January. The law's drafters were successful in giving something to everyone, which headed off both opposition to the bill's passage, but also repeal once it became clear how the ESEA and Civil Rights Act would work together to attack segregation (Orfield 1969, 2015; McGuinn and Hess 2005). A key to the design of ESEA was that money was targeted to disadvantaged students regardless of what school they attended. Federal funds from ESEA went to every congressional district and most schools, though those with higher percentages of low-income students received more funds under Title I. By allowing aid to go to parochial schools enrolling low-income children, ESEA garnered the support of Catholics, a key Democratic bloc.

BRANCHES OF GOVERNMENT UNDER THE JOHNSON ADMINISTRATION

With the passage of the Civil Rights Act and ESEA, the Johnson administration was tasked with implementation. A complex interplay between the federal branches began. Court supervision of desegregation led to automatic compliance with the Civil Rights Act for ESEA funding, which meant that desegregation requirements should not differ drastically between the branches. The Office of Education within HEW was now charged with evaluating desegregation in thousands of districts across the South that had been resisting *Brown*. To accomplish this task, HEW issued guidelines for desegregation, which were used to evaluate the plans that districts submitted for compliance and fund eligibility. Secretary Gardner noted that as HEW determined how to enforce Title VI, they were "plunged into a situation where we had no experience" (Halpern 1995, 64). HEW initially largely adopted fairly minimal judicial standards. In 1966, the guidelines became more specific, requiring districts to increase the percentage of blacks transferring to formerly white schools. Districts with lower rates of desegregation had to show more growth. These guidelines, referred to black student transfers only, but were comparable (if not more extensive) to a typical court-ordered plan (Cascio et al. 2010). During later years of the Johnson administration, HEW strengthened its standards in advance of the courts. Over time, as the guidelines demanded more desegregation progress, tangible, long-lasting progress was accomplished in the South.

Table 1. Summary of HEW Compliance Statuses in Southern and Border States, 1966–1967

Status	December 1966	March 1967	September 1967
Evidence of noncompliance	54	25	1
Evidence of noncompliance[a]	—	9	8
Deferred	143	161	89
Deferred[b]	—	11	50
Terminated	26	17	58
Total districts	4,774	4,890	4,785

Sources: U.S. Department of HEW, 1966, 1967a, 1967b.
[a]Evidence of noncompliance substantiated, negotiations being conducted, final approval of pending applications for federal assistance now being deferred by HEW-except no deferral is operative.
[b]No deferral is operative.

Impact of the New Laws

Contemporary accounts heralded the impact of the laws as accelerating desegregation (for example, USCCR 1966). Before ESEA, in 1964, federal education funding was $176 million for the southern and border states. An addition of nearly $590 million came from ESEA in 1966, making it such that districts could not risk fund termination without substantial disadvantage (*U.S. v. Jefferson Co. Bd. of Ed.*).

Overview of Laws' Impact

Many districts complied with Title VI of the Civil Rights Act in order to get federal funds, although this was not uniform across the South. As seen in the administrative procedure required to cut off funds, this was a last resort, and in many cases, threats of fund termination was enough to gain compliance. Periodic HEW compliance reports, testimony, and U.S. Commission on Civil Rights reports indicate that when threats were not enough, HEW deferred and terminated funds to districts not in compliance with HEW guidelines. For example, in the first year, 2 percent of nearly five thousand districts hadn't been certified to receive ESEA funds (Halpern 1995). In early 1966, sixteen districts had already been found in noncompliance and another twenty-three were pending (USCCR 1966). Later, Commissioner of Education Howe noted that thirty-seven districts had funds cut off in the fall of 1966 (Orfield 1969). Beginning in December 1966, HEW released reports documenting compliance statuses across the seventeen southern and border states. At the three times covered by these reports, hundreds of districts were in different stages of investigation, fund deferral, or termination (see table 1). At each point, some 150 districts had funds deferred, and from seventeen to fifty-nine had funds terminated illustrating that HEW did use the Title VI fund termination mechanism.

Studies assessing the impact of conditional funding and HEW enforcement complement case studies in southern locales finding a changed response due to the threat of the loss of funds (for example, Orfield 1969). A study of more than nine hundred districts not under court supervision in 1966 concluded that federal funding from ESEA, conditional on desegregation compliance, helped move southern districts beyond token desegregation (Cascio et al. 2010).[2] This estimate found that conditional funding accounted for 36 percent of the movement beyond token desegregation from 1964 to 1966. Because of the relatively minimal HEW requirements in 1966, there wasn't evidence of widespread increases in desegregation.[3] However, a small subset of districts had a substantial increase in the percentage of students in desegregated schools, which is perhaps due to the Civil Rights Act and ESEA giving these districts political cover to desegregate more than they felt the district's population would otherwise tolerate. At this time, the Civil

---

2. Defined as 2 percent of black students attending desegregated schools.

3. This analysis also found the ESEA and the Civil Rights Act furthered faculty desegregation in southern schools.

Rights Act and ESEA reduced the burden on the courts in furthering desegregation, which shifted back to the courts in 1970. Other analyses have reached similar conclusions about the effectiveness of HEW enforcement. A study analyzing school segregation in more than 1,300 southern districts in 1968 and 1970 found that racial segregation was lower in districts under HEW enforcement than under court oversight, after controlling for other district factors (Giles 1975). Yet, segregation fell more sharply in districts under court order, illustrating a weakening of HEW enforcement. Finally, a separate analysis of southern districts found those with more low-income students (for example, received more ESEA funding) were less likely to have had any desegregation by 1964, but had caught up to other districts by 1966 (Cascio et al. 2010).

Thus, studies conclude that when viewing desegregation across a variety of districts, the Civil Rights Act and ESEA made small but statistically significant improvements in school-level desegregation during the mid-1960s. Moreover, a small number of districts were investigated and in some cases, funds were deferred or briefly withheld. The pace of desegregation quickened in comparison to the prior decade of case-by-case litigation affecting relatively few districts.

Court Decisions
Court decisions also offer an example of the indirect effect of the Civil Rights Act and ESEA on school desegregation. The Fifth Circuit, which then had jurisdiction over much of the South, played a key role in furthering desegregation beyond what district judges had required (Bass 1990). In *Jefferson v. United States*, the court considered desegregation standards with respect to the HEW guidelines. This lengthy decision illustrates the complex interplay between the branches of the federal government as they confronted local resistance to *Brown*. *Jefferson* acknowledged that all three branches of the government are needed to "make meaningful the right of Negro children to equal educational opportunities. The courts acting alone have failed" (*U.S. v. Jefferson Co. Bd. of Ed.*, 847). Indeed, almost as if feeling reprimanded by the Civil Rights Act, the decision stated, "We read Title VI as a congressional mandate for change—change in pace and method of enforcing desegregation," which was due to wide variation in rulings and requiring case-by-case litigation (852–53).

Because of the ability of districts to qualify for ESEA funding, the court held that court-supervision could not be less stringent than HEW guidelines so that the courts would not be used as a means to evade Title VI. While expressing the opinion that courts could go beyond what HEW required, the court found that the HEW guidelines were due deference because they had been crafted by experts (rather than judges) and were part of a coordinated strategy to address segregation. The *Jefferson* decision (like earlier decisions) emphasized the importance of Congress, as the people's elected representatives, enacting the Civil Rights Act. The act and HEW guidelines, they said, "are belated but invaluable helps at arriving at a neutral, principled decision consistent with the dimensions of the problem" of undoing school segregation (*U.S. v. Jefferson Co. Bd. of Ed.*, 849). In fact, the decision noted that after HEW guidelines were announced, some districts that hadn't desegregated tried to subvert compliance with HEW guidelines by getting a court order, because judicial standards varied. The decision directed district courts to evaluate proposed desegregation plans in light of standards articulated in *Jefferson* and the HEW guidelines. Thus, the guidelines helped to give courts "cover" to demand more stringent requirements in the face of charges of intervention by an unelected branch. Further illustrating interplay among the branches, the HEW guidelines led the way for the courts to invalidate freedom of choice plans. The courts had declined to forbid such plans although they were ineffective, but following the issuance of the 1966 HEW guidelines, the Court issued its 1968 ruling in *Green v. County School Board of New Kent County* (391 U.S. 430), making freedom of choice invalid. In this way, the Civil Rights Act and ESEA indirectly contributed to school desegregation that resulted from compliance with *Green* and subsequent decisions.

Backlash to ESEA and Civil Rights Act Implementation

As desegregation enforcement took effect, recognition of the major changes wrought by Title VI and the expansion of federal funding under ESEA grew, but the ability of these laws to affect school desegregation in states without de jure segregation was less clear. The Johnson administration's attempt to expand Title VI enforcement outside of the South resulted in a stinging rebuke. Backlash to enforcement began, as did ultimately unsuccessful efforts to repeal the legislation. However, the Johnson administration made concessions of virtually no enforcement outside the South and selective enforcement in the South that restricted the laws' desegregative impact, illustrating the limits of this approach even with a supportive executive.

Desegregation Enforcement Outside the South

The Office of Education's first attempt to withhold funds outside the South (Chicago) went poorly, with a subsequent understanding that enforcement should not address districts that had "racial imbalance." Chicago, like many midwestern or northern cities, had high levels of de facto segregation. Although there was increasing evidence that the adverse impacts of de facto segregation were similar to the de jure segregation in southern schools, the two forms of segregation were viewed in quite different legal and political terms. HEW responded to a complaint from a Chicago civil rights group that public agencies were maintaining segregated schools by withholding funds in fall 1965. A provision of Title VI enforcement required that HEW officials provide a written report within thirty days detailing the grounds for withholding funds (Halpern 1995), but HEW could not provide evidence for their decision to terminate funds or specify what was necessary for the funds to be reinstated. Further, the complaints did not demonstrate clear constitutional violations absent of evidence showing school board intent to discriminate (Orfield 1969). A settlement was reached in which HEW released the funds and removed investigators for two months while the school board reaffirmed its commitment to ineffective resolutions and investigated school attendance boundaries, a political victory for the district.

The Chicago scandal highlighted the unresolved nature of Title VI in terms of de facto segregation. Top officials in the Office of Education debated about federal authority under Title VI, but ultimately concluded that the purview of Title VI did not address racial imbalance. In 1966, as reported in the bound Congressional Record, Commissioner Howe complained that when trying to address northern-style segregation, officials run into "quicksands of legal interpretation" and that when it came to de facto segregation, "[federal officials] can't do anything; we can only suggest and stimulate local school districts" (89 Cong. Rec. 25040). Despite failures in the non-South, the 1968 HEW guidelines did attempt to sanction some techniques common to de facto segregation. HEW withheld funds from at least one northern district, causing considerable controversy (Bolner and Shanley 1974). Cases outside the South were more painstaking due to the nature of proving de facto segregation and the lack of clear judicial or political support for doing so. The Johnson administration's Justice Department also began to bring nonsouthern desegregation cases (Bolner and Shanley 1974).

As a means to proactively address de facto segregation, in 1966 Senator Edward Kennedy proposed amending Title IV of the Civil Rights Act specifically to permit funds to assist districts facing racial imbalance in addition to desegregating districts. Regarding the proposed amendment, Kennedy was clear that de facto segregation was not caused by official action but resulted from the combination of residential segregation and school assignment based on residence (1996). He also specifically stated that his bill did not require "coercive" action but merely made resources available for nonsouthern districts interested in funds to help train teachers or design assignment policies to alleviate racial imbalance. The amendment initially seemed likely to pass, but increasingly lost support and did not get out of the Senate committee.

All told, at a time in which the Supreme Court had not explicitly extended desegregation beyond the South, some supporters of desegregation enforcement grew wary when nonsouthern cities were targeted. Although it was an open legal question as to whether the Fourteenth Amendment also required efforts to remedy racial imbalance where such patterns resulted from de facto residential segregation (itself caused, in part, by a variety of governmental actions), politically, the federal government was less ambiguous.[4] Although enforcement action or threats would prove useful in addressing segregation in the South, under Johnson, Title VI would be interpreted largely as not applying to areas where de jure intent could not be proven.

Repeal?
As time passed from Birmingham, which had allowed the "extraordinary extension of Federal power embodied in the Civil Rights Act," fear of big government overreach emerged (Orfield 1969, 361). The unique national moment where special conditions allowed the federal government to intervene in a way that created change in race relations began to fade. As enforcement proceeded, the HEW guidelines were strengthened. Token desegregation was no longer enough. Later guidelines—like court decisions—were skeptical of freedom of choice plans. Districts were increasingly required to restructure in a nondiscriminatory manner.

Commissioner of Education Keppel referred to ESEA as "'put[ting] funds in such quantity at particular points so that it is possible to get leverage to raise the quality'" in order to directly affect local practice (Orfield 1969, 314). One problem the Office of Education faced in 1966 with this "leverage" was that they had more power to affect local practice than the public believed was appropriate. Just as police response to nonviolent civil rights protestors in Birmingham shifted public opinion in support of the Civil Rights Act, subsequent violence helped break up the coalition supporting such federal action. In 1966, race riots occurred in a number of minority neighborhoods around the country. The nonviolent civil rights movement began to splinter, and the black power movement became more prominent.

These developments shifted white attitudes, lessening their support for continued federal involvement in civil rights issues.

As conservative influence grew in the House after the 1966 election, there was concern that ESEA would be altered due to fear of "big government." Proposals to change ESEA that would remove federal oversight in certifying desegregation compliance were floated (Orfield 1969, 314). The Johnson administration responded—ultimately successfully—by pointing out who would be harmed if the funding were no longer based on the number of poor students (the South, big cities, parochial schools). They also "neutralized" the race issue by stripping Commissioner Howe of his enforcement power and designating staff in the HEW secretary's office to monitor desegregation compliance. The ESEA was renewed for two years. The funding remained targeted to poor students and the GOP was not able to prohibit using federal money for busing.

Ironically, despite strengthening the HEW guidelines and the opposition in Congress that feared too much intrusion, the capacity of the Office of Education to enforce the guidelines was minimal. An assessment by the U.S. Commission on Civil Rights (USCCR) in February 1966 questioned the effectiveness of the Office of Education's enforcement efforts because some districts that filed compliance and desegregation plans were actually not in compliance. The USCCR concluded that lack of capacity limited the Office to investigating complaints in districts in which no plan whatsoever had been filed; further, some accepted court orders were below the minimum HEW guidelines. Taken together, analyses suggested that enforcement efforts were extremely limited as the Office largely focused on the worst violations of desegregation (USCCR 1966; Orfield 1969). Additionally, it's unclear as to whether HEW had enough data to be able to enforce its own guidelines (Cascio et al. 2010).

BRANCHES OF GOVERNMENT UNDER THE NIXON ADMINISTRATION

As the Johnson administration ended, desegregation across the South was expanding. How-

---

[4]. The courts later found HEW to have not enforced Title VI in thirty-three northern and western states.

ever, it was also becoming more complex outside the South and in urban areas, and had puzzled even the ardent integrationists of the Johnson administration. As these thorny questions took precedence, the lack of legal guidance stymied federal officials. Leadership and public support for desegregation fragmented as Nixon took office, removing important conditions for Title VI to be effective and the federal intrusion into local matters seem legitimate.

Changed Understanding of Desegregation

Nixon anchored his 1968 presidential campaign on the "southern strategy," in which he appeased the white South by being openly critical of policies ameliorating racial discrimination implemented during the Johnson administration, particularly HEW policies involving busing (Halpern 1995). When campaigning, Nixon attacked "forced busing" and asserted that judges and bureaucrats should not be making decisions for local districts. He also disagreed with threatening fund cut-offs to coerce local districts to carry out what federal officials thought was best (Orfield 1978). Soon after his election, Nixon faced whether to continue to desegregate the rural South and whether to develop a plan for desegregating urban areas; on both he opposed desegregation progress (Orfield 1978).

Central to the debate over de facto segregation was forced busing, which affected desegregation politics during the Nixon years. Through opposing the use of transportation for desegregation and prioritizing the good faith efforts of local officials, Nixon envisioned a limited federal role in desegregation. He acknowledged that *Brown* was settled law, but argued other considerations should be taken into account aside from remedying segregation "root and branch" as the *Green* decision required. In an extensive statement on desegregation, he said,

> I am dedicated to continued progress toward a truly desegregated public school system. But, considering the always heavy demands for more school operating funds, I believe it is preferable... to use limited financial resources for the improvement of education—for better teaching facilities, better methods, and advanced educational materials—and for the upgrading of the disadvantaged areas in the community rather than buying buses, tires, and gasoline to transport young children miles away from their neighborhood schools. (Nixon 1970)

He also outlined principles to govern how HEW and the Department of Justice would approach desegregation. Two included using the neighborhood school as the default student assignment and not requiring transporting students beyond "normal geographic zones for the purposes of racial balancing." He emphasized that neither the 1964 Civil Rights Act nor the 1966 ESEA amendments required transportation for racial balance. Nixon endorsed trying to make separate but equal while emboldening local officials' resistance to federal enforcement. Additionally, he thought that schools were not responsible for ameliorating the effects of de facto segregation.

The Executive Branch's Desegregation Efforts Recede

Title VI Enforcement

Nixon announced during his campaign that if elected he would pursue a different enforcement strategy under Title VI than his predecessor. The allowance for wide discretion in executive enforcement of Title VI is made possible through an ambiguous provision that stipulates administrators enforcing Title VI have the choice of terminating federal funds or enforcing Title VI by "other means authorized by law" (Halpern 1995, 33). This provision was discouraging to civil rights activists, who believed that given the option of whether to terminate funds, politicians would not use that device unless it were mandated. However, some southern congressmen and even liberals concerned with arbitrary executive power argued that Title VI gave too much influence to federal officials. Although Johnson's use of Title VI to terminate funds illustrates that some politicians would use this device, he represents an anomaly.

In July 1969, the administration issued the

Mitchell-Finch policy statement, articulating their new strategy toward Title VI enforcement to avoid using the fund cut-off mechanism under Title VI in favor of using their discretion to pursue litigation, ultimately eliminating the potential for federal financial incentives to advance desegregation efforts (Cascio et al. 2010). Two key changes were announced in the Mitchell-Finch policy statement. First, the administration would seek to minimize the number of cases where funds would be terminated and instead would emphasize gaining voluntary compliance from violators. Only when voluntary compliance was impossible would the Justice Department initiate lawsuits to enforce Title VI. The second change was eliminating the timeline previously established by HEW for the desegregation of southern schools, previously set as the beginning of the 1969–1970 school year (Halpern 1995).

Changes in Federal Agencies: Office for Civil Rights and the Justice Department

The new political climate under the Nixon administration led the Office for Civil Rights (OCR)—established in 1967 within HEW to oversee Title VI enforcement—and the Justice Department to adapt their mission. The shift in tone from the Johnson administration to the Nixon administration caused OCR to reconsider what could be done in the new political climate (Halpern 1995). OCR began to expand its work on discrimination by including a diversity of social change issues, but it was notably not pursuing school desegregation. The key task that had consumed OCR at its conception under the Johnson administration was being pushed aside as the political climate changed under Nixon. Likewise the Justice Department also shifted its work, deemphasizing segregation. Although de jure segregation in the South was a focus, urban segregation elsewhere received almost no attention from the Justice Department.

The strategy that HEW developed under the Nixon administration for investigating racial disparities rested on comparisons between schools under a framework of equal opportunity (rather than integration). Reviews of urban districts would include detailed attention to equal expenditures, courses, programs, and activities offered, and equality of health and food services (Orfield 1978). The assumption underlying HEW's approach during this period was that if equal resources were directed toward white students and minority students, the move would yield equal educational outcomes (see also Nixon 1970). Avoiding some of the most complex legal and political questions of de facto segregation, which was in line with Nixon's strategy announced in his March 1970 speech, was one of the ways the agency responded to the polarizing politics of busing often involved in urban segregation. The Justice Department was also coming down conservatively on evidence needed to prove unconstitutional segregation in urban areas (Orfield 1978, 2000). In some cases the Justice Department even acted against plaintiffs in desegregation cases. The attorney general, who is supposed to initiate litigation when Title VI is violated, gave low priority to desegregation and was against busing as a tool to achieve school desegregation. The effect was that both tools meant to enforce Title VI were absent or in weakened form under the Nixon administration (Orfield 1978).

Congress Prevents Greater Setbacks

Although executive enforcement was weakened, Congress continued, at the very least, to prevent additional rollback of federal support of desegregation while the courts also continued for a time to expand desegregation remedies. Southerners believed that congressional politics would change when other regions were forced to desegregate, and indeed antibusing fights previously headed by southern congressmen were now led by members from Michigan, Massachusetts, Colorado, and Delaware (Orfield 1978).[5] Public opinion against busing was strong causing no real threat of political loss for non-southern members of Congress if they were against busing. Despite a breakdown in the civil rights consensus in Congress, and the

---

5. In each state there was a pending desegregation case that would involve widespread busing.

added challenge of the executive branch now hostile to civil rights, they were not enough to lead to major backsliding on civil rights legislation in Congress during the Nixon years. Ironically, although Congress had prevented virtually all civil rights legislation from passing for more than seventy-five years, the legislative tools used to thwart such legislation were now used to impede efforts to weaken or repeal civil rights legislation (Orfield 1978).

From 1970 through 1972, a number of anti-busing amendments and a constitutional amendment were introduced in Congress. During the 1970 renewal of ESEA, the Stennis amendment sought to require a common policy to address northern and southern segregation and an end to the legal distinction between de facto segregation and de jure segregation (Orfield 1975). Because de facto segregation had no legal remedy at that time, a common policy would mean that enforcement action would be prevented in the South. The White House tacitly supported this amendment, but it was ultimately altered in congressional conference to leave Title VI obligations intact. Congress directed HEW to separately develop national policies for both de facto and de jure segregation though congressional debate made clear the lack of consensus for enforcing action to remedy de facto segregation outside the South.

Ultimately, despite Nixon administration efforts to use the legislative process to impede desegregation, Congress extended and expanded ESEA as well as funding and strengthening the Emergency School Aid Act. ESEA was finally renewed in 1974 with a variety of somewhat contradictory amendments pertaining to desegregation. The most significant was that federal courts or agencies could not require districts to implement a desegregation plan that bused students beyond the nearest school. Although it had little direct effect on courts, this provision had the potential to restrict HEW's ability to enforce the Civil Rights Act, particularly because it sought to comply with the *Adams v. Richardson* litigation (480 F.2d 1159).

The Courts Lead on Desegregation, for a While

The time of receding executive enforcement of desegregation coincided, for a time, with increasing judicial expectations of what was required for school districts to remedy segregation and become a unitary, desegregated district. Ultimately, the courts' influence as a champion of desegregation began to wane as Nixon appointed four conservative justices, which changed the Court's desegregation jurisprudence through a series of 5–4 decisions. Nevertheless, drawing in part on HEW guidelines, the Court repeatedly stifled the Nixon administration's attempts to slow desegregation.

Early on, the Supreme Court furthered school desegregation and disappointed the Nixon administration's hopes that desegregation efforts would be constrained. The Fifth Circuit's *U.S. v. Hinds County School Board* decision (417 F.2d 852, 5th Cir.) in July 1969 required that an ineffective freedom of choice plan in a Mississippi district be replaced by the start of the school year. In August, however, HEW asked for a several-month delay in submitting proposed plans and indefinite delay in implementation (Doherty 1970).[6] In its October *Alexander v. Holmes County School Board of Education* decision (396 U.S. 19), the Supreme Court declared desegregation delays ended and required immediate compliance. Two years later, the Court weighed in again, this time invalidating neighborhood assignment policies if they were not effective in desegregating schools, which was often the case due to segregated residential patterns. The Court endorsed a range of tools, including noncontiguous pairing of zones to help produce school diversity (*Swann v. Charlotte-Mecklenburg Bd. of Ed.*, 402 U.S. 1). The Court's unanimous decision upholding widespread busing went against the Nixon administration's brief arguing for a slower approach to desegregation.

The Court's jurisprudence outside the South was more mixed. In its 1973 *Keyes v. School District No. 1, Denver, Colorado* decision (413 U.S. 189), a fractured court found Denver

---

6. HEW asking for a delay in desegregation process was a break from prior actions.

guilty of intentionally segregating students and required that Latinos also be desegregated. One of the missed opportunities was getting five justices to join an opinion holding no legal difference between de jure and de facto segregation, which would have had major implications for nonsouthern districts (Ryan 2010). Some justices agreed that the distinction should be abandoned but disagreed about busing, which prevented a compromise majority opinion that would have eliminated the distinction (Jefferies 1994).

In 1973, the *Adams* case challenged the Nixon administration's lack of Title VI enforcement, seeking to limit the discretionary power that an administrative agency has to choose how and when to enforce the sanctions of a law. The Court found the Nixon OCR had not effectively been enforcing Title VI and later, in *Brown v. Weinberger* (417 F. Supp. 1215), that HEW had not applied Title VI outside the South. These decisions required a tighter timeline for investigating Title VI violations and other requirements to monitor desegregation compliance, but little evidence suggests that funds were actually cut off to noncompliant districts (Halpern 1995). Although the *Adams* ruling limited OCR's discretion on how to allocate resources toward investigation of complaints, it could not resolve the discretionary nature of Title VI. The mechanism that gave the provision the most power—fund termination—still depended on a president's approval, which carried substantial political risk, particularly outside the South.

The judicial branch's ability to further desegregation began to diminish with the 1974 *Milliken v. Bradley* decision (418 U.S. 717), which overturned a metropolitan desegregation plan that would have involved the city of Detroit and dozens of surrounding suburban districts. Such a decision limited the effectiveness of efforts in many areas, outside the South in particular, where boundary lines often separated students into smaller, homogenous districts. The *Milliken* decision was the first since *Brown* that limited desegregation efforts and it began a trend of others that lessened what was required of districts to eradicate segregation. This decision, with Nixon's appointees making up the majority, combined with the nonenforcement of Title VI effectively ended the active federal role in desegregation.

DISCUSSION

This examination of desegregation during the decade immediately after the Civil Rights Act of 1964 and ESEA were passed illustrates how legislation and executive action furthered desegregation after a decade following the *Brown* decision in which little desegregation progress occurred. The Johnson and Nixon administrations provide useful contrasts in understanding how the federal role can help further desegregation and what the limits of such approaches are.

Under both administrations, school desegregation expanded, albeit for different reasons. While Johnson was in office, the threat of fund cut-off and increasingly stronger HEW guidelines alongside the dramatically larger amount of federal education funding combined to change southern officials' resistance to desegregation to ensuring at least minimal compliance. During the Johnson administration, dozens of districts had their funds cut off, and more than a hundred districts were in earlier stages of the enforcement proceedings. As a result, the actual percentage of students in diverse schools in the South expanded in the 1960s (Cascio et al. 2010; Giles 1975; Orfield 1978). Courts were involved during the 1960s, but did not play as large a role as enforcement before 1970 (Giles 1975). However, as the threat of executive enforcement lessened during the Nixon administration, the courts had become increasingly unwilling to tolerate delays, particularly when they were being used by recalcitrant districts as a way to avoid more expansive desegregation requirements.

ESEA and the Civil Rights Act also indirectly affected court rulings. Because the HEW guidelines were the minimum required as part of a court desegregation order, they helped make judicial requirements more uniform across districts. Particularly during the later 1960s, HEW guidelines outpaced the courts' requirements; subsequent court decisions adopted the guidelines. Thus, though the consensus is the courts had a larger desegregation burden after 1970 (Cascio et al. 2010; Giles 1975), we might attribute some of the substance of judicial holdings to the expertise HEW developed during the 1960s monitoring compliance for ESEA and the Civil Rights Act. Further, the laws gave support to lower court decisions after *Brown* that struggled to implement desegregation in the face of local resistance. These laws passed by the nation's popularly elected representatives, along with HEW guidelines, gave the federal courts as an unelected branch cover to issue decisions expanding what desegregation actions were required of districts.

This progress was limited, however, because of staffing and expertise during the Johnson administration, and of popular and political support during the Nixon years. Although filled with staff committed to integration, Johnson's HEW was vastly understaffed. Its ability to monitor compliance in thousands of districts, many of which were seeking to do the least possible desegregation, was limited. HEW, like the courts in the preceding decade, was confronting how to conceptualize what desegregation required across districts that were vastly different. Ambiguity remained as to whether Title VI could require more of districts than the Constitution did. One important question was whether to examine only intent (for example, de jure policies) or racial impact as well; differing opinions led to accepting ineffective freedom of choice or neighborhood school policies for a while. The question of intent versus effect also had implications outside the South, where racial imbalance was the result of de facto patterns. Given a greater burden under the Nixon administration on private lawyers, desegregation suffered without the resources and coordination of the federal government behind it. Even in the South, technical and legal questions remained as to what should be done in urban areas to desegregate after freedom of choice plans were invalidated. By the time the Court legitimated cross-town busing to fully desegregate schools, federal officials were restricted from suggesting it as an option to districts.

Further, an obvious limit to the success of desegregation efforts is the sustainability of enforcement efforts. Although enforcement may have been less than complete during the Johnson administration, it had largely desegregated the rural South, and the Supreme Court preserved and extended these changes. The Nixon administration's Title VI enforcement strategy was a radical departure from the Johnson era. The Nixon administration's policies constrained OCR's investigations of school districts not in compliance with HEW guidelines and did not require HEW to terminate funds when school districts were found to be noncompliant. Despite the burden on the courts to enforce Title VI during the Nixon administration, administration policy limited the Justice Department's efforts to advance school desegregation through the courts, particularly when it came to de facto segregation outside the South.

IMPLICATIONS: THE ROLE OF FEDERAL LEGISLATION

What can we learn from this examination about how legislation can work with the courts to help desegregation? The courts are rightly recognized as the governmental branch most able to protect the rights of minority groups because it is an unelected, nonmajoritarian branch. Indeed, the *Brown* decision provided the legal framework for asserting that state action segregating students was unconstitutional. Yet, in part because the way in which *Brown I* and *II* were decided, progress in desegregation was scant for the next decade (Orfield 1969; *U.S. v. Jefferson Co. Bd. of Ed.*). Indeed, this decade illustrated the limits of the federal role (which was largely the federal courts) in affecting local practice as, for example, officials in the Justice Department were committed to desegregation but lacked the legal authority to intervene in any substantial way. Given current jurisprudence, the federal courts may not to be the best arena for furthering racial integration.

Today, students of color are almost a majority in the nation's schools, and students attend schools stratified by race and poverty (for example, Orfield and Frankenberg 2014). What are the implications of these patterns of school segregation for our understanding of the federal role in both contributing to and remedying these trends? First, to the extent possible, civil rights legislation must be crafted to minimize variation in interpretation and implementation. The final text of the Civil Rights Act was altered in subtle ways to gain passage that likely limited its impact. In particular, clarifying that Title IV authority did extend to racial imbalance and removing the phrase "other means authorized by law" from Title VI, which allowed the executive branch to avoid implementing fund deferral and termination, could have meant the laws had longer, more far-reaching effect. Second, the federal government has an important role not only in enacting policies to promote integration, but also in effectively enforcing them. As seen, the enforcement of the Civil Rights Act and ESEA were limited: staff capacity, incomplete evidence, and lack of expertise as desegregation cases grew more complex. Under the Nixon administration, the unwillingness to terminate funds greatly reduced the effectiveness of enforcement, putting the onus back on the judicial system. Thus, future efforts—especially if not embraced by local districts—require sufficient federal capacity and expertise as well as sustained political will to enforce legislation. Third, if the judicial system, particularly the Supreme Court, had clarified earlier ambiguous aspects of law pertaining to desegregation while an administration committed to enforcement efforts was still in office, it might have changed the scope of HEW enforcement efforts. A federal agenda would be boosted if courts found de facto segregation to be a compelling interest to justify integration policies (as four justices did in the 2007 *Parents Involved* decision).

Conditions Necessary for Legislation to Further Desegregation

A larger question remains as to whether some of the problems identified in the implementation of legislation mean that popularly elected branches will be fundamentally limited in their approach to desegregation. We conclude that such flaws are not inherent to federal legislation and efforts to change local practice around student assignment, though we do think it is likely to be challenging. First, the policy window for reforms is typically narrow; in this case, it took the televised assault on nonviolent protestors in Birmingham to galvanize public support in favor of unprecedented federal intervention. Even then, the bill had to overcome a lengthy filibuster before becoming law. Thus, despite widespread public support, resistance was strong enough that it was hard to marshal a majority in Congress to gain approval. ESEA had a considerably easier time gaining passage the following year, given that it was providing needed financial resources (for example, being the carrot and not the stick of enforcement).

A year later, however, the policy window had already begun to close, and efforts such as Edward Kennedy's attempt to amend Title IV of the Civil Rights Act to encompass racial imbalance failed. Later, public opinion had shifted such that cutting off funds to districts was seen as unreasonable, lessening the use of threats that were effective in Johnson's HEW. This illustrates a disadvantage of seeking to enforce minority rights through popularly elected branches of government. Today, many Americans, particularly whites, profess a colorblind ideology in which they believe that racial discrimination no longer exists and therefore race-conscious policies are not needed to address existing racial inequalities, favoring instead policies that treat everyone equally (see, for example, Bonilla-Silva 2010; Frankenberg et al. 2015). Such beliefs make it difficult, unlike in the 1960s, to justify support for federal intervention to redress persisting (and rising) inequality.

We also saw the technical challenges of lacking expertise to implement the laws. HEW repeatedly revised its guidelines as southern districts found new ways to resist desegregation. Though judges deferred to HEW's expertise, analysts questioned what experience HEW had in enforcing desegregation guidelines on such a wide scale. Given extremely limited staff capacities, the Office of Education focused on the worst districts or those that refused to submit a plan (Orfield 1969). Even if the plan was ineffective, districts were likely judged to be in compliance (USCCR 1966). Of course, judges were no more likely to have expertise than federal officials in judging the merits of desegregation plans. A benefit of HEW enforcement is that although enforcement proceedings could be drawn out, given that threats of cut-off were often enough to motivate action, they were quicker than many legal cases that extended years before plans were implemented. Thus, the Civil Rights Act and ESEA, along with executive enforcement, came at a critical time to step into the void caused by the slow, piecemeal judicial process after *Brown*. They, in turn, promoted more far-reaching actions by the judiciary in subsequent years.

Finally, an important lesson is that it is unlikely that either piece of legislation would have had a remotely similar impact alone—it was through their combined effects that segregation was overcome in the South. This suggests future efforts to affect desegregation must be cognizant of ensuring that legislation is complementary and comprehensive to change local practice. Moreover, the story of federal desegregation efforts in the two decades after *Brown* illustrates the strengths and weaknesses of each branch in terms of responsiveness to certain kinds of arguments, decision-making process and criteria, and public–interest group influence, particularly in regard to protecting the rights of a minority group.

Moving Forward: Addressing De Facto Segregation

Many current-day challenges preventing further school integration have their origins in the pushback to Civil Rights Act and ESEA enforcement. The federal government has done little to further desegregation in the last four decades. In the 1960s, all branches of the federal government struggled with questions of how to treat de facto segregation outside the South. These questions splintered the congressional civil rights consensus, and HEW was unclear about technical and political aspects of proving de facto violations. The Supreme Court's first desegregation decision outside the South came in 1973, after the civil rights era had ended. Even then, the Court failed to clarify that both de jure and de facto segregation required districts to remedy such segregation (Ryan 2010). The consensus that the federal government should intervene to address de jure segregation led to the South being the most integrated region for black and white students by 1970, which remains true today (Orfield and Frankenberg 2014). Meanwhile, the legacy of the ambiguity about addressing de facto segregation through enforcement or judicial remedy means that de facto segregation remains high. The North is the most segregated region for black students, and the only region where segregation has risen since the late 1960s (Orfield and Frankenberg 2014). Many areas also have high levels of segregation between districts instead of within districts—another dimension of de facto segregation.

Moreover, as the civil rights consensus dissolved in the late 1960s, although congressional allies staved off possible setbacks to civil rights enforcement during the Nixon administration through tactical moves, less focus was on challenging the narrative questioning the need for desegregation. The shift in enforcement under Nixon to focusing on equalizing resources rather than integrating black and white schools—a shift subsequently adopted by the courts—changed the framing about educational equality. Today, local politics reflect this framing and, at a time of economic stress with little overt federal support for integration, many districts are cutting transportation for students that is needed to ameliorate the effects of persisting residential segregation. *Brown* remains a cherished legal decision, but the federal effort to enforce the right it enshrined has been whittled away and whether the rights remain in practice is questionable for many students.

Our analysis suggests several avenues for the federal government to further desegregation. First, it could provide rhetorical framing of—public support for—the need for policies to address racial segregation in an ostensibly postracial society. This has been done occasionally during the Obama administration, most prominently in the form of guidance about how districts could voluntarily pursue integration. The minimal funding to provide districts the opportunity to retain social science or legal expertise in designing new assignment plans came before this guidance and thus many districts adopted policies that may result in less integration (Frankenberg et al., 2015). Yet, as discussed, such messages from the federal government could give localities political cover to implement more far-reaching policies. Our second recommendation stems from the lack of coordination: one reason these two laws were so effective was that they worked in tandem and with other branches. Federal policy should be aligned such that it does not create incentives working against school integration (for a discussion of federal policy conflicting with integration, see National Coalition for School Diversity 2014). Third, though enforcement efforts were limited in various ways during the first decade after the Civil Rights Act was passed—and despite a subsequent Supreme Court decision that has further limited the right of individuals to sue under Title VI—filing Title VI complaints with the federal government may still be a useful tool, particularly as the Obama administration recently outlined an expansive interpretation of complaints they would consider (see U.S. Department of Education 2014). Finally, a longer-term effort to clarify our understanding of discrimination to include de facto segregation could address Title VI's ambiguity and reinvigorate federal efforts to expand access to high-quality integrated schools.

Legislative and enforcement efforts played an under-recognized role in furthering desegregation across the South, but became more limited in their direct effect as the public perceived a lessened need for such efforts where segregation was de facto. Nevertheless, these efforts had a long-lasting impact and an indirect judicial impact in subsequent years. Together, they provide useful lessons for our contemporary understanding of how the federal government could continue to help increase the diversity of public schools.

REFERENCES

Abernathy, Charles F. 1981. "Title VI and the Constitution: A Regulatory Model for Defining 'Discrimination.'" *Georgetown Law Journal* 70(1): 1–49.

Bass, Jack. 1990. *Unlikely Heroes*. Tuscaloosa: University of Alabama Press.

Bolner, James, and Robert A. Shanley. 1974. *Busing: The Political and Judicial Process*. New York: Praeger Publishers.

Bonilla-Silva, Eduardo. 2010. *Racism without Racists: Color-Blind Racism and the Persistence of Racial Inequality in America*, 3rd ed. Lanham, Md.: Rowman & Littlefield.

Cascio, Elizabeth, Nora Gordon, Ethan Lewis, and Sarah Reber. 2010. "Paying for Progress: Conditional Grants and the Desegregation of Southern Schools." *Quarterly Journal of Economics* 125(1): 445–82.

Doherty, Patric J. 1970. "Integration Now: A Study of *Alexander v. Holmes County Board of Education*." *Notre Dame Law Review* 45(3): 489–514.

Frankenberg, Erica, Kathryn McDermott, Elizabeth DeBray, and Annie Blankenship. 2015. "The New Politics of Diversity: Lessons from a Federal Technical Assistance Grant." *American Educational Research Journal* 52(3): 440–74.

Giles, Michael W. 1975. "H.E.W. Versus the Federal Courts: A Comparison of School Desegregation Enforcement." *American Politics Research* 3(1): 81–90.

Halpern, Stephen C. 1995. *On the Limits of the Law: The Ironic Legacy of Title VI of the 1964 Civil Rights Act*. Baltimore, Md.: Johns Hopkins University Press.

House of Representatives Subcommittee No. 5 of the Committee on the Judiciary. 1963. "Civil Rights" 88th Congress, 1st session committee print. Washington: U.S. Government Printing Office. Available at ProQuest Congressional (accessed March 24, 2015).

Jeffries, John C. 1994. *Justice Lewis F. Powell, Jr.* New York: C. Scribner's Sons.

Kennedy, Edward M. 1996. "The Case for New Desegregation Legislation." *Equity and Excellence in Education* 4(3): 41–44.

Kennedy, John F. 1963. "Radio and Television Report to the American People on Civil Rights," June 11, 1963. Online by Gerhard Peters and John T. Woolley, *The American Presidency Project*. Available at: http://www.presidency.ucsb.edu/ws/?pid=9271 (accessed July 17, 2015).

Klarman, Michael. 2005. *Brown v. Board of Education and the Civil Rights Movement*. New York: Oxford University Press.

McGuinn, Patrick, and Frederick Hess. 2005. *Freedom from Ignorance? The Great Society and the Evolution of the Elementary and Secondary Education Act of 1965*. Amherst: University of Massachusetts Press.

Marshall, Burke. 1962. *Federalism and Civil Rights*. New York: Columbia University Press.

Meranto, Philip J. 1967. *The Politics of Federal Aid to Education in 1965*. Syracuse, N.Y.: Syracuse University Press.

Miller, Mark C., and Jeb Barnes. 2004. *Making Policy, Making Law: An Interbranch Perspective*. Washington, D.C.: Georgetown University Press.

National Coalition for School Diversity. 2014. "Federal Support for School Integration: A Status Report." Washington, D.C. Available at: http://www.school-diversity.org/pdf/DiversityIssueBriefNo4.pdf (accessed October 21, 2015).

Nixon, Richard. 1970. "Statement About Desegregation of Elementary and Secondary Schools," March 24, 1970. Online by Gerhard Peters and John T. Woolley, *The American Presidency Project*. Available at: http://www.presidency.ucsb.edu/ws/?pid=2923 (accessed July 17, 2015).

Orfield, Gary. 1969. *The Reconstruction of Southern Education: The Schools and the 1964 Civil Rights Act*. New York: Wiley-Interscience.

———. 1975. *Congressional Power: Congress and Social Change*. New York: Harcourt Brace Jovanovich.

———. 1978. *Must We Bus? Segregation and National Policy*. Washington, D.C.: Brookings Institution Press.

———. 2000. "The 1964 Civil Rights Act and American Education." In *Legacies of the 1964 Civil Rights Act*, edited by Bernard Grofman. Charlottesville: University of Virginia Press.

———. 2015. "Lyndon Johnson and American Education." In *LBJ's Neglected Legacy: Reshaping the Federal Government*, edited by Robert H. Wilson, Norman J. Glickman, and Laurence E. Lynn Jr. Austin: University of Texas Press.

Orfield, Gary, and Erica Frankenberg. 2014. *Brown at 60: Great Progress, a Long Retreat and an Uncertain Future*. Los Angeles, Calif.: Civil Rights Project/Proyecto Derechos Civiles.

Reed, Douglas S. 2014. *Building the Federal Schoolhouse: Localism and the American Education State*. New York: Oxford University Press.

Ryan, James E. 2010. *Five Miles Away, a World Apart: One City, Two Schools, and the Story of Educational Opportunity in Modern America*. New York: Oxford University Press.

U.S. Commission on Civil Rights (USCCR). 1966. "Survey of School Desegregation in the Southern and Border States 1965–66." Washington: Government Printing Office.

U.S. Department of Education. 2014. "Office for Civil Rights Resource Comparability Materials." Available at: http://www2.ed.gov/about/offices/list/ocr/resourcecomparability.html (accessed August 15, 2015).

U.S. Department of Health, Education, and Welfare (HEW). Office of Education. 1966. "Status of Compliance Public School Districts Seventeen Southern and Border States: Report No. 1." Washington: Government Printing Office.

———. 1967a. "Status of Compliance Public School Districts Seventeen Southern and Border States: Report No. 4." Washington: Government Printing Office.

———. 1967b. "Status of Compliance Public School Districts Seventeen Southern and Border States: Report No. 7." Washington: Government Printing Office.

Follow the Money: School Spending from Title I to Adult Earnings

RUCKER C. JOHNSON

Title I funding has been the largest federal program of K–12 education for the past fifty years, the objective being to eliminate the educational disadvantage associated with poverty. I provide new evidence on the long-term effects of school spending from Title I on children's educational and adult economic outcomes. To study effects of Title I, I link school district spending and administrative data on Title I funding to nationally representative data on children born between 1950 and 1977 and followed through 2011. Models include controls for birth cohort and school district fixed effects, childhood family–neighborhood characteristics, and other policies. I find that increases in Title I funding are significantly related to increases in educational attainment, high school graduation rates, higher earnings and work hours, reductions in grade repetition, school suspension or expulsion, incarceration, and reductions in the annual incidence of poverty in adulthood; effects on educational outcomes are more pronounced for poor children.

Keywords: school spending, Title I, educational attainment, poverty

Title I, originally enacted as one of the provisions of the Elementary and Secondary Education Act (ESEA) of 1965, currently accounts for one-third of federal government support for K–12 education. Title I funding represented $14.3 billion in 2014 appropriations and has been the largest federal program of K–12 education for the past fifty years with an objective of eliminating the educational disadvantage associated with poverty. The program allocates money (nonmatching grants) for compensatory education to school districts based on child poverty. Currently, more than half of all public schools receive such Title I funding. The program's central goal is to increase achievement of poor students by providing more funding to poor schools. Despite its fiscal importance, evidence on the effectiveness of Title I is mixed (Matsudaira, Hosek, and Walsh 2012; Cascio, Gordon, and Reber 2013; Van der Klaauw 2008). Research has shown that one of the reasons it may not have worked as successfully is the ways in which it may crowd out local funding (Gordon 2004).[1]

Rucker C. Johnson is associate professor of public policy at the University of California, Berkeley.

I wish to thank the PSID staff for access to the confidential restricted-use PSID geocode data. This research was prepared for the Russell Sage Foundation Conference "ESEA at 50," organized by David Gamson, Kathryn McDermott, and Doug Reed and benefited from their comments and those from conference participants Sheldon Danziger, Nora Gordon, and Sarah Reber. Direct correspondence to: Rucker C. Johnson, ruckerj @berkeley.edu, University of California, Berkeley, Goldman School of Public Policy, 2607 Hearst Ave., Berkeley, CA 94720.

1. This relates to the flypaper effect in the public finance literature. For example, Nora Gordon (2004) finds full crowd-out of Title I for the average district during the 1990s.

EXAMINING THE EFFICACY OF TITLE I

This article provides new evidence on the long-term effects of school spending from Title I on children's subsequent educational and adult economic outcomes. To study the effect of Title I, and resultant changes in school spending, on long-term adult outcomes, I link school district spending and administrative data on Title I funding to detailed, nationally representative data on children born between 1950 and 1977 and followed through 2011. In particular, the analysis focuses on the first fifteen years of the roll-out of Title I (from 1965 to 1980) and their long-term impacts for cohorts born between 1950 and 1970 who straddled the period in which federal funding toward low-income districts via Title I rapidly expanded.

With the passage of the Elementary and Secondary Education Act of 1965, school districts with a high percentage of low-income students received additional funding for the first time from the federal government; the regulations gave priority to low-achieving schools. *Poor districts* here refer to those in which a high percentage of students come from low-income families. In some cases, these may be relatively high-spending districts, but they also have high needs. The high degree of residential segregation by economic status and heavy reliance on local property taxes to fund public schools typically leads to a positive correlation between the level of school spending on the one hand, and both childhood family–neighborhood socioeconomic status and student outcomes on the other, in a cross-sectional analysis. However, many of the changes to how schools have been funded since the 1960s have been compensatory, directed to economically disadvantaged districts to narrow educational opportunity gaps driven by funding inequities. Differences in per-pupil spending across wealthy or high-income districts and poor ones are significant, but not all low-income districts are also low-spending, and not all high-spending districts are high-income. The stated program goal of Title I is to improve educational opportunities and outcomes for low-achieving students from schools with high concentrations of poverty. The program is based on the premise that children from poor families living in high-poverty school districts are doubly disadvantaged: they have fewer nonschool learning opportunities and attend schools with inferior instructional programs relative to children from more economically advantaged backgrounds. This compensatory funding policy likely generates a negative relationship between Title I funding and student achievement that would negatively bias the observed relationship between school spending and student outcomes.[2]

One of the primary empirical challenges in estimating the effects of Title I funding is that there are many differences between Title I and non–Title I schools and the students attending them (especially the poverty level). The multistage allocation procedure for distribution of Title I funds involves the federal government providing money to counties to support K–12 education based on census county poverty counts, and states give money to districts based on these same need-based measures of poverty. The key identification challenge is that, though a district's poverty determines its Title I allotment, poverty also influences both a district's and children's outcomes in a variety of other ways. Thus, separately distinguishing the effects of Title I on state and local revenue from the effects of poverty on Title I, state, and local revenue streams, as well as student outcomes, is extremely difficult. Failure to control for nonrandom assignment of Title I status will generally understate any potential benefits of the program. The research design for this article better addresses the nonrandom allocation of funds and services to facilitate causal inference (that is, attempts to account for the nonrandom selection of students and schools for program participation).

The basic funding structure of the Title I program has remained essentially unchanged over the past fifty years. Although the goal of Title I is to increase school funding in poorer districts to improve student performance, both the intradistrict allocative funding and curricular design of Title I programs to meet

---

2. An additional concern is whether districts face a disincentive by which improving schools may result in reductions in funding (some scholars have suggested this was the case for some time during the 1980s).

these goals is far from uniform. Some districts target Title I dollars toward disadvantaged children within schools and hold separate classes to provide remedial services to these students and to those identified as at-risk (the pull-out approach). In other districts, the funding is used for schoolwide programs with no targeting of aid at all. Thus, variation is significant in how Title I programs have been implemented across time and geographic areas. Some prior studies of Title I fail to measure whether this additional compensatory funding led to substantive changes in the level or distribution of school funding as well as when and for how long. Without sufficient attention to this first-order question, one cannot definitively conclude whether evidence from Title I can shed light on the role of school spending for student outcomes from poorer districts. That is, if we are to assess the extent to which Title I funding and resultant school spending changes matter, we must first establish how the money is being spent. In the case of no relationship between Title I and outcomes, it is important to understand whether the services funded by Title I are ineffective because they are poorly designed or because they do not represent net service increases.

Other articles that examine the effects of Title I in this issue consider numerous important questions, such as

- Does Title I increase funding of poor schools? Does Title I funding appear to displace other sources of funding? If so, what other sources of funding decline? How does ESEA influence the composition of school spending (expenditures on instruction, the number of guidance counselors, the number of teachers, capital expenditures on school facilities)?
- Does Title I boost measurable school inputs, such as teacher-to-pupil ratios, teacher salary, teacher quality?
- Do schools engage in strategic behavior to gain Title I funding?
- How does the role of socioeconomic status intersect with that of race with regard to ESEA and school functioning in different educational contexts?

This article, however, focuses on whether Title I increases children's long-run socioeconomic attainment, particularly among poor and minority children targeted by Title I programs. That is, has Title I been successful at one of its chief stated objectives in particular?

BACKGROUND AND PRIOR LITERATURE

A higher proportion of Title I resources were allocated to lower grade levels under the assumption that they would have the greatest impact at that level. Such heterogeneity in resource allocation within districts provides an additional rationale to examine a longer time horizon of educational outcomes for cohorts initially exposed during elementary school. For example, Launor Carter (1984) found that Title I students achieved greater gains in the earlier grades than in the upper, and in math programs than in reading.

Related evidence from prior studies shows that schools appear to respond to Title I incentives, possibly by enrolling more eligibles in free-lunch programs (Fisher and Papke 2000). The welfare consequences of such behavior—involving zero-sum competition among poor schools—are likely negative. As well, increases in Title I funding have been shown to be partially offset by local education agency behavior—local funds are redistributed to partially compensate non–Title I schools (Matsudaira, Hosek, and Walsh 2012). Although ESEA explicitly prohibits such substitution that violate the maintenance of effort mandate of the legislation, it is difficult for the federal government to enforce compliance.

During the 1960s and early 1970s, Title I was deemed ineffective because localities did not implement it as intended. Early federal reports of this era explicitly identified major problems in design implementation of Title I, including the misuse of funds and the exclusion of disadvantaged and minority children in low-income areas (McLaughlin 1977), which undermined the program's goals. Ruby Martin and Phyllis McClure's evaluative study (1969) showed how school districts used millions of dollars across the country to make purchases that had little to do with helping poor students. In fact, they documented that districts used Title I funds to continue racial segregation by offering African American children free food, medical care, shoes, and clothing as long as they remained in predominantly black schools. As well, audits exposed Title I programs whose funds had not been equitably distributed to urban schools but had instead flowed disproportionately to suburban districts. Money intended for poor children was used illegally as a welcome infusion of extra cash to meet overhead expenses, raise teacher pay, and other such general aid. Their investigation helped prompt a flurry of efforts to monitor use of Title I money and ensure that it was being targeted for low-income children and remedial education services.[3]

Early studies of Title I from this era also charged that the program had perhaps contributed to a dual system of education (and more tracking), in which poor children were systematically subjected to low expectations, watered-down curricula and inexperienced teachers. As documented in an early survey on Title I–funded remedial education programs (Wargo et al. 1972; Rossi et al. 1977), many districts adopted pull-out programs in which reading specialists and teacher aides taught separate compensatory education classes, paid with Title I funds. Although the most popular delivery model for compensatory education was the pull-out program, many educators consider it ineffective and have found it has a stigmatizing effect on students, thus leading to adverse outcomes. As Wilbert Van der Klaauw summarizes it (2008, 754),

> Pull-out programs have been found to add little extra instruction time (on average less than 30 minutes a day) and predominantly use drill and practice exercises involving basic thinking skills (Millsap et al. 1993). The additional time Title I students receive in reading and mathematics instruction, replaces the class time that regular students usually receive in more advanced subjects, such as science and social studies (LeTendre 1991). Thus it is not clear that Title I students enjoy much of a net gain in total instruction.... Remedial classes, especially those in high-poverty schools, are often taught by inexperienced teacher aides, the majority of whom do not have college degrees (Millsap et al. 1993; Jendryka 1993). There also have been complaints in the past about a lack of coordination between Title I teachers and regular classroom teachers (Peterson 1987).

Evidence on the effectiveness of Title I improving academic achievement has come primarily from two large congressionally mandated studies (mentioned), one meta-analysis of seventeen studies (cited), and two regression-discontinuity studies using recent cohorts of students in a large, urban northeastern city. The latter two recent studies use quasi-experimental research designs to assess the causal effect of Title I (Matsudaira, Hosek, and Walsh 2012; Van der Klaauw 2008). They compare outcomes of schools just above and just below the district-wide poverty threshold. Their approach to distinguish the effect of Title I from the effect of poverty exploits the fact that eligibility for Title I funding within a given district is determined by the poverty rate of each school's attendance area. This formula for eligibility renders schools with a poverty rate below a given cutoff to be ineligible and to receive no funds whatsoever, and all schools with a rate above the cutoff to receive Title I funds. This feature is amenable to a regression discontinuity approach and is valid if they are similar in other characteristics that may affect outcomes. Neither study found a significant effect of Title I funding on either reading or math at the school level for recent student cohorts from the 2000s. Wilbert Van der Klaauw found no Title I effects on school-level spending, and Jordan Matsudaira and his colleagues found very small effects on spending. However, both of these studies analyzed only two to three years of cross-sectional, administrative data from elementary and middle-school records and were not able to use panel-data methods or follow cohorts to examine longer-run educational outcomes beyond short-run test-score gains.

A limitation of studies of the effects of Title

---

3. For example, see also summary of results of Department of Health, Education, and Welfare (HEW) audits of forty states conducted between 1966 and 1969.

I on achievement is the focus solely on short-run test scores, which are imperfect measures of learning and may be weakly linked to adult earnings and success in life. Indeed, recent studies have documented that effects on long-run outcomes may go undetected by test scores (Heckman, Pinto, and Savelyev 2013; Deming 2009; Jackson 2012; Chetty, Friedman, and Rockoff 2013; Ludwig and Miller 2007; Kemple 2008; Cortes, Goodman, and Nomi 2015). I address the limitations of focusing on test scores as the main outcome by analyzing the effects of Title I school spending on long-run outcomes such as educational attainment and earnings.

DESCRIPTION OF THE LONGER-RUN OUTCOME DATA

I use nationally representative data from the longest-running longitudinal panel in the world—the Panel Study of Income Dynamics (PSID) spanning 1968 through 2011—matched to administrative data about Title I funding at the county level. The study analyzes the life trajectories of original sample children born between 1950 and 1977 and followed through 2011, using the PSID and its supplements on educational experiences from pre-K through grade twelve.[4] Using the restricted, confidential, geocoded version of the PSID with identifiers at the level of the neighborhood blocks in which children grew up, the PSID data are linked with neighborhood and school characteristics as well as information on other key policy changes (such as the timing of school desegregation, hospital desegregation, rollout of War on Poverty initiatives, and expansion of safety-net programs) from multiple data sources on the conditions that prevailed when these children grew up. This data construction allows for a rich set of control variables.[5] Most importantly for this project, these data are linked to federal Title I funding at the county level during the first fifteen years of the program, when these individuals were in their school-age years, acquired from the National Archives and Records Administration (NARA). This historical county-level data enables me to compile an estimate of Title I program expenditures per student and per poor student in the county for all years between 1965 and 1980, and the average Title I per-pupil expenditure during their K–12 school years.

The PSID oversampled low-income and black families, which enables large enough sample sizes of Title I–eligible children among these birth cohorts. The roll-out of Title I and implementation of other War on Poverty policy initiatives during these birth cohorts' childhood provide a unique opportunity to evaluate the long-run impacts of groundbreaking legislation designed to improve educational investment opportunities for poor children.

Figures 1 through 4 show the birth-cohort variation in ESEA–Title I school funding and how the share of individuals exposed to Title I expenditures during childhood increases significantly with birth year over the 1950 through 1970 birth cohorts analyzed in the PSID sample. Specifically, cohorts born in 1950 were the last cohort without access to Title I funding during their school-age years; for cohorts born

---

4. The PSID began interviewing a national-probability sample of families in 1968. These families were reinterviewed each year through 1997, when interviewing became biennial. All persons in PSID families in 1968 have the PSID "gene," which means they are followed in subsequent waves. When children with the gene become adults and leave their parents' homes, they become their own PSID "family unit" and are interviewed in each wave. The original geographic-cluster design of the PSID enables comparisons in adulthood of childhood neighbors who have been followed over the life course.

5. The data I use include measures from 1968–1988 Office of Civil Rights (OCR) data; 1960, 1970, 1980, and 1990 Census data; 1962–1999 Census of Governments (COG) data; Common Core Data (CCD) compiled by the National Center for Education Statistics; Regional Economic Information System (REIS) data; a comprehensive case inventory of court litigation regarding school desegregation over the 1955–1990 period (American Communities Project); and the American Hospital Association's Annual Survey of Hospitals (1946–1990) and the Centers for Medicare and Medicaid Services data files (dating back to the 1960s) to identify the precise date in which a Medicare-certified hospital was established in each county of the U.S. (an accurate marker for hospital desegregation compliance).

Figure 1. Birth Cohort Variation in Per-Pupil Title I Funding, All Children

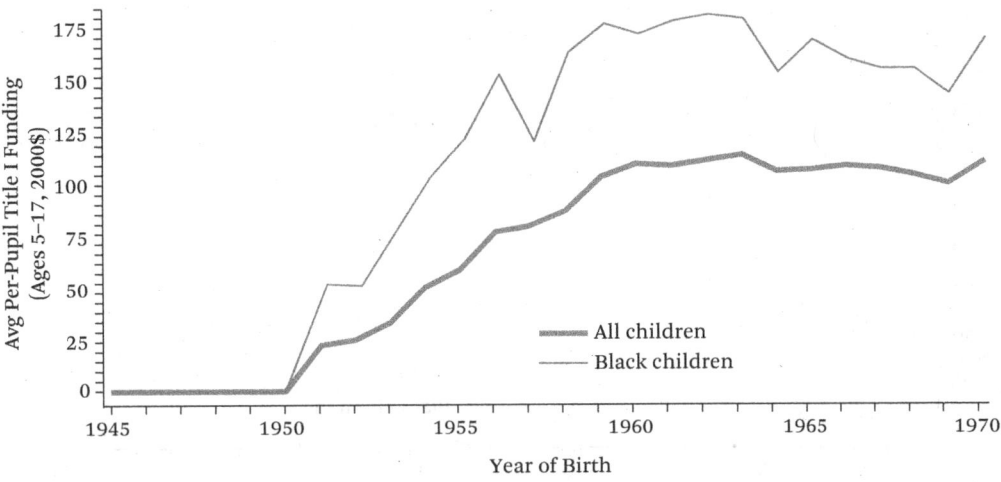

Source: Author's calculations based on nationally-representative data from the Panel Study of Income Dynamics (PSID) of original sample children born between 1950 and 1977 followed into adulthood (1968–2011), matched with administrative data of county-level Title I funding from the National Archives and Records Administration (NARA) covering 1965 to 1980 and county-level census counts of the number of children and number of poor children (Surveillance, Epidemiology, and End Results (SEER) data).

in 1960 and through 1970, the average child was in a public school district that received roughly $110 in per-pupil Title I funding in each year of their school-age years. For the average child, this figure corresponds to about $950 in Title I funding per poor child received by the public-school district in each year of their school-age years (figures 3 and 4). These increases are especially pronounced for poor and minority children. As shown, the average black child was in a public school district that received roughly $175 in per-pupil Title I funding in each year of their school-age years (figures 1 and 2), which corresponds to about an average of $1,150 in Title I funding per poor child during K–12 (figures 3 and 4).

After combining information from these data sources, the main sample used to analyze adult attainment outcomes consists of PSID original sample children born between 1950 and 1977 followed until at least survey wave 1995 (that is, individuals who were children up to age eighteen in the 1968 wave who have been followed into adulthood).[6] It includes 7,182 individuals from 2,221 childhood families, 567 school districts, 296 childhood counties, across forty states—a total of 1,572 poor children and 5,610 nonpoor children.[7] To compare individuals from different cohorts at around the same age, I focus on those adult-economic observations between the ages of thirty and forty. The mean age is thirty-five years for the economic-outcome measures considered.

I begin the analysis by examining the relationship between the 1960 county-poverty rate and Title I funding, then I estimate models of Title I effects on per-pupil spending. The set of adult outcomes examined chronologically over the life cycle include educational outcomes—whether ever repeated a grade, whether ever placed in a gifted program, whether ever suspended or expelled from school, whether grad-

---

6. The PSID maintains high wave-to-wave response rates of 95 to 98 percent. Studies have concluded that the PSID sample of heads of households and spouses remains representative of the national sample of adults (Fitzgerald, Gottschalk, and Moffitt 1998).

7. The average school district has thirteen PSID sample children: half have at least nine, fewer than 6 percent only one, three-quarters at least three, and one-quarter at least twenty-five.

Figure 2. Birth Cohort Variation in Per-Pupil Title I Funding, 90 Percent CI

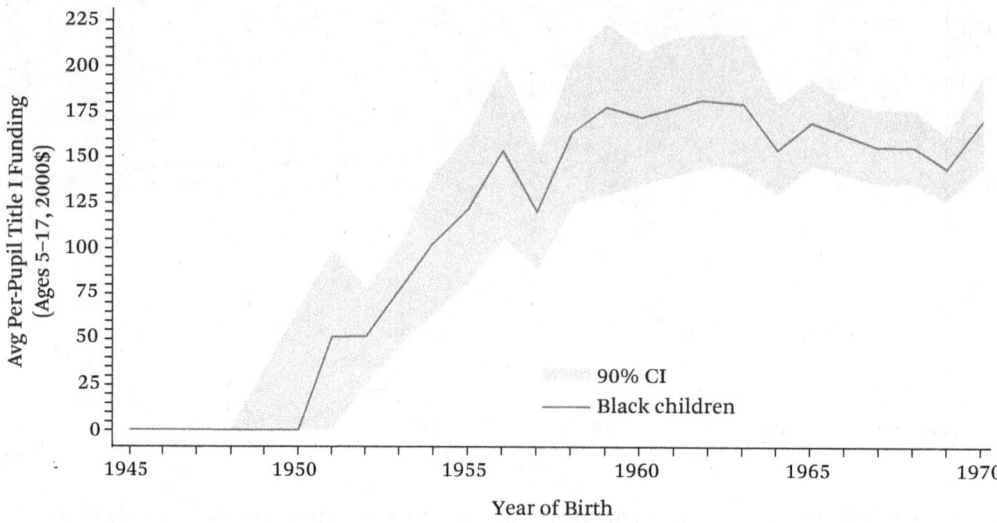

Source: Author's calculations based on nationally-representative data from the Panel Study of Income Dynamics (PSID) of original sample children born between 1950 and 1977 followed into adulthood (1968–2011), matched with administrative data of county-level Title I funding from the National Archives and Records Administration (NARA) covering 1965 to 1980 and county-level census counts of the number of children and number of poor children (Surveillance, Epidemiology, and End Results (SEER) data).

Figure 3. Birth Cohort Variation in Title I Funding per Poor Child, All Children

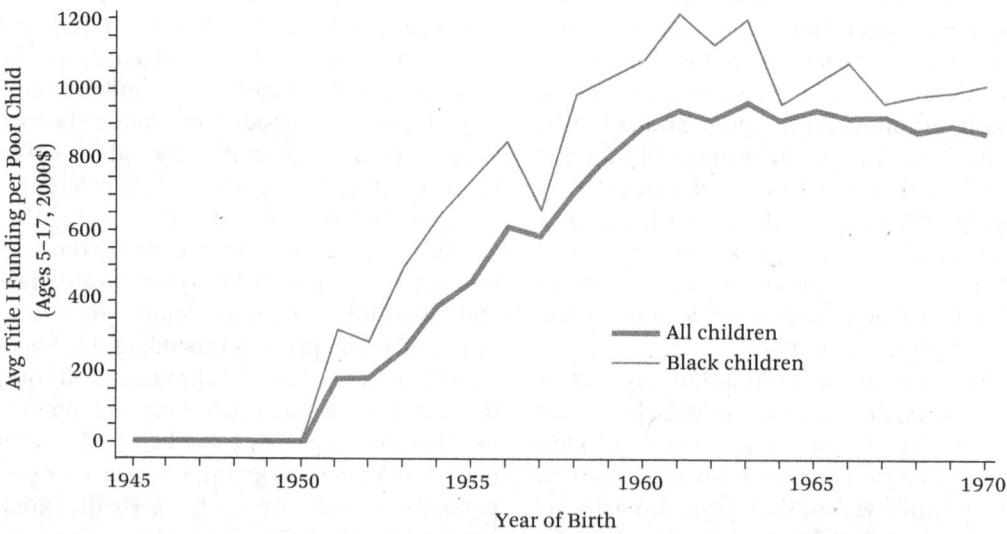

Source: Author's calculations based on nationally-representative data from the Panel Study of Income Dynamics (PSID) of original sample children born between 1950 and 1977 followed into adulthood (1968–2011), matched with administrative data of county-level Title I funding from the National Archives and Records Administration (NARA) covering 1965 to 1980 and county-level census counts of the number of children and number of poor children (Surveillance, Epidemiology, and End Results (SEER) data).

Figure 4. Birth Cohort Variation in Title I Funding per Poor Child, 90 Percent CI

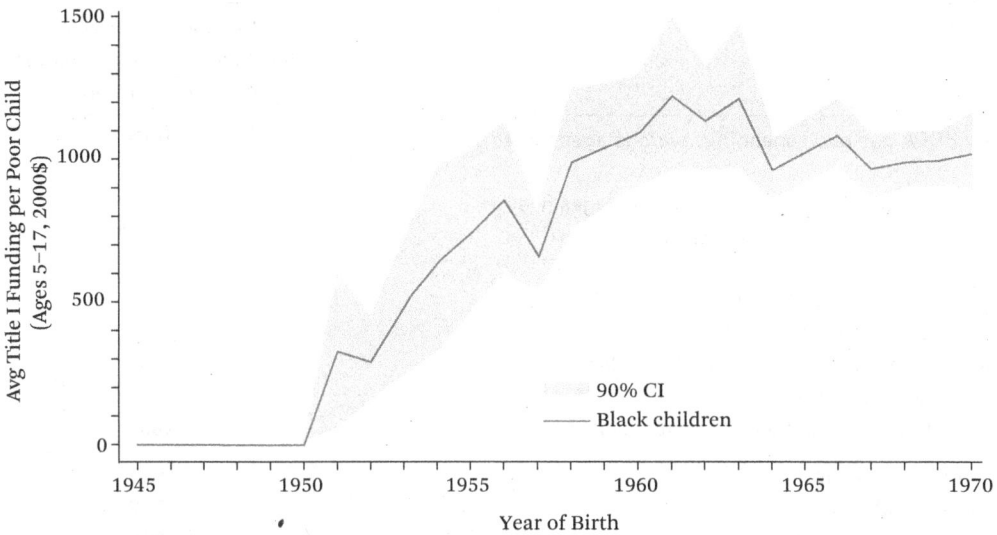

Source: Author's calculations based on nationally-representative data from the Panel Study of Income Dynamics (PSID) of original sample children born between 1950 and 1977 followed into adulthood (1968–2011), matched with administrative data of county-level Title I funding from the National Archives and Records Administration (NARA) covering 1965 to 1980 and county-level census counts of the number of children and number of poor children (Surveillance, Epidemiology, and End Results (SEER) data).

uated from high school,[8] years of completed education; labor-market and economic-status outcomes (all in 2000 dollars)—wages, annual work hours, earnings, family income, and annual incidence of poverty in adulthood (ages thirty through forty); and whether ever incarcerated by age thirty-five. The child behavioral outcomes (ever repeated a grade, ever suspended or expelled) are important to examine in part because early manifestations of problem behavior in children have been shown to often be a risk factor for dropping out of high school and a precursor to more serious involvement in deviant behavior in adolescence and criminal involvement in adulthood. All analyses include men and women with controls for gender. Childhood family poverty status is assessed by matching a child's total family-income average in the period between ages twelve and seventeen with the corresponding poverty thresholds based on income and family size. Summary statistics are presented in table 1.

Spells of incarceration are recovered from information on PSID respondents collected in each survey that includes whether a respondent was incarcerated at the time of the interview. This data on incarceration alone has limitations. Among the most important is that the survey identifies incarceration in a given year only if ongoing at the time of the interview. As a result, we are likely to miss individuals serving shorter sentences that did not coincide with the time of the interview. The 1995 wave added an education and crime-history module to the PSID, including several key questions I use to augment and obtain more precise information about the timing and duration of incarceration and minimize measurement error. In particular, information was collected for all adults in the 1995 wave on grade repetition, placement in gifted programs, whether respon-

---

8. High school graduate here refers to earning a high school diploma. Individuals earning GEDs are treated as high school dropouts here, following Heckman's work showing that the economic returns to GEDs are closer to that of dropouts than those who earn high school diplomas.

Table 1. Effects of Title I Funding on School District Spending

	Dependent Variable: Per-Pupil Spending, Average, Ages Five to Seventeen
County ESEA per-pupil spending, average ages five to seventeen	0.9976*
	(0.5647)
County ESEA per-pupil spending, average ages five to seventeen*(1960 county poverty rate - 45)	0.1292*
	(0.0777)
School district fixed effects?	yes
Race-specific year of birth fixed effects?	yes
Race*census division FE*year of birth?	yes
Childhood family and neighborhood controls?	yes
School desegregation controls?	yes
Other local/state/federal government expenditure programs?	yes
Number of individuals	6,817
Number of childhood families	1,920
Number of school districts	518

Source: Author's calculations based on nationally-representative data from the Panel Study of Income Dynamics (PSID) of original sample children born between 1955 and 1977 followed into adulthood (1968–2011), matched with administrative data of county-level Title I funding from the National Archives and Records Administration (NARA) and school district per-pupil spending from the Individual Government Finances Database and Census of Governments.
Note: Robust standard errors in parentheses (clustered on childhood county).
Sample: PSID original sample children born 1955 to 1977 followed to adulthood.
*$p < .10$; **$p < .05$; ***$p < .01$

dents had ever been expelled or suspended from school, been booked or charged with a crime, been placed in a juvenile correctional facility, or served time in jail or prison, as well as the number of times and the month and year of release as respectively applicable. For the adult incarceration outcome, the sample consists of PSID children born between 1950 and 1970 followed into adulthood who answered the criminal history questions in the 1995 wave of the PSID or were positively identified as incarcerated in any wave of the survey between 1968 and 2011.

I use the census block as the definition of neighborhood, which is a smaller geographic area than most previous studies use, and I match childhood residential address histories to blocks and school-district boundaries that prevailed in 1969 (the algorithm is outlined in the appendix).[9] Each record is merged with data on school spending for 1960 through 2000, the Title I funding information at the county level, neighborhood-level variables from the 1970, 1980, and 1990 census that corresponds with the prevailing levels during their school-age years. I use the census block or tract contained in the geocode file based on the 1968 residential location—the earliest available address in childhood (or county of birth when census block information is unavailable)—to avoid potential bias from endogenous residential mobility in response to Title I–induced school spending changes.

EMPIRICAL STRATEGY FOR ESTIMATING TITLE I EFFECTS ON ADULT OUTCOMES

The central aim of the empirical analysis is to investigate whether Title I funding, and resultant changes in school spending, have long-term impacts on adult outcomes. Particular at-

---

9. Many school districts were counties during this period, including more than half of southern school districts.

tention is given to determine whether the increased Title I funding experienced by children in lower-income communities had any lasting effects on their adult socioeconomic well-being. The empirical approach uses changes in Title I expenditures across cohorts from the same district, and differences in Title I expenditures among observationally similar children and families in different districts, experienced during one's school-age years, to isolate the effect of Title I as distinct from the effects of childhood poverty and other trends and coincident policies.

The main regression models used to analyze the impacts of Title I on the difference in adult attainment between treated and untreated cohorts involve estimating equations of the form

$$Y_{idb} = \beta_1 TitleISpend_{db} + \beta_2 TitleISpend_{db} * NonPoorKid_{idb} + X_{idb}\theta + Z_{db}\gamma + (W_{1960d} * b) \phi + \eta_d + \lambda_b^r + \varphi_g^r * b + \varepsilon_{idb}$$

where i indexes the individual, d the school district, b the year of birth, g the region of birth (defined by nine census division categories), and r the racial group. The measure of exposure to Title I funding is $TitleISpend_{5-17}$, the average per-pupil Title I expenditure in an individual's birth district during the individual's school-age years (ages five through seventeen). A doubling of this average can be interpreted as a doubling of Title I per-pupil spending for all twelve years of an individual's school career. In alternative specifications, I also examine the average Title I expenditures per poor child in the county during K–12 as the key explanatory variable. The rationale for this latter measure is that, if Title I funding is targeted toward resources and services for disadvantaged students within the district, then the effective school resources this funding supports would partly depend on how many of those students are in the district. No information is available on intradistrict resource allocation of Title I funding toward specific school inputs nor on the extent to which it is targeted.

I test for differential Title I effects by childhood poverty status, as prior research has shown that children from low-income families may be more sensitive to changes in school quality and school-related interventions (such as the Tennessee Star class-size experiment) than children from more advantaged family backgrounds. Furthermore, because both residential mobility across counties and private school attendance are more common among children from affluent families than those from low-income ones, one might expect larger effects among children from low-income families.[10] The equation includes school-district fixed effects (η_d), race-specific birth year fixed effects (λ_b^r), and race-by-region of birth cohort trends ($\varphi_g^r * b$), and it controls for an extensive set of child and childhood family-neighborhood characteristics (X_{idb}): parental education and occupational status, parental income, mother's marital status at birth, birth weight, child health insurance coverage, gender, neighborhood poverty, neighborhood racial composition, and neighborhood average-education level).

To account for the effect of the other coincident policies, I include county-by-birth-year measures of school desegregation, community health centers, and state funding for kindergarten, in addition to per capita expenditures on Head Start (at age four), and average childhood spending on food stamps, Aid to Families with Dependent Children (AFDC), Medicaid, and unemployment insurance (Z_{cb}) (for the data sources used to compile these measures, see Johnson 2011). To control for trends in factors hypothesized to influence Title I funding, the equation also includes interactions between 1960 characteristics of the county of birth and linear trends in the year of birth ($W_{1960d} * b$): 1960 county poverty rate, percent black, average education level, percent urban, and population size). Standard errors are all clustered at the childhood county level.

---

10. Prior research has demonstrated that though residential instability is significantly greater for poor families, and they experience intracounty moves more frequently, they most often move to neighborhoods of similar observable quality (Johnson 2009). Poor families are far less mobile, as measured by upward residential-mobility patterns, and less responsive to policy changes due to the greater residential location constraints they face.

Ideally, one would want information on Title I funding at the school or district level, but for this historical time period, per-pupil Title I funding and Title I funding per poor child at the county level are the most detailed measures one can construct from the available National Archives Record Administration (the only data source one can use to compile this information for this period). Although this limitation undoubtedly results in some measurement error, including school-district fixed effects and controls for detailed neighborhood characteristics will minimize potential bias. Moreover, many school districts were counties during this period, including more than half of southern school districts.

One potential parental response to existing school quality differences across public schools is to move to a different city or enroll children in a private school. Moreover, changes in how local school expenditures are financed may affect local residential-sorting patterns and property values. For example, it is possible that, instead of affecting learning per se, a school's Title I status may affect who enrolls and leaves a school. In that case, the estimated effects could be due to changes in the composition of students attending a school. This would constitute a true causal effect of Title I receipt on average educational outcomes, but obviously would have very different policy implications. If Title I services actually lead to improved educational outcomes, one would expect attrition rates (the main component of mobility rates) to be lower instead of higher in Title I schools. Because I did not want to include endogenous residential moves (that is, selective mobility of students to non–Title I schools during these years), I identified the neighborhood and school of upbringing based only on the earliest childhood address, 1968, which predates most of the major increases in Title I funding.[11] Because of this limitation, we can interpret the results as providing intention-to-treat estimates of the impacts of Title I school spending. The analysis aims to capture the quality of the public schools potentially attended by a given individual, rather than simply the quality of schools and classes actually attended; this approach also lessens measurement error and helps circumvent issues of endogeneity of both school choice and intradistrict resource allocation. In particular, I examine district-level measures of school resource inputs that reflect the quality of the overall school system available to an individual during their K–12 years, based on the district lived in that corresponds with the earliest residential address.[12] By using the earliest residential address of children, I minimize potential bias from endogenous residential mobility.[13]

RESULTS

To put things in context and provide perspective before proceeding to the regression results, I present a set of descriptive statistics compiled for this historical period. In a series of maps, I first display the geographic variation in county-poverty rates in 1960, which highlights the substantial concentration of poverty in the South during the time period leading up to ESEA (figure 5). Figure 6 shows the geographic variation in the racial composition in 1960, which demonstrates the concentration of blacks in the South that overlaps the high-poverty counties. Geographic variation in Title

---

11. Among original sample children in the PSID, the average proportion of childhood spent growing up in the 1968 neighborhood was roughly 65 percent.

12. We recognize that classroom sizes and teacher characteristics vary even within districts and schools, and some children move across school systems, which will induce some measurement error. However, if this measurement error is of a classical variety, the resultant attenuation bias will lead us to understate the importance of school spending. Districts are not typically required to report school-level expenditures.

13. I find a similar pattern of results (with larger point estimates for Title I effects) among the subsample of cohorts born between 1963 and 1977 for whom the earliest residential address information used predates their school-age years. This suggests that endogenous residential mobility is not a significant source of bias and is not likely a factor that would result in an overstatement of Title I effects in this analysis.

Figure 5. U.S. County Poverty Rates in 1960

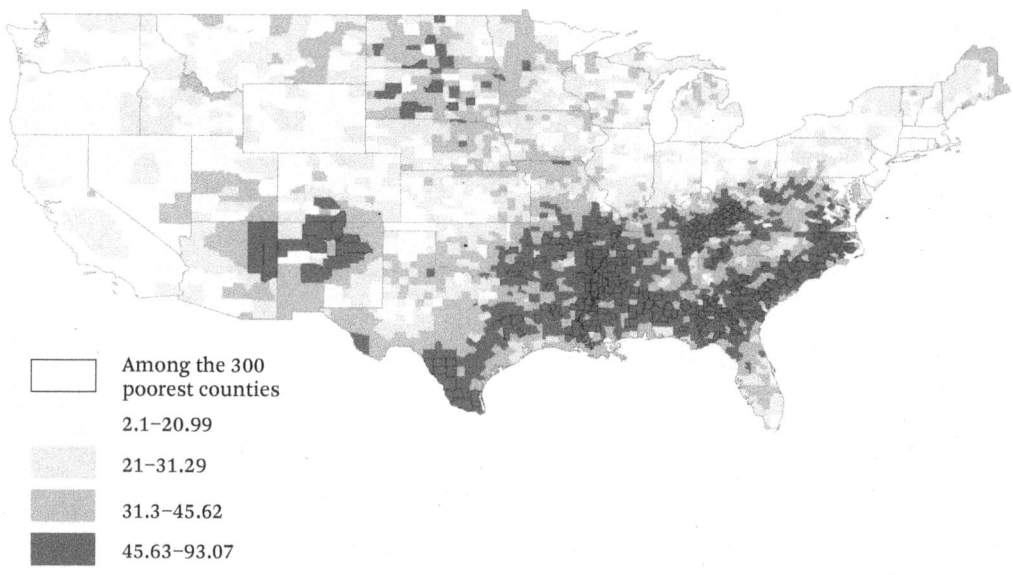

Source: Author's calculations based on county-level poverty rates for all U.S. counties in 1960 based on 1960 census data and data from the National Archives and Records Administration (NARA). Calculations verified from a study conducted by Jens Ludwig and Doug Miller (2007).

Figure 6. County Population: Percent African American, 1960

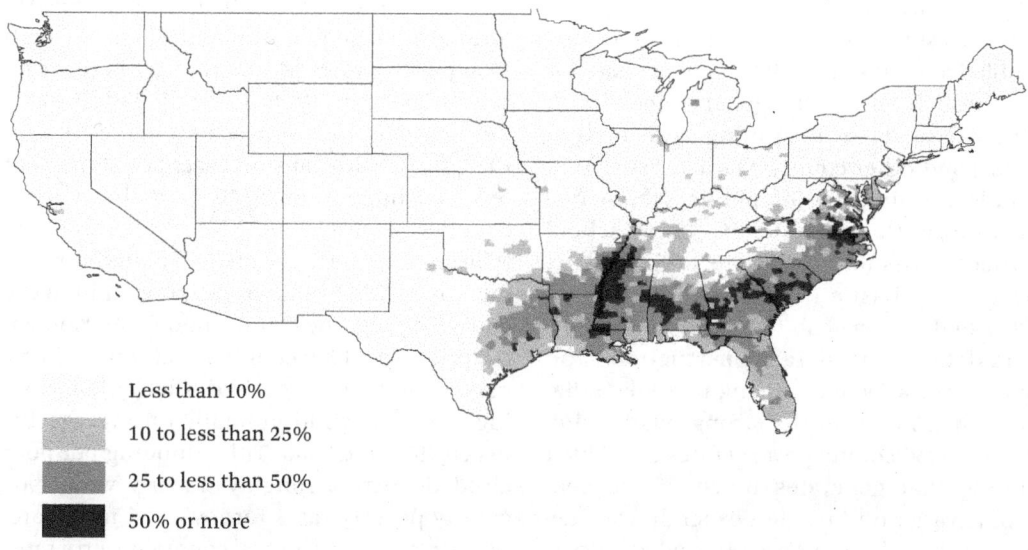

Source: Author's calculations based on county-level racial composition for all U.S. counties in 1960 based on 1960 census data.

Figure 7. Per-Pupil Title I Funding and 1960 County Poverty Rate

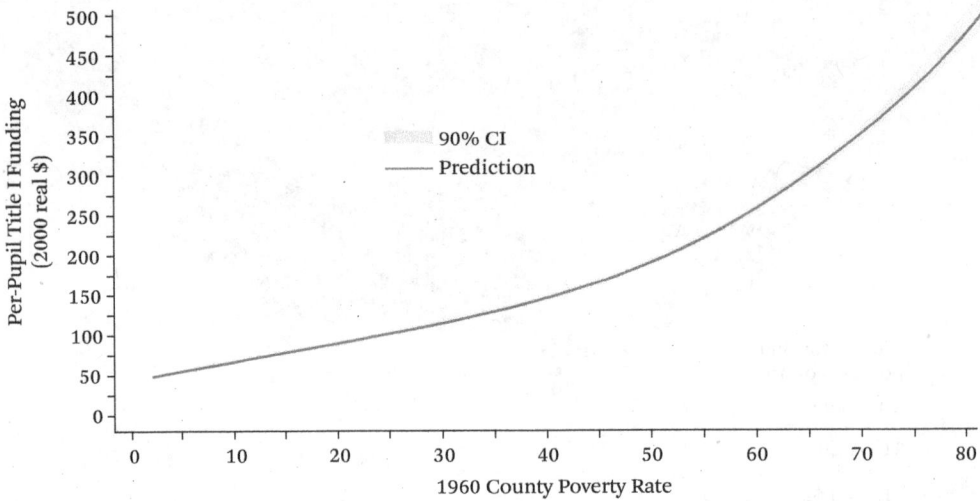

Source: Author's calculations based on annual school district data of the full universe of U.S. public school districts from the Individual Government Finances Database and Census of Governments, 1970–1980. These data are matched with county-level Title I funding information (NARA) and county-level demographic characteristics from census data.
Note: District spending and Title I funding CPI-U deflated in real 2000 dollars. Analysis sample includes 10,735 school districts; forty-five states. Results are based on regression models of per-pupil Title I funding on 1960 county poverty rates (quadratic specification allowing flexible functional form) that include year fixed effects as controls.

I funding and its increases in successive years between 1965 and 1980 is substantial, as shown in figures 1 through 4.

To investigate this variation further, I assembled annual school-district panel data for 1967 through 1990 (NBER 2003) matched with county-level Title I funding information (NARA) and other county characteristics that include the universe of public school districts in the United States (N=10,735 school districts across forty-five states). The district spending and Title I funding measures are CPI-U deflated in real 2000 dollars (for further details on data construction and sources, see appendix). Using these data, figures 7 and 8 present the strong relationship between 1960 county poverty rates and Title I funding that generates much of the geographic variation in Title I expenditures. Results are based on regression models of per-pupil Title I funding on 1960 county poverty rates (quadratic specification allowing flexible functional form) that include year fixed effects as controls to account for national time trends (figure 7). Per-pupil Title I funding increased rapidly with 1960 county poverty rates. In particular, although counties with 1960 poverty rates of less than 20 percent received less than $100 per-pupil Title I funding annually on average between 1970 and 1980, those with rates in excess of 50 percent received more than $200, and the poorest counties received $500. Figure 8 presents the relationship between 1960 county poverty rates and Title I funding per poor child in the county using the same model. As shown, counties with 1960 county poverty rates in excess of 30 percent received $700 Title I funding per poor child annually on average between 1970 and 1980. Title I funding per poor child decreases roughly linearly with 1960 county poverty rates for low- and moderate-poverty counties (that is, county poverty rates up to 25 percent), going from roughly $1,200 for counties with less than 10 percent to $800 for counties with 20 percent. These increases

Figure 8. Title I Funding per Poor Child and 1960 County Poverty Rate

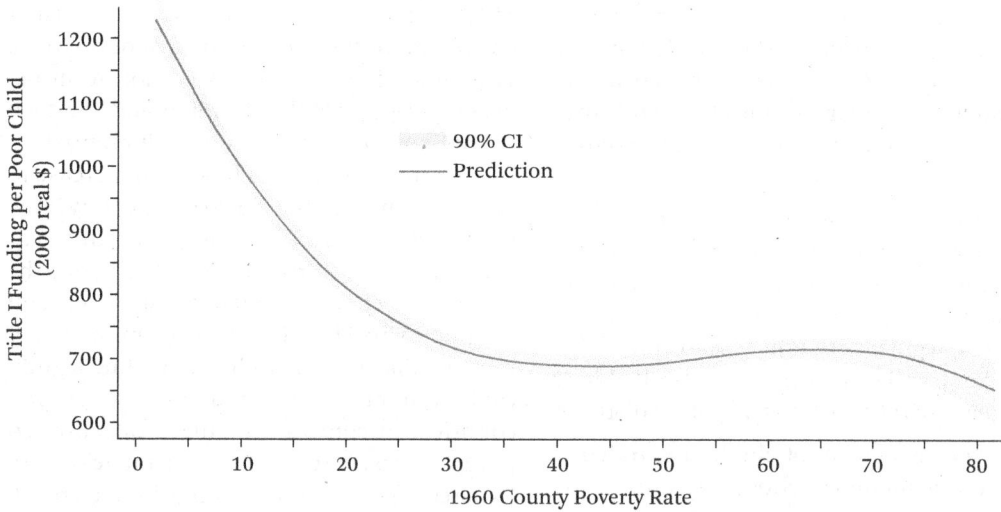

Source: Author's calculations based on annual school district data of the full universe of U.S. public school districts from the Individual Government Finances Database and Census of Governments, 1970–1980. These data are matched with county-level Title I funding information (NARA) and county-level demographic characteristics from census data.
Note: District spending and Title I funding CPI-U deflated in real 2000 dollars. Analysis sample includes 10,735 school districts; forty-five states. Results are based on regression models of per-pupil Title I funding on 1960 county poverty rates (quadratic specification allowing flexible functional form), estimating the same model as figure 7 with Title I funding per poor child as the dependent variable.

are significant, given that the average total per-pupil spending in 1967 was about $2,900 (in 2000 dollars). Whether per-pupil Title I spending or Title I spending per poor child is the most important measure to consider depends in part on the degree of targeting of Title I–funded resources to the most disadvantaged children within the district.

The descriptive summary statistics for the PSID sample are presented in table A1 (see appendix). Some additional descriptive statistics are drawn directly from congressional reports and surveys conducted in the first decade when Title I funding was first distributed (Wargo et al. 1972), supplemented with my own analyses:

In 1970, 13.5 percent of school-age children in the United States were from families with incomes below the poverty line; moreover, 39 percent of all black school-age children were poor but only 9.5 percent of all white children were. These rates were substantially higher in the South.

As of 1969, the end of the study period, minority children made up 20 percent of public school enrollment. However, 77 percent of all black students were enrolled in schools with minority concentrations above 50 percent and 98 percent of white children attended schools with minority proportions below 49 percent.

More black (24.2 percent) than white children (16.5 percent) were achieving below grade level in one or more subjects, and fewer blacks (65 percent) than whites (74 percent) were at grade level. Although 14 percent of all elementary school children had severe reading problems, 20 percent of children from low-income families and 25 percent of students enrolled in large urban schools had such problems.

Descriptive statistics on the Title I program's operational context follow:

> Poor children tended to be enrolled in a relatively few large districts that had low to moderate regular per-pupil expenditures and high concentrations of low-income children.

> As of 1969, the majority of low-income children were enrolled in Title I schools, 90 percent of them concentrated in districts with low (under $1,885) to moderate ($1,885 to $2,770) regular per-pupil expenditures (2000 dollars), and 68 percent were enrolled in 12 percent of the Title I participating districts.

> In 1968, 29 percent of children enrolled in Title I elementary schools were from minority groups. Within Title I elementary schools, 83 percent of students were assigned to classrooms in which 90 percent or more of the children were of one race, white or black. Only 17 percent were in classrooms where the racial composition corresponded to that of the student population in Title I schools, and even fewer were in classrooms with a racial composition corresponding to national standards for integration (Wargo et al. 1972). In stark contrast, only 0.2 percent of white children in Title I elementary schools were enrolled in classrooms with a 90 percent or higher concentration of blacks.

> The extensive segregation by race and class reflected by these descriptive statistics was partially due to a tendency to group minority and poor children by ability in classrooms, and white children and children from more economically advantaged families by subject.

> Approximately 75 percent of children attended schools with low concentrations of poor children, but 9 percent were in schools where more than half of children were from poor families, and these were disproportionately located in large urban cities.

> Between 1966 and 1969, participation intensity in compensatory education programs averaged about only one hour per day (Wargo et al. 1972).

REGRESSION RESULTS

Figure 9 presents estimated effects of per-pupil Title I funding on per-pupil spending using panel data of the universe of school districts. The model includes an interaction term between per-pupil Title I funding and the 1960 county poverty rate to test for differential responsiveness of districts to a given increase in Title I depending on the district's poverty level, using school-district fixed effects and year fixed effects as controls. Figure 9 highlights the differential effect of a $100 dollar increase in per-pupil Title I funding on per-pupil spending by county poverty rate, wherein we find significant crowd-out for low- and moderate-poverty counties. In contrast, for high-concentrated poverty areas, particularly in the range of 35 to 55 percent poverty, there is only limited crowd-out and every additional Title I dollar translates into between $0.75 to $1 in additional total school district spending. For example, the results indicate that a $100 dollar increase in per-pupil Title I funding leads to an $88 dollar increase in total per-pupil spending for county poverty rates of 40 to 50 percent, a $79 increase for county poverty rate of 30 percent, a $59 increase for poverty rate of 20 percent, but only a (statistically insignificant) $26 increase for a county with a 10 percent rate. Thus, on average, not only did higher concentrated poverty areas receive more Title I funds, but they also experienced less crowd-out, which led to larger increases in total district spending for a given Title I funding increase.

Table 1 presents results of a similar analysis of the estimated effects of Title I on average per-pupil spending between the ages of five and seventeen using the subset of districts that overlap the PSID sample. The pattern of results is similar. Despite significant increases in Title I funding, they led to very modest increases in per-pupil spending in low- and moderate-poverty districts due to significant crowd-out of local revenue for public schools. However, in high-concentrated poverty areas, a $100 increase in per-pupil Title I funding is associated with about a $100 increase in average per-pupil spending, which corresponds to roughly a 3 percent increase for a county with a 45 percent poverty rate. I find that per-pupil spending increased by about twice as much per dollar of

Figure 9. Effect of $100 Increase in Per-Pupil Title I Funding on Per-Pupil Spending by 1960 County Poverty Rate

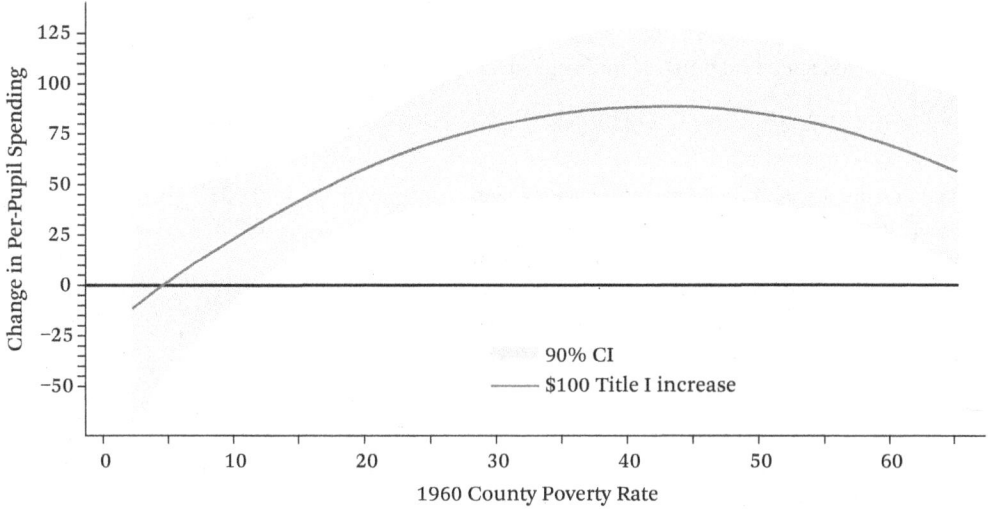

Source: Author's calculations based on annual school district data of the full universe of U.S. public school districts from the Individual Government Finances Database and Census of Governments, 1970–1980. This data is matched with county-level Title I funding information (NARA) and county-level demographic characteristics from census data.
Note: District spending and Title I funding CPI-U deflated in real 2000 dollars. Analysis sample includes 10,735 school districts; forty-five states. Results are based on regression model of district per-pupil spending on per-pupil Title I funding interacted with 1960 county poverty rates (quadratic specification allowing flexible functional form) that include school district fixed effects and year fixed effects as controls.

federal revenue in both high-poverty districts and high black-enrollment-share districts, due to less local offset. Federal guidance on how school districts are to use Title I funds is imprecise, especially during the first twenty years after ESEA was enacted. Over time, local guidance on the use of Title I funds has become far more specific, and the degree to which Title I funds are restricted varies by district. Title I did not impose a student performance requirement in its original 1965 enactment, and the requirement was introduced in 1994 and was not fully implemented until the No Child Left Behind Act (NCLB) of 2001. In the current Title I policy context within school accountability systems, even if being a Title I school does not lead to a significant increase in average per-pupil expenditures, the Title I program itself could still have an effect, as it may put restrictions on the minimum amount of resources to be spent on low-achieving students, on the way it is spent, and also makes the school accountable for its students' achievements.

ESTIMATED EFFECTS ON LONGER-RUN OUTCOMES

Educational Attainment

Differences are large and significant in educational attainment by child poverty status, as evidenced in the summary statistics: the high school graduation rate among poor children in the sample was 0.63 but among nonpoor children 0.87; poor children completed 11.9 years of education and nonpoor children 13.4 years on average (table A1). Tables 2 and 3 present the results for the effects of Title I funding on the likelihood of high school graduation and years of completed education, respectively. The results indicate that a $100 increase in per-pupil Title I funding experienced throughout one's K–12 years (which is

Table 2. Effects of Title I Funding on the Likelihood of Graduating from High School

	Dependent Variable: Prob(HS Graduate)		
County Title I per-pupil spending (00s), average ages five to seventeen	0.0225** (0.0093)		
County Title I per-pupil spending (00s), average ages five to seventeen*poor child		0.0533*** (0.0164)	
County Title I per-pupil spending (00s), average ages five to seventeen*nonpoor child		0.0087 (0.0096)	
County Title I spending per poor child (00s), average ages five to seventeen*poor child			0.0121*** (0.0036)
County Title I spending per poor child (00s), average ages five to seventeen*nonpoor child			0.0008 (0.0013)
School district fixed effects?	yes	yes	yes
Race-specific year of birth fixed effects?	yes	yes	yes
Race*census division FE*year of birth?	yes	yes	yes
Childhood family and neighborhood controls?	yes	yes	yes
School desegregation controls?	yes	yes	yes
Other local/state/federal government expenditure programs?	yes	yes	yes
Number of individuals	7,035	7,035	7,035
Number of childhood families	2,171	2,171	2,171
Number of school districts	563	563	563

Source: Author's calculations based on nationally-representative data from the Panel Study of Income Dynamics (PSID) of original sample children born between 1950 and 1977 followed into adulthood (1968–2011), matched with administrative data of county-level Title I funding from the National Archives and Records Administration (NARA).
Note: Robust standard errors in parentheses (clustered on childhood county).
*p < .10; **p < .05; ***p < .01

the average increase across districts and also represents a standard deviation change) is associated with a 2.2 percentage point increase in the likelihood of graduating from high school (table 2, column 1) and a 0.25 increase in completed years of education (table 3, column 1) on average among all children. The estimated effects are both statistically significant at the 0.05 level. Furthermore, we find statistically significant differences in these effects for the likelihood of high school graduation by childhood poverty status; effects are more pronounced for poor children. In particular, for poor children the estimated effect of a $100 increase in per-pupil Title I funding leads to a 5.3 percentage point increase in the likelihood of graduating from high school. Title I spending has a negligible and statistically insignificant effect for nonpoor children, however (table 2, column 2). The estimated effects of per-pupil Title I funding for poor and nonpoor children are similar for years of education (table 3, column 2).

The results indicate that for poor children, a $1,000 increase in Title I funding per poor child (a standard deviation change, the average increase across districts being $800) is associated with a 12.1 percentage point increase in the likelihood of high school graduation and 0.6 more years of completed education, all of which are statistically significant at the 0.01 level (tables 2 and 3, column 3). The corresponding effects for nonpoor children are roughly half the magnitude found for poor children on years of education, and the effects for non-poor children are small and insignificant for high school graduation (tables 2 and 3, column 3).

Table 3. Effects of Title I Funding on Educational Attainment

	Dependent Variable: Years of Education		
County Title I per-pupil spending (00s), average ages five to seventeen	0.2459** (0.0531)		
County Title I per-pupil spending (00s), average ages five to seventeen*poor child		0.2763*** (0.0680)	
County Title I per-pupil spending (00s), average ages five to seventeen*nonpoor child		0.2225*** (0.0557)	
County Title I spending per poor child (00s), average ages five to seventeen*poor child			0.0600*** (0.0151)
County Title I spending per poor child (00s), average ages five to seventeen*nonpoor child			0.0297*** (0.0107)
School district fixed effects?	yes	yes	yes
Race-specific year of birth fixed effects?	yes	yes	yes
Race*census division FE*year of birth?	yes	yes	yes
Childhood family and neighborhood controls?	yes	yes	yes
School desegregation controls?	yes	yes	yes
Other local/state/federal government expenditure programs?	yes	yes	yes
Number of individuals	7,035	7,035	7,035
Number of childhood families	2,171	2,171	2,171
Number of school districts	563	563	563

Source: Author's calculations based on nationally-representative data from the Panel Study of Income Dynamics (PSID) of original sample children born between 1950 and 1977 followed into adulthood (1968–2011), matched with administrative data of county-level Title I funding from the National Archives and Records Administration (NARA).
Note: Robust standard errors in parentheses (clustered on childhood county).
*p < .10; **p < .05; ***p < .01

Other School-Related Outcomes

To examine intermediate educational outcomes leading up to high school graduation, looking beyond overall years of education reveals a similar pattern of significant results for the likelihood of grade repetition and other school-related outcomes. Among poor children, 20 percent repeated a grade at some point, and 28 percent were suspended or expelled from school. Among nonpoor children, 11 percent were held back and 17 percent were suspended or expelled. The results presented in table 4 indicate that a $100 increase in per-pupil Title I funding leads to a 2 percentage point reduction in the likelihood of grade repetition (column 1, marginally significant), a 2 percentage point increase in the likelihood of placement in an advanced or gifted class (column 2), and roughly a 2 percentage-point reduction in the likelihood of ever being suspended or expelled from school (column 3, marginally significant). These results are particularly noteworthy because, as mentioned, grade repetition and suspension or expulsion from school are often early antecedents to high school dropout and behavior problems. They are also key risk factors for subsequent criminal involvement among individuals raised in high-poverty, high-crime neighborhoods. The final column of table 4 shows that a $100 increase in per-pupil Title I funding is significantly associated with a 0.44 percentage-point reduction in the likelihood of ever being incarcerated by age thirty-five, which corre-

Table 4. Effects of Title I Funding on Other School-Related Outcomes

	Dependent Variable:			
	Prob(Ever Grade Repetition)	Prob(Ever Placed in Gifted Program)	Prob(Ever Suspended/ Expelled)	Prob(Ever Incarcerated) by Age Thirty-Five
County Title I per-pupil spending (00s), average ages five to seventeen	−0.0197+ (0.0138)	0.0196* (0.0118)	−0.0196+ (0.0127)	−0.0044* (0.0025)
School district fixed effects?	yes	yes	yes	yes
Race-specific year of birth fixed effects?	yes	yes	yes	yes
Race*census division FE*year of birth?	yes	yes	yes	yes
Childhood family and neighborhood controls?	yes	yes	yes	yes
School desegregation controls?	yes	yes	yes	yes
Other local/state/federal government expenditure programs?	yes	yes	yes	yes
Number of individuals	5,715	5,715	5,715	9,446
Number of childhood families	1,939	1,939	1,939	2,415
Number of school districts	538	538	538	589

Source: Author's calculations based on nationally-representative data from the Panel Study of Income Dynamics (PSID) of original sample children born between 1950 and 1977 followed into adulthood (1968–2011), matched with administrative data of county-level Title I funding from the National Archives and Records Administration (NARA).
Note: Robust standard errors in parentheses (clustered on childhood county).
+$p < .10$ (one-tailed test); *$p < .10$ (two-tailed test); **$p < .05$; ***$p < .01$

sponds with about a 10 percent reduction in the risk, on average, for poor children. Recall that a $100 increase in per-pupil Title I funding corresponds with about an $800 increase in Title I funding per poor child for the average district.

Labor Market Outcomes, Adult Family Income, and Poverty Status

As with educational achievement, differences are stark in adult economic attainments by childhood poverty status. Among poor children, the average family income at age thirty was $33,169 and 26 percent were in poverty at age thirty. Among nonpoor children, the average family income at age thirty was $48,736 and only 5 percent were in poverty at age thirty (see table A1). The next series of results reveals modest, but significant, effects of Title I funding on children's subsequent adult economic status and labor market outcomes, using the same model specifications. As shown in table 5, the results indicate that a $100 increase in per-pupil Title I funding throughout the school-age years leads to a 6.1 percent increase in adult wages, 49 additional annual work hours, 7.9 percent increase in annual labor market earnings, a 5.5 percent increase in annual family income, and a 1.7 percentage-point reduction in the annual incidence of adult poverty at ages thirty to forty. All but one of the estimated effects are statistically significant at the 0.05 level and many at the 0.01 level.

Table 6 presents the estimated effects of Title I funding per poor child by child poverty status across the main socioeconomic outcomes considered. The broad pattern is that the estimated effects of Title I funding per poor child are between one and a half and two times larger for poor children than for nonpoor children on years of education, likelihood of place-

Table 5. Effects of Title I Funding on Adult Economic Outcomes

	Dependent Variable:				
	Ln(Wage), Ages Thirty to Forty	Annual Work Hours (Include 0s), Ages Thirty to Forty	Ln(Annual Earnings), Ages Thirty to Forty	Ln(Annual Family Income), Ages Thirty to Forty	Annual Incidence of Poverty, Ages Thirty to Forty
County Title I per-pupil spending (00s), average ages five to seventeen	0.0610*** (0.0204)	49.1535* (29.7015)	0.0793*** (0.0292)	0.0553** (0.0269)	−0.0168*** (0.0062)
School district fixed effects?	yes	yes	yes	yes	yes
Race-specific year of birth fixed effects?	yes	yes	yes	yes	yes
Race*census division FE*year of birth?	yes	yes	yes	yes	yes
Childhood family and neighborhood controls?	yes	yes	yes	yes	yes
School desegregation controls?	yes	yes	yes	yes	yes
Other local/state/federal government expenditure programs?	yes	yes	yes	yes	yes
Number of person-year observations	30,979	36,389	31,095	36,948	37,079
Number of individuals	4,734	4,932	4,740	4,966	4,970
Number of childhood families	1,903	1,929	1,903	1,931	1,933
Number of school districts	509	517	509	518	518

Source: Author's calculations based on nationally-representative data from the Panel Study of Income Dynamics (PSID) of original sample children born between 1950 and 1977 followed into adulthood (1968–2011), matched with administrative data of county-level Title I funding from the National Archives and Records Administration (NARA).
Note: Robust standard errors in parentheses (clustered on childhood county).
*$p < .10$; **$p < .05$; ***$p < .01$

ment in a gifted program, likelihood of incarceration, and adult wages. For example, the results indicate that, on average, a $1,000 increase in Title I funding per poor child during the school-age years is associated with a 10.8 percent increase in adult wages and a 5.8 percent increase for nonpoor children (table 6, column 6).

Discussion of Magnitudes in Perspective

Given the small increase—between $100 and $400 per student—in school spending, what is a reasonable expectation of the effect of Title I? A few caveats on how to interpret the magnitudes of the estimates are important. Given the lack of information on the extent of targeting of Title I programs, the effects of Title I funding on treated students remains unclear. That is, whether one considers the estimated effects as large or small would ideally be informed by the extent to which funds are targeted within schools. For example, if funds are targeted to 20 percent of students, expected effects should be five times as large. Targeting issues, and the effective progressivity of school spending, include not only whether resources are targeted to poor schools within districts, but also whether they are targeted to educationally disadvantaged students within schools. Early reports of blatant misappropriation of funds and large-scale violations in the operation of the program are referenced in early reports.

The precise interpretation of the results de-

Table 6. Effects of Title I Funding on Socioeconomic Outcomes, by Child Poverty Status

	Prob (HS Graduate)	Years of Education	Prob(Ever Placed in Gifted Program)	Prob(Ever Suspended/ Expelled)	Prob(Ever Incarcerated) by Age Thirty-Five	Ln(Wage), Ages Thirty to Forty
County Title I spending per poor child (00s), average ages five to seventeen*poor child	0.0121*** (0.0036)	0.0600*** (0.0151)	0.0078** (0.0032)	−0.0089*** (0.0031)	−0.0016* (0.0009)	0.0108* (0.0062)
County Title I spending per poor child (00s), average ages five to seventeen*nonpoor child	0.0008 (0.0013)	0.0297*** (0.0107)	0.0038** (0.0017)	−0.0013 (0.0024)	−0.0010*** (0.0002)	0.0058* (0.0034)
School district fixed effects?	yes	yes	yes	yes	yes	yes
Race-specific year of birth fixed effects?	yes	yes	yes	yes	yes	yes
Race*census division FE*year of birth?	yes	yes	yes	yes	yes	yes
Childhood family and neighborhood controls?	yes	yes	yes	yes	yes	yes
School desegregation controls?	yes	yes	yes	yes	yes	yes
Other local/state/federal government expenditure programs?	yes	yes	yes	yes	yes	yes
Number of person-year observations	—	—	—	—	—	30,979
Number of individuals	7,035	7,035	5,715	5,715	9,446	4,734
Number of childhood families	2,171	2,171	1,939	1,939	2,415	1,903
Number of school districts	563	563	538	538	589	509

Source: Author's calculations based on nationally representative data from the Panel Study of Income Dynamics (PSID) of original sample children born between 1950 and 1977 followed into adulthood (1968–2011), matched with administrative data of county-level Title I funding from the National Archives and Records Administration (NARA).

Note: Robust standard errors in parentheses (clustered on childhood county).

*$p < .10$ (two-tailed test); **$p < .05$; ***$p < .01$

pends on the source and nature of the variation in a school's Title I status over time and its links with the distribution of school budget and expenditure patterns in these years. One of the lessons from decades of education evaluation research on the effectiveness of school reforms is that the how matters more than the what—that is, how programs are implemented must be carefully considered and understood. That concept applies for the context of this study as well, though a lack of data availability prohibits focus on these issues. Decisions on how the money is spent are left to local governance. There is no single Title I treatment effect because of the diverse ways in which federal spending was used and the program implemented across districts. The results section discussed the average effects, but substantial heterogeneity is likely in treatment effects across geographic areas because of the diverse ways in which Title I funding was implemented. Relatively small samples prohibit exploring this heterogeneity in detail in this study given substantial precision issues and the lack of available information on how funds were used.[14]

An alternative way to gauge the magnitudes of Title I effects is to consider them alongside impacts of other major K–12 education interventions, such as class size reductions. For example, the Project Star experiment (a randomized experiment investigating the effects of small class size) cost about $3,800 per student. This large-scale experiment reduced class size by seven students from a base of twenty-two for several early-elementary grades and increased student achievement by between 0.2 and 0.25 standard deviations. A reasonable starting benchmark may be to assume that effects are linear in program costs, so Title I effects may be slightly less than one-tenth of Project Star's effects. Following this logic, one may reasonably expect effects of roughly a 0.7 reduction in student-teacher ratios, and a 0.02 to a 0.025 increase in test scores—a very small effect indeed.

Other recent studies use quasi-experimental designs to analyze the impacts of school inputs and school spending on long-run outcomes (see Jackson, Johnson, and Persico 2015; Chetty et al. 2011; Fredriksson, Ockert, and Oosterbeek 2013). Raj Chetty and his colleagues (2011) report that Project Star students who were randomly assigned to a kindergarten teacher with more than ten years of experience earn 6.9 percent higher income on average at age twenty-seven relative to students with less experienced teachers. They also find that assigning students to a classroom that is one standard deviation better than average in kindergarten (where class quality captures the combined influences of peer effects, teacher effects, and all other classroom characteristics that affect test scores) generates a 9.6 percent increase in annual earnings at age twenty-seven. Kirabo Jackson, Rucker Johnson, and Claudia Persico (2015), using evidence from court-ordered school finance reforms, find that, for children from low-income families, a 10 percent increase in per-pupil spending throughout one's K–12 years leads to 0.46 additional years of completed education, 9.6 percent higher earnings, and a 6.1 percentage-point reduction in the annual incidence of adult poverty. In light of the fact that these reforms generated substantially larger changes in spending and school inputs than Title I, and back-of-the-envelope calculations, the results on long-run outcomes presented here may be viewed as sizeable.[15]

That the Title I effects on long-term attainment outcomes documented here are larger than previous effects highlights the importance of evaluating educational interventions. It also raises concerns about accountability policies that rely exclusively on test scores, because long-run analyses of educational interventions may yield very different conclusions

---

14. I explored heterogeneous effects by 1960 county poverty rate, initial level of local revenue, region (South versus non-South), and race, but small sample sizes resulting in significant precision issues failed to produce useful evidence along these lines.

15. I thank Jordan Matsudaira (Cornell) for helpful discussions about alternative ways of thinking through the magnitudes of the estimated Title I effects.

than short-run analyses that focus on test scores.

Other Unresolved Issues and Directions for Future Research

A dynamic analysis of whether a state responds to its poor districts' receipt of large Title I grants by redirecting money away from education aid in poor districts toward welfare (public assistance), criminal justice, health care, or tax reduction could have implications for educational outcomes. Such analysis could provide greater insight into the dynamics of the flypaper effect and shed light on the form the crowd-out responses to Title I might take and how they affect educational outcomes.

The results presented here suggest that the incidence of benefits and costs of Title I–induced changes in school expenditure patterns favor children from poor families. One unanswered question is whether this relationship operates similarly or differently by race. Other related questions include how the effectiveness of Title I is related to the way Title I funds are spent, whether participation in Title I narrows educational achievement differences between program participants and (otherwise similar) nonparticipants, and whether this gap would widen without the existence of Title I services (that is, whether Title I students learn more than they would have without Title I).

CONCLUSION

This article provides fresh evidence on the long-term effects of school spending from Title I on children's subsequent educational and adult economic outcomes, focusing on the first fifteen years of the roll-out of Title I. To isolate the effect of Title I on long-run adult outcomes, all models include controls for school-district fixed effects, race- and region-specific birth-cohort trends, an extensive set of childhood, family, and neighborhood characteristics, and other coincident policies (such as desegregation and War on Poverty initiatives and related safety-net programs). I find that increases in Title I funding are significantly related to increases in the likelihood of graduating from high school, reductions in both the likelihoods of grade repetition and school suspension or expulsion, more years of completed education, higher earnings and work hours, a reduction in the annual incidence of poverty in adulthood (ages thirty to forty), and a reduction in the likelihood of ever being incarcerated by age thirty-five. The effects on educational outcomes are more pronounced for children from poor families. Although the magnitudes of these effects are modest, they are economically important and noteworthy because a significant amount of Title I funding led to only modest increases in school district spending due to crowd-out of local funding.

One of the factors undermining the effectiveness of ESEA is that it crowds out local provision of school funding (Gordon 2004). This suggests an alternative matching-funds school-finance formula design that rewards local effort so that overall spending in poor districts is increased and per-pupil spending between poor and affluent districts narrowed. Such formulas are effective because they affect taxes directly, allowing such districts to have more than a dollar in spending for each dollar raised in taxes. The lesson from state school finance reform is that design features are central to effectiveness both in narrowing disparities in spending and in improving the long-term educational and adult economic outcomes (Jackson, Johnson, and Persico 2015).

Today, a majority of the per-pupil spending disparities by socioeconomic status occur between states rather than between districts within a state. This is in large measure due to the role of court-mandated school finance reforms and legislative reforms at the state level (Jackson, Johnson, and Persico 2014). On a federal level, additional questions remain related to the efficiency of fifty fragmented state school finance systems.

The effectiveness of school spending is a perennial issue in education policy and has spawned a large literature and contentious debate. Concerns that school spending inequalities undermine the provision of equal educational opportunities fueled the initial passage of ESEA in 1965 and movement toward school finance reform litigation and legislation over the past several decades. Money alone may not be enough, but provision of adequate and equitable distribution of spending is a necessary condition. These efforts may need to be adjoined with accountability systems that help ensure spending is allocated to its most productive uses to narrow gaps in educational opportunity, which may be key sources of the growing socioeconomic status gaps in student achievement. Other nonmonetary factors may also influence school quality, such as school accountability policies, curricular standards, role of tracking and ability grouping, improving incentives in schools, and competition between schools for students.

One of the main factors that may moderate the influence of school spending on student outcomes is how the money is spent. An unresolved question and high-priority issue for future research concerns the relative efficacy of specific school resource inputs that the marginal dollar of targeted educational spending can determine, such as smaller classes versus higher teacher salaries versus capital or building expenditures and other spending categories. Arguably, ensuring a quality education for all students has never been more important given the substantial increases in the labor market returns to skills. A collage of recent evidence paints a collective picture that, with well-designed and targeted incentives, Title I alongside school finance reform policies can be a part of the solution to reduce the intergenerational transmission of poverty.

APPENDIX
Data on Title I Funding

I compiled administrative data about federal outlays for Title I acquired from the National Archives and Records Administration (NARA) for 1965 through 1980. The information (of historical annual county-level Title I funding) was culled from NARA records by searching program titles and program codes. I identified the pool of grants potentially for ESEA (included string searches in ESEA grant titles). For most records, ESEA spending are listed by community and funding, and information on "stock" of programs at a particular time allows verification of accuracy of grant flows. Historical annual data of county-level age-specific population counts from 1965 to 2000 from SEERS data are used to put the county-level federal ESEA program outlay measures in per-pupil terms.

To verify that the Title I spending information I compiled was accurate, I was able to successfully match the NARA data to published figures for total (ESEA) federal spending and Title I spending at the national and state levels.

Although data on school-level Title I spending are unavailable (because districts are not required to report intradistrict resource allocation) and the use of county-level Title I expenditures leads to some measurement error, no other data source or analysis has investigated long-run impacts or used data at this level of geographic detail, particularly for this historical period.

Matching PSID Individuals to Their Childhood School Districts

Using GIS mapping techniques, I was able to match childhood addresses to the school district boundaries that prevailed in 1969 (to avoid complications arising from endogenously changing district boundaries over time). I obtained addresses for the full universe of elementary and secondary schools in the United States in 1969 along with a geocoded match file of district boundaries and census tract codes. I have done this in my prior work that examines the long-run effects of school desegregation, school finance reforms, and Head Start (separate papers).

To limit the possibility that school district boundaries were drawn in response to pressure for SFRs, we use 1969 school district geographies. The "69-70 School District Geographic Reference File" (U.S. Bureau of Census 1970) relates census tract and school district geographies. For each census tract in the country, it provides the fraction of the population that is in each school district. Using this information, I aggregated census tracts to 1970 district geographies with Geographic Information Systems (GIS) software. I assigned census tracts from 1960, 1980, and 1990 to school districts using this resulting digital map based on their centroid locations.

To construct demographic information on 1969–1970 school districts, I compiled census data from the tract, place, school district and county levels of aggregation for 1960, 1970, 1980, and 1990. I constructed digital (GIS) maps of 1970 geography school districts using the

Table A1. Descriptive Statistics by Childhood Poverty Status

	All (N=7,182)	Poor (N=1,572)	Nonpoor (N=5,610)
Adult Outcomes			
High school graduate	0.84	0.63	0.87
Years of education	13.29	11.87	13.44
Ever repeated a grade	0.11	0.20	0.11
Ever suspended/expelled	0.17	0.28	0.17
Ever placed in gifted program	0.19	0.09	0.20
Ln(wages), at age thirty	2.60	2.13	2.64
Annual work hours (includes 0s), at age thirty	2,112	1,858	2,132
Adult family income, at age thirty	$47,605	$33,169	$48,736
In poverty, at age thirty	0.07	0.26	0.05
Ever incarcerated, by age thirty-five	0.02	0.04	0.01
Year born (range: 1950–1977)	1963	1962	1963
Female	0.52	0.57	0.51
Black	0.12	0.50	0.08
Childhood school variables			
Per-pupil spending average ages five to seventeen	$4,187	$3,739	$4,232
Per-pupil Title I funding average ages five to seventeen	$96	$128	$93
Title I funding per poor child average ages five to seventeen	$805	$744	$812
1960 district poverty rate (%)	22.49	33.80	21.31
Childhood family variables			
Income-to-needs ratio average ages twelve to seventeen:	3.12	0.71	3.37
Mother's years of education	12.05	11.32	12.66
Father's years of education	12.05	10.91	12.93
Born into two-parent family	0.89	0.61	0.92
Low birth weight (<5.5 pounds)	0.07	0.08	0.06
Childhood neighborhood variables			
Neighborhood poverty rate	0.11	0.16	0.10
Residential segregation dissimilarity index$_{county}$	0.72	0.71	0.72

Source: Author's calculations based on nationally representative data from the Panel Study of Income Dynamics (PSID) of original sample children born between 1950 and 1977 followed into adulthood (1968–2011), matched with administrative data of county-level Title I funding from the National Archives and Records Administration (NARA) and school district per-pupil spending from the Individual Government Finances Database and Census of Governments.

Note: All descriptive statistics are sample weighted to produce nationally representative estimates of means. Dollars are CPI-U deflated in real 2000 dollars.

1969–1970 School District Geographic Reference File from the Census. This file indicates the fraction by population of each census tract that fell in each school district in the country. Those tracts split across school districts I allocated to the school district comprising the largest fraction of the tract's population. Using the resulting 1970 central school district digital maps, I allocated tracts in 1960, 1980, and 1990 to central school districts or suburbs based on the locations of their centroids. The 1970 definition central districts located in regions not tracted in 1970 all coincide with county geography that I use instead.

REFERENCES

Carter, Launor. 1984. "The Sustaining Effects Study of Compensatory and Elementary Education." *Educational Researcher* 13(7): 4–13.

Cascio, Elizabeth, Nora Gordon, and Sarah Reber. 2013. "Federal Aid and Equality of Educational Opportunity: Evidence from the Introduction of Title I in the South." *NBER* working paper no. 17155. Cambridge, Mass.: National Bureau of Economic Research.

Chetty, Raj, John N. Friedman, Nathaniel Hilger, Emmanuel Saez, Diane W. Schanzenbach, and Danny Yagan. 2011. "How Does Your Kindergarten Classroom Affect Your Earnings? Evidence from Project Star." *Quarterly Journal of Economics* 126(4): 1593–660.

Chetty, Raj, John N. Friedman, and Jonah E. Rockoff. 2013. "Measuring the Impacts of Teachers II: Teacher Value-Added and Student Outcomes in Adulthood." *NBER* working paper no. 19424. Cambridge, Mass.: National Bureau of Economic Research. Available at: http://www.nber.org/papers/w19424 (accessed July 24, 2015).

Cortes, Kalena, Joshua Goodman, and Takako Nomi. 2015. "Intensive Math Instruction and Educational Attainment: Long-Run Impacts of Double-Dose Algebra." *Journal of Human Resources* 50(1): 108–58.

Deming, David. 2009. "Early Childhood Intervention and Life-Cycle Skill Development: Evidence from Head Start." *American Economic Journal: Applied Economics* 1(3)(July): 111–34.

Fisher, Ronald C., and Leslie E. Papke. 2000. "Local Government Responses to Education Grants." *National Tax Journal* 53(1): 153–68.

Fitzgerald, John, Peter Gottschalk, and Robert Moffitt. 1998. "An Analysis of Sample Attrition in Panel Data: The Michigan Panel Study of Income Dynamics." *Journal of Human Resources* 33(2): 251–99.

Fredriksson, Peter, Bjorn Ockert, and Hessell Oosterbeek. 2013. "Long-Term Effects of Class Size." *Quarterly Journal of Economics* 128(1): 249–85.

Gordon, Nora. 2004. "Do Federal Funds Boost School Spending? Evidence from Title I." *Journal of Public Economics* 88(9–10): 1771–92.

Heckman, James, Rodrigo Pinto, and Peter Savelyev. 2013. "Understanding the Mechanisms Through Which an Influential Early Childhood Program Boosted Adult Outcomes." *American Economic Review* 103(6): 2052–86.

Jackson, Kirabo. 2012. "Non-Cognitive Ability, Test Scores, and Teacher Quality: Evidence from 9th Grade Teachers in North Carolina." *NBER* working paper no. 18624. Cambridge, Mass.: National Bureau of Economic Research.

Jackson, Kirabo, Rucker C. Johnson, and Claudia Persico. 2014. "The Impacts of School Spending on Educational and Economic Attainments: Evidence from School Finance Reforms." *NBER* working paper no. 20118. Cambridge, Mass.: National Bureau of Economic Research. Available at: http://socrates.berkeley.edu/~ruckerj/Jackson_Johnson_Persico_SFR_LRImpacts.pdf (accessed July 24, 2015).

———. 2015. "The Effects of School Spending on Educational and Economic Outcomes: Evidence from School Finance Reforms." *Quarterly Journal of Economics* 130(4). Available at: http://socrates.berkeley.edu/~ruckerj/QJE_resubmit_final_version.pdf (accessed July 24, 2015).

Johnson, Rucker C. 2009. "Race Differences in the Incidence and Duration of Exposure to Concentrated Poverty over the Life Course: Upward Mobility or Trapped in the Hood?" Unpublished manuscript, University of California Berkeley.

———. 2011. "Long-Run Impacts of School Desegregation and School Quality on Adult Attainments." *NBER* working paper no. 16664, updated January 2014. Cambridge, Mass.: National Bureau of Economic Research. Available at: http://socrates.berkeley.edu/~ruckerj/johnson_schooldesegregation_NBERw16664.pdf (accessed July 24, 2015).

Kemple, James J. 2008. "Career Academies: Long-Term Impacts on Labor Market Outcomes, Educational Attainment, and Transitions to Adulthood." New York: MDRC. Available at: http://www.mdrc.org/publication/career-academies-long-term-impacts-work-education-and-transitions-adulthood (accessed July 24, 2015).

Ludwig, Jens, and Douglas L. Miller. 2007. "Does Head Start Improve Children's Life Chances? Evidence from a Regression Discontinuity Design." *Quarterly Journal of Economics* 122(1)(February): 159–208. doi:10.1162/qjec.122.1.159.

Martin, Ruby, and Phyllis McClure. 1969. "Title I of ESEA: Is It Helping Poor Children?" Washington,

D.C.: Washington Research Project and NAACP Legal Defense and Educational Fund.

Matsudaira, Jordan D., Adrienne Hosek, and Elias Walsh. 2012. "An Integrated Assessment of the Effects of Title I on School Behavior, Resources, and Student Achievement." *Economics of Education Review* 31(3): 1–14.

McLaughlin, Donald H. 1977. "Title I, 1965–1975: Synthesis of the Findings of Federal Studies." Palo Alto, Calif.: American Institutes of Research.

National Bureau of Economic Research. 2003. "Annual Survey of Governments Finance Data." Available at: http://www.nber.org/asg/ASG_release/ASG_Documentation.pdf (accessed August 24, 2015).

Rossi, Robert J., Donald McLaughlin, Elizabeth Campbell, and B.E. Everett. 1977. "Summaries of Major Title I Evaluations, 1966–1976." Palo Alto, Calif.: American Institutes of Research.

United States Department of Commerce. Bureau of the Census. 1970. *School District Geographic Reference File, 1969-1970.* ICPSR version. Washington: U.S. Government Printing Office. doi:10.3886/ICPSR03515.v1.

Van der Klaauw, Wilbert. 2008. "Breaking the Link Between Poverty and Low Student Achievement: An Evaluation of Title I." *Journal of Econometrics* 142(2): 271–309.

Wargo, Michael J., Guy K. Tallmadge, David D. Michaels, Dewey Lipe, and Sarah J. Morris. 1972. *ESEA Title I: A Reanalysis and Synthesis of Evaluation Data from Fiscal Year 1965 Through 1970.* Palo Alto, Calif.: American Institutes of Research.

Schooling the State: ESEA and the Evolution of the U.S. Department of Education

PATRICK MCGUINN

This article examines the evolution of the role of the "state" in American K–12 education and analyzes the history of the Elementary and Secondary Education Act (ESEA) through the entity responsible for its implementation, the U.S. Department of Education. More specifically, it explores how and why national administrative capacity and the design and implementation of federal policy in education in the United States underwent a dramatic shift between 1965 and 2014. It will address these questions through an analysis of the ways in which the mission and activities of the Department of Education have changed since the passage of ESEA in 1965. For the department to be effective in gaining states' compliance with federal education policies, it needs sufficient statutory authority, administrative capacity, and political support. However, throughout most of the history of the department these resources have not been present.

Keywords: federal education policy, U.S. Department of Education, Elementary and Secondary Education Act

This article analyzes the history of the Elementary and Secondary Education Act (ESEA) through the entity that is responsible for its implementation, the U.S. Department of Education (ED). More specifically, it explores how and why national administrative capacity and the design and implementation of federal policy in education in the United States underwent a dramatic shift between the 1965 passage of ESEA and 2015. The United States' multilevel and fragmented education governance structure has made the creation of national policy in education very complex, both politically and administratively (Bailey and Mosher 1968, vii; for more on the history of educational politics and policymaking in the United States, see McGuinn 2006; Manna 2006). Yet, persistent racial and socioeconomic achievement gaps, global economic competition, and concerns about the performance of U.S. students on international tests have led to an increasingly active federal role in American public schools.

Education in the United States historically has been characterized by local control and the federal government has no constitutional authority to dictate education policy to the states. Beginning with the National Defense Education Act of 1958 and the Elementary and Secondary Education Act of 1965, however, national policymakers have used the grant-in-aid system to pursue federal goals in public education. To claim their share of a growing pot of federal education funds, states have had to agree to comply with a wide array of federal policy mandates. These mandates initially focused on ensuring more equitable school

---

Patrick McGuinn is associate professor of political science and education and chair of the Department of Political Science and International Relations at Drew University.

Direct correspondence to: Patrick McGuinn, pmcguinn@drew.edu, Drew University, Department of Political Science, 36 Madison Ave., Madison, NJ 07940.

funding and access rather than the academic performance of students and schools. A new federal focus on accountability for student achievement and school reform was outlined in the Improving America's Schools Act of 1994 and was given more "teeth" in the No Child Left Behind Act (NCLB) in 2001. These developments have involved the federal government for the first time in core matters of school governance—such as academic standards, student assessment, teacher quality, school choice, and school restructuring—and fundamentally altered the relationship between the federal government and the states in education policy. They have also severely strained the federal grant-in-aid system and the administrative capacity of the Department of Education. For the ED to be effective in gaining state compliance with federal education policies, it needs sufficient statutory authority, administrative capacity, and political support. Still, throughout most of the thirty-five-year history of the department, these resources have not been present.

This article provides an overview of the evolution of national administrative capacity and the implementation of federal education policy in the United States between 1965 and 2015 to examine the process by which federal power over schools has become institutionalized over time. The relationship between Washington and the states in the area of education has historically been predicated on cooperation rather than conflict, due to state education agencies' long dependence on the Department of Education for a considerable portion of their budgets (about 40 percent on average), and because the federal government rarely interfered with core state education policies before the 1990s. (The department did, however, intervene forcefully on behalf of the civil rights of minority, English-language learners, and special education students in response to a series of Supreme Court rulings between 1950 and 1975.)

The challenge in the post-NCLB era is that the feds have demanded that states develop new systems for tracking and disseminating student achievement data and intervening in struggling schools. States resent this new level of federal involvement and have struggled to meet all of the federal mandates. Consequently, as federal goals and methods have diverged from those of the states, the intergovernmental relationship has undergone a significant transformation. A central contribution of this article is thus to offer a detailed analysis of the new educational federalism in the post-NCLB era. It assesses how the policy mandates of the law have affected the institutional capacities and incentives for reform in state and federal departments of education to illuminate the administrative mechanisms through which this new federalism operates. Writing in the 1960s, Stephen Bailey and Edith Mosher articulate the many challenges to using federal power to drive school reform, challenges that continue to ring true today. "Both in the innovative and administrative aspects of public policy, a grant-in-aid agency must operate in a complex political environment. It must function in an intricate web of tensions spun by historical circumstance and by both coordinate and cross-purposes: congressional, presidential, judicial, group interest, intra-agency, inter-agency, inter-governmental, personal, societal, and even international. When as is the case with aid to education, the magnitude of Federal involvement is increased with dramatic suddenness, these tensions are particularly illuminated and exacerbated" (1968, vii).

The original ED was a classic example of a "captive agency"—created for and largely operated by members of the education establishment and therefore unwilling to fundamentally challenge it. As a result, the ED has faced three distinct challenges in implementing NCLB. The first challenge is a systemic one due to the complicated nature of public administration in a federal system where political and administrative power is highly fragmented and contested. Second, the purposes of ESEA have changed due to the recognition of new educational problems, the adoption of new remedies, and shifts in partisan control in Washington. Third, the agency itself has undergone its own institutional transformation in recent years as it has reorganized itself in response to new political demands and a new policy mission. Reformers from both the Left and Right now seek to use the department as a change agent in driving educational improvement and have pushed it to break free of the hold of the educational clientele groups to which it has long been beholden. The "liberation" of a "captured" agency has necessitated creating new institutional norms, structures, and tools in the ED to implant a new operational mission.

ORIGINS: THE EARLY FEDERAL ROLE IN EDUCATION

Education policymaking in the United States has traditionally been very decentralized and dominated by local and (to a lesser extent) state governments. The U.S. Constitution's silence on a federal role in education, supplemented by tradition and the reserved powers clause of the Tenth Amendment, meant that schooling was a very locally run affair from colonial times through the early days of the Republic. It was not until the common school movement of the nineteenth century that the states began to develop organized systems of public schools, with Massachusetts opening the first public high school in 1821 and passing the nation's first compulsory school attendance law in 1852. It was not until 1918, however, that such laws were in force in the other forty-seven states (Newman 1994). Even then, state supervision and control over the education policies of locally financed and run public schools remained weak, as evidenced by the fact that, in 1890, on average, state departments of education employed only two staffers, one of whom was the superintendent (Tyack and Cuban 1997). The origin of federal involvement in education can be traced to the Land Ordinance Act of 1785 and the Northwest Ordinances of 1787, which linked the drawing of property lines with the creation of schools. Beginning with the admission of Ohio as a state in 1803, Congress required that all subsequent states guarantee public education in their state constitutions as a condition of statehood. The federal government became more directly involved in education—and set a precedent for grant-in-aid programs—with the passage of the Morrill Act in 1862. The act authorized the creation of a network of what became known as land-grant colleges and committed the federal government to support them financially through the sale of federally owned lands.

Although the federal government played a crucial early role in the development of K–12 education, it stayed virtually absent from the management of public schools until the second half of the twentieth century. The size and scope of national administrative power in education has, until the past decade or so, been quite small—a fact that is both a cause and a consequence of limited federal educational goals. A U.S. Office of Education (USOE) was created in 1867 but was given little staff or resources and a very proscribed mandate to gather statistical data on schools. Its founding legislation declared that the office was "for the purpose of collecting such statistics and facts as shall show the condition and progress of education in the several states and territories, and of diffusing such information respecting the organization and management of schools and school systems, and methods of teaching, as shall aid the people of the United States in the establishment and maintenance of efficient schools systems, and otherwise promote the cause of education throughout the country" (Kursh 1965, 11–12).

Even this limited role encountered a great deal of opposition from states' rights advocates, who saw any federal role in education as inappropriate and threatening to their sovereignty. Harry Kursh notes "a lingering fear that almost any Federal activity—even an ingenuous attempt to gather statistics on the per capita expenditures of the states for education—would sharpen the entering wedge for complete government control of education" (1965, 13). Opposition to the original office resulted in its receiving a tiny initial budget and a staff of only six, and these were expanded only slowly and amid much political infighting. The federal role in education increased in 1917 with the passage of the Smith-Hughes Act, which provided the first annual federal appropriation for K–12 schooling for vocational education programs. Even as late as the first half of the twentieth century, however, the nation's school system remained extremely decentralized. The day-to-day management of schools—including such matters as personnel, curriculum, and pedagogy—remained in the hands of local authorities, with state and federal governments having little influence.

EXPANSION: ESEA, GRANT-IN-AID CONDITIONS, AND CATEGORICAL COMPLIANCE

In the 1950s, growing elite concerns around educational equity and economic and military competitiveness led to a more expanded federal role in education. The National Defense Education Act (NDEA) of 1958 and the Elementary and Secondary Education Act of 1965 fundamentally expanded and transformed the federal role in schools by providing sustained, large-scale education aid to the states for the first time. The aim of the combination of the NDEA and the ESEA was to dramatically increase federal funding for education, both in absolute terms and as a proportion of total education spending. Even as federal spending and programs in education grew over time, however, the ends and means of federal policy were clearly circumscribed—the national government would limit its efforts to improving educational equity by providing targeted categorical programs and supplemental funding for schools serving high percentages of low-income students.

The creation of federal categorical programs in the NDEA and ESEA required that federal educational institutions shift from what had been largely an information gathering and disseminating role to a more supervisory responsibility in the administration of the new federal funds and programs. This shift necessitated the creation of new federal and state administrative capacities to oversee the administration of the programs and ensure state compliance. State eligibility for federal education funds often depended on state matching funds, central implementing offices, and a variety of statistical data, which necessitated that state education agencies expand their size and activities and become more institutionalized. This was a clear objective of ESEA, as Title V of the original legislation provided $25 million over five years for the agencies to build up their administrative capacity so that they would be better equipped to handle their new, federally imposed responsibilities. The result, as Paul Hill notes, was that state education agencies often became so dependent on federal funding and pliable to federal direction that they were effectively "colonized" (2000, 25–26).[1]

State education agencies (SEAs)—that had generally been poorly funded and staffed before ESEA—became a crucial partner of the USOE and the key implementing agency for federal education policy. For most of the next thirty years, this was a cooperative and symbiotic relationship, as the federal government depended on SEAs to funnel national grant monies to local school districts. Moreover, the states were thrilled to accept such funds, particularly when not accompanied by federal mandates. However, the federal reliance on state education agencies created the potential for a serious principal-agent challenge for USOE and the department would later struggle to get SEAs to align state priorities and resources with federal educational goals.[2]

From the start, the USOE faced tremendous challenges in implementing ESEA (Bailey and Mosher 1968). First, the legislation incorporated multiple goals and methods, some of which were incompatible with one another. Second, the original ESEA gave federal administrators few tools to force compliance with federal directives in the use of ESEA funds. (Given the political opposition to federal control in education, it had been impossible to include even the kind of basic requirements that were normally attached to categorical grants in other policy areas such as AFDC.) Third, even if they had been available, for several years after the law's passage, the USOE was either not inclined or unable to make use of

---

1. By 1993, state education agencies nationwide relied on federal funds for on average 41 percent of their operating budgets, with the federal share as high as 77 percent in some states.

2. John Nugent notes that "The delegation of authority to another entity to define, fund, or implement a federal policy creates the possibility of principal-agent problems, in which the entity to which authority has been delegated (the agent) uses it in ways not intended by the delegator (the principal). . . . When state governments are invited, induced, or compelled to participate in the implementation of federal policies, their own interests may clash with those embodied in the federal policy" (2009, 176).

such compliance tools. Fourth, lingering opposition to federal control of education ensured that attempts to rigorously administer ESEA would generate a strong political backlash. Finally, the politics and implementation of ESEA were greatly complicated by the addition of new purposes and programs and an increasingly contentious racial politics around school integration in the years after 1965.

Though the goal of ESEA—to improve educational opportunity for the poor—was clear, the legislation was vague on how this goal was to be achieved. The ESEA distributed funds to school districts according to the number of poor children enrolled, but did not specify which services districts should provide to "educationally deprived" children (Jennings 2000, 4). The consequence of ESEA's initial flexibility was that federal funds were used in a wide variety of ways and for a wide variety of purposes and local districts often diverted funds away from redistributive programs (for a more detailed discussion of the local tendency to shift federal funds, see Peterson, Rabe, and Wong 1986, 136–40). As Hugh Graham observes, "the upshot of all this is that when Title I was implemented, it produced not *a* Title I program, but something more like 30 thousand separate and different Title I programs" (1984, 204). The original ESEA legislation gave the USOE little power to coerce states to comply with federal regulations or goals or to punish states and school districts that failed to do so. The great level of discretion accorded to states and school districts in spending the new federal money ensured that compliance with federal goals was spotty at best. In his examination of the implementation of ESEA, Joel Berke notes that "federal aid is channeled into an existing state political system and pattern of policy, and a blend distilled of federal priorities and the frequently different state priorities emerges. . . . Federal money is a stream that must pass through a state capitol; at the state level, the federal government is rarely able—through its guidelines and regulations—radically to divert the stream or reverse the current" (1974, 143).

Initially, the USOE relied on the assurances of state education officials that they were in compliance with federal guidelines.[3] However, one of the fundamental premises behind the idea of compensatory education, and of ESEA more generally, was that state and local education authorities had failed to ensure equal educational opportunities for their students and that they could not be trusted to do so in the future without federal intervention. The distrust of local education authorities—and mounting evidence that states and localities were diverting federal funds to purposes for which they were not intended—ultimately led Congress and federal bureaucrats to increase the regulation and supervision of federal aid. By the 1970s, the additional resources available to the Office of Education and the agency's gradual adjustment to its new administrative role led the USOE to more aggressively enforce federal education mandates (Hughes and Hughes 1972, 57). The ongoing consolidation of school districts across the country facilitated this effort as administrative centralization at the state level ultimately made schools more susceptible to federal regulation.[4]

As Frankenberg and Taylor detail elsewhere in this issue, the implementation of ESEA also quickly became enmeshed in the highly charged struggles over integration and busing during the 1960s and 1970s. Although the 1964 Civil Rights Act declared that federal funds could not be allocated to support segregated institutions or programs, it was ESEA funding that became a key carrot (and stick) for federal integration efforts. States that failed to comply with court integration decrees would lose their share of federal education funds, which as noted were very sizable after the creation of

---

3. The USOE was ill suited to a compliance role—it had long been a small, passive organization that focused on collecting and disseminating statistical data on education and did little else. The result, as John and Anne Hughes note, was that "if USOE had limitations on its policymaking authority and capability—and these have been legion—its ability to enforce its policies has been even more limited. The state agencies and the local districts, by and large, were used to going their own ways, which often meant disregarding federal requirements" (1972, 50).

4. The number of districts declined from approximately 150,000 in 1900 to 15,000 in 1993 (Newman 1994, 166).

ESEA. The original *Brown* decision in 1954, though declaring that states must integrate their public schools, was silent on the crucial issues of when and how this was to be accomplished. The court's 1955 *Brown II* decision declared that integration should proceed "with all deliberate speed," but the Court again declined to set firm deadlines or methods for integration. Recalcitrant states such as Virginia engaged in "massive resistance" and were able to postpone large-scale integration efforts (for more on the Supreme Court's *Brown* and *Brown II* decisions and southern desegregation efforts, see Wilkinson 1978). The initial flexibility and discretion that the Supreme Court accorded state desegregation efforts came to an end, however, with the 1968 *Green v. County School Board of Kent County, Virginia*, case (391 U.S. 430) when the court declared that school boards must develop integration plans that promise "realistically to work *now*" (for more on the judicial and political context of this period, see Orfield and Eaton 1996; Armor 1995; Wright Edelman 1973).

In response to the decision, lower courts mandated the widespread busing of students and the Department of Health, Education, and Welfare (HEW) ultimately played a central role in forcing southern school districts to desegregate. As Gary Orfield notes in his classic book *The Reconstruction of Southern Education*, the Office of Education initially was hesitant to engage race or desegregation as it tried to preserve cozy relationships with districts and states because they needed their cooperation (Orfield 1969). The Court's 1972 ruling in *Adams v. Richardson* (351 F. Supp. 636, D.C. Cir.), however, forced a reluctant HEW to resume the funding termination process for districts that had not desegregated, which was the final straw that led many districts to comply.[5]

In the 1980s, John Chubb would note that "in federal programs that are not explicitly regulatory, as well as those that are, policy has come to be carried out by increasingly detailed, prescriptive, legalistic, and authoritative means" (1985, 287). Between 1964 and 1976, for example, the number of pages of federal legislation affecting education increased from eighty to 360, and the number of federal regulations increased from ninety-two in 1965 to nearly one thousand in 1977 (Ravitch 1983, 312). The lack of consensus on the goals of public education and how to measure the effectiveness of school reform efforts, however, led federal administrators to focus on school districts' spending patterns and administrative compliance. The result of this shift was that large numbers of bureaucratic regulations were created during the 1970s without any kind of concomitant focus on student or school results—everything was judged by procedure and process. Federal spending on elementary and secondary education, meanwhile, continued to grow, increasing more than tenfold between 1958 and 1980, from $651 million to $9.5 billion in constant dollars. During the same period, the federal share of total K–12 education spending expanded from 4.4 percent to about 10 percent of total school funding; it has hovered in the 6 to 12 percent range since (NCES 2014, table 235.10).

Strong institutional and ideological obstacles to an expansion of federal influence in education persisted long after the passage of ESEA in 1965 and a bipartisan consensus of sorts developed around these limits imposed on the federal role. National administrative authority in education was severely fragmented, with operational authority for federal categorical programs dispersed across a number of federal agencies, including Defense, Labor, and Health, Education, and Welfare. Liberals, meanwhile, fought to keep the federal role redistributive and focused on disadvantaged students. In addition, because of their alliance with teachers' unions and the belief that inadequate school resources were the primary problem, Democrats also sought to keep the federal role centered on school inputs rather than on outputs or curricular or governance issues. Conservatives, however, were willing to tolerate a small federal role in education, as long as it was unobtrusive and did not threaten local control over schools. These structural and political constraints produced a strange dynamic in which the increase in federal education spending and pro-

---

5. I would like to thank Doug Reed for bringing this point to my attention.

grams was not accompanied by a comparable strengthening of national administrative power over core school governance issues, or by expanded influence over state school improvement efforts.

INSTITUTIONALIZATION: THE CREATION OF THE DEPARTMENT OF EDUCATION

As the quantity and size of federal education programs grew in the wake of ESEA, calls from some quarters were heard to consolidate national administrative capacity in the form of a single-cabinet level agency. Although legislation to create a new federal department for education had been introduced 130 times between 1908 and 1975, the idea had always generated a great deal of political opposition from a variety of interests that had a stake in preserving the status quo (Stallings 2002, 677). Small government conservatives opposed the idea because it would expand the size of the federal bureaucracy and the power of the federal government, which they were committed to rolling back. Moreover, state rights advocates believed that education was a state and local responsibility and that any federal role would be intrusive and counterproductive (Stephens 1984, 651).

The primary goal of the advocates who fought to create the ED was to protect and expand federal education spending and programs, rather than to build an organization that could pressure states to reform their school systems. President Carter led the successful effort to create the department in 1980, fulfilling an earlier campaign promise he had made to win the first presidential endorsement of the National Education Association. That Congress viewed ED largely as a clientele agency was manifest in the legislation itself and the way in which the department was structured, staffed, and empowered. Congress limited the managerial flexibility of the department's leadership by embedding a detailed organizational structure in the authorizing legislation. This was somewhat unusual and was to have important consequences; as one observer noted, "unlike many reorganization efforts, most decisions concerning the ED reorganization structure were made in the adoption stage of the policy process by Congress" (Radin and Hawley 1988, 176).

In *The Politics of Federal Reorganization: Creating the Department of Education*, Beryl Radin and Willis Hawley observe that the political compromises in the drafting of the authorizing legislation limited the flexibility and resources accorded to the department's leadership and diluted the effectiveness of the new department in the short term. The practical task of merging a large number of programs with their disparate organizational structures, cultures, and procedures would take time and meant that "true" reorganization of the executive department would take many years. From the very beginning, the administrative functions of the department were underfunded and understaffed and these issues persisted as the number and size of federal education programs grew over time. This reflected the vision of ED as a mere grant-making and information-gathering organization, rather than one charged with pushing states to embrace school reform (1988, 188). The new department also needed to adapt to the demands of rigorous oversight. Protective of certain Education Department programs and staff, members of Congress were quite willing to intervene to protect them, which limited the managerial flexibility of the secretary even further (Balogh et al. 2002).[6]

When Carter was defeated in the 1980 presidential election (shortly after the department was created), the Department of Education lost its most powerful proponent. President Carter's successor, Republican Ronald Reagan, announced his desire to abolish the department entirely and secured the passage of the 1981

---

6. Shirley Hufstedler quoted Reagan on this point: "with respect to one man on the Hill, if I didn't call him up on Wednesday and wish him a happy Thursday, he would be petulant and would give me trouble on some aspects of departmental work. In terms of turf, there are projects that are protected either by staff or by a congressman or by a senator. They believe they own those programs and if you try to do something that you think is important to change the priorities of the department, they are all over you like a nest of bees" (1990, 66–67).

Education Consolidation and Improvement Act (ECIA), which dramatically reduced its size and power.[7] Although Reagan's efforts to disband the department were ultimately unsuccessful, the attacks succeeded in substantially reducing its staffing and budget and its regulatory authority, thereby further limiting its ability to promote educational coordination or improvement. Some scholars have estimated that the number of regulatory mandates imposed on states through federal education programs was reduced by 85 percent during the Reagan administration (Glendening and Reeves 1984, 243). The budget for the Department of Education was cut by 11 percent between fiscal year (FY) 1981 and FY1988 (in real dollars), and the National Institute of Education (the federal educational research and development body) lost 70 percent of its funding during the period (Verstegen and Clark 1988, 137). As Maris Vinovskis notes, these reductions significantly reduced the number and quality of program evaluations within the department and thus made it more difficult for the agency to gauge the effectiveness of its educational improvement efforts (1999). Moreover, the assault on the department's legitimacy occupied the time and energies of both policymakers within the department and of its supporters in Congress. Consequently, the new department and its allies were preoccupied with its survival rather than on the difficult task of adapting the organization to its new responsibilities.

The 1980s thus witnessed two contradictory trends in national administrative power in education. On one hand, the opening of a cabinet-level national Department of Education in 1980 represented the expansion and institutionalization of federal authority over public schools. On the other hand, however, this expansion was not accompanied by an increase in the administrative capacity or political will that would have enabled the ED to hold states accountable for the outputs of their school systems or to force them to adopt major reforms. By 1980, federal spending and influence on schooling had expanded dramatically and the new Department of Education administered approximately five hundred federal education programs.[8] As federal spending at the state and local level increased, however, federal funding for the operations of the Department of Education did not increase even close to proportionally. As a result, the department has been tasked with overseeing a growing enterprise, but has been specifically hamstrung by Congress to prevent it from engaging in that oversight with rigor.[9] Between 1965 and 2010, the budget for the department increased from $1.5 billion to about $60 billion, an increase of forty times, yet the number of department employees overseeing those funds barely doubled, from 2,100 to 4,300 (U.S. Department of Education 2010). In 2012, the Department of Education had the third largest discretionary budget of the fifteen federal cabinet agencies but the smallest staff (U.S. Department of Education 2012).

In addition, the federal focus remained on access and equity issues rather than on improving schools' or students' academic performance and little effort was made to measure the educational progress of students that received federal funds or protection. This became increasingly problematic as a number of prominent studies were released that found that ESEA funds and programs had largely failed to improve educational opportunity for disadvantaged students (see, for example, those by Bailey and Mosher 1968; Berke and Kirst 1972; Berke 1974; McLaughlin 1975; Thomas 1975; and Jeffrey 1976). Berke and Kirst, for example, analyzed data from more than five hundred school districts and concluded that ESEA aid had done little to redress

---

[7]. The 1980 Republican platform called for "deregulation by the federal government of public education and ... the elimination of the federal Department of Education." The platform fretted that "parents are losing control of their children's schooling" and that Democratic education policy had produced "huge new bureaucracies to misspend our taxes" (CQ Press 1981, 583–84).

[8]. For an extended discussion of the expansion of federal compensatory education programs and the accompanying increase in federal education regulations, see Peterson 1983.

[9]. I would like to thank Doug Reed for encouraging me to explore this dynamic further.

the large inequality in per-pupil expenditures between rich and poor districts.[10] In addition, because ESEA was premised on the provision of additional resources, rather than the promotion of school reform, federal education aid generally went to support existing state and local programs. Over time, this approach came under fire, as the additional resources failed to generate either new reform approaches or improvement in student achievement.

The creation of a national department of education and the release of the widely discussed *A Nation at Risk* report (which the department commissioned) in 1983, created the potential for a reconfiguration and expansion of the federal role in school reform. Nonetheless, the new administrative capacity that the creation of the Department of Education was intended to provide did not develop during the 1980s because of the control of the executive branch (and for part of the time Congress) by a Republican party that was extremely hostile to increasing federal power over schools. The same political dynamics redirected the national momentum generated by *A Nation at Risk* to advancing state school reform efforts, despite the report's call for a more robust federal role.

REDIRECTION: NEW FOCUS ON STANDARDS AND ACCOUNTABILITY

The election of a Democratic president and a Democratic Congress in 1994 created a political environment more favorable to an expansion of federal education policy. In the 1994 ESEA reauthorization, President Clinton—a former "education governor" and "New Democrat"—secured changes that would push states to increase performance reporting and embrace educational accountability. Under this new ESEA and a companion piece of legislation, Goals 2000, states were required to establish academic standards in each grade and create tests to assess whether students had mastered the standards. The tests were to be administered to all poor children at least once in grades three through five, six through nine, and ten through twelve. Enforcement by the Department of Education was lax, however, in that Democrats were opposed to withholding funds from state education systems and Republicans resisted federal micromanagement of states. In the end, most states failed to comply: as late as 2002, two years after the target date for full compliance, just sixteen states had fully complied with even the central components of the 1994 law. Meanwhile, on the heels of the passage of the 1994 ESEA reauthorization, Republicans won control of both the House and Senate for the first time in decades—partly on the strength of their "Contract with America" and its call to roll back the expanse and power of the federal government. Republicans used their control of Congress—and of the appropriations for the ED—to undermine the ED's ability to pressure states on school reform. During the next ESEA reauthorization debate in 1999, conservative Republicans in Congress introduced the Academic Achievement for All Act ("Straight A's"), which sought to reduce federal influence by combining most federal education programs into block grants.

ENFORCEMENT: NCLB AND THE NEW MISSION OF THE DEPARTMENT OF EDUCATION

The previous discussion demonstrates that the ED has historically been unable or unwilling to use federal education dollars as leverage to force systemic change in state education systems (with the notable exception of ending de jure segregation). The ED lacked the combination of three resources essential to undertaking such an effort—statutory authority, administrative capacity, and political will. The passage of the No Child Left Behind Act in 2001 fundamentally expanded and redirected fed-

---

10. It found that though Title I—which was explicitly focused on disadvantaged students—had a somewhat redistributive effect, this was erased by the effects of the other titles of ESEA and vocational aid, which went disproportionately to wealthier districts. By dispersing ESEA funds widely across school districts, not only was federal assistance poorly targeted to its intended beneficiaries, but the additional resources that came to any particular school were limited (Berke and Kirst 1972, 45).

eral education policy. Furthermore, it placed the ED at the center of a bipartisan effort to use federal education spending to pressure states to embrace test-based accountability and introduce a host of reforms to reduce racial and socioeconomic achievement gaps. Although the 1994 Goals 2000 and the Improving America's Schools Act reforms put in place much of the statutory scaffolding for a shift in federal policy, the ED lacked the administrative capacity and political will to enforce the law's mandates vigorously.

NCLB requires states to create accountability systems, annually test children in reading and math in grades three through eight (and once in high school), identify proficient students as well as schools where an insufficient number of students were proficient, ensure that specified measures were taken with regard to schools that failed to make adequate yearly progress (AYP), and set targets that would ensure that 100 percent of children were proficient in reading and math by 2014. One of the most important mandates in the law is that school report cards must disaggregate student test score data for subgroups based on race and ethnicity, economically disadvantaged status, limited English proficiency, and classification as in need of special education. Crucially and controversially, a school that does not meet the proficiency target for any one of these groups is placed in "in need of improvement status" and states are required to take an escalating series of steps and interventions (including the offering of public school choice, tutoring, technical assistance, and restructuring) aimed at schools and districts that persistently fail to meet AYP targets.

The scope, specificity, and ambition of the law's mandates signaled something akin to a revolution in federal education policy. As written, however, the NCLB legislation was a complex mix of federal mandates and state discretion—although states are required to put standards and tests in place and create a system for dealing with failing schools, they are also entrusted with setting the rigor of these. Given these cross-cutting currents, much would depend on the way in which the law was implemented by the Bush Department of Education, and how the department handled states' requests for flexibility, extensions, and waivers. On this count, states hoped that the administration would be as amenable as the Clinton administration had proved to be in implementing the 1994 legislation. Deeming it the most promising path to deliver the cultural shift in schooling it sought, the Bush administration took a hard line and pushed states to comply with the letter of the law. Although this forced states to take the law's mandates more seriously than they otherwise would have, it unsurprisingly sparked vocal complaints among educators, who argued that the law's goals and timetables were unrealistic and that the resources and guidance provided were insufficient.

One awkward question was how the Bush administration would respond to states that pushed back against the law's requirements in the name of federalism. The administration faced a thorny choice: acquiescing and accepting the efforts to undercut the reach of NCLB or aggressively challenging states that threatened to forfeit federal dollars in order to opt out of the NCLB regime. In a decision that caused consternation among conservatives concerned about federal overreach and the integrity of federalism, the administration opted to use every tool at its disposal to keep states in line. Given the noble promise of NCLB's pledge that every child would be proficient in reading and math by 2014, along with its belief that allowing states to backslide would launch the nation on a slippery slope and undercut its effort to transform the culture of schooling, the administration successfully brought substantial pressure to bear when Utah and Connecticut publicly challenged NCLB.

The aggressive implementation approach of the Bush administration Department of Education succeeded in getting states to comply with federal mandates and intervene to a greater extent than ever before in districts with failing schools. As Phyllis McClure, a long-time member of the Title I Independent Review Panel observes, "NCLB has grabbed the education community's attention like no previous ESEA reauthorization. It has really upset the status quo in state and local offices.... For the first time, district and school officials are actually being required to take serious and urgent action in return for federal dollars" (2004). NCLB's requirement that states conduct annual testing and report student scores foreed states to build new data gathering and dissemination systems and resulted in a greater degree of transparency in public education than ever before. Scholars Tiffany Berry and Rebecca Eddy write that the law has "transformed the landscape of educational evaluation" and is "redefining what evaluation is within the education evaluation community" (2008, 2). By holding states clearly accountable for the performance of their public schools, NCLB has also prompted state departments of education to expand their capacity to monitor local districts, provide technical assistance, and intervene where necessary (see Hess and Finn 2007).

The major policy shifts imbedded in NCLB necessitated a corresponding shift in the structure, staffing, and operations of the ED, which is charged with implementing the law. In particular, NCLB's new focus on raising student achievement necessitated that the department develop new research capacities that could permit the effective monitoring of state compliance, the implementation of new longitudinal student data systems, and the identification of effective classroom interventions (McGuinn, Berger, and Anderson 2012). The Institute of Education Sciences (IES) was created by the Education Sciences Reform Act of 2002, replacing the Office of Educational Research and Improvement (OERI) and its predecessor the National Institute of Education (NIE), which had been the primary federal education research institutions since 1972. The methodology and quality of the research studies funded by OERI and NIE was widely criticized and they were generally seen as exerting little if any influence on state education policies or classroom practice. In response, IES adopted a new strategy of conducting and funding research, which is primarily based on randomized trials that can more precisely measure the effects and effectiveness of state and federal policies (Whitehurst 2003).

Another important arm of the new ED was the Office of Innovation and Improvement, which was created early in President George W. Bush's first term. According to its website, the OII is "the nimble, entrepreneurial arm of the U.S. Department of Education. It makes strategic investments in innovative educational practices through two dozen discretionary grant programs and coordinates the public school choice and supplemental educational services provisions of the Elementary and Secondary Education Act as amended by No Child Left Behind" (U.S. Department of Education, n.d.). These institutional changes at ED served a dual purpose. In the short term, they were intended to enable the department to more effectively carry out its new mission of monitoring state compliance with NCLB mandates. In the longer term, however, it was hoped that the reorientation and reorganization of the ED would institutionalize the new, more aggressive federal approach to school reform into the bureaucracy and make it harder for the approach to be undone by subsequent presidential administrations or congressional pressure.

IMPLEMENTATION: STATE EDUCATION AGENCIES

As Sandra Vergari notes, states have rebelled against federal mandates in education and sought to reshape them on the ground (2012). However, NCLB mandates—combined with the rigorous ED enforcement—pushed states to rapidly and fundamentally transform their student testing, data collection, and district monitoring systems. A 2008 RAND study, for example, concluded that "states, districts, and schools have adapted their policies and practices to support the implementation of NCLB" (Stecher et al. 2008, 64). The ED has closely monitored state compliance efforts on both the front end—through the use of detailed accountability plans that each state must submit for review—and on the back end, through regular state reporting and federal audits (for more information on the ED review process for state accountability plans, see GAO 2009). The ED's Office of Inspector General has conducted audits of state policies and their compliance with NCLB mandates and demanded that states make changes where necessary.

In New Jersey, for example, a federal audit in 2005 criticized the Department of Education for not disseminating state assessment results effectively and for not exerting sufficient oversight of district compliance with either the choice or Supplemental Educational Services (SES) provisions of NCLB (U.S. Department of Education 2005). The highly critical federal audit was sufficient to generate significant changes in state policies and has led to the creation of a more robust role for the NJ Department of Education in implementing NCLB and providing technical assistance to schools and districts. This vision became the basis for Collaborative Assessment and Planning for Achievement (CAPA) teams, which conduct week-long school reviews in low-performing Abbott and Title I schools (for additional information on the CAPA process, see New Jersey Department of Education 2010). In 2005, the Department of Education's monitoring and evaluation system was completely transformed with the creation of the New Jersey Quality Single Accountability Continuum (NJQSAC) and the development of a statewide student-level database.

This New Jersey example demonstrates the historically unprecedented level of federal monitoring and enforcement activities in state education systems in the wake of NCLB. In implementing NCLB, the Bush administration fundamentally altered the role of the federal Department of Education—shifting it from its historical role as a grant-maker and compliance monitor to a more active (if still relatively toothless) role as a compliance-enforcer and agitator. The administration has emphasized the importance of bottom line results in student achievement, shifting the traditional focus from regulation and process. Despite all of the political controversy surrounding NCLB, one of the enduring legacies of the Bush administration has been the institutionalization of assessment and accountability in education. In this sense, NCLB's influence may ultimately be compared to the original ESEA in 1965—which, for all its flaws and shortcomings, cemented in place a new and substantial federal role in education.

A NEW APPROACH: RACE TO THE TOP AND NCLB WAIVERS

The election of Barack Obama as president in 2008—combined with Democratic control of Congress—gave the Democratic Party an opportunity to assert a new vision of education reform. Many observers initially assumed that this would lead to a move away from federal school accountability and a reassertion of the traditional liberal focus on school resources, integration, and social welfare programs. Although his administration did in fact offer states waivers from some of NCLB's ambitious accountability requirements, it did so only on the condition that individual states were willing to support key elements of the Obama reform agenda (Cavanaugh 2012). President Obama has also increased the federal role in important ways in calling for the growth of annual testing in ESEA, expanding federal efforts to restructure the worst performing schools, and creating a new focus on innovation, charter schools, and teacher accountability. The centerpiece of the Obama education agenda was the $4.35 billion Race to the Top (RTT), $3.5 billion School Improvement Grant (SIG), and $650 million Investing in Innovation (i3) programs (McGuinn 2012c).

Historically, almost all federal education funds have been distributed through categorical grant programs that allocated money to districts on the basis of need-based formulas. According to this traditional model, states and districts received funding automatically, regardless of the performance of their schools or the promise of their particular school reform policies. Long-standing variation across states and districts in the amount of federal funds received has been due to differences in state educational needs (the number of poor, ESL, or special education students, for example), rather than differences in school policies. The RTT, SIG, and i3 funds, by contrast, were distributed through a competitive grant process in which states and districts were only rewarded for developing school reforms that were in line with federal goals and guidelines. In particular, state applications were graded according to the rigor of the reforms proposed and their compatibility with five administration priorities: the development of common standards and assessments; improving teacher training, evaluation, and retention policies; developing better data systems; the adoption of preferred school turnaround strategies; and building stakeholder support for reform.

ED also established a number of criteria

that states had to meet to even be eligible to apply for the RTT funds. These requirements have had a major effect on state school reform efforts, independent of the specific grant proposals the states have submitted. Among the fourteen criteria for RTT eligibility was that a state did not have a cap on the number of charter schools that are permitted to operate and that it did not have a firewall preventing the linking of student achievement data with individual teacher information. This served to stir the pot politically over school reform as never before, by forcing different interest groups to publicly stake out their positions on the various reform components of RTT in the debate over whether to apply them and under what conditions (McGuinn 2012b). The competition also attracted tremendous media attention to the issue of school reform, shone a bright light on dysfunctional state policies, and helped create new political coalitions at the local and state levels to drive reform. Some evidence indicates, for example, that RTT's emphasis on expanding charter schools and revamping teacher evaluations helped change the political climate around these controversial issues, paving the way for the passage of reform legislation in many states. The Obama administration has initiated a second Race to the Top competition and announced its desire to distribute more federal education funding though competitive grant programs in the future.

In the area of teacher evaluation and compensation, Obama and Duncan have supported their tough talk with some important steps to tie federal funds to significant reform. They have expanded the federal Teacher Incentive Fund, which has distributed resources to experiment with alternative evaluation systems and performance pay systems. So far thirty-four states, districts, and nonprofit groups have received money to develop approaches that use "objective measures" of student performance to compensate the most effective teachers. Most significantly, the Obama administration is leveraging the RTT funds to spur improvements in state teacher data collection and evaluation systems, as well as to link such information to student achievement information. As Stephen Sawchuk notes, "the stimulus application for the first time, sets a federal definition of teacher effectiveness" and states receiving RTT funds "must commit to using their teacher effectiveness data for everything from evaluating teachers to determining the type of professional development they get, to making decisions about granting tenure and pursuing dismissals" (2009, 1). These changes are pushing states to embrace the types of teacher evaluation, compensation, and tenure reforms that they have long resisted.

NCLB was scheduled to be reauthorized in 2007 but a divided Congress has been unable to agree on the appropriate role of the federal government in education. The law remains in effect, however, and an estimated 48 percent of schools nationwide failed to make AYP and faced NCLB-related penalties in 2011. That year the Obama administration took matters into its own hands by announcing an ESEA flexibility plan that would enable states to apply to the Department of Education for a waiver from NCLB's accountability provisions. In a speech announcing the program, President Obama stated, "I've urged Congress for a while now, let's get a bi-partisan effort to fix this. Congress hasn't been able to do it. So I will. . . . Given that Congress cannot act, I am acting" (quoted in Simendinger 2011, 1).

Secretary Duncan cited his regulatory authority under NCLB—and in particular section 9401 of ESEA—as justification for the waiver program. Most observers agree that he has the authority to issue waivers, but the administration made granting waivers conditional, which is much more controversial and appears to be unprecedented in education. The administration declared that to be eligible to receive a waiver, states must adopt college and career-ready standards (such as the Common Core), develop a plan to identify and improve the bottom 15 percent of schools, and develop teacher and principal evaluation systems "based on multiple valid measures, including student progress over time." As Riley observes, "This proposal . . . takes many of the ideas underlying RTTT [sic] and expands their application in order to slay the NCLB zombie" (Riley 2012, 2). Members of Congress criticized the conditional waiver program as essentially using administrative discretion to rewrite the law in violation of the separation of powers. Representative John Kline (R-MN), for example, remarked, "In my judgment, he is exercising an authority and power he doesn't have. We all know the law is broken and need to be changed. But this is part and parcel with the whole picture with this administration: they cannot get their agenda through Congress, so they're doing it with executive orders and rewriting rules. This is executive overreach" (quoted in Viteritti 2012, 5). The waiver program nonetheless proved irresistible to the forty-five states that applied and received them, eager as they were to escape NCLB's accountability system even if in exchange for promising to enact several Obama administration reforms. The use of competitive grants and NCLB waivers to drive states' reform efforts is a new and potentially transformative role for the ED in American education.

THE COMMON CORE EFFORT

Another important recent development has been the effort by the National Governors Association (NGA) and the Council of Chief State School Officers (CCSSO) to develop a "Common Core" of national academic standards and parallel assessments. Earlier efforts to develop national standards and assessments in the United States—such as those by President George H. W. Bush and President Bill Clinton in the 1990s—were met with passionate opposition from across the political spectrum by those who feared federal power in education or the idea of a national curriculum that would overwhelm traditional state prerogatives (for more of the standards-setting effort during this period, see Ravitch 1995). The implementation of NCLB, however, increased the pressure to develop national standards and assessments, as states used their discretion in this area to manipulate the accountability system by lowering their standards, making their tests easier, or decreasing their proficiency cut scores. Such actions were widely criticized for dumbing down the curriculum and undermining the law's school accountability system. The result was that school reformers from across the political spectrum came to see the creation of common standards and assessments—and the increased accuracy and transparency they would bring to school performance—as an essential part of the effort to improve schools going forward (Busyh and Klein 2011).

In the wake of the many centralizing and coercive NCLB mandates, however, concerns regarding federal authority had only increased and this led to the mantra that common standards and assessments should be "national, not federal" (Heise 2006). In July 2009, the NGA and CCSSO created a task force comprising representatives from higher education, K–12 education, and the research community and released standards in language arts and mathematics in June 2010. Given the voluntary nature of this approach, each state must make its own decision about whether to adopt the common core, and thereby substitute the national standards and assessments for the state's own. By encouraging states to sign on as part of their RTT applications, the Obama administration was able to get forty-eight states to pledge to sign on to the Common Core Standards Initiative (only Alaska and Texas declined to participate). Moreover, as of July 2012, forty-five states had gone further and formally adopted the common standards to replace their own state standards. (The Common Core encountered mounting political opposition in 2014 and 2015, however, with several states dropping the standards and others contemplating doing so.) In addition, three consortia competed for the $350 million in RTT funding provided by the Department of Education to develop next-generation assessments. Timothy Conlan and Paul Posner see RTT and the common core approach as part of the Obama administration's "hybrid model of federal policy innovation and leadership, which mixes money, mandates, and flexibility in new and distinctive ways.... The model represents a blend of, but is different from, both cooperative and coercive federalism" (2011, 443–444).

The Department of Education—like many state education agencies—is also shifting from primarily administering grants and monitoring compliance to focusing more on supporting school improvement efforts. It worked closely with states that received RTT grants through what is called a Reform Support Network, which aims to build capacity to implement and sustain their reform efforts, particularly around adopting high-quality standards and assessments, developing effective data systems, recruiting and retaining great teachers and leaders, and turning around the lowest-performing schools. And, in October 2014, the department announced a major reorganization that includes a new Office of State Support that will consolidate a variety of offices to better provide technical assistance to states with their school improvement work.

CONCLUSION

American K–12 education has undergone a significant transformation since the passage of the ESEA in 1965 as increasingly ambitious federal policies push states to embrace a school reform paradigm centered around standards, testing, accountability, and choice. As the main interpreter and implementer of federal education policy, the Department of Education has played a crucial (if underexplored) role in this transformation. A larger federal role in education—and increased administrative capacity—may very well not lead to better educational outcomes. If federal education policies are misguided—or if a more active ED uses its authority in counterproductive ways—then student learning may remain stagnant or even decline.

Federalism, and the lack of national constitutional authority to directly impose school reform on the states, has greatly complicated American politics and policymaking in education because it has forced the federal government to pursue its goals for school reform indirectly—through the grant in aid system and state education agencies. The intergovernmental relationship in education in the United States in the contemporary era is both cooperative and coercive—a duality that makes it complex and contingent on broader political forces. The relationship has a cooperative element because the department must rely on state education agencies as a conduit for federal education spending and as the implementer of federal policies on the ground in school districts. It is also coercive, however, because federal spending and policies have increasingly been used to push states to undertake politically unpopular changes they likely would not have undertaken in the absence of federal pressure. For the ED to be effective in gaining state compliance with federal education policies, it needs adequate statutory authority, administrative capacity, and political support. However, throughout most of the thirty-five year history of the department, these resources have been lacking.

The 2001 No Child Left Behind Act represented a major shift in ESEA and an ambitious and controversial expansion of federal power over an educational system that has long been based on the principle of local control. With its prescriptive mandates, timetables, and aggressive enforcement, NCLB represents nothing less than a transformative shift in educational governance in the United States. However, the ultimate impact of the law—as well as recent Obama initiatives, such as Race to the Top and the Common Core—on schools is contingent on ongoing efforts to restructure state and federal departments of education to expand their administrative capacity and reconfigure intergovernmental relationships to adapt to the new demands placed on them. The Bush and Obama administrations initiated an unprecedented effort to empower and reorient the Department of Education to pressure states to embrace federal school assessment and accountability mandates and to support their preferred reform strategies.

Nonetheless, ongoing administrative capacity deficits within federal, state, and local education departments present a formidable challenge to the current ambitious education reform agenda. The ED has long lacked the staff, resources, and technical expertise to provide sustained supervision and guidance of state compliance with federal education programs. Although its programs and grant expenditures have grown dramatically in the past thirty years, the department itself has not. As its website notes, "In fact, with a planned fiscal year 2010 level of 4,199, ED's staff is 44 percent below the 7,528 employees who administered Federal education programs in several different agencies in 1980, when the Department was created" (U.S. Department of Education 2012). Ironically then, the department's push to expand states' administrative capacity to implement education reform may ultimately be undone by the lack of adequate administrative capacity at the federal level.

And as states have struggled to meet NCLB's ambitious goals and chafed at the reforms rewarded by RTT, some of the initial philosophical reservations within the Democratic and Republican Parties regarding the new federal emphasis on testing and accountability have come storming back to the surface. Many Republicans resent the coerciveness of the new federal role, while many Democrats are concerned about the impact of standardized testing on instruction and teacher evaluation and the focus on schools over broader economic and social change (McGuinn 2012a). The November 2014 elections resulted in Republican control of both chambers of Congress, and the party has pledged to reduce federal activism in a variety of policy areas, including and especially in education. Led by Senator Lamar Alexander (TN), a former secretary of education, Republicans are pushing the long overdue congressional reauthorization of NCLB and early signs indicate that they will attempt to roll back the law's federal accountability provisions as well as rein in the authority of the ED. Republican presidential candidates campaigning in advance of the 2016 election have likewise indicated they would act vigorously to reduce federal authority over public education if elected, with several going so far as to call for the outright elimination of the ED. While the latter appears unlikely to occur and the outcome of the ESEA reauthorization remains unclear, it is possible that we may well have witnessed the apogee of federal power in education. Even if true, ESEA and federal policy—and the way in which it was implemented by the ED—will have left an enormous legacy for education in the United States by pushing states to reorient their school systems around the principles of standards, assessment, accountability, and choice.

REFERENCES

Armor, David. 1995. *Forced Justice: School Desegregation and the Law*. New York: Oxford University Press.

Bailey, Stephen, and Edith Mosher. 1968. *ESEA: The Office of Education Administers a Law*. Syracuse, N.Y.: Syracuse University Press.

Balogh, Brian, Joanna Grisinger, and Philip Zelikow. 2002. "Making Democracy Work: A Brief History of Twentieth-Century Federal Executive Reorganization." *Miller Center* working paper. Charlottesville, Va.: University of Virginia.

Berke, Joel. 1974. *Answers to Inequity: An Analysis of the New School Finance*. Berkeley, Calif.: McCutchan Publishing.

Berke, Joel, and Michael Kirst. 1972. *Federal Aid to Education*. Lexington, Mass.: Heath.

Berry, Tiffany, and Rebecca M. Eddy. 2008. Editor's notes. "Consequences of No Child Left Behind on Educational Evaluation." Special Issue, *New Directions for Evaluation* 117(2008): 2.

Busyh, Jeb, and Joel Klein. 2011. "The Case for Common Educational Standards." *Wall Street Journal*, June 23.

Cavanaugh, Sean. 2012. "Some States Skeptical of NCLB Waivers: Big Strings Attached to Bid for Flexibility." *Education Week*, January 18.

Chubb, John. 1985. "Excessive Regulation: The Case of Federal Aid to Education." *Political Science Quarterly* 100(2): 287.

Conlan, Timothy, and Paul Posner. 2011. "Inflection Point? Federalism and the Obama Administration." *Publius: The Journal of Federalism* 41(3): 443–44.

CQ Press, ed. 1981. *Historic Documents of 1980*. Washington, D.C.: CQ Press.

Glendening, Parris, and Mavis Reeves. 1984. *Pragmatic Federalism*. Pacific Palisades, Calif.: Palisades Publishers.

Graham, Hugh Davis. 1984. The Uncertain Triumph: Federal Education Policy in the Kennedy and Johnson Years. Chapel Hill: University of North Carolina Press.

Heise, Michael. 2006. *"The Political Economy of Education Federalism." Emory Law Journal* 56(125): 125–58.

Hess, Frederick, and Chester Finn, Jr. 2007. *No Remedy Left Behind: Lesson from a Half Decade of No Child Left Behind*. Washington, D.C.: AEI Press.

Hill, Paul. 2000. "The Federal Role in Education." *Brookings Papers on Education Policy* 3: 11–57.

Hufstedler, Shirley. 1990. "Organizing the Department of Education." In *The Presidency and Education*, edited by Kenneth Thompson. Lanham, Md.: University Press of America.

Hughes, John, and Ann Hughes. 1972. *Equal Education: A New National Strategy*. Bloomington: Indiana University Press.

Jeffrey, Julie Roy. 1978. *Education for Children of the Poor: A Study of the Origins and Implementation* of the Elementary and Secondary Education Act of 1965. Columbus: Ohio State University Press.

Jennings, Jack. 2000. "Title I: Its Legislative History and Its Promise." *Phi Delta Kappan* 81(7): 516–22.

Kursh, Harry. 1965. The United States Office of Education: A Century of Service. New York: Chilton Books.

Manna, Paul. 2006. *School's In: Federalism and the National Education Agenda*. Washington, D.C.: Georgetown University Press.

McClure, Phyllis. 2004. "Grassroots Resistance to NCLB." *Education Gadfly* 4(11). Available at: http://www.edexcellence.net/commentary/education-gadfly-weekly/2004/march-18/grassroots-resistance-to-nclb-1.html (accessed July 23, 2015).

McGuinn, Patrick. 2006. *No Child Left Behind and the Transformation of Federal Education Policy, 1965–2005*. Lawrence: University Press of Kansas.

———. 2012a. "The Federal Role in Educational Equity: The Two Narratives of School Reform and the Debate over Accountability." In *Education, Democracy, and Justice*, edited by Danielle Allen and Robert Reich. Chicago: University of Chicago Press.

———. 2012b. "Fight Club: How New School Reform Advocacy Groups Are Changing the Politics of Education." *Education Next* (Summer 2012): 25–31. Available at: http://www.academia.edu/12384535/Fight_Club_How_New_School_Reform_Advocacy_Groups_Are_Changing_the_Politics_of_Education (accessed July 23, 2015).

———. 2012c. "Stimulating Reform: Race to the Top, Competitive Grants and the Obama Education Agenda." *Educational Policy* 26(1): 136–59.

McGuinn, Patrick, Larry Berger, and David Anderson. 2012. "Incentives, Information, and Infrastructure: The Federal Role in Educational Innovation." In *Carrots, Sticks, and the Bully Pulpit: Sobering Lessons from a Half-Century of Federal Efforts to Improve America's Schools*, edited by Frederick Hess and Andrew Kelly. Cambridge, Mass.: Harvard Education Press.

McLaughlin, Milbrey. 1975. *Evaluation and Reform: Elementary and Secondary Education Act of 1965, Title I*. New York: HarperCollins.

National Center for Education Statistics. 2014. "Table 235.10. Revenues for Public Elementary and Secondary Schools, by Source of Funds: Selected Years, 1919–20 through 2011–12." *Digest of Education Statistics 2013*. Washington: U.S. Department of Education. Available at: https://nces.ed.gov/programs/digest/d14/tables/dt14_235.10.asp?current=yes (accessed July 23, 2015).

New Jersey Department of Education. 2010. "Collaborative Assessment for Planning and Achievement." http://www.state.nj.us/education/title1/archive/program/ (accessed July 23, 2015).

Newman, Joseph W. 1994. *America's Teachers: An Introduction to Education*, 2nd ed. New York: Pearson Publishing.

Nugent, John. 2009. *Safeguarding Federalism: How States Protect Their Interests in National Policymaking*. Norman: University of Oklahoma Press.

Orfield, Gary. 1969. *The Reconstruction of Southern Education: The Schools and the 1964 Civil Rights Act*. New York: John Wiley & Sons.

Orfield, Gary, and Susan Eaton, ed. 1996. *Dismantling Desegregation: The Quiet Reversal of Brown v. Board of Education*. New York: The Free Press.

Peterson, Paul E. 1983. "Background Paper." In *Making the Grade: Report of the Twentieth Century Fund Task Force on Federal Elementary and Secondary Education Policy*. New York: Twentieth Century Fund.

Peterson, Paul E., Barry G. Rabe, and Kenneth K. Wong. 1986. *When Federalism Works*. Washington, D.C.: Brookings Institution Press.

Radin, Beryl, and Willis Hawley. 1988. *The Politics of Federal Reorganization: Creating the U.S. Department of Education*. New York: Pergammon Press.

Ravitch, Diane. 1983. *The Troubled Crusade: American Education 1945–1980*. New York: Basic Books.

———. 1995. *National Standards in American Education*. Washington, D.C.: Brookings Institution Press.

Riley, Benjamin. 2012. "Waive to the Top: The Dangers of Legislating Education Policy from the Executive Branch." *Education Outlook* 1(March 8): 1–6. Available at: https://www.aei.org/wp-content/uploads/2012/03/-waive-to-the-top-the-dangers-of-legislating-education-policy-from-the-executive-branch_151023576072.pdf (accessed July 23, 2015).

Sawchuck, Stephen. 2009. "Teachers and the Race to the Top Fund." *Teacher Beat*, July 24, 2009. Available at: http://blogs.edweek.org/edweek/teacherbeat/2009/07/teacher_provisions_in_the_race.html (accessed July 23, 2015).

Simendinger, Alexis. 2011. "Feeling Legislative Chill,

Obama Flexes Executive Muscles." *Real Clear Politics*, September 26. Available at: http://www.realclearpolitics.com/articles/2011/09/26/feeling_legislative_chill_obama_flexes_executive_muscles_111471.html (accessed July 23, 2015).

Stallings, D. T. 2002. "A Brief History of the U.S. Department of Education, 1979–2002." *Phi Delta Kappan* 83(9): 677.

Stecher, Brian, Scott Epstein, Laura S. Hamilton, Julie A. Marsh, Abby Robyn, Jennifer Sloan McCombs, Jennifer Russell, and Scott Naftel. 2008. *Pain and Gain: Implementing No Child Left Behind in Three States, 2004–2006*. Santa Monica, Calif.: RAND Corp. Available at: http://www.rand.org/content/dam/rand/pubs/monographs/2008/RAND_MG784.pdf (accessed July 23, 2015).

Stephens, David. 1984. "President Carter, the Congress, and NEA: Creating the Department of Education." *Political Science Quarterly* 98(4): 641–63.

Thomas, Norman C. *Education in National Politics*. New York: David McKay Company.

Tyack, David and Larry Cuban. 1997. *Tinkering Toward Utopia: A Century of Public School Reform*. Boston, Mass.: Harvard University Press.

U.S. Department of Education. 2010. "An Overview of the U.S. Department of Education." Available at: http://www2.ed.gov/about/overview/focus/whattoc.html (accessed January 5, 2015).

———. 2012. "The Federal Role in Education." Available at: http://www2.ed.gov/about/overview/fed/role.html (accessed July 23, 2015).

———, Office of Innovation and Improvement. n.d. "Connect with the Office of Innovation and Improvement." Available at: http://www.ed.gov/about/offices/list/oii/index.html (accessed July 23, 2015).

———, Office of Inspector General. 2005. "Audit of NJDOE's Compliance with Public School Choice and SES Provisions." ED-OIG/A02-F0006. Washington: Government Printing Office. Available at: http://www.ed.gov/about/offices/list/oig/auditreports/a02f0006.doc (accessed July 23, 2015).

U.S. Government Accountability Office (GAO). 2009. "No Child Left Behind Act: Enhancements in the Department of Education's Review Process Could Improve State Academic Assessments." GAO-09-911. Washington: Government Printing Office.

Vergari, Sandra. 2012. "The Limits of Federal Activism in Education Policy." *Educational Policy* 26(1): 15–34.

Verstegen, Deborah, and David Clark. 1988. "The Diminution in Federal Expenditures for Education During the Reagan Administration." *Phi Delta Kappan* 70(2): 137.

Vinovskis, Maris. 1999. "Missing in Practice? Systematic Development and Rigorous Program Evaluation at the U.S. Department of Education." Paper presented at the Conference on Evaluation of Educational Policies, American Academy of Arts and Sciences. Cambridge, Mass. (May 13–14, 1999).

Viteritti, Joseph. 2012. "The Federal Role in School Reform: Obama's Race to the Top." *Notre Dame Law Review* 87(5): 2087–122.

Whitehurst, Grover. 2003. "The Institute of Education Sciences: New Wine, New Bottles." Presentation to the American Education Research Association 2003 Annual Meeting. Washington, D.C. (April 23, 2003).

Wilkinson, J. Harvie III. 1978. "The Supreme Court and Southern School Desegregation, 1955–1970." *Virginia Law Review* 64(4): 485–559.

Wright Edelman, Marian. 1973. "Southern School Desegregation, 1954–1973: A Judicial-Political Overview." *Annals of the American Academy of Political and Social Science* 407(May): 32–42.

PART II
Limitations and Proposals for Change

Getting to Sesame Street? Fifty Years of Federal Compensatory Education

GLORIA LADSON-BILLINGS

"Sunny day, sweeping the clouds away,
On my way to where the air is sweet,
Can you tell me how to get,
How to get to Sesame Street?"

—Stone and Hart Theme Song,
 Sesame Street

Education research primarily draws from the social science disciplines of psychology and sociology (and to some extent, economics). Each of these disciplines contributes much to our understanding of education in complex societies. This article argues for the inclusion of anthropological or cultural perspectives in understanding the policy known as the Elementary and Secondary Education Act (ESEA) of 1965. Rethinking culture might help policymakers be more aware of and challenged to include culture as an important construct to factor into decision-making when serving traditionally underserved communities.

Keywords: culture, culture and policy

I must start with a confession, I was one of those parents who placed her children squarely in front of the television each afternoon to watch the Children's Television Workshop's *Sesame Street* in its earliest days. I thought of it as a virtuous thing to do because the only things the program was selling were letters and numbers. I appreciated its educational value and its innovative way of reaching children without patronizing them. Also I must confess I did not think much about the program's actual premise and purposes—to reach those children who did not have the advantage of high-quality preschool or highly educated parents. I did not think of *Sesame Street* as a compensatory education program because of its availability to and use by families across the racial, ethnic, and socioeconomic spectrum. Everyone loved Big Bird, Cookie Monster, Gordon, and the entire *Sesame Street* cast. More recently, *Sesame Street* has extended its audience across the globe and in each instance the show has tailored its programming to the local culture and conditions. For example, *Sesame Street* in Israel deals with the tensions that exist between Arab- and Jewish-descent peoples and seeks to ensure that young children do not foster the prejudices of the adults. In South Africa, *Sesame Street* has made deliberate strides toward explaining the scourge of HIV-

---

Gloria Ladson-Billings is the Kellner Family Chair of Urban Education at the University of Wisconsin–Madison.

Direct correspondence to: Gloria Ladson-Billings, gjladson@wisc.edu, University of Wisconsin–Madison, Department of Curriculum & Instruction, 225 N. Mills St., Madison, WI 53706.

AIDS that was ravaging the nation. Interesting, a recent study suggests that *Sesame Street* has a Head Start–like effect on children's cognitive skills (Kearney and Levine 2015). *Sesame Street* provides this cognitive impact at a fraction of the cost. Head Start typically costs about $7,600 per child each year while the annual per-child cost of *Sesame Street* is just $5 in today's dollars.

This wide reach of *Sesame Street* in some ways serves as a metaphor for the construction of this article. I argue that despite its most earnest efforts the fifty years of the Elementary and Secondary Education Act (ESEA) have not helped to close the achievement disparities between low-income students and their middle-class peers. I begin with a look at the contribution of anthropology to education research and policy.

WHAT ANTHROPOLOGY CONTRIBUTES TO EDUCATION RESEARCH AND POLICY

The work of an anthropologist is to document the cultural practices of a specific group or subgroup of people. This work is rarely predictive or speculative. Instead, anthropologists provide very detailed and specific information about how groups function. Analytically, anthropology sometimes uses analogy, metaphor, and parallels in its "thick description" and works to "make the familiar strange" (Geertz 1977). Anthropology began as a field designed to study "the other." Much like the field of geography the British early on dominated the field of anthropology. As an empire Britain understood the need to map the world it was set to conquer. It used anthropology as a way to rate and rank cultural groups where those of northern and western European stock always came out as superior to every other group. Despite Franz Boas's emphasis on cultural relativity and the need to assess cultures by their internal standards, American anthropologists maintained this practice of cultural ranking and in the United States the concept of race was promulgated by anthropology (Smedley and Smedley 1993).

To do their work, anthropologists often study either very traditional, less complex societies (for example, the Nuer of Southern Africa or the Arunta of Australia) or small segments of a society (such as Santeria priests or Vietnamese fishermen) because studying culture up close is labor intensive and time consuming. However, as anthropologists began to study more complex societies (including their own) the scope of the inquiry required highly specific foci. Studies of single schools, classrooms, and teachers became popular (see, for example, Spindler and Spindler 1994; Rosenfeld 1983). This work helped construct narratives of teaching and learning that elaborated the more statistical explorations and analysis of schools and classrooms detailed by social scientists in disciplines such as sociology, psychology, and economics. The ethnography of schooling grew throughout the 1970s and 1980s and has become an accepted form of educational research and inquiry. Despite growth in the field of educational anthropology, rarely is anthropology used to analyze education policy and legislation. This article attempts to do just that. It will look at a specific piece of education legislation, the Elementary and Secondary Education Act (ESEA) of 1965, and describe it as a "cultural phenomenon" that helped shape education practice.

I do not want to suggest that anthropology has nothing to add to policymaking and policy debates. Indeed, a special interest group of the American Anthropological Association, the Association for the Anthropology of Policy, is charged specifically with addressing policy. Its mission statement asserts the following:

> The study of policy deals with issues at the heart of anthropology such as: institutions and power; ideology and discourse; identity and culture; and interactions between the global and the local, public and private, and bureaucracy and market. Understanding the dynamics of policy processes is ever more important because of greater global interconnectedness; decisions made in one place or arena increasingly have major effects in other places and arenas. Policy connects disparate and diverse peoples—many of whom never interact personally or directly—yet who are dispersed among the multiple arenas of interaction that policy processes trigger or touch across place and time. (Association for the Anthropology of Policy 2012)

Rather, I argue that what anthropology contributes to policy is a way to think about the cultural context of policymaking and the way anthropological knowledge can provide background knowledge to inform and improve policymaking. For example, anthropology can be useful for government agencies that deal with indigenous populations. Anthropological knowledge can help decide what constitutes a fair and just settlement of resources and ongoing government relations. Or, anthropology can help avoid awkward or coercive policies that deal with health or nutritional regulations between mainstream societies and those regarded as culturally separate and distinct.

Two paradigms dominate educational anthropology—cultural ecology and cultural difference theory. Cultural ecology is best known as a theory John Ogbu promoted (1978, 1987; Gibson and Ogbu 1991). The premise of the cultural ecology theory is that "caste-like minority" status affects motivation and achievement and depresses IQ scores. More specific to the U.S. context, Ogbu argued that cultural differences associated with being a member of a minority group alone does not account for educational differences. Some minority groups appear to do quite well. To explain those differences, Ogbu contended that some minority groups fall into voluntary minority status while others are in what he terms involuntary minority status. Voluntary minorities are those groups who chose to immigrate to the United States with the hopes of securing a better life for their families and quality education for their children. Thus, many of the groups that immigrated to the United States from Asia (for example, Koreans, Chinese, Vietnamese, Indians, and others) of their own volition are more likely to find academic success in U.S. schools. On the other hand, involuntary or caste-like minorities are groups who found themselves in the United States (or under U.S. jurisdiction) against their own will (for example, African Americans, Latinos, and American Indians). Ogbu's theory represents a macro-social approach to the issue of minority school achievement.

The theorists Frederick Erickson, Henry Trueba, and Shirley Brice Heath argue that the problems of minority student achievement are rooted in cultural differences and our inability to account for those differences in the delivery of school services (Erickson and Mohatt 1982; Trueba 1988, 1990; Heath 1983). Cultural difference theorists point to the micro-social practices that occur in classrooms through instruction, specifically, linguistic and social practices. They argue that Ogbu's perspective lacks historical context and explanatory power for those members of so-called involuntary minorities who are successful. Cultural ecological theorists argue that cultural difference theorists miss the broad structural determinants of minority status that result in differential outcomes despite similar socioeconomic status.

Anthropologists privilege culture over socioeconomic status and class in their analysis. However ESEA is aimed at low-income children and some low-income members of cultural groups (as Ogbu and others argue) experience success in U.S. schools but others struggle generation after generation. Anthropologists are more interested in the way "cultural practices" determine educational outcomes (Gutierrez and Rogoff 2003). One powerful example of the salience of culture appears in the evidence that suggests middle-class African Americans continue to lag academically behind their white counterparts. If the more significant explanatory variable is class, what explains this disparity? Cultural factors may provide some insight. It is here that anthropologists can contribute to the debate since they are more likely to argue that one-size-fits-all solutions are unable to account for the way culture is differentially deployed and differentially accessible to various groups.

Education policy rarely accounts for culture because the concept is difficult to manipulate as a variable. For instance, if a researcher uses race, class, socioeconomic status, or gender as variables they are relatively discrete notions even if they are sometimes inaccurate or crudely determined. Graduate students often fall into the category of low income although culturally they are more likely to be very different from families who have experienced generational poverty. The category of race is particularly problematic because it has little scientific validity. It is, however, an agreed-upon category in U.S. society. Fewer policies are racially specific and those that are face increasing scrutiny. California, Washington, and Michigan have all struck down state-level policies that take race into consideration. At the federal level, public colleges and universities are awaiting a U.S. Supreme Court decision on the use of race as a "value-added"[1] component in college admissions policies. Culture is not considered in these state and federal policy decisions. Only when culture is encapsulated in other specific elements, such as language or religion, are policymakers able to identify cultural practices that may matter in the public arena. For example, the landmark *Lau v. Nichols* decision (414 U.S. 563, 1974) links directly to students' language. Language groups may overlap with cultural groups. In the case of religion increasing numbers of students from Muslim cultures find it important to emphasize that aspect of their cultural identities. Female Muslim students who cannot wear shorts in physical education classes may be exempt from that requirement for religious reasons, not cultural reasons. However, pulling apart the religion from the culture is difficult and may make little sense from the standpoint of the person engaged in these cultural practices.

Despite the difficulty of operationalizing the concept of culture so that policymakers can consider it as they make decisions, it may still be useful to consider culture as a rubric for thinking about the foundations that ultimately undergird policy. In the next sections of the paper I provide a brief history of ESEA and its shortcomings from a cultural vantage point.

BRIEF HISTORY OF ESEA

As a part of President Lyndon B. Johnson's War on Poverty, the U.S. Congress enacted the Elementary and Secondary Act (ESEA, P.L. 89-10) on April 9, 1965.[2] Johnson, a former teacher on the Texas border, believed that equal education access was crucial to insure the futures of the nation's most needy children. Symbolically, President Johnson signed the act at a rural school in Stonewall, Texas, with his own first grade teacher, Katherine Deadrich Loney, seated at his side. Through a special funding source (Title I), the law allocated large resources to meet the needs of those children considered "educationally deprived" through compensatory programs for the poor, especially in the basic skills areas of reading, writing, and mathematics. Some of the specific wording from the act states

> In recognition of the special educational needs of low-income families and the impact that concentrations of low-income families have on the ability of local educational agencies to support adequate educational programs, the Congress hereby declares it to be the policy of the United States to provide financial assistance . . . to local educational agencies serving areas with concentrations of children from low-income families to expand and improve their educational programs by various means (including preschool programs) which contribute to meeting the special educational needs of educationally deprived children. (Section 201, ESEA)

The principle under which the Title I section of ESEA was developed was that of redress—that children from poor families needed more educational services than those from more affluent families. Title I therefore provided $1 billion in funding for schools serving the nation's poorest children. Although the legislation was designed to focus on low-income children regardless of race and ethnicity, it would be culturally and historically naïve to overlook the significant role that the civil rights movement had on shaping and encouraging the law (see Cohen and Moffit, this issue). It is also important that race and socio-

---

1. The use of the term *value added* here is not to be confused with the statistical technique currently used to determine teachers' contributions to students academic achievement as measured by standardized test scores.

2. See editors' introduction. This section includes information retrieved electronically from Elementary and Secondary Act of 1965. Available at: http://www.socialwelfarehistory.com/events/elementary-and-secondary-education-act-of-1965/ (accessed October 30, 2014).

economic status covary and most analyses of poor children in public schools will have higher proportions of children of color, particularly African American children. The goal of the legislation was to reach five million children from poor and low-income families in an attempt to level the educational playing field. Johnson declared this legislation to be the nation's most far-reaching education act since 1870 and it would maintain that stature until President George W. Bush signed the 2001 ESEA reauthorization known as No Child Left Behind (NCLB).

In 1965 ESEA contained six sections: Title I, Financial assistant to local education agencies (LEAs) for the education of children of low-income families; Title II, School library resources, textbooks, and other instructional aids; Title III, Supplementary educational centers and services; Title IV, Educational research and training; Title V, Grants to strengthen state departments of education; and Title VI, General provisions. In 1968, the act was amended to include Title VII, Aid to schools to assist with the educational needs of limited-English speaking students.

On the surface, ESEA appears to be an example of affirmative steps that the federal government took to right the perceived wrongs of the past. However, as is true with most education policy in the nation, ESEA reflects the political wrangling and deal making that result from legislators and an electorate of disparate ideological positions and political interests. Johnson's first inclination may have been to distribute funds in a wholesale fashion to all public schools. However, such a decision would alienate constituents in Catholic schools—particularly when many Catholic schools in urban communities served a population similar to those in urban public schools. A second tack would have been to allocate funds to all K–12 schools, public and private, but that strategy would raise strong constitutional concerns regarding the separation of church and state. Thus, the third tack, which Johnson took, was to link the funding to the income of the families. Few could argue the need to provide assistance to the poor. The other advantage of this strategy was that instead of suggesting that the federal government was participating in a takeover of local schools and subverting states' rights, the federal government could establish itself as providing only categorical aid linked to national policy such as defense, poverty, and economic growth. ESEA, as written, also permitted the federal government to assist low-income children attending parochial (and other religious) schools by arguing its support of students, not institutions. In addition, ESEA greatly expanded the power and scope of state departments of education (SDEs) because of the need for SDEs to grow in order to administer the federal funds.

Given the incredible infusion of money ESEA has provided for children from low-income families, one might wonder why what is regularly referred to as the achievement gap has not been substantially closed. It is important to acknowledge the good ESEA has done in its attempt to mitigate disparities that exist between poor children and their middle-income peers. Unfortunately, much of the public discourse focuses on academic disparity along racial (specifically black-white) lines. Sean Reardon argues, however, that the "income achievement gap" is nearly twice that of the black-white gap, and that almost fifty years ago racial achievement disparity was one and a half times that of income academic disparity (2011). However, the interesting aspect of this gap is that it is less fueled by the inability of children of families at the low-income level to advance than by the increased investments that children of families of middle and higher income levels seem to make on their behalf. Specifically, raising those on the bottom is almost always accompanied by additional supports for those on the top through personal and private resources. The other cultural challenge the society has in its public debate about academic disparity is that the face of poverty is regularly represented as black. Everything from Ronald Reagan's infamous "welfare queen" to George H. W. Bush's "Willie Horton" political ads have superimposed race on to poverty. Thus, the conflation of an entire set of social problems—drug use, crime, poverty, failing schools, and so on—often are associated with specific racial groups and the public discourse sometimes creates a less than sympathetic response to particular groups.

In the remainder of this article, I focus on two classroom-level shortcomings I think contributed to the reasons that compensatory education (that is, ESEA) failed to live up to the promise of 1965. These include the failure to recognize, first, the assets that low-income families do have that can be leveraged in school classrooms and, second, the importance of appropriate pedagogies for low-income students.

WHAT LOW-INCOME CHILDREN BRING

Discussions about the lack of achievement among children from low-income parents typically focus on deficiencies. Popular depictions of poor families tend to highlight dysfunction that works against achievement. Each week America's airways are filled with television programs such as *Cops*, *Here Comes Honey Boo Boo*, *The Wire*, and *Treme*, but in the 1970s TV producer Norman Lear dared to show a positive example of a poor family living in a public housing project in the sitcom *Good Times* (Blair 2014). Critics argued that Lear's depiction of the Evans family was too optimistic and failed to highlight the terrible outcomes and life chances such families were likely to suffer. However, in 1974, when *Good Times* appeared, the nation was in the midst of a recession. Many households knew what it was to struggle to make ends meet. *Good Times* was emblematic of a common condition. However, today with increasing income disparity empathy between haves and have-nots is almost nonexistent. What *Good Times* did not (and probably could not) tell us is the way structural forces such as institutional racism helped to create the policies that impoverished African Americans in particular.

In the 1950s, suburban communities developed by Levitt & Sons began offering single-family homes to returning veterans (Lambert 1997). However, the homes were not available to black or any other nonwhite veterans and their families. Although not alone in imposing restrictive covenants, Levittown is emblematic in the construction of the wealth gap that emerged in the 1950s. Buyers in Levittown were permitted to move in with zero down payments to purchase the $8,000 home. African Americans were encouraged to take advantage of the newly built public housing that only provided rental units. Today, Levittown homes are valued at about $450,000. Over time, Levittown residents have been able to accumulate wealth, but families relegated to public housing were often left with no wealth, despite paying about the same in rent that their white peers in the suburbs paid in mortgage payments. Thus, the poverty we bemoan may be a result of deliberate policies that disenfranchise segments of our society. It is not endemic to specific groups of people.

What Lear attempted to do in his sitcom forty years ago was to suggest certain strengths in poor families. Indeed, given their circumstances, often they were required to find strengths to survive. The research literature in child and family studies supports Lear's assertion. Dennis Orthner, Hinckley Jones-Sanpei, and Sabrina Williamson examined a random sample of low-income households with children (2004). Their work used an instrument called the Family Strength Index to assess strength according to economic, problem solving, communication, family cohesion, and social support assets. Their findings indicate that relationship assets such as communication, problem solving, and social support predict positive outcomes for low-income families. Similarly, Walter Mullin and Miguel Arce were able to identify factors such as positive beliefs, positive thinking, and taking action steps as key to producing resilience among low-income families (2008). They stress that these factors must take place in a context of supportive internal family relations and external community connections.

Documenting strength and resilience among low-income families might prompt researchers to ask which specific aspects of these qualities do low-income school-age children exhibit and how can these qualities be leveraged to improve their academic performance? Joseph Williams identifies protective factors for African American high school graduates from low-income families in urban contexts

(2011).[3] He finds that participants in his study benefitted from identifying at least one adult who served as a source of support and inspiration, education-specific parenting practices, nontraditional ways of supporting education, maintaining kinship networks, school as an agent of families, resilience-promoting features of schools, supportive relational networks within the community, promoting ecological resilience to improve student outcomes, and relational strategies to promote educational resilience. Geoffrey Borman and Laura Rachuba studied various school-level models that might promote and support resiliency among low-income students (2001). Their findings indicate greater engagement in academic activities, an internal locus of control, efficaciousness in math, a more positive outlook toward school, and a more positive self-esteem were characteristic of all low-SES students who achieved resilient outcomes. The most powerful school characteristics for promoting resiliency were represented by the supportive school community model, which, unlike other school models, included elements that actively shielded children from adversity.

Each of the strength and resilience studies tends to look for ways that low-income students can better assimilate into extant school models. Some might argue that this approach of fitting students into already problematic school structures is not the best way to support and encourage their intellectual, social, emotional, and civic development. Rather, it is merely a mechanism for helping them appear more like middle-class children. Thus, an alternate look at what low-income children bring to school might be a cultural resources model.

Marcelle Christian and Oscar Barbarin, for example, find that African American children from low-income families are more likely to experience school success if their parents attend church regularly (2001). Thus, some sense of spiritual connection could support not just an individual child but foster a classroom culture of justice, fairness, and reciprocity. Perhaps the most powerful "existence proof" of building academic excellence from the cultural resources of low-income students comes in the form of the African-Centered Schools movement. Begun in the 1970s, these schools were an attempt on the part of low-income African American communities to gain control over their schools to ensure that their children received academic, socioemotional, and cultural support. The philosophy of these schools emphasized unity, self-determination, collective work and responsibility, cooperative economics, purpose, creativity, and faith. These principles comprise what is called the Nguzo Saba (the basis of the holiday Kwanzaa) as core beliefs and cultural characteristics that are a part of African American culture.

Similarly, Wade Boykin and Caryn Bailey explore a "talent development" model to point out the resources that low-income African American students bring to classrooms. In their work, they examine

> certain home cultural factors, cultural orientations, and learning preferences of African American school children from low-income backgrounds in order to document the relationship of prior cultural socialization experiences to enhanced cognitive, performance, and motivational outcomes. In their work they attempt to offer a conceptual basis for how certain Afro-cultural themes—Movement, Communalism, and Verve—in low-income African American children's proximal experiences outside of school are transmitted and acquired, and the consequences of such acquisitions on their orientation and preferences for learning. Specifically, their research documents the cultural integrity residing in the experiences of African American children from low-income backgrounds and offers ways to proactively build upon these assets for enhancing school achievement. (2000, v)

This work in African American communities began to gain traction in other low-income

---

3. It is important not to assume that research done on African Americans or other "minoritized" groups have no applicability to those in the general public. Early work done in cooperative learning was done primarily on African American students entering desegregated schools. Today, cooperative learning is an accepted practice regardless of classroom composition.

communities of color where Latino, immigrant, and Native peoples began to inquire about how cultural models might increase academic performance for their children.

The point of addressing issues of strength, resilience, and cultural resources is to remind us that policies like ESEA are based on a presumption of lack or deficiency on the part of families and children. However, the school and classroom experiences of their middle-class peers presume they bring assets such as family involvement and engagement, prior knowledge, an achievement orientation, and networks rich in social and cultural capital. Similar presumptions may actually support the academic success of low-income students.

Anthropologists are more likely to ask, "How might the culture of under-served communities help inform the planning and programming associated with broad scale policies such as ESEA?" This approach moves away from the standardization of service delivery and incorporates more local cultural resources to ensure positive outcomes. For example, instead of accepting attending school improvement plan (SIP) meetings and signing the SIP document as evidence of parent engagement, anthropologists examine the cultural practices that may be compatible with increased parent engagement. This may mean SIP meetings that take place in churches, mosques, or community centers. It may mean curriculum materials selection committees that include parents. It may mean recruiting what Patricia Collins calls "other mothers"—people (generally, women) who have influence in a particular community despite not being a parent attached to a youngster in a neighborhood school (2008).

In one community, a woman who was actually a great-grandmother was referred to as Super Gram and was one of the most reliable sources of information to the community and understood how to negotiate school bureaucracy. From a typical ESEA policy perspective, Super Gram would most likely not be asked to participate on the SIP Council, but she could be one of the best people to engage to improve governance and compliance. In another community, a teacher noticed how confused her students were when children from her class were pulled out of the room to receive compensatory education services. She decided to ask the Title I reading teacher whether she could bring her entire class to the reading center so they could see what happened there. After the class visit to the reading center, individual students wanted to volunteer to visit the center with their classmates. The teacher set up a schedule that allowed individual students to go once a week to the reading center with the Title I students. Legally, that non–Title I students were visiting the reading center was an issue of noncompliance. Culturally, including friends and classmates was a way to demystify the Title I program and allow the students receiving Title I services to continue to share with their academically more able classmates.

These examples represent the ways that culture could have an impact on policy formation and implementation. They point to the way specific cultural contexts may require changes in standard regulations where the ends—improved academic performance—may require very different means. In the next section, I address the impact of teaching or instruction on academic performance and its obvious absence from ESEA.

TEACHING MATTERS

Almost all of the resources that came with the Elementary and Secondary Act of 1965 were for personnel and curriculum. Schools were permitted to hire additional teachers and instructional aids and to order supplementary curriculum materials. The predominant Title I program model involved removing eligible students from their classrooms to receive more individualized or small group instruction, as described. This strategy, called *pull-out* instruction, was legally supposed to supplement and not supplant regular classroom instruction (see Gordon and Reber, this issue). Thus, students who received Title I services were not supposed to receive those services during the reading and mathematics instruction block of their regular classroom. Title I was supposed to provide eligible students with added instruction. However, in far too many instances, students' Title I reading and math instruction were their only instruction in those areas.

The other problem with the pull-out services was that children felt the stigma of not being a part of the classroom community—sometimes leaving and reentering their classrooms midstream. So pronounced were the differences between who was and was not eligible for Title I services in one first grade classroom that whenever a student of color enrolled in the school and was assigned to this class, white middle-income students would ask the teacher, "Is he Title?" (see, for example, Weinstein et al. 2009). The very services that were supposed to eliminate the classroom achievement gaps were actually exacerbating the sociocultural gaps and labeling students in the program.

In some instances, schools determined that the best use of Title I resources was to hire instructional aids to go into classrooms to assist the eligible students with the ongoing work of the classroom. The problem with this model was that often the instructional aids were unsure of exactly who they should be serving and their human inclination was to help any student who asked for help. Also, as paraprofessionals they were often in no position to make instructional decisions. They followed the direct instructions of the classroom teachers. In this model, it was difficult to see how students were actually benefiting from the Title I resources. State and local agencies provided the resources; they did not provide the instructional know-how.

After the release of the Commission on Excellence in Education's widely publicized 1983 report *A Nation at Risk*, addressing the needs of the nation's low-income children shifted to sounding an alarm that the nation's entire public school system was in jeopardy. This report focused on the cafeteria-like offerings of the high school curriculum and demanded a more coherent, rigorous approach to secondary education. However, despite the stir that *A Nation at Risk* caused, the report also failed to address the need to build teacher capacity and expand pedagogical repertoires. It would be the Carnegie Forum on Education and the Economy that in 1986 focused the nation on the dire need to upgrade its teaching force. The next year, 1987, Lee Shulman published "Knowledge and Teaching: Foundations of the New Reform" to provide some theoretical and conceptual coherence to the field of teaching. Shulman's work provided the impetus for creating a national assessment to professionalize teaching by focusing on content knowledge, pedagogical knowledge, and pedagogical content knowledge.

Shulman's paper was followed by work that raised questions about the role of culture in teaching. Scholars such as Lis Delpit (1986, 1988), Gloria Ladson-Billings (1995a), and Michele Foster (1998) introduced the idea that the teachers' culture and perspectives affect student achievement. An underlying premise of much of this work was that a generic vision of "good teaching" was unlikely to help low-income students who have struggled with traditional teaching be successful. On the ground, studies of excellent teaching revealed that teachers who understood students' culture and incorporated that culture into their teaching were having more success with low-income African American students. Additionally, work with Native Hawaiian students and American Indian students revealed similar results (Au and Kawakami 1985; Erickson and Mohatt 1982). Ladson-Billings calls this teaching "culturally relevant pedagogy" and in a three-year study of eight exemplary teachers was able to isolate three major propositions—conceptions of self and others, conceptions of social relations, conceptions of knowledge—as ways to make sense of outstanding practice that is likely to support the academic, cultural, and socio-civic success of students who traditionally struggle in schools (1995a, 1995b).

Conceptions of Self or Others

A big challenge for the teaching profession is in elevating the status of teachers. Although teachers are among the nation's more widely "admired" professionals (second only to fire fighters), the profession ranks low on prestige. Additionally, the perception of low status is exacerbated when teachers work with what they consider to be low-status students (Foster 1986). But teachers who practice a culturally relevant approach to teaching do not think of their students, their families, and their communities as deficient or defective. They believe their students are capable of academic success and that they as teachers are capable of contributing to that success. These teachers are less likely to have a technical orientation toward teaching, are instead open to more fluid, less predictable classroom experiences and willing to change their practices when necessary. These teachers also connect with their students' communities in meaningful ways, such as attending local church services, athletic contests, block parties, and community cultural celebrations such as Juneteenth, Kwanzaa, and students' *quinceñeras*. Their approach to teaching reflects a belief that their students came to school with knowledge as opposed to being "empty vessels." This orientation stands in stark contrast to the one seemingly promulgated by deficit-based programs that advocate an approach that suggests that getting students away from home and community was essential for school success (see, for example, Payne 2005).

Conceptions of Social Relations
In their 1997 volume, *Working for Equity in Heterogeneous Classrooms*, Elizabeth Cohen and Rachel Lothan build on Cohen's early work to argue that how we structure classroom relations can support learning. The literature on classroom social interactions is plentiful and long-standing and teachers engaged in culturally relevant practice work to maintain fluid and flexible student-teacher relationships, attempt to connect with all students, develop a community of learners and encourage their students to learn collaboratively and take responsibility for each other (see, for example, Brophy and Good 1970; Rist 1970; Wilcox 1982; Ryan and Patrick 2001).

Classrooms structured this way try to minimize individual competition and instead work toward a team or family concept. Teachers working in this framework are willing to share power without relinquishing authority. Thus, in some instances students can expect to assume the role of teacher as they demonstrate knowledge and skills they have acquired. The collaborative grouping of students in these classrooms is not viewed as an opportunity to merely try something novel. Teachers are purposeful and systematic in making sure that students develop deep and extensive relationships with all of their classmates, not just those whose academic performance mirrors their own. Even in those instances character- ized by some ability grouping, these groups remained fluid. Teachers encouraged peer tutoring and mentoring to remind students that they were in interdependent relationships with each other.

Conceptions of Knowledge
Finally, the research on culturally relevant pedagogy revealed that teachers in this pedagogical paradigm have a critical stance to the curriculum, knowledge, and skills they teach. They believe that knowledge is not static, that it should be shared, recycled, constructed and reconstructed. In addition to viewing knowledge critically, the teachers were passionate about knowledge and learning and build scaffolding to facilitate students' learning. In these classrooms, assessment is multifaceted and incorporates multiple ways for students to demonstrate competency and mastery.

In the well-researched work on cognitive guided instruction (CGI), Thomas Carpenter and Elizabeth Fennema and their colleagues argue that all children come to school with problem-solving abilities (1992). However, few classrooms offer meaningful, challenging problems for young children (especially classrooms serving low-income students) and consequently never really help students improve and develop additional problem-solving abilities (Carey et al. 1995). In their model, teachers may pose a problem but start by giving children time to solve problems, recruit responses from students that ask not what the answer is but rather how they arrived at an answer, listen beyond the answer, listen to the children's comments and vocabulary, and invite alternate problem-solving strategies. In this process, children learn that multiple paths to solving problems are respected and encouraged. Instead of focusing on right answer thinking, children learn that divergent thinking is more likely to yield deeper understanding of mathematical concepts than simply an answer.

In each of the classrooms where teachers practiced culturally relevant pedagogy, students were in multiple instances encouraged and rewarded for developing more robust problem-solving repertoires, not only in mathematics but in all subject areas and classroom interactions as well.

HOW ESEA COULD BE A BETTER POLICY

The significant changes in public education that have transpired since the passage of the legislation and its subsequent reauthorizations reflect the dynamic and shifting environment in which we attempt to educate all students.

How People Learn

Since 1965 scholars of learning sciences have come to prominence with more robust theories of learning that have a profound impact on how education can take place (Bransford, Brown, and Cocking 2000). We are seeing an exponential growth in what we now know as the *learning sciences*. Instead of separate and distinct disciplinary domains, learning sciences pulls on cognitive psychological, social psychological, and cultural psychological foundations of human learning. Drawing on fields as diverse as psychology, anthropology, cognitive science, computer sciences, and applied linguistics, the learning sciences extend the scope of learning beyond the classroom to include informal learning environments such as the home, church, community, after school experiences, and peer networks. This new approach to learning and teaching demands different ways to think about curriculum design and pedagogical strategies. Although ESEA has been reauthorized six times, the last round ushering in what became known as No Child Left Behind, little attention has been given to pedagogical innovation. This is clearly an area in which ESEA can be improved.

Because of the growing income inequality in the society (the largest disparity in the highly technological Western or G-7 world) and the increasing resegregation of schools we now see more schools where ESEA funding is allotted schoolwide. These are characterized by concentrations of poverty, inexperienced teaching staffs, and increased mobility of both students and staff. Because the NCLB reauthorization was more focused on standardized test score results these schools often are known for their "drill and kill" approach to teaching and learning where schools function as "test prep" factories. By using more research from the learning sciences, the policy can offer more opportunity for teaching and learning innovation and exploration.

Another way ESEA could be improved is by paying close attention to the shifts in the teaching profession. We should be considering the impact of the proliferation of fast track alternative certification for teaching and learning. Programs such as Teach for America (TFA), Teach-Now, Troops to Teachers, and state-sponsored alternative certification almost exclusively produce teachers who are assigned to low-income schools. Fast-track alternative teaching programs are not new. The same year ESEA was passed, the Higher Education Act made provision for the Teacher Corps (Rogers 2009). Teacher Corps, another of Lyndon Johnson's War on Poverty programs, was designed to provide elementary and secondary teachers for low-income, hard-to-staff schools. Unlike many of today's alternative teacher education programs, Teacher Corps programs were developed in conjunction with higher education institutions and their local school district partners. Rogers described the program as an attempt to attract the "smartest" non-education majors to work in urban and rural schools. Unfortunately, many of the participants in the first cohort did come from education. The second cohort drew more male participants perhaps because of the built-in draft deferment. In many ways, today's alternative certification programs mimic the Teacher Corps model except that they are linked to more entrepreneurial, neoliberal perspectives that run counter to a notion of a public school system.

Another way ESEA could improve would be to factor in the ways that U.S. students will increasingly compete with students throughout the world. In 1957, the U.S. public school system received what it thought of as its first international wake-up call. Always proud of its attempt to offer free public education to almost all of its students (children with disabilities were regularly excluded from public schools before legislative changes), American public schooling was the envy of the world. However, once the Soviet Union launched a space satellite, the public discourse was centered on a need to improve U.S. schools. Although many programs and groups benefited from this increased emphasis on public schooling, no straight line could be drawn from the classroom to space exploration. Rather, historians of science have argued that the involvement of schools in the space race was merely a tactic to garner more support from the public for the scientists the United States already had (Rudolph 2002). But the tactic worked. A greater infusion of resources was funneled into the sciences, mathematics, world languages, and college loan support.

Today, the work of the Organization of Economic Cooperation and Development (OECD) has made international comparison of the educational status of nations a kind of gold standard. Interesting, the United Nations Education, Scientific, and Cultural Organization (UNESCO), established as the intellectual arm of the United Nations, has almost no clout in the discussion of education in Western, highly technological nations. Rather, UNESCO seems to be relegated to helping "poor" countries improve their schools and recruit more teachers. How the United States does on PISA (the international science measure) and TIMSS (the mathematics measure) have become the gauges to determine progress. Despite the United States' remaining decidedly in the middle of the pack on these measures over time, a sense of heighted alarm and urgency is now prevalent. ESEA was not concerned with international comparisons when it realized that the national system had too much internal inequality. Nations with the highest average scores on international comparative tests typically have the lowest variation in scores. Score gaps between children from low- and upper-income families are smaller in the highest performing countries. One of the emphases on improving federal policy could be on raising the performance of low-income children to that of international students in highly technological nations.

In addition to having ESEA attend to changes in the teaching profession, it seems important for demographers to help policymakers think seriously about how shifting population demographics can impact a changing public school landscape. Reproduction theorists have long argued that our public schools are operating exactly the way they were designed to work (see, for example, Apple 2011; Bowles and Gintis 2001). Middle-class and wealthy students are succeeding and poor children are failing. Such failure was tolerable they argue because there would always be a need for low-skilled, low-wage workers. However, the nation was not prepared for a global, interconnected economy that would require many more skilled and highly educated workers. It was not prepared for a world economy where manufacturing could be exported to factories and sweatshops where people earned pennies a day. It also was not prepared for a move to a bifurcated economy filled with "knowledge workers" and service workers, many of whom would earn minimum wage.

This demographic shift that produced many more low-skilled workers meant that the need for ESEA services would grow exponentially, especially when their numbers would accompany an exodus of middle-class families from urban areas who would elect to send their children to suburban or private schools. This intense concentration and growth of poverty is something ESEA can begin to consider in its reauthorization to ensure that all students experience school success.

CONCLUSION

The entire nation can and should celebrate the accomplishments of the Elementary and Secondary Education Act of 1965 and the political will to fight for its multiple reauthorizations. The act itself is a landmark in shaping the federal role in public schooling. But no law is perfect. The premise here is that ESEA, with all of its good intentions, experienced some significant fails. These include the failure to consider the assets and strengths of children and families from low-income circumstances and the failure to consider pedagogy or teaching expertise in the implementation of the act. Research on the resilience and resources of low-income families suggests that schools can engage with families beyond a deficit-based paradigm. Instead of presuming that professional educators know better, a reauthorized ESEA can open up opportunities for significant and meaningful parent and family engagement. Despite these failures, I am hopeful that future reauthorizations will and can take into account major changes in technology, teacher preparation, and increasing globalization that may radically reorient our thinking about public schooling.

This article began with a reference to the award-winning and celebrated children's program *Sesame Street* because of its link in time and intent to ESEA. But *Sesame Street* was not limited by the slow, ponderous ways of law. As a part of a nimble and creative industry, *Sesame Street* can and does change with the external social and cultural changes. It has taken up issues of disability, child abuse, and even AIDS in its national and international iterations. *Sesame Street* also pays close attention to pedagogy. Its rapid, attention-getting, commercial-like appeals to learning numbers and letters reflects an understanding that from an early age infants and toddlers will stop what they are doing to pay attention to a jingle or catchy tune. The program uses rhythm, rhyme, and repetition to teach both skills and concepts. Viewers learn how to make analogies and moral judgments as they acquire basic skills like counting and recognition of sound-symbol relationships. Unfortunately, this combination of conceptual and skill-based knowledge is woefully absent in many of the practices embedded in ESEA Title I programming.

Also, *Sesame Street* never characterized the homes and communities of its audience as deficient or lacking. By basing the program solidly in an urban community, the creators of *Sesame Street* were deliberate in emphasizing the strengths and resources of the urban community. The program never considered various family configurations as problematic or "wrong." Some characters had two parents, some had one, and some lived in extended family relations with grandparents and fictive kin. Community members on *Sesame Street* all were thought capable of both teaching and learning to enrich each other. The intergenerational relations and various family configurations were reminiscent of urban life in low-income communities.

However, with all of the wonderful assets that *Sesame Street* brought to young children in low-income urban communities, it had no way to exclude middle- and upper-income families from both benefiting from and building on what the program offered. For example, although low-income children could watch an hour of *Sesame Street* each day, middle-income and wealthy families could enhance the viewing hour with ancillary materials such as books, talking Muppets (like Tickle-me-Elmo), and later videos of the program. Although *Sesame Street* could help low- income students become ready for formal school settings, it also provided middle- and upper-income students with a boost given that their more highly educated parents were likely to create extensions that would extend their literacy and mathematics skills beyond those that *Sesame Street* offered.

The intent and results of the Elementary and Secondary Education Act of 1965 should not be minimized. The act represents a deliberate attempt through schooling to close the opportunity gap and pay down the education debt (Carter and Welner 2013; Ladson-Billings 2006). The problems that low-income families face, however, are broader and deeper than what schools can remedy. Issues of under- and unemployment, health disparities (from prenatal to dental, optical, auditory screenings, and increased childhood obesity), environmental threats (such as lead paint poisoning, rising asthma rates due to air pollution and vermin, and so on) and food insecurity (such as living in food deserts, neighborhood saturated with fast food restaurants, and a lack of access to fresh produce) all affect the education outcomes of children from low-income families. In addition, material lack is not the sole basis for the disparity. The limited access to political power is a major factor in closing down opportunity for children from low-income families. Without the ability to choose their representatives to city government and school boards, low-income families remain without a voice and disenfranchised when it comes to decision making that directly influences the educational lives of their children. My notion of an education debt asserts that despite legal or policy decisions such as school desegregation and funding equity, U.S. public schools have failed to fully implement either (Frankenberg and Taylor, this issue).

New Orleans is a classic case of low-income disenfranchisement. The catastrophe of Hurricane Katrina allowed neoliberal interests to make wholesale changes in low-income communities. Firing all public school teachers meant that those with long-standing community relationships would not be a part of rebuilding the school system. By creating market-like school choice, the poorest of the poor were more likely to be relegated to the least desirable schools. The entire concept of neighborhood schools was destroyed for low-income families. Conversely, middle-income and wealthy communities continue to have access to the best school facilities, the best curricular offerings, and the best teachers. What has been advertised as choice is not choice for all (Carr 2013; Dixson 2011). As was true with traditional school patterns, the "new" approaches to schooling, creating something called portfolio districts, creates winners and losers. And, through the use of market language, these portfolios include a variety of "investments" where "losers" are dumped and "winners" receive even greater investments. However, it is no surprise that the poorest children continue to attend "loser" schools (Dowdall 2011). Their schools lack adequate physical facilities, strong instructional leadership, well-prepared teachers, expansive curricular offerings, and positive home-school-community relationships.

Omnibus bills like ESEA always require refinement and adjustment. We must presume that policymakers can learn from past practices and previous mistakes. The goals of ESEA are the "right" goals. The anthropological contribution to a policy issue such as ESEA can be a more in-depth look at the resources and strengths of the culture or cultures the policy intends to affect. Instead of focusing on what a policy can do for a group, anthropological perspectives may force the question of what a policy can do with a group. We should be doing everything we can to close the education opportunity gap between low-income and middle-income communities. More recently, districts and municipalities have sought legal remedies for narrowing resource differentials between wealthy and poor districts (see for example, *Abbeville County School District et al. v. the State of South Carolina*, 335 S.C. 58, 68, 515 S. E.2d 535, 540, 1999 and *Campaign for Fiscal Equity v. State of New York*, 86, NY 2nd 306, 1995). Because the nation seems to have little appetite for pursuing school desegregation cases, cases have been brought in New York and South Carolina to argue for funding equity. If we cannot get commitments to dismantle "separate and unequal" some communities are willing to settle for a version of "separate and equal funding." Ultimately, we will need policy, personnel, and practices that show our most vulnerable students how to get to *Sesame Street*.

REFERENCES

Apple, Michael W. *Education and Power*, 3rd ed. New York: Routledge, 2011.

Association for the Anthropology of Policy (ASAP). 2012. "Mission." *ASAP*. Available at: http://www.aaanet.org/sections/asap/goals/ (accessed July 8, 2015).

Au, Kathryn H., and Alice Kawakami. 1985. "Talk Story and Learning to Read." *Language Arts Journal* 62(4): 406–11.

Blair, Elizabeth. 2014. "From 'Good Times' to 'Honey Boo-Boo:' Who Is Poor on TV?" NPR, August 5. Available at: http://www.npr.org/2014/08/05/337779030/from-good-times-to-honey-boo-boo-who-is-poor-on-tv (accessed October 29, 2014).

Borman, Geoffrey D., and Laura T. Rachuba. 2001. "Academic Success Among Poor and Minority Students: An Analysis of Competing Models of School Effects." Report no. 52. Washington, D.C.: Center for Research on the Education of Students Placed at Risk. Available at: http://www.csos.jhu.edu/crespar/techReports/report52.pdf (accessed July 27, 2015).

Bowles, Samuel, and Herbert Gintis. 2001. "Schooling in Capitalist America, Revisited." Paper presented at the annual meeting of the American Educational Research Association, Seattle (March 2001).

Boykin, A. Wade, and Caryn T. Bailey. 2000. "The Role of Cultural Factors in School Relevant Cognitive Functioning: Description of Home Environmental Factors, Cultural Orientations, and Learning Preferences." Report no. 43. Washington, D.C.: Center for Research on the Education of Students Placed at Risk.

Bransford, John D., Ann L. Brown, and Rodney R. Cocking, eds. 2000. *How People Learn: Brain, Mind, Experience, and School*. Washington, D.C.: National Academy Press.

Brophy, Jere, and Thomas L. Good. 1970. "Teachers' Communication of Differential Expectations for Children's Classroom Performance." *Journal of Educational Psychology* 61 (1970): 365–74.

Carey, Deborah A., Elizabeth Fennema, Thomas P. Carpenter, and Megan L. Franke. 1995. "Equity and Mathematics Education." In *New Directions for Equity in Mathematics Education*, edited by Walter G. Secada, Elizabeth Fennema, and Lisa Byrd, 93–125. New York: Cambridge University Press.

Carpenter, Thomas P., and Elizabeth Fennema. 1992. "Cognitively Guided Instruction: Building on the Knowledge of Students and Teachers." In *Curriculum Reform: The Case of Mathematics in the United States*, edited by Walter G. Secada, 457–70. Special issue of *International Journal of Research in Education*. Elmsford, N.Y.: Pergamon, 1992.

Carr, Sarah. 2013. *Hope Against Hope: Three Schools, One City, and the Struggle to Educate America's Children*. New York: Bloomsbury.

Carter, Prudence L., and Kevin G. Welner, eds. 2013. *Closing the Opportunity Gap: What America Must Do to Give Every Child an Even Chance*. New York: Oxford University Press.

Christian, Marcelle D., and Oscar Barbarin. 2001. "Cultural Resources and Psychological Adjustment of African American Children: Effects of Spirituality and Racial Attribution." *Journal of Black Psychology* 27(1): 43–63.

Cohen, Elizabeth G., and Rachel A. Lothan. 1997. *Working for Equity in Heterogeneous Classrooms: Sociological Theory in Practice*. New York: Teachers College Press.

Collins, Patricia Hill. 2008. *Black Feminist Thought: Knowledge, Consciousness and the Politics of Empowerment*. New York: Routledge.

Commission on Excellence in Education. 1983. *A Nation at Risk: The Imperative for Educational Reform*. Washington, D.C.: National Commission on Excellence in Education.

Dowdall, Emily. 2011. "Closing Public Schools in Philadelphia: Lessons from Six Urban Districts." Philadelphia, Pa.: Pew Charitable Trusts.

Delpit, Lisa D. 1986. "Skills and Other Dilemmas of a Progressive Black Educator." *Harvard Educational Review* 56(4): 379–86.

———. 1988. "The Silenced Dialogue: Power and Pedagogy in Educating Other People's Children." *Harvard Educational Review* 58(3): 280–99.

Dixson, Adrienne. 2011. "Whose Choice? A Critical Race Perspective on Charter Schools." In *Neo-Liberal Deluge: Hurricane Katrina, Late Capitalism and the Remaking of New Orleans*, edited by Cedric Johnson. Minneapolis: University of Minnesota Press.

Erickson, Fred, and Gerald Mohatt. 1982. "Cultural Organization of Participation Structures in Two Classrooms of Indian Students." In *Doing the Ethnography of Schooling*, edited by George Spindler. New York: Holt, Rinehart & Winston.

Foster, Herbert L. 1986. *Ribbin' Jivin' and Playin' the Dozens*. Cambridge, Mass.: Ballinger.

Foster, Michele. 1998. *Black Teachers on Teaching*. New York: The New Press.

Geertz, Clifford. 1977. *The Interpretation of Cultures*. New York: Basic Books.

Gibson, Margaret A., and John U. Ogbu, eds. 1991. *Minority Status and Schooling: A Comparative Study of Immigrants and Involuntary Minorities*. New York: Garland Publishing.

Gutierrez, Kris D., and Barbara Rogoff. 2003. "Cultural Ways of Learning: Individual Traits or Repertoires of Practice." *Educational Researcher* 32(5): 19–25.

Heath, Shirley Brice. 1983. *Ways with Words: Language, Life and Work in Communities and Classrooms*. New York: Cambridge University Press.

Kearney, Melissa S., and Philip B. Levine. 2015. "Early Childhood Education by MOOC: Learning from Sesame Street." *NBER* working paper no. 21229. Cambridge, Mass.: National Bureau of Economics Research.

Ladson-Billings, Gloria. 1995a. "Toward a Theory of Culturally Relevant Pedagogy." *American Educational Research Journal* 32(3): 465–91.

———. 1995b. *The Dreamkeepers: Successful Teachers of African American Children*. San Francisco: Jossey Bass.

———. 2006. "From the Achievement Gap to the Education Debt: Understanding Achievement in U.S. Schools." *Educational Researcher* 35(1): 3–12.

Lambert, Bruce. 1997. "At 50, Levittown Contends with Its Legacy of Bias." *New York Times*, December 28. Available at: http://www.nytimes.com/1997/12/28/nyregion/at-50-levittown-contends-with-its-legacy-of-bias.html (accessed June 13, 2015).

Mullin, Walter J., and Miguel Arce. 2008. "Resilience of Families Living in Poverty." *Journal of Family Social Work* 11(1): 424–40.

Ogbu, John U. 1978. *Minority Education and Caste: The American System in Cross-Cultural Perspectives*. San Diego, Calif.: Academic Press.

———. 1987. "Variability in Minority School Performance: A Problem in Search of an Explanation." *Anthropology and Education Quarterly* 18(4): 312–34.

Orthner, Dennis K., Hinkley Jones-Sanpei, and Sabrina Williamson. 2004. "The Resilience and Strengths of Low-Income Families." *Family Relations* 53(2)(March): 159–67.

Payne, Ruby K. 2005. *A Framework for Understanding Poverty*, 4th ed. Highlands, Tex.: aha! Process.

Reardon, Sean. 2011. "The Widening Achievement Gap Between the Rich and the Poor: New Evidence and Possible Explanations." In *Whither Opportunity? Rising Inequality, Schools, and Children's Life Chances*, edited by Greg J. Duncan and Richard Murnane. New York: Russell Sage Foundation.

Rist, Ray C. 1970. "Student Social Class and Teachers' Expectations: The Self-Fulfilling Prophecy in Ghetto Schools." *Harvard Educational Review* 40(3): 411–50.

Rogers, Bethany. 2009. "'Better' People, Better Teaching: The Vision of the National Teacher Corps, 1965–1968." *History of Education Quarterly* 49(3): 347–72.

Rosenfeld, Gerry. 1983. *"Shut Those Thick Lips:" A Study of Slum School Failure*. Long Grove, Ill.: Waveland Press.

Rudolph, John L. 2002. *Scientists in the Classroom: The Cold War and the Reconstruction of American Science Education*. New York: Palgrave.

Ryan, Allison M., and Helen Patrick. 2001. "The Classroom Social Environment and Changes in Adolescents' Motivation and Engagement in Middle School." *American Educational Research Journal* 38(2): 437–60.

Shulman, Lee S. 1987. "Knowledge and Teaching: Foundations of the New Reform." *Harvard Educational Review* 57(1): 1–21.

Smedley, Audrey, and Brian D. Smedley. 1993. *Race in North America: Origin and Evolution of a Worldview*. Boulder, Colo.: Westview Press.

Spindler, George, and Louise Spindler, eds. 1994. *Pathways to Cultural Awareness: Cultural Therapy with Teachers and Students*. Thousand Oaks, Calif.: Corwin Press.

Trueba, Henry T. 1988. *Raising Silent Voices: Education the Linguistic Minorities for the 21st Century*. New York: Heinle ELT.

———. 1990. *Cultural Conflict and Adaptation: The Case of Hmong Children in American Society*. New York: Routledge.

Weinstein, Meryl G., Leanna Stiefel, Amy Ellen Schwartz, and Luis Chalico. 2009. "Does Title I Increase Spending and Improve Performance? Evidence from New York City." *Institute for Education and Social Policy* working paper no. 09-09. New York: New York University.

Wilcox, Kathleen. 1982. "Differential Socialization in the Classroom: Implications for Equal Opportunity." In *Doing the Ethnography of Schooling*, edited by George Spindler. Prospect Heights, Ill.: Waveland.

Williams, Joseph M. 2011. "Home, School, and Community Factors that Contribute to the Educational Resilience of Urban African American High School Graduates from Low-Income Single-Parent Families." Ph.D. diss. University of Iowa.

Charting the Relationship of English Learners and the ESEA: One Step Forward, Two Steps Back

PATRICIA GÁNDARA

The signing of the Bilingual Education Act in 1968 presumed that the federal government had a role to play in the equitable education of immigrant and English learner students, who had been largely invisible to most of the country. Initial language of the Act was intended to build on these students' assets. Nonetheless, the language that survived in the BEA limited its effectiveness and created ongoing challenges for educators, including an ever-changing definition of the goals and purposes of funding; a deficit rather than an asset-based orientation that cast English learners as "remedial students"; unresolved tensions between the goals of desegregation and bilingual education; and fluctuating and inadequate attention to the capacity development needs of the field. The latest iteration of the ESEA removed the BEA from federal legislation altogether, failed to resolve any of the ongoing issues, and reinforced the remedial framing of ELs, arguably placing them at even greater educational risk.

Keywords: bilingual education, Bilingual Education Act, English (language) learners, Title VII, Title III

In 1968, two and a half years after President Lyndon Johnson signed the Elementary and Secondary Education Act (ESEA) into law, it was amended to add Title VII, the Bilingual Education Act (BEA). This was the first time that the federal government had acknowledged that English learners—at that time termed limited English-speaking (LES) or limited English proficient (LEP) students[1]—experienced unique challenges in meeting the same educational goals as English-speaking children, and that the federal government should play a role in helping them meet those challenges. Thus not only had the federal government stepped up to help equalize resources for children with significant economic need, but it had also declared through the new Title VII that it would also address the needs of children who did not speak English or did not speak it well. The passage of the BEA was an important turning point in the role of the federal government, yet several aspects of the new law and the debates that shaped it limited its effectiveness and created ongoing challenges for educators. Those challenges include an ever-changing definition of the goals and purposes of the funding, making it difficult to sustain bilingual programs over time; a deficit

---

Patricia Gándara is co-director of the Civil Rights Project at the University of California, Los Angeles.

Direct correspondence to: Patricia Gándara, gandara@gseis.ucla.edu, University of California, Los Angeles, Graduate School of Education & Information Studies, 3329 Moore Hall, Box 951521, Los Angeles, CA 90095.

1. Labels for students who are not proficient in English have changed over time, including LES (limited English-speaking), LEP (limited English proficient), EL (English learners), ELL (English-language learners), Emerging Bilinguals, among others. Here, EL and LEP are used interchangeably to refer to this population, as many government documents used and continue to use LEP, though the term is no longer preferred in the field.

rather than an asset-based orientation that cast English learners (ELs) as remedial students; unresolved tensions between the goals of desegregation and bilingual education; and fluctuating and inadequate attention to the capacity development needs of the field.

Because the BEA was framed as targeting poverty as much as language needs, only children living in homes with an income below $3,000 and from homes where English was not spoken were allowed to receive the benefits, and the targeted children could not include English speakers. Thus, if programs were to be designed to benefit only LEP students who were also poor, it required that the English learners be separated from their nonpoor and English-speaking peers. Hence the funds were generally restricted to linguistically and economically segregated schools (Moran 1988). The law thus perhaps inadvertently supported the segregation of EL students. This would set the stage for an ongoing tension between segregation and bilingual education that would resonate through the years, and be revisited each time Title VII was reauthorized.

Arguments for serving only LEP students included that the impact of the limited funding should not be diluted by serving children who did not need language assistance. In the early years of the BEA, the benefits were especially modest: no funds were appropriated in 1968, and in the following year only $7.5 million were provided. Rachel Moran asserts that between 1968 and 1973 no more than $5 to $6 per child in need was appropriated (1988). Thus it was understandable that many educators would want to preserve these modest funds for children with the greatest need. Of course, arguments in favor of including non-LEP students primarily focused on reducing the linguistic isolation and segregation of EL students, and on the role they could serve as important English-language models. Research since that time has tended to support this belief, though education policy has not generally reflected it (Gass, Mackey, and Pica 1998; Gifford and Valdés 2006).

The first iteration of the BEA only sought to provide very modest grant in aid funds to "carry out new and imaginative elementary and secondary school programs designed to meet these special educational needs" (Title VII, 1968, Sec. 702, 81 stat. at 816). Thus it was intentionally vague in its goals and purposes, and carefully crafted to not appear to usurp local authority. Although titled the Bilingual Education Act, the law actually skirted any definition of bilingual education. Senator Yarborough of Texas, the bill's chief sponsor, had gone on record in 1967 as wanting "the creation of bilingual-bicultural programs, the teaching of Spanish as a native language" "designed to impart to Spanish-speaking students a knowledge and pride in their culture" (Schneider 1976, 22). This was a far cry from the compensatory education frame of the ESEA, which sought to remediate the deficits wrought by poverty. But, as Natalia Mehlman Petrzela recounts, passage of the bill depended on its fitting into the overall objectives of the ESEA and not challenging the popular notion of the melting pot into which immigrants were expected to relinquish their distinctive cultural features (2010). As Moran notes, "The vague statement of purpose masked fundamental differences over whether the programs were designed to promote assimilation by overcoming a language 'deficiency' or were intended to foster pluralism by acknowledging a linguistic asset" (1988, 1273). The definition and goals of the program under the ESEA would continue to be debated in Congress and to create confusion and instability in the funding of programs at the state level.

Finally, in good part because the goals and purposes of bilingual education were left ill defined, it was assumed that good educators could simply come up with a strong program out of whole cloth to support their English learners. But in fact teachers had not been trained to provide bilingual instruction, good materials and curriculum had not been developed, and both basic and applied research on effective practice was just beginning in the United States. In other words, no capacity had been built to mount the programs in the early years of the act, and the meager funds appropriated were supposed to be used for developing "innovative" programs. Yet there was little to no infrastructure with which to innovate.

REAUTHORIZATIONS AND THE EVOLVING LEGISLATION

The first reauthorization of the BEA came in 1974 and clarified some of the issues left vague in the initial writing of the law. It specifically incorporated language to address equal educational opportunity and linked it to bilingual education programs: "the Congress declares it the policy of the United States to establish equal educational opportunity for all children (a) to encourage the establishment and operation . . . of education programs using bilingual education practices, techniques, and methods" (Title VII, 1974, Sec. 702[a]). Bilingual education was defined as "instruction given in, and study of, English, and, *to the extent necessary* to allow a child to progress effectively through the educational system, the native language" (Wiese and Garcia 1998, 5 [emphasis added]). This would set the tone for two decades, defining bilingual instruction as *transitional*, use of the first language being only a temporary means to another end. The 1974 reauthorization also importantly removed the poverty requirement and allowed English-speaking children to enroll in bilingual education programs to "acquire an understanding of the cultural heritage of the children of limited English-speaking ability" (Title VII, 1974, Sec. 703 [a][4][B]). Thus, this version of the BEA also attempted to promote cultural understanding and to reduce the segregation implied in the implementation of a program that could only serve poor LEP children. Another addition to the BEA in 1974 was significant: a graduate fellowship program for study in the field of training teachers for bilingual education programs, a clear acknowledgment that educators were expected to mount programs without any pipeline of qualified candidates to implement them. The 1974 reauthorization also included a program to support the development of materials to be used in bilingual programs.

This honeymoon for bilingual education, however, was to be short lived. The civil rights era was coming to a close and conservative forces sought to restore the old order. The programs would quickly come under attack just as desegregation efforts were also being turned back by increasingly conservative courts and presidential administrations (Gándara, Moran, and Garcia 2004). In the 1978 reauthorization, support for bilingual education would begin to evaporate. Language was added to the act to emphasize acquisition of English skills over bilingualism, and by the 1984 reauthorization the legislation made clear that only transitional bilingual education was favored—75 percent of all funds had to be expended on such programs. The goal of the Bilingual Education Act was now to provide "structured English-language instruction, and, to the extent necessary to allow a child to achieve competence in the English language, instruction in the child's native language" (Title VII, 1984, Sec. 703 [a][4][A]). That is, the native language was to be used only insofar as it furthered the goal of English acquisition. It is also important that because English was the goal, little was mentioned and nothing measured with respect to primary language achievement. Integration of these students into the mainstream was assumed as a by-product of becoming more Americanized through acquisition of English.

In a seminal 1984 article describing the orientations or philosophies of policymakers regarding language policies, Richard Ruiz (1984) contends three basic orientations: language as a problem, something that needs to be fixed; language as a right, something that must be legally protected; and language as a resource, something that is an asset. By creating legislation that casts language as a problem, it results in practices that focus neither on social justice (a right), nor on asset development (a resource). Clearly, by 1984, if not before, languages other than English were seen as a problem.

In 1984, the door was also opened for purported bilingual programs that did not incorporate a primary language at all: Special Alternative Instructional Programs (SAIPs) were written into the law and 4 percent of funds were to go to these programs. In the 1988 reauthorization, the door was opened further to nonbilingual programs, increasing the funding to 25 percent for SAIPs and limiting the time that a student could spend in a bilingual program: "No student may be enrolled in a bilingual program . . . for a period of more than 3 years" (Title VII, 1988, Sec. 7021 [d][3][A]). This effectively ended the notion that bilingual education could be used for the purpose of developing bilingual individuals because the program was designed to end as soon as enough English was acquired. No research supported the idea that enough English to keep pace with native English speakers in academic subjects could be acquired within a maximum of three years. In fact, the research has long since concluded otherwise (Weise and Garcia 1998). Many factors determine how quickly a student becomes proficient in a second language, including prior schooling, age, parents' socioeconomic status, contact with the language outside of school, and quality of education, but as a general rule researchers have converged on the finding that it takes at least five to seven years to develop mastery of academic English (Hakuta, Butler, and Witt 2000).

During the Clinton (Democratic) administration, the march away from primary language instruction took an about face. The 1994 reauthorization of the ESEA, under the title Improving America's Schools Act (IASA), retained Title VII but changed its focus considerably. This time an emphasis on bilingualism was written into the law. Although it actually allowed the 25 percent cap on funding of SAIPs to be lifted if districts could show they were not able to mount a bilingual program, this version of Title VII gave "priority to applications which provide for the development of bilingual proficiency both in English and another language for all participating students" (Title VII, 1994, Sec. 7116[i][1]). By including "all participating students," the law invoked the possibility that ELs could be studying alongside English speakers, breaking down their isolation and providing a potential asset for all students. With support to build a cadre of well-prepared teachers, instructional materials, and pedagogical strategies that could equalize education for English learners, it appeared that support for bilingual instruction was back. However this was not to be, as the pendulum would again swing back with the next reauthorization of the ESEA in 2001.

Although support for the BEA fluctuated, its passage probably helped spur the development of policy in the states. Whereas before 1968 no state had a pro-bilingual education policy on the books (Moran 1988), by 1983 all fifty permitted bilingual education and nine required some form of dual language instruction (Ovando and Collier 1985).

HISTORIC TRENDS IN EDUCATION OF ENGLISH LEARNERS

Bilingual education was not new to the United States at the time of the passage of the BEA. In fact, during the history of the nation it had thrived in many parts of the country, and especially in the Midwest. By the end of the nineteenth century, about a dozen states had passed pro-bilingual laws (Kloss 1998). However, an unprecedented wave of immigration to the country and a war with Germany (the language group with the most bilingual schools in the United States) in the first decades of the twentieth century brought a swift end to pro-bilingual education policies. Americanization became the policy regarding children of immigrants and included transitioning them to English as rapidly as possible. Speaking a language other than English was inconsistent with the American melting pot.

The Immigration and Nationality Act of 1965, which was signed into law the same year as the ESEA, would launch a stream of immigration that would begin to change the face of the nation. There had long been large pockets of children who did not speak English along the southern border and throughout the Southwest, a legacy of the war with Mexico in 1848, which had incorporated a third of the landmass of Mexico and its citizens into the United States. These children, however, remained invisible to most of the country.

The only immigrants that were highly visible in the late 1950s and early 1960s were Cubans fleeing the Castro regime. They were warmly received by the American public in the anticommunist tenor of the times and legislation was quickly passed to aid their integration into American society. The Cuban migration to South Florida had an important impact on the way that bilingual instruction came to be viewed. Unlike the Mexicans of the Southwest in almost every way (such as wealth, status, education, race) except language, the Cubans established bilingual schools where their children could learn in two languages while they waited to return to the Spanish-speaking island as soon as Castro was deposed. The Coral

Way School, the first established to meet the needs of the Cuban children, became a model of bilingual education for the nation, and it clearly supported maintenance of the Spanish language.

A BRIEF OVERVIEW OF THE RESEARCH ON PROGRAMS FOR ENGLISH LEARNERS

Bilingual programs has often been used as an umbrella term for all programs serving ELs, even those in which no primary language is used (Lessow-Hurley 2004). Thus the first study commissioned by the Department of Education to examine the effectiveness of bilingual education was conducted by American Institutes for Research in 1977 and 1978 (Danoff 1978). It compared students in thirty-eight Title VII programs with similar students in English as a Second Language (presumably English only) classrooms and found no particular impact of the bilingual programs on test scores. The study was criticized by many researchers for including programs in the two groups solely on the basis of program labels without examining the actual educational treatment provided or controlling for differences in the students assigned to the programs (August and Hakuta 1998; Willig 1985). This and other methodological problems left the findings of the study in significant dispute. Perhaps most important, however, the study paid little attention to the fundamental questions of teacher skill and preparedness, curriculum, materials, and pedagogy, and it tested differences after only a few months of exposure to the programs.

A second, large-scale comparative study was commissioned, again by the Department of Education, about a decade later. Conducted by David Ramirez and his colleagues (1991), it was much more complex and involved a four-year comparison of English immersion, early-exit transitional bilingual (usually lasting no more than three years), and late-exit bilingual programs (normally continued through the end of elementary grades and focusing on biliteracy) on various achievement outcomes in both English and Spanish. The researchers were careful to examine the instruction provided in each, and the time dedicated to instructing in each language and in eliciting language from students, as well as teacher characteristics and pedagogical strategies. Unfortunately, the researchers found significant differences in the students assigned to each program type, late-exit students being much more low income and having a significantly lesser chance of having attended preschool—all characteristics not controlled in the nonrandomly assigned classrooms. Also, programs could not usually be compared with others in the same district or school (because they did not exist) so that school and district effects were likely powerful contributors to uncontrolled differences among the groups (Meyer and Fienberg 1992). Moreover, very heavy attrition of students called many of the results into question. Still, the researchers found a small positive difference in first grade reading outcomes for the early-exit bilingual model over the English immersion, but overall no significantly different outcomes for the three groups of students. The researchers did, however, note that the trend lines for test scores were in a steep upward trajectory for the bilingually educated students at the point of termination of the study at fourth grade. Longitudinal studies since that time find that bilingual and dual language program test scores tend to exceed those of English-only programs at about fifth grade (see, for example, Genesee et al. 2006; Umansky and Reardon 2014; Valentino and Reardon 2015). Among the more influential smaller studies during the period was the one Keith Baker and Adriana de Kanter conducted in 1981, in which they reviewed twenty-eight studies that met sufficient methodological rigor to be included in their qualitative analysis of the programs: yes, the evaluation found positive effects for bilingual instruction or, no, it did not. No attempt was made to quantify the degree of effectiveness, and they had no firsthand knowledge of the "treatments." This very widely cited study found that "the case for the effectiveness of transitional bilingual education is so weak that exclusive reliance on this instructional method is clearly not justified" (Baker and de Kanter 1981, 1).[2] In other words, they did not find a

---

2. A Google search returns 324 citations to this study in other published articles.

definitively superior outcome for either of the two methods tested. Yet this study, coupled with the American Institutes for Research (AIR) study, had a very important impact on the language of the reauthorization of Title VII in 1984. The new amendments included language that specifically opened up funding for English-only programs; it was no longer necessary to incorporate the students' primary language to gain funding under the Bilingual Education Act.

A NEW GENERATION OF RESEARCH ON BILINGUALISM AND ITS BENEFITS

Both the knowledge base regarding language acquisition and methodological techniques for studying it have developed substantially over the last several decades. Newer studies address many of the limitations of earlier research. In a best evidence meta-analytic study, Robert Slavin and Alan Cheung find that among the seventeen studies that met their strict methodological criteria for inclusion, thirteen favored bilingual programs (all Spanish-English), and four found no differences (2005).[3] This study, in contrast to the earlier Baker and de Kanter study, incorporated quantitative methods to determine the actual effect sizes of the treatments. The effect size for the averaged score differences was between 0.33 and 0.45, indicating a medium positive effect. Across both the Slavin and Cheung study and four other rigorous meta-analyses reviewed by Diane August and her colleagues, the researchers find "differences in favor of native-language instruction, with effect sizes ranges from small to moderate" (August, Goldenberg, and Rueda 2010, 143). They also note that the better the technical quality of the studies, the larger were the effect sizes. In a synthesis of the most rigorous research on reading instructional approaches for English learners, Claude Goldenberg also concludes that "teaching students to read in their first language promotes higher levels of reading achievement in English" (2008, 14). This finding is often thought to be counterintuitive, though it is well supported by theory as well as by data (Durgunoğlu, Nagy, and Hancin-Bhatt 1993; Verhoeven 1994). The theories underlying this finding are that of *transfer*, knowledge acquired in one language is transferred to additional languages as they are acquired, and *comprehensible input*, individuals learn more efficiently when they can understand at least part of what is being communicated (Cummins 1981; Krashen 1987).

Most evaluation research on bilingual education has focused narrowly on short-term outcomes for reading and sometimes math in English only. Very little attention has been paid to longer-term effects or to other potential outcomes. In fact, many of the studies that have found no difference or less positive effects for bilingual instruction have been based on very short-term analyses. Fred Genesee and his colleagues, reporting on a synthesis of research on English learners, note that

> Evaluations conducted in the early years of a program (Grades K-3) typically reveal that students in bilingual education scored below grade level . . . [but] Almost all evaluations of students at the end of elementary school and in middle and high school show that the educational outcomes of bilingually educated students, especially those in late-exit and two-way programs, were at least comparable to and usually higher than their comparison peers. (Genesee et al. 2006, 201)

A recent study that followed thousands of students in one large school district in transitional bilingual (aka early exit), dual language bilingual (longer term, incorporating English speakers and English learners), and English-only programs beginning in kindergarten and following them into high school found that the EL students who had remained in bilingual instruction, and especially dual language bilingual programs, outperformed the students in English only instruction on all measures. Specifically, they ultimately reclassified to English proficient at higher rates and scored higher on both English-language arts and measures of English proficiency (Umansky and Reardon 2014).

---

3. A best evidence meta-analytic study is one that uses strict methodological criteria for inclusion, eliminating those studies that do not meet these standards.

With respect to outcomes other than test scores or English proficiency, the body of research on a host of outcomes is large and growing. Ellen Bialystok and her colleagues find in a series of innovative studies that bilingually educated students have greater cognitive flexibility, working memory, and executive functioning, such as concentration (Bialystok 2001; Bialystok and Majumder 1998; Bialystok and Craik 2010). Alejandro Portes and Lingxin Hao find that bilingual students have more cohesive family relations and fewer behavior problems in school (2002). They attribute this, as have others, to greater communication and parental authority fostered by parents and children communicating in the same language. Lucrecia Santibañez and Maria Estela Zárate, analyzing longitudinal data from the Educational Longitudinal Study (ELS) of the Department of Education, find that students from bilingual homes who maintain their bilingualism into high school are more likely to go to college than those who lose the home language, and that bilingual Latinos are more likely to go to four-year colleges (2014).[4] Rubén Rumbaut, in analyses of two longitudinal data sets with more than six thousand subjects from the southern California region, finds that those students from immigrant backgrounds who maintain bilingual skills are less likely to drop out of high school and more likely to secure higher level positions in the workforce, and to earn more at those jobs than monolinguals (2014). Most of these studies also find that the benefits of bilingualism increase with the level of fluency the individual has in both languages (Gándara 2015). These findings call attention to the need to be more specific about the goals of instructional programs for English learners when comparing outcomes. If the goal is simply oral English proficiency, it may not matter greatly which program is provided as long as the quality is high. However, if educators are concerned about a host of other potential outcomes, research suggests that bilingual instruction may be desirable, at least as an option.

LEGAL RIGHTS OF ENGLISH LEARNERS

Educational policies for the instruction of English learners are created in the courts and through administrative regulations as well as by acts of Congress, and the BEA has proved a catalyst for some of these rights. (Sometimes they are also created at the ballot box, as in the anti-bilingual initiatives that were voted on in California, Arizona, and Massachusetts between 1998 and 2002.) The Office for Civil Rights (OCR) has played an active role in advocating for the rights of EL students to receive appropriate services. It first entered the fray in interpreting the national origin clause of the Title VI of the Civil Rights Act of 1964 as prohibiting discrimination based on language. This stance remains the law of the land today. Following on the passage of the BEA, in 1970 OCR issued a memorandum that came to be known as the May 25th Memorandum, putting school districts on notice that they "must take affirmative steps to rectify the language deficiency in order to open its instructional program to these [LEP] students" (Office for Civil Rights 1970). The memorandum also included notice that districts would be reviewed for compliance and would have to prove they had such a program in place and that it did not operate as an educational dead end. OCR was highly conscious of the segregative potential of programs that grouped ELs separately and so included that the ELs' needs should be met "as soon as possible."

In 1973, the Supreme Court ruled in *Keyes v. School District No.1* (13 U.S. 189) that the Denver schools must provide relief from segregation for "Hispano" students as well as for blacks. In 1975 the district court, to which *Keyes* had been remanded to develop a desegregation plan, clarified the guarantee of a bilingual education program for the Latino students in its ruling (Moran 2013). The next critical event in the development of legal rights for English learners occurred in 1974 with the Supreme Court ruling, *Lau v. Nichols* (414 U.S. 563), in which 1,856 Chinese-speaking children in San Francisco argued that they were being

---

4. ELS data collection began in 2002 with students in the tenth grade and has now followed these young people to their mid-twenties, with the latest data collection occurring in 2012. Data used for this study were from the 2006 follow-up of approximately sixteen thousand students

denied an equal education because they could not understand the classroom instruction and no accommodations were made for their language difference. The Court ruled that the school district had to take affirmative steps to provide access to the same curriculum that English-speaking students received, but did not instruct the schools about how this should happen.

Days after the *Lau* ruling, Congress passed the Equal Educational Opportunities Act (EEOA), which helped clarify *Lau*, requiring school districts to "take appropriate action to overcome language barriers that impede equal participation by its students in its instructional programs." Appropriate action was defined by the Fifth Circuit in the 1981 *Castañeda v. Pickard* decision (648 F.2d 989), setting the three-prong standard that has survived, at least in theory, to the present and includes a program based on recognized theory; faithfully implemented according to the theory, including adequate resources for implementation; and that demonstrated effectiveness over time.

Finally, in 1982, the Supreme Court ruled against the state of Texas, which had passed a statute requiring undocumented children to pay the state for the costs of their public education. The Court found that "Public education has a pivotal role in maintaining the fabric of our society" and "the deprivation of education takes an inestimable toll on the social, economic, intellectual, and psychological well-being of the individual" (*Plyler v. Doe*, 457 U.S. 203). In other words, because the children found themselves in the United States through no fault of their own, to deprive them of an education because their parents could not afford to pay for it served no rational purpose. Although *Plyler* did not direct itself to the language education of the children, it clarified that all children within U.S. borders were to be provided with a public education at the state's expense, and it had to be an education that would overcome language barriers that impeded their equal participation in school, as already stipulated in *Lau v. Nichols* and in the EEOA.

THE UNDOING OF LEGAL RIGHTS

As Congress was redefining the BEA with each reauthorization, the rights for English learners that had been hard won through a series of court decisions were also being redefined. Congressional actions and court rulings would gradually come into alignment to undermine the protections that existed. Although *Lau v. Nichols* appeared to require that school districts provide access to the regular curriculum for all EL students, the right to sue a district for not providing this access was taken away from individuals in a 1983 Supreme Court decision. The Court found that Title VI of the Civil Rights Act authorized compensatory relief only for purposeful wrongs, not actions involving adverse effects, or "disparate impact." *Lau* suffered another blow in 2001 when the Court decided in *Alexander v. Sandoval* (532 U.S. 275) that there is no private right of action under Title VI disparate impact regulations. Private plaintiffs can sue only for intentional discrimination, which is virtually impossible to prove. As a result, if federal agencies are too overburdened, or not interested in filing an action, children are left without recourse under Title VI.

The loss of Title VI protections made the EEOA the best alternative to seek redress because it allows for private right of action. That is, an individual or a group of individuals can bring a case against a school district for failing to meet its obligations to provide equal access to the curriculum for its English learners. This is exactly what Miriam Flores did in 1992 in Arizona, claiming that the state did not invest enough funding in her education to make true access possible. In 2009, the case ended up in the Supreme Court, which ruled in *Horne v. Flores* (557 U.S. 433) that the federal court had overstepped its bounds in ordering the school district to increase its investment in the education of its English learners, as there was no rational relationship between the amount of funds expended and the quality of an instructional program. The Court effectively obviated the second prong of *Castañeda* requiring that schools provide sufficient resources to ensure faithful implementation of the program. The Court also added in dicta that in imposing a statewide requirement that schools serving English learners provide Structured English Immersion (SEI), Arizona had implemented a program that was "significantly more effective than bilingual education." This appeared to suggest that the state had also met the third prong—that a program must demonstrate its effectiveness over time. However, the Court's claim that SEI is more effective than bilingual instruction was not warranted by research (Martinez-Wenzl, Pérez, and Gándara 2012). Although the courts have attempted to rein in the legal protections for EL students, OCR has once again engaged the battle. On January 7, 2015, OCR and the Department of Justice released guidance for schools and districts on their civil rights obligations to EL students, reiterating the legal requirements under *Lau* and the EEOA.

A NEW ERA OF ESEA AND THE DISAPPEARANCE OF THE BEA

The last reauthorization of the ESEA came in 2001 with a bipartisan effort to set high standards for America's schools and to place accountability at the center of the framework. Titled the No Child Left Behind Act (NCLB), it declared that all children would be proficient in basic academic standards by the year 2014. Of course, because it has never been possible for all children to meet any particular goal, many educators immediately predicted its failure (Sunderman et al. 2004). This time, the reauthorization did another about face and eliminated the Bilingual Education Act altogether. In its place was a new Title III, renamed Language Instruction for Limited English Proficient and Immigrant Students. The Office of Bilingual Education and Minority Language Affairs established in 1974 as the arm of the Department of Health, Education, and Welfare (HEW) to deal with the implementation of the law disappeared. It was replaced by the Office of English Language Acquisition, Language Enhancement, and Academic Achievement for Limited English Proficient Students. This new name reflected the shift away from bilingualism as a goal and emphasized the perspective that EL students' defining characteristic is their lack of English proficiency.

Title III of NCLB states its purpose as "to help ensure that children who are limited English proficient, including immigrant children and youth, attain English proficiency, develop high levels of academic attainment in English, and meet the same challenging State academic content and student academic achievement standards as all children are expected to meet" (Title III, 2001, Sec. 3102 (1)). It aims to do this by providing "flexibility to implement language instruction educational programs, based on scientifically based research on teaching limited English proficient children, that the agencies believe to be the most effective for teaching English" (Title III, 2001, Sec. 3102 (9)). The focus of Title III is entirely on English proficiency outcomes and schools may use any method they "believe" is most effective for this purpose. Moreover, in the strict accountability system of NCLB, schools have had to show progress on three Annual Measurable Achievement Objectives (AMAOs) for their ELs to receive formula grants from the federal government. That is, unlike past practices in Title VII when funds were competitive, Title III provides funds on a formula basis, but the funds depend on achieving specific accountability goals.

AMAO 1 requires that districts and schools show measurable improvement in the percentage of ELs who "make progress" in learning English. Progress is to be defined by the state and varies widely among states. The 2010 evaluation of Title III accountability found that the range was between 20 percent and 85 percent of students achieving the state standard (Boyle et al. 2010). AMAO 2 requires that EL students make annual progress toward achieving English proficiency, which is generally described as the percent of students who achieve English proficiency. However, this measurement is also fraught with variability, because states can adopt their assessments and set their own standards for proficiency, so that as in AMAO 1, outcomes are dependent on where the states set the bar for proficiency. Finally, AMAO 3 requires that a set percentage of EL students achieve proficiency in math and English language arts, and now science using the same tests that all students are tested on under Title I. Thus, with respect to assessment requirements, ELs are governed by both Title I and Title III. Given that by definition ELs do not have enough command of English to be instructed in an English only setting without some kind of language support, it seems inconsistent to test them in English and have those scores count toward an evaluation of a school's or district's academic program. It is well established that tests given in English to students who do not have a good command of English are likely to be both unreliable and invalid (Abedi 2004; Abedi and Gándara 2006).

Title III acknowledged this problem:

> [ELs] shall be assessed in a valid and reliable manner and provided reasonable accommodations on assessments administered to such students under this paragraph, including, to the extent practicable, assessments in the language and form most likely to yield accurate data on what such students know and can do in academic content areas, until such students have achieved English language proficiency. (Title III. Sec. 1111[C][III])

In the following subsection, it is noted that this practice should normally continue for at least three years and on a case-by-case basis for up to five years. Yet this language has never been enforced. Across the nation, EL students have been subjected to tests in English as soon as a matter of months after enrolling in school (Menken 2010). With high stakes attached to these testing outcomes, some schools and districts have found themselves in a no-win situation.

In June 2005, nine school districts in California—the state that accounts for at least one-third of all English learners—and three statewide nonprofit organizations banded together under the lead district, Coachella Unified School District, to sue the state of California for failing to comply with the provisions of NCLB that ELs should be assessed in a valid and reliable manner. A survey of districts conducted for the court found that only 3 percent of students were actually provided with accommodations, and most accommodations provided to EL students were not of a kind that have been shown to have any particular impact on their ability to perform on a test they do not fully understand (Haertel 2007). It was also relevant that the state had already developed a Spanish version of the statewide achievement exam, which made "to the extent practicable" very possible at least for this one language group that comprises about 85 percent of the ELs in the state. Moreover, the expert who oversaw the development of the California Standards Test (CST) asserted in a declaration to the court that the test should not be used with students who did not speak English because it was specifically not designed for their use (Haertel 2007). Despite these arguments, in 2007 the plaintiffs lost the case. California has continued to test in English-only even though one-fourth of all students in the state are English learners, and predictably those schools with large numbers of EL students routinely fail to meet adequate yearly progress (AYP) (Bryant et al. 2008).

The consequences of low test scores that result in the subsequent sanctioning of schools with large numbers of EL students have pushed many districts to simply focus on quick-fix English drill programs that ignore the students' broader learning needs in an effort to raise their test scores in English (Menken 2010; Ravitch 2011). Maryann Zehr reported in 2007 that many schools were abandoning bilingual programs in favor of English-only instruction in order to meet the pressures of NCLB. In Arizona, state policy became four hours of English drill daily to the exclusion of other coursework such as science, math, social studies and other courses offered to mainstream students, in what is an apparent challenge to *Lau*. Some high school ELs have been unable to graduate with their class because of the requirement to take several hours of English drill daily (Gándara and Orfield 2012; Lillie et al. 2012).

NCLB's impact has not been entirely negative, however. It is widely believed that its focus on subgroups, and holding schools accountable for their achievement as well as that of their more advantaged students, was and is an important step forward in achieving more equitable educational opportunities. Without a light shining on the problems, no one was likely to pay attention. However, it is obvious that overall EL students have been more hurt than helped by the law. According to National Assessment of Educational Progress (NAEP) scores, they have made no appreciable progress toward closing the gaps with their non-EL peers since before NCLB was instituted and have often been stigmatized as the reason their schools have carried the label of failing (Novak and Fuller 2003).

Nationally, since 1996, the first year for which NAEP shows the gap trend lines for ELs, the gap has not closed for fourth grade math; in fact, over the last decade of NCLB, the gaps have begun to widen between ELs and all others. In 2003, the gap between English learners and English speakers in fourth grade mathematics was 23 points, in 2013 the gap had grown to 25 points; fourth grade reading showed a similar widening, 3 points, over the same period. Gaps at the eighth grade had grown even larger (NAEP 2014). At least from the perspective of math and reading score gaps nationally, educational achievement has not improved for English learners.

THE CURRENT STATE OF EDUCATION POLICY FOR ENGLISH LEARNERS

The legacy of the BEA remains even though the act itself has disappeared. The vagueness about the purposes of bilingual education, the language-as-problem orientation of the law, the failure to adequately address the capacity needs of schools, and the increasing segregation of English learners (programmatically as well in the schools they attend) continue to challenge the field. Ironically, as the research has converged on the many benefits of bilingualism, both for academic as well as for noncognitive outcomes, education policy appears to have moved in the opposite direction. Even while the secretary of education touts the importance of bilingualism—saying, it "is clearly an asset that these kids are coming to school with" that should be "maintained" and "that our kids don't grow up [bilingual] puts them at a competitive disadvantage"—the federal government actually has no policy to foster bilingualism and maintains no office dedicated to this goal (Maxwell 2013). The focus of the ESEA (NCLB) continues to be on the acquisition of only English, and as quickly as possible. This focus is embodied in the test-driven accountability of NCLB that holds children accountable on tests given in English before they actually know the language.

A group of the nation's foremost researchers on English learner education formed in 2010 to provide advice to Congress on the reauthorization of Title III of ESEA and those recommendations were updated in 2015.[5] A primary problem that the ELL Working Group identified was the lack of longitudinal data on EL students. Once ELs are redesignated as proficient in English, the school is required to track them for two years to ensure that they are progressing adequately without additional services, but no particular intervention is required if they are not, and after two years the students are absorbed into the mainstream. We do not know whether they flounder later, though indications are that this may be so (Slama 2014; Robinson 2011). Another area of concern the ELL Working Group highlighted was the need for enhanced training of teachers who serve EL students. Although NCLB requires that all children have a highly qualified or highly effective teacher, it is silent on what constitutes high qualifications for teachers of EL students. Because it does not, no policy focuses on recruiting teachers with specialized skills for the classrooms serving these students. Surveys suggest that this is the one area of instruction teachers feel most inadequately prepared to undertake (Editorial Projects in Education Research Center 2013; Gándara, Maxwell-Jolly, and Driscoll 2005). Some research suggests that the best qualified teachers are those who meet all the standard definitions of highly qualified and additionally are bilingual (Loeb, Soland, and Fox 2014; Hopkins 2013; de Jong and Harper 2005), but both research and policy are clearly lacking in this area. Moreover, financial support to train the individuals who prepare these highly qualified teachers has not been restored in the current version of the ESEA.

Because the emphasis at the federal level has been solely on the acquisition of English, the great majority of students are placed in temporary programs dedicated to that goal. Thus, a major debate has been raging across the country with respect to when to exit English learners from these special programs designed to teach them English. Some have argued that lowering the bar to program exit (reducing the number and level of test scores required to demonstrate English or subject

---

5. See The Working Group on ELL Policy 2015, available at: http://www.ellpolicy.org (accessed July 27, 2015).

matter proficiency) benefits these students by introducing them into the mainstream earlier (Hill, Weston, and Hayes 2014; Flores et al. 2009). Others have argued that the evidence that students actually gain greater access to high level coursework on exit is inconsistent (Robinson 2011), and that in fact many fall behind because they exit too early (Slama 2014). It would seem, however, that this debate has missed the point. If programs for English learners were truly strong, there should be no rush to exit them, and if the programs were actually additive, producing high-level skills in two languages, perhaps the students should never exit. Instead the debate has centered on how to more quickly remove students from programs under the assumption that they are stigmatizing, limit access to appropriate coursework, and retard student progress. This may all be true, and some evidence does suggest that it is (Callahan, Wilkinson, and Muller 2010), but one must ask: why not focus on strengthening the programs rather than avoiding them?

THE DEMOGRAPHIC IMPERATIVE

When the BEA was first signed into law, no accurate count of how many students needed services had been taken. Schools did not collect these data and actually had no standard or way to assess them. However, the Congress estimated, based on testimony by Bruce Gaarder at the Office of Education, that even in this period of historically low immigration, approximately three million students used a primary language other than English and needed such services (Moran 1988). Much has changed in the ensuing years. Today the population of ELs has mushroomed, in part because of the changes in immigration law. Since 1980, the number of people five years old and older who speak a language other than English at home in the United States has nearly tripled. Today more than sixty million people, some 20 percent of the total population, use another language at home. Two-thirds of these individuals speak Spanish, the next most common languages being Chinese, French, Tagalog, Vietnamese, and Korean (Ryan 2013). One in five students in American public schools comes from a home in which English is not the primary language, and about 10 percent of all students are designated as English learners at any given time (NCES 2014). Moreover, the overwhelming majority (estimated now as high as 90 percent) of these students are native-born Americans. This is no longer an issue that can be put on the back burner of education policy. But it can either be framed as a problem or a tremendous opportunity for this nation in a globalizing world.

LOOKING FORWARD

EL students are now found in virtually every state and in all the major cities of America, and they are the least likely of any subgroup to graduate high school (Callahan 2013) and rarely are they prepared to enroll in college (Martinez-Wenzl 2014). Today the challenges that ELs face have become a central issue for most large school districts in the country. The stakes are very high. Some studies have predicted that per capita income will decline substantially in the next decade in those states with high EL populations because of the failure to adequately educate these and other underrepresented students (National Center for Public Policy and Higher Education 2005; Kelly and Strawn 2011). California alone is predicted to be one million bachelor's degrees short of meeting its labor force needs in the next decade (Johnson and Sengupta 2009).

When the BEA was first conceived, Congress evidently believed that these students, who were faring so poorly in the nation's public schools, could be brought into the mainstream if their language "problem" were remediated. More recently, Title III of NCLB was fashioned in the belief that simply holding these students and their teachers accountable to higher standards would force improvement. But laws have been made and remade without much attention to the research on what these students actually do need. A new ESEA should incorporate what we have learned over the nearly fifty years since the BEA was designed. First, it should revisit the initial impetus for the Bilingual Education Act as articulated by Senator Yarborough, and it should define these students as having both linguistic and cultural assets on which to build. Because overwhelmingly, English learners are also low-income students,

Title I should continue to provide support to ameliorate these students' social and economic disadvantages, which most ELs have in abundance, due in part to the increasingly unequal distribution of income and wealth in the country (Desilver 2013). The successor to Title III, however, could best focus on these students' assets while supporting their acquisition of academic English.

A new ESEA should identify the students who speak a language other than English with assessments that are standardized across the states. It should also support the states in developing assessment measures that allow them to validly and reliably chart their progress. The students should be assessed in all languages in which they are being taught and progress in all languages should be "counted" as meaningful educational achievements. To track the performance of these students and ensure that adequate services are provided for the period they are needed, EL students' academic performance should be monitored throughout their K–12 careers. There has been pushback on this by some groups that worry that the label of EL is itself stigmatizing and therefore these students should no longer be identified after exiting a language assistance program. But an education program oriented toward building on assets should not be stigmatizing, and therefore monitoring student performance over time should not invite concern.

Given that EL students who manage to maintain strong dual language skills graduate and go on to college at higher rates than their monolingual peers, and that all ELs benefit from having a teacher who can communicate with them and their families (Hopkins 2013), the new ESEA should provide the wherewithal to train highly skilled bilingual teachers and principals. This would also allow for opening many more dual language and international baccalaureate programs that incorporate both English learners and English speakers. Such programs help reduce the increasing segregation of these students so that they have the opportunity to learn alongside students from different backgrounds, different language groups, and different socioeconomic statuses. In this way they can become much more aware of the opportunities that exist for them in school and in the broader society. Advanced placement (AP), international baccalaureate (IB), Gifted and Talented, and other high-level curricular offerings should be expanded for these students, helping them to stretch their limits. The Seal of Biliteracy is another way of rewarding EL students for building on their assets. It is now awarded by eight states, from Washington to New York, and several other states are actively considering it. The seal on a student's diploma is earned by demonstrating proficiency in all four modalities (speaking, understanding, reading, and writing) in two or more languages. Research we have conducted suggests that many employers would value this designation in their hiring practices and a new ESEA could encourage these opportunities (Porras, Ee, and Gándara 2014).

Certainly a new ESEA should learn from past errors and avoid the high-stakes accountability system that has had a particularly negative impact on English learners. A new and improved ESEA would emphasize formative assessment that helps teachers better meet their EL students' needs. Accountability should be achieved through a system that is more sensitive to both the unique challenges and resources that different schools and districts experience. A system such as the education inspectorate used in some European countries can help schools analyze their strengths and weaknesses and find meaningful solutions to their problems. This does not obviate accountability, it simply makes it more sensitive to local circumstances and makes more clear what needs to be changed internally in a school, and can more easily differentiate the particular needs of students, such as English learners (Grubb 2000).

The Common Core State Standards (CCSS) are sweeping the land as forty-three states endeavor to put into place either a national set of common core standards or something like them (some states have rebelled against the *homogenization* of curriculum but have created something similar but with a different name). The CCSS have particular relevance for EL students because, depending on how a new ESEA interprets accountability for

ELs, the CCSS can encourage teachers to focus more of their instruction on language development broadly or can place greater emphasis on English acquisition in an effort to comply with test accountability in English. In the latter case, the testing regimen is likely to place English learners at a greater disadvantage. (Early returns from CCSS testing of ELs in New York, for example, have shown drastic declines in scores for ELs.) If the ESEA continues to pursue the path of high stakes, English-only testing, the potential benefit of CCSS for ELs can be lost and will most likely further erode support for bilingual education at the same time that the research has achieved consensus on its many benefits.

To clarify, I propose a reauthorized ESEA that strengthens the assets that ELs bring to school while attending to their socioeconomic needs both in school and out through Title I (or something like it). This would remove the stigma of being an English learner, invest more in the development of "highly effective" educators for ELs, and provide incentives to create many more dual language programs and integrate ELs with other high-performing peers. In sum, these changes would address the problems outlined in the original BEA and its successors. However, moving beyond merely ameliorating problematic aspects of past legislation to actually valuing those students who bring other languages and cultures to the classroom as assets to the nation could result in a new ESEA much more aligned with twenty-first-century reality.

REFERENCES

Abedi, Jamal. 2004. "The No Child Left Behind Act and English Language Learners: Assessment and Accountability Issues." *Educational Researcher* 33(1): 4–14.

Abedi, Jamal, and Patricia Gándara. 2006. "Performance of English Language Learners as a Subgroup in Large-Scale Assessment: Interaction of Research and Policy." *Educational Measurement: Issues and Practice* 25(4): 36–46.

August, Diane, Claude Goldenberg, and Robert Rueda. 2010. "Restrictive State Language Policies: Are They Scientifically Based?" In *Forbidden Language: English Learners and Restrictive Language Policies*, edited by Patricia Gándara and Megan Hopkins. New York: Teachers College Press.

August, Diane and Kenji Hakuta. 1998. *Educating Language Minority Children*. Washington, D.C.: National Academy Press.

Baker, Keith, and Adriana De Kanter. 1981. "The Effectiveness of Bilingual Education. A Review. Final Draft Report." Washington: U.S. Department of Education. Available at: http://files.eric.ed.gov/fulltext/ED215010.pdf (accessed July 27, 2015).

Bialystok, Ellen. 2001. *Bilingualism in Development: Language, Literacy, and Cognition*. New York: Cambridge University Press.

Bialystok, Ellen, and Fergus I. M. Craik. 2010. "Cognitive and Linguistic Processing in the Bilingual Mind." *Current Directions in Psychological Science* 19(1): 19–23.

Bialystok, Ellen, and Shilpi Majumder. 1998. "The Relationship Between Bilingualism and the Development of Cognitive Processes in Problem Solving." *Applied Psycholinguistics* 19(1): 69–85.

Boyle, Andrea, James Taylor, Steven Hurlburt, and Kay Soga. 2010. "Title III Accountability: Behind the Numbers." Palo Alto, Calif.: American Institutes for Research. Available at: http://www2.ed.gov/rschstat/eval/title-iii/behind-numbers.pdf (accessed July 27, 2015).

Bryant, Michael J., Kimberly A. Hammond, Kathleen M. Bocian, Michael F. Rettig, Cathy A. Miller, and Richard A. Cardullo. 2008. "School Performance Will Fail to Meet Legislated Benchmarks." *Science* 321(5897): 1781–82.

Callahan, Rebecca. 2013. "The English Learner Dropout Dilemma: Multiple Risks and Multiple Resources." Santa Barbara: California Drop out Research Project. Available at: http://www.cdrp.ucsb.edu/ pubs_reports.htm (accessed January 12, 2014).

Callahan, Rebecca, Lindsey Wilkinson, and Chandra Muller. 2010. "Academic Achievement and Course Taking Among Language Minority Youth in U.S. Schools: Effects of ESL Placement." *Educational Evaluation and Policy Analysis* 32(1): 84–117.

Cummins, James. 1981. "The Role of Primary Language Development in Promoting Educational Success for Language Minority Students." In *Schooling and Language Minority Students: A Theoretical Framework*. Los Angeles: California

State University Evaluation, Dissemination, and Assessment Center.

Danoff, Malcolm N. 1978. "Evaluation of the Impact of ESEA Title VII Spanish/English Bilingual Education Programs." ED154634. Washington, D.C.: American Institute for Research.

de Jong, Esther. J., and Candace A. Harper. 2005. "Preparing Mainstream Teachers for English-Language Learners: Is Being a Good Teacher Good Enough?" *Teacher Education Quarterly* 32(2): 101–24.

Desilver, Drew. 2013. "U.S. Income Inequality, on Rise for Decades, Is Now Highest Since 1928." Washington, D.C.: Pew Research Center. Available at: http://www.pewresearch.org/fact-tank/2013/12/05/u-s-income-inequality-on-rise-for-decades-is-now-highest-since-1928/ (accessed November 12, 2014).

Durgunoğlu, Aydin Y., William E. Nagy, and Barbara J. Hancin-Bhatt. 1993. "Cross-language Transfer of Phonemic Awareness." *Journal of Educational Psychology* 85(3): 453–65.

Editorial Projects in Education Research Center. 2013. "Findings from a National Survey of Teacher Perspectives on the Common Core." Bethesda, Md. EPERC. Available at: http://www.edweek.org/media/epe_survey_teacher_perspctives_common_core_2013.pdf (accessed July 27, 2015).

Flores, Edward, Gary Painter, Zachary Harlow-Nash, and Harry Pachon, 2009. "¿Qué Pasa? Are English Language Learning Students Staying in English Learning Classes Too Long?" Policy Brief. Los Angeles: Tomás Rivera Policy Institute, University of Southern California. Available at: http://trpi.org/wpcontent/uploads/archives/LAUSD%20Policy%20Brief.pdf (accessed July 27, 2015).

Gándara, Patricia. 2015. "Is There Really a Labor Market Advantage to Bilingualism in the U.S.?" Princeton, N.J.: Educational Testing Service.

Gándara, Patricia, Julie Maxwell-Jolly, and Anne Driscoll. 2005. "Listening to Teachers of English Language Learners: A Survey of California Teachers' Challenges, Experiences, and Professional Development Needs." Santa Cruz, Calif.: Center for the Future of Teaching and Learning. Available at: http://www.wested.org/resources/listening-to-teachers-of-english-language-learners-a-survey-of-california-teachers-challenges-experiences-and-professional-development-needs (accessed July 27, 2015).

Gándara, Patricia, Rachel Moran, and Eugene Garcia. 2004. "Legacy of *Brown*: *Lau* and Language Policy in the United States." *Review of Research in Education* 28(1): 27–46.

Gándara, Patricia, and Gary Orfield. 2012. "Segregating Arizona's English Learners: A Return to the 'Mexican Room?'" *Teachers College Record* 114(9): 1–27. Available at: http://www.tcrecord.org/content.asp?contentid=16600 (accessed July 27, 2015).

Gass, Susan M., Alison Mackey, and Teresa Pica. 1998. "The Role of Input and Interaction in Second Language Acquisition: Introduction to the Special Issue. *The Modern Language Journal* 82(3): 299–307.

Genesee, Fred, Kathryn Lindholm-Leary, William Saunders, and Donna Christian. 2006. *Educating English Learners: A Synthesis of Research Evidence*. Cambridge: Cambridge University Press.

Gifford, Bernard R., and Guadalupe Valdés. 2006. "The Linguistic Isolation of Hispanic Students in California's Public Schools: The Challenge of Reintegration." *Yearbook of the National Society for the Study of Education* 105(2): 125–154.

Goldenberg, Claude. 2008. "Teaching English Language Learners." *American Educator* (Summer): 8–44. Available at: http://www.aft.org/sites/default/files/periodicals/goldenberg.pdf (accessed July 27, 2015).

Grubb, W. Norton. 2000. "Opening Classrooms and Improving Teaching: Lessons from School Inspections in England." *Teachers College Record* 102(4): 696–723.

Haertel, Edward. 2007. "Declaration of Edward Haertel in Support of Plaintiff's Motion for Issuance of Writ of Mandate in *Coachella Valley Unified School District et al. v. State of California, Arnold Schwarzenegger et al.*" April 23, 2007.

Hakuta, Kenji, Yuko Goto Butler, and Daria Witt. 2000. "How Long Does It Take English Learners to Attain Proficiency?" Policy Report no. 2000–01. Santa Barbara: University of California Linguistic Minority Research Institute.

Hill, Laura E., Margaret Weston, and Joseph M. Hayes. 2014. "Reclassification of English Learner Students in California." San Francisco: Public Policy Institute of California. Available at: http://www.ppic.org/content/pubs/report/R_114LHR.pdf (accessed July 27, 2015).

Hopkins, Megan. 2013. "Building on Our Teaching Assets: The Unique Pedagogical Contributions of

Bilingual Educators." *Bilingual Research Journal* 36(3): 350–70.

Johnson, Hans, and Ria Sengupta. 2009. "Closing the Gap: Meeting California's Need for College Graduates." San Francisco: Public Policy Institute of California. Available at: http://www.ppic.org/content/pubs/report/R_409HJR.pdf (accessed July 27, 2015).

Kelly, Patrick, and Julie Strawn. 2011. "Not Just Kid Stuff Anymore: The Economic Imperative for More Adults to Complete College." Boulder, Colo.: National Center for Higher Education Management Systems. Available at: http://www.nchems.org/pubs/docs/NotKidStuffAnymoreAdultStudentProfile-1.pdf (accessed July 27, 2015).

Kloss, Hans. 1998. *The American Bilingual Tradition*, 2nd ed. Washington, D.C.: Delta Systems and Center for Applied Linguistics.

Krashen, Stephen D. 1987. *Principles and Practice in Second Language Acquisition*. New York: Prentice Hall.

Lessow-Hurley, Judith. 2004. *The Foundations of Dual Language Instruction*, 4th ed. New York: Pearson Higher Education.

Lillie, Karen, Amy Markos, Beatriz Arias, and Terence Wiley. 2012. "Separate and Not Equal: The Implementation of Structured English Immersion in Arizona's Classrooms." *Teachers College Record* 114(9): 1–33.

Loeb, Susanna, James Soland, and Lindsay Fox. 2014. "Is a Good Teacher a Good Teacher for All? Comparing Value-Added of Teachers with Their English Learners and Non-English Learners." *Education Evaluation and Policy Analysis* 36(4): 457–75.

Martinez-Wenzl, Mary. 2014. "¿Listo para el Colegio? Examining College Readiness Among Latino Newcomer Immigrants." Ph.D. diss., University of California, Los Angeles.

Martinez-Wenzl, Mary, Karla Pérez, and Patricia Gándara. 2012. "Is Arizona's Approach to Educating Its English Learners Superior to Other Forms of Instruction?" *Teachers College Record* 114(9): 1–32.

Maxwell, Leslie. 2013. "Arne Duncan Touts Advantages of Bilingualism." Learning the Language Blog. *Education Week*, May 30, 2013. Available at: http://blogs.edweek.org/edweek/learning-the-language/2013/05/arne_duncan_touts_advantages_o.html (accessed May 17, 2015).

Mehlman Petrzela, Natalia. 2010. "Before the Federal Bilingual Education Act: Legislation and Lived Experience in California." *Peabody Journal of Education* 85(4): 406–24.

Menken, Kate. 2010. "Teaching to the Test: How No Child Left Behind Impacts Language Policy, Curriculum, and Instruction for English Language Learners." *Bilingual Research Journal* 30(2): 521–46.

Meyer, Michael E., and Stephen M. Fienberg. 1992. *Assessing Evaluation Studies: The Case of Bilingual Education Strategies*. Washington, D.C.: National Academies Press.

Moran, Rachel. 1988. "The Politics of Discretion: Federal Intervention in Bilingual Education." *California Law Review* 76(6): 1249–351. Available at: http://scholarship.law.berkeley.edu/californialawreview/vol76/iss6/2/ (accessed November 14, 2014).

Moran, Rachel. 2013. "Untoward Consequences: The Ironic Legacy of *Keyes v. School District No. 1*." *Denver University Law Review* 90(5): 1209–229.

National Assessment of Educational Progress (NAEP). 2014. "The Nation's Report Card: 2013 Mathematics and Reading Grade 12 Assessments." NCES 2014087. Washington: National Center for Education Statistics. Available at: http://www.nationsreportcard.gov/reading_math_g12_2013/#/ (accessed May 13, 2015).

National Center for Education Statistics (NCES). 2014. "English Language Learners." Available at: https://nces.ed.gov/programs/coe/pdf/Indicator_CGF/coe_cgf_2014_05.pdf (accessed July 27, 2015).

National Center for Public Policy and Higher Education. 2005. "Income of U.S. Workforce Projected to Decline If Education Doesn't Improve." *Education Policy Alert*. San Jose, Calif.: National Center for Public Policy and Higher Education. Available at: http://www.highereducation.org/reports/pa_decline/pa_decline.pdf (accessed May 13, 2015).

Novak, John R., and Bruce Fuller. 2003. "Penalizing Diverse Schools? Similar Test Scores, but Different Students, Bring Federal Sanctions." *PACE* Policy Brief no. 03–4. Berkeley: Policy Analysis for California Education. Available at: http://nepc.colorado.edu/files/EPRU-0312-48-RW.pdf (accessed July 27, 2015).

Office for Civil Rights. 1970. "DHEW Memo Regarding Language Minority Children." Washington: U.S. Department of Education. Available at:

http://www2.ed.gov/about/offices/list/ocr/docs/lau1970.html (accessed July 27, 2015).

Ovando, Carlos, and Virginia Collier. 1985. *Bilingual and ESL Classrooms*. New York: McGraw-Hill.

Porras, Diane, Joy Ee, and Patricia Gándara. 2014. "Employer Preferences: Do Bilingual Applicants and Employees Experience an Advantage?" In *The Bilingual Advantage: Language, Literacy, and the U.S. Labor Market*, edited by Rebecca Callahan and Patricia Gándara. Bristol, UK: Multilingual Matters.

Portes, Alejandro, and Lingxin Hao. 2002. "The Price of Uniformity: Language, Family, and Personality Adjustment in the Immigrant Second Generation." *Ethnic and Racial Studies* 25(6): 889–912.

Ramirez, David J., Sandra D. Yuen, Dena R. Ramey, David J. Pasta, and David K. Billings. 1991. *Longitudinal Study of Structured-English Immersion Strategy, Early-Exit and Late-Exit Transitional Bilingual Education Programs for Language-Minority Children*. Final Report. Volumes I & II. San Mateo, Calif.: Aguirre International.

Ravitch, Diane. 2011. *The Death and Life of the Great American School System*. New York: Basic Books.

Robinson, Joseph. 2011. "Evaluating Criteria for English Learner Reclassification: A Causal-Effects Approach Using a Binding-Score Regression Discontinuity Design with Instrumental Variables." *Educational Evaluation and Policy Analysis* 33(3): 267–92.

Ruiz, Richard. 1984. "Orientations in Language Planning." *NABE Journal* 8(2): 15–34.

Rumbaut, Rubén. 2014. "English Plus: Exploring the Socio-Economic Benefits of Bilingualism in Southern California." In *The Bilingual Advantage: Language, Literacy and the U.S. Labor Market*, edited by Rebecca Callahan and Patricia Gándara. Bristol, UK: Multilingual Matters.

Ryan, Camille. 2013. "Language Use in the United States: American Community Survey Reports." ACS-22. Washington: U.S. Census Bureau. Available at: https://www.census.gov/prod/2013pubs/acs-22.pdf (accessed July 27, 2015).

Santibañez, Lucrecia, and Maria Estela Zárate. 2014. "Bilinguals in the United States and College Enrollment." In *The Bilingual Advantage: Language, Literacy and the U.S. Labor Market*, edited by Rebecca Callahan and Patricia Gándara. Bristol, UK: Multilingual Matters.

Schneider, Susan Gilbert. 1976. *Revolution, Reaction or Reform? The 1974 Bilingual Education Act*. New York: Las Americas.

Slama, Rachel B. 2014. "Investigating Whether and When English Learners Are Reclassified into Mainstream Classrooms in the United States: A Discrete-Time Survival Analysis." *American Educational Research Journal* 51(2): 220–52.

Slavin, Robert E., and Alan Cheung. 2005. "A Synthesis of Research on Language of Reading Instruction for English Language Learners." *Review of Educational Research* 75(2): 247–84.

Sunderman, Gail L., Christopher A. Tracey, Jimmy Kim, and Gary Orfield. 2004. "Listening to Teachers: Classroom Realities and No Child Left Behind." Cambridge, Mass.: Civil Rights Project, Harvard University. Available at: http://civilrightsproject.ucla.edu/research/K-12-education/nclb-title-i/listening-to-teachers-classroom-realities-and-no-child-left-behind/sunderman-tracey-kim-orfield-listening-teachers.pdf (accessed July 27, 2015).

Umansky, Ilana M., and Sean F. Reardon. 2014. "Reclassification Patterns among Latino English Learner Students in Bilingual, Dual Immersion, and English Immersion Classrooms." *American Educational Research Journal* 51(5): 871–912.

Valentino, Rachel, and Sean F. Reardon. 2015. "Effectiveness of Four Instructional Programs Designed to Serve English Language Learners: Variation by Ethnicity and Initial English Proficiency." *Educational Evaluation and Policy Analysis* forthcoming in print. Online April 1, 2105. Available at: http://epa.sagepub.com/content/early/2015/04/01/0162373715573310.full (accessed July 27, 2015).

Verhoeven, Ludo T. 1994. "Transfer in Bilingual Development: The Linguistic Interdependency Hypothesis Revisited." *Language Learning* 44(3): 381–415.

Wiese, Anne-Marie, and Eugene E. Garcia. 1998. "The Bilingual Education Act: Language Minority Students and Equal Educational Opportunity." *Bilingual Research Journal* 22(1): 1–18.

Willig, Ann C. 1985. "A Meta-Analysis of Selected Studies on the Effectiveness of Bilingual Education." *Review of Educational Research* 55(3): 269–317.

Zehr, Mary Ann. 2007. "NCLB Seen as a Damper on Bilingual Programs: Some States and Districts Say Testing Requirements May Discourage Efforts." *Education Week*, online May 8, 2007.

The Quest for a Targeted and Effective Title I ESEA: Challenges in Designing and Implementing Fiscal Compliance Rules

NORA GORDON AND SARAH REBER

Title I ESEA faces a fundamental tension in achieving its goal of improving outcomes for disadvantaged students. On the one hand, districts may fail to target federal funds to the intended recipients. On the other hand, regulations meant to ensure proper targeting can interfere with the efficient use of funds. Congress attempted to address concerns that Title I's fiscal regulations limit flexibility and lead to fragmented instructional programs by authorizing the use of schoolwide programs. We argue that, despite increasing uptake of the schoolwide option, misconceptions of Title I's fiscal rules likely still prevent many schools operating schoolwide programs from taking full advantage of the flexibility the schoolwide designation allows and putting Title I funds to their best uses.

Keywords: Title I, intergovernmental grants, federal education aid, fiscal rules

Fifty years after its passage as part of President Lyndon Johnson's War on Poverty, Title I of the Elementary and Secondary Education Act (ESEA) remains at the center of the federal role in elementary and secondary education in the United States. Title I aimed to increase opportunity for disadvantaged children through an influx of federal funds to the public and private schools serving them, awarding funds to school districts based largely on a proxy for child poverty counts. Congress intended for local districts to target their grants to their highest poverty schools and, within those schools, to direct services to the most educationally deprived children. From the start, it has proved challenging for the federal government to ensure that districts direct their Title I money solely to the program's intended beneficiaries.

Beginning with the 1994 reauthorization, and consistent with research findings from the Coleman Report (1966) suggesting that revenue alone does not guarantee student success, another key federal goal emerged for the program: ensuring the effective use of funds in improving student outcomes. We argue that the goal of preventing any leakage of federal funds beyond the target population can be at odds with the goal of using those funds most effectively to improve educational outcomes for disadvantaged students.

Early in the program's history, and in response to highly publicized and egregious misuses of funds, Title I's fiscal rules transformed it from something close to general aid into a much more restricted and closely monitored source of categorical aid for the disadvantaged.

Nora Gordon is associate professor of public policy at Georgetown University and research associate at the National Bureau of Economic Research. **Sarah Reber** is associate professor of public policy at the University of California, Los Angeles, and research associate at the National Bureau of Economic Research.

Direct correspondence to: Nora Gordon, nora.gordon@georgetown.edu, Georgetown University, McCourt School of Public Policy, 37th and O Sts. N.W., Old North #100, Washington, D.C. 20057; Sarah Reber, sreber@ucla.edu, University of California, Los Angeles, Luskin School of Public Affairs, 3250 Public Affairs Bldg., Box 951656, Los Angeles, CA 90095.

Observers soon noted that these restrictions hindered the ability of schools to best use their grants, and new rules soon emerged attempting to preserve the targeting of aid while simultaneously seeking to promote effective uses of funds by allowing some flexibility in the use of funds. That tension is the subject of this article: how successful are the fiscal rules governing Title I today and especially its schoolwide program option—both on paper and as perceived by program administrators—at striking this balance? We argue that many programs are schoolwide in name only, and more needs to be done to address these long-standing but low-profile issues.[1]

In this article, we argue that though progress toward more effective use of Title I funds has been made, the problem is far from resolved. Our argument draws on three main categories of evidence: the policy history up to and including the fiscal rules in place today; interviews with school district Title I administrators, which provide information not only on how they spend their funds but also on how they understand the fiscal rules; and analysis of how Title I funds are spent in two large, highly disadvantaged districts.

In sum, we find that in many cases perceptions of the fiscal rules have not caught up with the legal reality for schools operating schoolwide programs. Many of these schools appear to still use Title I funds to pay for things that appear more extra or supplemental, as opposed to core, though it is difficult to assess just how integrated Title I expenditures are with the rest of a school's functioning from available data sources. This may be in part due to the fact that total Title I funding in many schools is not enough to finance substantial components of the core instructional program on its own, but we also find evidence of misperceptions about what is allowed on the part of administrators. The interviews also revealed that district Title I administrators rely on state administrators, more than federal documents or actors, for information about permissible uses of funds.

Thus, any federal or other efforts to provide more transparent guidance on Title I rules should pay particular attention to the role of state education agencies in disseminating such information and to the variation in capacity across state education agencies.

METHODS AND SOURCES

We begin by reviewing the policy history of ESEA Title I, leading up to the current compliance requirements, with particular attention to schoolwide programs. For this discussion, we draw on the law itself; the U.S. Department of Education's body of nonregulatory policy guidance documents, written for an audience of state and local education agency federal program administrators; the compliance circular produced by the Office of Management and Budget (OMB) providing more detailed guidance for the auditors; and technical assistance documents from nongovernmental sources that translate these complex original sources. This description and interpretation of Title I's key fiscal rules is a necessary foundation for describing the impact of these rules on practice and for understanding why practitioners may view the rules differently from the way Congress does.[2]

We also describe the federal single-audit process, which has been widely criticized for generating inaccurate findings. The outcomes of this process are critical to administrators, because the Department of Education may choose to follow up on negative findings with a process that can lead to a mandate to return funds to the federal government. To learn how often this feared outcome was realized, we submitted Freedom of Information Act (FOIA) requests to the Department of Education for all program determination letters related to Title I Part A for the calendar years 2011 through 2013; the request yielded 112 such letters to state and local education agencies, which we read to determine whether repayment of funds was required.

We selected a sample of target districts in four states, chosen for variety in embrace of

---

1. Some of the clearest and most detailed writing on this topic comes from attorneys Melissa Junge and Sheara Krvaric (2011, 2012).

2. For a political history of ESEA, see Jennings 2015.

school reform and for regional diversity. We limited potential districts to those with at least eight schools—this is the 25th percentile in the number of schools per district nationally when weighting by free and reduced-price lunch eligible (FRPLE) enrollment—and with a district-wide FRPLE rate of at least 30 percent. These precise cut-offs are arbitrary but motivated by the goal of ruling out districts with little program involvement and expertise. We divided these remaining districts into four quadrants, above and below their state's median enrollment and FRPLE rate, and randomly selected two districts per quadrant. We referenced each district's website to identify its Title I or federal grants administrator and contacted that individual in July 2014 via e-mail at least twice and if we received no response, via phone at least once. We also attempted to include the largest district in each state. Our sample of interviewees is necessarily limited to people who were willing to talk with us, who may or may not be representative of Title I administrators more generally. We emphasized in all contacts that all conversation would be off the record and the identity of the district and state would be obscured in our writing. We ultimately conducted eight interviews in the summer of 2014. One of the four states had administrators from four districts respond, one state had two, and the remaining two states each had only one.

Policy History of Title I Fiscal Rules and Enforcement

When ESEA was passed in 1965, the U.S. Department of Health, Education and Welfare's (HEW's) Office of Education found itself tasked with managing a program substantially larger than anything it had previously; simply writing the checks occupied most of the available staff's time (Bailey and Mosher 1968). The regulations accompanying the law did discuss some fiscal requirements, but in practice enforcement was quite limited and even those districts identified by audits as violating the law were not subject to financial penalty (Cohen and Moffitt 2009). In this context, it is not surprising that many districts chose to use Title I in ways that would not benefit the students Congress intended to help. In 1969, the Washington Research Project (which later became the Children's Defense Fund) and the Legal Defense Fund (LDF) of the NAACP issued a highly influential report documenting egregious misuse of Title I funds across many districts and states (Martin and McClure 1969). The report does not claim to describe a representative sample, but the sheer number of cases and the outrageousness of many of them proved quite persuasive.[3] Soon after the release of the LDF report, the 1970 amendments to the ESEA strengthened the fiscal requirements and added enforcement teeth.

A major change in the new regime was that districts and states could be forced to pay back program funds if audits revealed they had violated program requirements. Perceptions about the likelihood of a given use of funds producing a negative audit finding thus became critical in shaping the use of funds. In addition to the uncertain educational benefits associated with any particular use of funds, and political costs (either locally or with the state education agency) of changing the service mix, districts considering new uses of Title I funds now face the additional risk that they may be required to defend the expenditure or pay back funds following the audit.[4]

Not only can it be difficult for administrators to know whether a given use of funds is truly permissible, but the auditors also frequently get it wrong. A recent study of federal audits revealed that audits of all but the largest recipients of federal funds are of remarkably low quality. About two-thirds of audits of large agencies (federal funds exceeding $50 million per year) were deemed acceptable; just under half of the audits of smaller agencies (with

---

3. For example, they describe that "an HEW audit of Louisiana school districts ... in 1966 ... found that 23 parishes (counties) 'loaned' equipment ... to schools that were ineligible to participate in Title I programs. The auditors noted that much of the 'loaned' equipment was 'set in concrete or fastened to the plumbing'" (Martin and McClure 1969, 9).

4. Back and forth between the LEA and SEA can be costly because delays in submitting the application can lead to delays in the availability of funds for the relevant school year.

$500,000 to $50 million of federal grants per year) were.[5] So even if a district makes some effort to determine a particular use of funds is legally permissible, it still might reasonably worry the auditor will not know this. On the other hand, expenses that have previously passed an audit will almost certainly pass again.[6] This dynamic mitigates against innovation in the use of Title I funds in general and in response to policy changes, such as the expansion of schoolwide programs.

Although the regulations governing fiscal compliance with Title I have been modified many times since 1970, their key elements—maintenance of effort (MOE), comparability, and supplement not supplant—remain with us today. We discuss each in turn, with particular attention to supplement not supplant, which appears to exert the greatest influence on how districts use their funds.

MOE requirements are used in a variety of intergovernmental grants programs, not just Title I, and are meant to prevent recipient governments from reducing their fiscal effort in response to a federal grant, effectively diverting federal funding to an unintended purpose. For example, if districts decrease local property tax rates following an influx of Title I funds, federal funds would effectively be diverted toward increases in private consumption, commensurate with increases in residents' after-tax income.[7] Because school districts have revenue from both state and local sources, Title I MOE requirements apply to combined state and local revenue. Ideally, the MOE regulation would require revenue to a school district from all nonfederal sources to be at least as much as it would have been in the absence of Title I funding. In practice, this counterfactual is impossible to know, and calibrating the MOE requirement is difficult. The most the law has ever required is that state and local contributions not decline relative to previous years. Although this prevents state governments and local districts from reducing funding levels in response to Title I, it does not prevent them from increasing funding less than they would have in the absence of Title I. This is particularly relevant because per-pupil spending has been increasing rapidly, funded by state and local sources, throughout most of the history of the Title I program. Finally, MOE does not relate to how districts or schools spend revenue, only to how much different sources contribute revenue. We therefore focus the remainder of our discussion on those compliance requirements related to how districts may spend their Title I grants.

Maintenance of effort regulations are meant to prevent Title I funds from being diverted beyond district budgets. The two other fiscal requirements for Title I, comparability and supplement not supplant, are meant to prevent diversion of funds to ineligible schools within districts and ineligible students within schools, respectively.[8] Districts with uniform salary schedules are permitted to show comparability by demonstrating that state and local revenue fund an equal number of full-time equivalent (FTE) teachers per student across all schools in the district, so that Title I funds are layered on top of already equalized distri-

---

5. The National Single Audit Sampling Project used a stratified random sample to select 208 single audits of public agencies from more than thirty-eight thousand audits submitted from April 1, 2003, through March 31, 2004. A panel of experts conducted quality-control reviews (QCRs) for the sections pertaining to federal grants on these audits (President's Council on Integrity and Efficiency 2007).

6. Larry Stanton and Alison Segal's observation that "Schools and districts act as though federal Title I grant supported activities are permanent and fixed regardless of their impact on school performance" is consistent with this line of reasoning (2013).

7. Although such reallocation might be optimal from a social welfare perspective, we present this from the perspective of a federal policymaker specifically concerned with spending on educational services.

8. See appendix A for the relevant statutory language. Current nonregulatory policy guidance on fiscal issues in Title I describes comparability as the requirement that a district "provide *services* in its Title I schools with State and local funds that are at least comparable to *services* provided in its non-Title I schools" and later on the same page, states that "comparability requires an LEA to ensure that each Title I school receives its fair share of *resources* from State and local *funds*" (U.S. Department of Education 2008, emphasis added).

bution of revenue. Some refer to this practice as the comparability loophole because it allows different amounts of state and local revenue per pupil across schools, because the typically less experienced teachers in Title I schools cost less. In practice, this reporting of FTEs rather than funds is the dominant form of compliance with the requirement.[9]

The supplement not supplant requirement is perhaps the most confusing and influential of the three fiscal rules. Historically, it has aimed to prevent districts from buying things for students not participating in Title I with state and local funds, and using Title I funds to buy those same things for Title I students, hence supplanting the services that should have been funded with state and local dollars. When Title I students are in a school with other students, these regulations rule out many things schools might want to do with their funds (for example, buy anything potentially accessed by an entire school, such as curriculum or certain technologies, or support teachers in any way that might benefit non–Title I students). Even if Title I and other students were perfectly segregated by school, supplement not supplant rules out district-wide initiatives. This requirement puts pressure on districts to find standalone activities to fund with Title I, and led to widespread use of "pull-out" instruction, whereby students are pulled out of their regular (core) classroom to receive Title I services. This mode has been criticized on many fronts: it may stigmatize students, pull-out services were typically provided by paraprofessionals rather than teachers, and pull-out services take students away from the regular instructional program.

The supplement not supplant rules are particularly opaque: The statutory language is brief (see appendix A) and while the Department of Education's 2008 nonregulatory fiscal guidance includes a number of example data tables a district could produce to demonstrate compliance with MOE and comparability, the supplement not supplant "examples" are buried in text, and specific examples of data or tables a district might provide to show compliance are not provided. The guidance advises, "Keep in mind that any determination about supplanting is very case specific and it is difficult to provide general guidelines without examining the details of a situation." In essence, the Department of Education says it knows supplanting when it sees it.

SCHOOLWIDE PROGRAMS IN TITLE I: HOW ARE THEIR RULES DIFFERENT?

It did not take long for observers to note the unintended consequences of the new fiscal regime. Brenda Turnbull and Marshall Smith each provide excellent accounts of how the supplement not supplant regulations were perceived as fragmenting programming and requiring excessive administrator savvy and time to comply (Turnbull 1981; Smith 1986). Smith summarized the impact of supplement not supplant:

> In their attempt to implement this requirement, the U.S. Office of Education and state departments of education . . . issued regulations, guidelines, and other non-regulatory guidance and provided technical assistance to LEAs to help them design delivery mechanisms which were legal. The dominant choice to create a 'clean' fiscal trail was to create, in effect, a separate system within the school. Their goals were to keep the Chapter 1 teachers as separate as possible from the core program of the school, deliver Chapter 1 services in separate settings, and have separate technical assistance and reporting lines. By and large they succeeded. (1986, II-82)

Congress responded to these concerns by introducing in 1978 and later expanding eligibility for a schoolwide program (SWP) option for Title I schools serving particularly high concentrations of poor children.[10] The fiscal rules for SWPs are significantly more flexible, allowing schools to use funds for services and

---

9. Marguerite Roza finds that within urban districts she studied, lower poverty schools had more expensive FTEs, a greater number of staff FTEs per pupil, and more unrestricted funds per pupil; nonetheless, these districts met the legal requirements for comparability (2008).

10. This is not a coincidence. For example, Smith actively pushed for expansion of schoolwide programs in his writing (1986).

materials benefiting the entire school, though they do face some additional compliance requirements: they must produce a plan, and must self-evaluate (in very loose terms) annually. Schools that receive Title I funding but do not operate SWPs, either because they are not poor enough to qualify for an SWP or choose not to take up that option, are referred to as targeted assistance schools (TAS) and are governed by fiscal rules similar to those governing all Title I schools in the 1970s.

When the schoolwide program was first introduced as an option, it was attractive for very few districts: a school needed to have 75 percent of its enrollment eligible and federal funds were conditional on a dollar-for-dollar match. There was little take-up of the schoolwide program option in the decade following its introduction, and pull-outs remained a key part of Title I (Wong and Meyer 1998). Marshall Smith references the District Practices Study of 1983, in which 18 percent of surveyed districts reported choosing pull-out designs for educational reasons, and 73 percent reported choosing pull-outs for compliance purposes (1986). His paper articulating problems with supplement not supplant had a specific policy recommendation—to expand use of schoolwide programs—and in 1988, the match requirement was eliminated.

The threshold for schoolwide program eligibility continued to be lowered over time, and take-up continued to increase. Title I schools are now eligible for schoolwide programs if at least 40 percent of their students are eligible for free or reduced price meals, and take-up is perceived to be generally high but variable by state and not universal. National data on the use of schoolwide programs are surprisingly hard to come by. The Public School Universe of the Common Core of Data includes variables for public schools on whether they are eligible for Title I and eligible to use the schoolwide model, but does not provide data on whether the schools participate in Title I, and if so, whether they use the targeted assistance or schoolwide model (see appendix B; Keaton 2012). The eligibility data reveal that two-thirds of public schools nationally are eligible for Title I programs, and of those, nearly three-quarters are eligible to operate schoolwide programs (Keaton 2012). Our interviews suggest that in large districts with many high-poverty schools, districts are likely to take up the schoolwide model in most if not all eligible schools.

However, we know little about the extent to which schools actually took advantage of the additional flexibility allowed in schoolwide programs in a way that promoted a more integrated and, potentially, productive approach to the use of Title I funds. That the schools exhibited so little initial demand for SWPs (as well as current incomplete take-up) and evidence of ongoing confusion about Title I's fiscal rules in general (such as the 2003 GAO report) both point to the possibility that the problems of fragmentation of funding and instruction identified in the 1980s may persist.[11]

Recall that supplement not supplant is meant to ensure that funds are targeted to participating students, not just schools. So what does this regulation require in a schoolwide program, where funds can be used to benefit all students in the school? Program administrators and auditors could refer to one of several sources of information to answer this question (see table 1).

The A-133 supplement (appendix C), referenced by auditors, begins by detailing three presumptions of supplanting (Executive Office of the President 2014). Using Title I funds for an activity is presumed to be supplanting nonfederal funds if any of the three are true: the activity is required by state or local law; the activity was funded with nonfederal funds in the prior year; or the activity was funded for children not participating in Title I with nonfederal funds in the current year. Auditors test these presumptions on a cost-by-cost basis; that is, the district must be able to show that every single good or service purchased with program funds meets each of the three presumptions. Informal discussions with state

---

11. This finding is consistent with an extensive literature emphasizing the importance of implementation and examining the frequent disconnect between policy intent and how programs operate in practice (for recent examples, see Spillane 2004; Honig 2006).

Table 1. Sources of Information on Compliance Requirements

Documents	Authors	Mode of Dissemination
Statute *Appendix A*	Congress	Easy to find, including on ED website and many SEA websites
Regulations	ED, with OMB process	*Federal Register* (online)
Federal nonregulatory guidance *Multiple documents, see appendix B for examples*	ED, with OMB process	Federal Department of Education website; most state education agencies offer links to at least some of these documents
State policy guidance	SEAs or their legal counsel or consultants	Many states offer state-specific guidance posted on their website for district reference, though this often takes the form of PowerPoint slides or webinars
Compliance circular A-133 Department of Education cross-cutting section *Appendix C*	OMB	OMB website
Program determination letters	ED	Sent to individual agency in question. Available from ED via FOIA request or with paid subscription to LRP Publications
Handbooks, newsletters, CD-ROMs	Private sector (or public sector employees outside of public role)	For sale by for-profit publishers
Toolkits	Private sector	Made freely available by advocacy organizations, such as CCSSO and MassInsight
"Supporting School Reform by Leveraging Federal Funds in a Schoolwide Program"	U.S. Department of Education	Letter to Chief State School Officers

Source: Authors' compilation.

and local Title I administrators suggest widespread familiarity with the substance of the three presumptions.

However, the administrators we spoke with did not mention what the A-133 supplement explains immediately following the three presumptions: they must apply to targeted assistance schools, but schools operating schoolwide programs do not need to use federal funds to provide supplemental services, and instead can show that the federal funds are supplemental to the state and local funds that would have been allocated to the school absent its Title I program.[12] This is clear from a close read of the full supplement, but could easily be missed. To be clear, the schoolwide pro-

12. Although grants administrators, particularly in smaller districts, are unlikely to read the compliance circular, its content shapes their decisions nonetheless as they observe their own audit findings over time. Local administrators also learn about audit findings in other districts in their states through their discussions with state program administrators, who approve LEA Title I applications before they are submitted to the federal government each year.

grams of today have no legal reason to demonstrate the separateness between Title I programming and the core functioning of the school bemoaned in the past. In fact, eliminating this need—and the fragmentation of the instructional program it promoted—was a key goal of schoolwide programs.

Although the language in the A-133 supplement is relatively clear (if one perseveres in reading beyond the three presumptions), the clarity and completeness of the explanations provided in the Department of Education's nonregulatory guidance is more mixed. The department's 2006 "Designing Schoolwide Programs," a fifty-four-page document, provides extensive guidance on how to comprehensively assess a school's needs, set goals, and devise an appropriate evidence-based plan. It does not, however, speak to any concern a district might have about whether particular evidence-based strategies for school improvement would be interpreted as supplanting other resources, and the word *supplant* does not appear in the document a single time. Appendix B reproduces an excerpt of the department's 2008 nonregulatory guidance on "Title I Fiscal Issues," which clearly translates the supplemental funds test consistent with the A-133; however, the clear text appears in a section under "General Fiscal Issues" rather than in the sections for "Supplement not Supplant" or "Schoolwide Programs" and could easily be missed by federal grants administrators attempting to determine permissible uses of funds. The Department of Education recently clarified this point in a July 2015 "Dear Colleague" letter: "A schoolwide program school does not need to demonstrate that Title I funds are used only for activities that supplement, and do not supplant, those the school would otherwise provide with non-Federal funds" (2015, 5).

The extent to which the guidance is both salient and correctly interpreted by its readers in state and local education agencies is an open question. But the demand for professional interpretations of the guidance provides at least some evidence that federal grants administrators do not find the guidance completely straightforward.[13] The department provides only a few hypothetical cases in its nonregulatory guidance, and does not make public the program determination letters (PDLs) summarizing the resolution of specific cases in which the single-audit findings prompt a more intensive response from the department, or even how many such cases exist.[14] The private sector has responded to the demand for a larger sample of real cases: LRP Publications' Title1 Admin service obtains PDLs via Freedom of Information Act (FOIA) requests and makes them available to its customers via paid subscriptions.[15] Although many single-audit findings do not prompt PDLs, any find-

---

13. LRP Publications, the same publisher offering the subscription service to ED letters obtained via FOIA requests, also sells a $250 CD with a ninety-minute video presentation by a federal grants administrator in the South Carolina Department of Education, "Can Title I Pay for This? A Guide to Allowable Costs." The Council of Chief State School Officers commissioned "Maximizing Federal Education Funds for Student Achievement: A Toolkit for States Seeking to Enhance Flexibility and Reduce Burden" from education attorneys and federal compliance specialists Melissa Junge and Sheara Krvaric. MassInsight also partnered with Junge and Krvaric to produce "The Money You Don't Know You Have for School Turnaround: Maximizing the Title I Schoolwide Model," available at: http://www.massinsight.org/publications/stg-resources/240/file/1/pubs/2013/07/12/FedEd_SDN_supplemental_funds_toolkit_FINAL_7_11_13.pdf (accessed July 29, 2015).

14. All state and local agencies receiving at least $500,000 in federal funds (across all federal agencies, including the Department of Agriculture) are required to be audited annually, while others must be audited at least every three years. These single audits are available publicly via the Federal Audit Clearinghouse (https://harvester.census.gov/facweb/default.aspx/). The Department of Education pursues a subset of single audits with findings. In these cases, the agency under review has the opportunity to respond to the findings, and the assistant secretary of elementary and secondary education then issues his or her "determination." The letters summarizing this process are referred to as program determination letters.

15. We mention the market demand for PDLs to motivate the need for clearer exposition of the rules. The PDLs include vast amounts of boilerplate text and, though these are somewhat helpful in determining what is not

Table 2. Program Determination Letters Issued by Department of Education, January 1, 2011–December 31, 2013

Recipient Agency	Total PDLs	PDLs Not Requiring Repayment of Funds	PDLs Requiring Repayment of Funds
State education agency	104	94	10
Local education agency	8	3	5
Total	112	97	15

Source: Authors' calculations. Letters obtained via Freedom of Information Act request.

ing ultimately resulting in repayment of funds to the department or involving significant "corrective action" will generate a PDL.

A PDL letter typically discusses more than one audit finding per agency. In some cases, agencies received more than one PDL concerning different audit periods or findings during the time period covered by our request. Table 2 summarizes the distribution of letters (rather than findings or agencies).

Over the three years, the total of 112 cases generated enough ED interest to result in a determination. Thirty-nine states (or their education agencies), the District of Columbia, and Puerto Rico received at least one such a letter in this period, the department requiring repayment in just under 10 percent of the cases. Whereas most states—which are tasked with monitoring compliance of their districts—received at least one PDL, only eight local school districts received PDLs, a vanishingly small share of districts receiving Title I funds. In those few cases when local districts did receive PDLs, however, they were more likely to be required to repay federal funds.[16] Although school districts were highly unlikely to be subject to formal federal intervention following their single audits, the high rate at which the Department of Education intervened regarding audits of their state agencies means that state education agency (SEA) administrators have a clear interest in passing on the importance of compliance to the local education agencies (LEAs) they oversee.

WHAT DISTRICTS DO WITH THEIR TITLE I FUNDS AND WHY

Have schools and districts taken advantage of the additional flexibility that the schoolwide designation allows? Do they use Title I to fund the core instructional program? Unfortunately, data on school-level budgets are largely unavailable, and we know surprisingly little about whether schoolwide programs have altered how schools spend Title I funds. The American Recovery and Reinvestment Act of 2009 (ARRA) required school districts receiving Title I funds to report school-level per-pupil expenditures from state and local sources, but these data have a number of problems and ultimately provide little insight into what schools buy with those funds (Heuer and Stullich 2011).[17]

---

allowed, PDLs are not the best way to provide this information. Instead, as discussed, we recommend the federal government clarify the guidance.

16. We do not have direct evidence explaining the much higher rate of required repayment among local districts receiving PDLs. However, we expect the low rate of PDL receipt and the relatively high rate of required repayments for local districts are related: if the threshold for filing a PDL against a local district is high, the chance of finding a severe violation is likely also higher.

17. This also poses a significant problem for researchers wishing to evaluate the impact of Title I, as they are fundamentally limited in their ability even to measure what Title I buys in terms of educational services (see Puma et al. 1993; van der Klaauw 2008; Gordon 2004; Chambers et al. 2009; Matsudaira, Hosek, and Walsh 2012; Cascio, Gordon, and Reber 2013; Borman and D'Agostino 1996). Evaluating the impact of Title I is particularly challenging as the federal allocation is a function of child poverty counts, which are closely correlated with other forces driving fiscal conditions and student outcomes.

We are interested in what schools do differently when they have Title I funds, compared with what they would have done in the absence of the program. We are also interested in whether the answer to this question changed with the advent of schoolwide programs. We face at least two obstacles in addressing the question using the available data. First, finding an appropriate counterfactual is difficult, because Title I schools differ from non–Title I schools along a variety of dimensions. Second, we would need to observe how schools spend all their funds, but we only observe how Title I funds are spent in the application data. That is, the available data do not even allow us to say descriptively how spending in Title I and non–Title I schools differs.[18] Nevertheless, we report what we can from the available data. Districts report how they use Title I and other federal funding in some detail when they apply for Title I funding. To gain some insight into how districts spend Title I funds in general and specifically in schoolwide programs we obtained and analyzed Title I application data for two districts. We also interviewed a small sample of district Title I administrators. We discuss our findings in turn.

For the reasons described, the application data do not allow us to determine how Title I funding affects what schools do. Nor is it straightforward to determine whether any particular Title I line item is funding the core instructional program; determining whether it is an efficient use of funds is of course even more difficult. But the data may provide some insight into a narrower question. Are Title I schools operating schoolwide programs taking advantage of the flexibility the law allows, spending money in ways they could not have thirty years ago—or in a targeted assistance program today? If schoolwide programs do not change Title I spending patterns, they may not have resolved the fragmentation problem they were designed to address. We find evidence that at least some districts do spend in schoolwide programs in ways that would not be allowed in targeted assistance schools. We also find some support for the idea that districts may use a "targeted assistance" approach to allocating and justifying Title I expenditures even when they operate schoolwide programs; this is consistent with "input from the field," cited in the Department's 2015 "Dear Colleague" letter that there appear to be "some schoolwide program flexibilities that are not being used to their full extent."

Both district A and district B are large, urban districts serving disadvantaged populations. Nearly all their Title I schools operate schoolwide programs. Consistent with other evidence about how schools spend Title I funds (Chambers et al. 2009), we find that both districts spent somewhat more than three-quarters of their Title I budget on personnel.[19] To understand whether Title I purchases services that are part of the "core instructional program," we need to know what the personnel purchased with Title I funds do. In district B, nearly half of spending for personnel (and over one-third of the total Title I budget) pays for regular classroom teachers for class size reduction. Class size reduction is not allowed in targeted assistance schools, so district B is clearly taking advantage of the flexibility the schoolwide program affords.[20] District A, on the other hand, appears not to use any Title I funds to

---

18. Ruth Heuer and Stephanie Stullich do analyze spending for Title I and non–Title I schools, but the included expenditures do not cover all funds that were spent at the school and are reported in very broad categories—total personnel salaries for all school-level instructional and support staff, salaries for instructional staff, salaries for teachers, and nonpersonnel expenditures (if available). These data do not contain nearly enough detail to discern whether spending is core and integrated or supplemental (2011).

19. In this analysis, we focus on the basic grant under Title I Part A, the largest component of Title I. Part A is titled "Improving Basic Programs Operated by Local School Districts." The other parts of Title I are earmarked more specifically (such as for reading, migrant children, dropout prevention).

20. It is possible that district A chooses other uses of funds (other than for class size reduction) because administrators do not perceive class size reduction to be an effective use of resources, rather than because they perceive it to be an impermissible use of resources.

reduce class size (none of the descriptions include references to class size or smaller classes). District A does devote substantial Title I resources (about 5 percent of its budget) to extending the kindergarten day, a program that would not be permitted in a targeted assistance school.

Other line items are more difficult to classify. For example, the description for many line items indicates that teachers will provide "supplemental instruction" in core subjects, or "to support" core subjects; in many cases, the line item references "eligible students" or indicates that this will happen during the regular school day. Sometimes the description indicates that the role will be filled by a "highly qualified teacher." These line items appear to refer to some form of small group or one-on-one supplemental instruction. This could be funding for traditional *pull-outs*, where students are taken out of class to work with a specialist or paraprofessional individually or in groups, or *push-ins*, where similar activity takes place inside the classroom. But we cannot tell from the description whether the supplemental instruction is well integrated with the regular instructional program or more separate, as in much-criticized pull-out programs. Similarly, both districts report substantial spending on instructional coaches, paraprofessionals, and interventionists—purchases that may seem more supplemental or separate, but if well-integrated with the regular instructional program could well be core.

Perhaps the most interesting difference between the two districts is that, in district A, line item descriptions commonly use language suggesting a targeted assistance approach to justifying spending. For example, a nontrivial share of line items mention "eligible students" or refer to "Title I students" or equipment, a distinction that is critical in targeted assistance schools, but not necessary in schoolwide programs.[21] We want to emphasize (again) that we cannot make conclusions about the efficacy of any particular Title I line item or Title I spending overall. Rather, we view this exercise as pointing out the difficulty of understanding how schools use Title I funds based on what they report in the applications (though what they report there is voluminous), and showing that some districts clearly do take advantage of the flexibility schoolwide programs allow, but other districts and schools may not fully perceive or act on the added flexibility the schoolwide designation permits.

To better understand how Title I administrators decide how to allocate Title I funds, how they understand the rules that govern those allocations, and where they get information about those rules, we interviewed eight district Title I administrators. District administrators consistently referred to their state education agencies, or consultants retained by those agencies, as the key decision makers in judging which uses of funds were permissible. They understood that the principle of supplement not supplant is a federal one, not a state one, but perceive their states to be the arbiters of that concept.[22] This points to the importance of targeting communication about what is allowable to state education agencies; we return to this point later.

Overall, the administrators were quite consistent in these interviews in characterizing their use of Title I funds as supplemental. We emphasize here and throughout that though some supplemental practices of the past (for example, pull-out instruction delivered by paraprofessionals who today would not be described as highly qualified) were widely criticized, we do not affix a value judgment to supplemental per se. For example, a district using Title I funds to provide struggling students with personalized support from a well-trained reading specialist may well be an effective use

---

21. We are not able to match line items to schools in district A. However, less than 5 percent of schools in the district operate targeted assistance programs, and these terms appear frequently enough that those line items are unlikely to all belong to the targeted assistance schools. The justification for about 6 percent of line items, accounting for 12 percent of Title I funding, include either of two phrases, "eligible students" or "Title I students."

22. This raises the important question, which is beyond the scope of the current article, of how state education agencies (SEAs) interpret the federal rules, and why. This is also a little-studied topic (see GAO 2003; Hanna 2014; Murphy 2014).

of funds. The extent to which it is effective depends not only on what the specialist is doing with the students, but also on how those activities align with the core instructional program the students experience in their regular classes.

We asked about common uses of funds in both schoolwide programs and targeted assistance schools, as relevant to district circumstances. Based on the activities they described, we conclude that their common use of the terms *supplemental* and *intervention* and avoidance of the term *core* does accurately reflect how they spend Title I funds, rather than being driven by reporting bias favoring activities they perceive to be compliant. The types of supplemental supports they described generally included expenditures on personnel: specialists or interventionists, instructional coaches, paraprofessionals, and in some cases, retired teachers working part time. When administrators reported using Title I funds for such personnel, we asked whether the personnel were working with students on content from the core curriculum, or on supplemental content: administrators typically responded that the content in the intervention, not simply its delivery format, was supplemental, though in some cases described the content as core support. These personnel provided services inside or outside the regular classroom during the regular school day (push-in or pull-out respectively) or before or after school via extended day programs. In some cases, students were served during the summer. Some administrators reported schoolwide programs using funds for regular classroom teachers for class size reduction. Professional development was also reported as a use of funds.

Administrators frequently referred to the interventions by their tiers in the response to intervention (RTI) framework.[23] In this framework, tier 1 refers to what we think of as regular classroom instruction with ongoing screening to identify students in need of further supports, tier 2 is the first line of response, often in a small group, and tier 3 is the most intensive, individualized level intervention. RTI is a permissible and encouraged use of funds, and provides another example of how difficult it is to classify Title I expenditures as comprehensive versus fragmented, or core versus supplemental, in their contributions to school improvement. One can imagine a school implementing RTI faithfully as viewing all three tiers as essential parts of individualized, core instruction. It is also easy to imagine today's administrators describing programs much like the pull-out programs of the past—so distinct from the core curriculum as to be disjointed—as tier 2 or tier 3 interventions. In practice, the administrators we spoke to not only consistently referred to their Title I interventions as supplemental, but also mentioned their use of supplemental materials as separate from the regular curricular materials. One administrator clarified that these materials "are only allowed to be used by our intervention team," as required by supplement not supplant in a targeted assistance school.

Administrators often described supplemental instruction via an extended day or extended year. In each case, we asked whether this was a uniform schedule for the entire school or an option for participating students (in the case of schoolwide programs, potentially for all students in a school). In all cases, the extra hours were optional, so regular classroom teachers could not expect all their students to receive any particular content via that program; extended day programs were often described as providing tutoring or supplemental educational services, but never core instruction.[24] Again, seeing a line-item description on a budget (for example, "extended day ELA instruction") does not communicate the full context needed to judge the likely efficacy of the

---

23. RTI is discussed explicitly in the Individuals with Disabilities Education Act (IDEA), but not in the statutory language of ESEA. Schools receiving Title I funds are also implementing special education services to be in compliance with IDEA, so it is in not surprising that they reference RTI concepts in this context.

24. In the case of supplemental educational services, we interpret the use of the term *supplemental* as describing a required policy action rather than reflecting an administrator's judgment on the pedagogical nature of services.

funded activities or whether they represent an improvement over the old style of Title I services fragmenting educational programming. Some schoolwide programs offered extended day options for all students, and it is clearly legal to do so; targeted assistance schools are limited to offering this to their Title I–identified students. Yet when describing a schoolwide program offering before- and after-school tutoring to all its students, one administrator concluded, "We're probably breaking some rule."

The interviews not only were helpful in decoding the types of expenditures described tersely in the application budgets, but also reveal why districts had chosen to allocate their funds as they did. Administrators rarely mentioned concern with future audits, but often mentioned the need for approval from their state education agency or its consultants during the application phase. One said, "They'll come back to me and say, listen, this is what you need to say, and then we'll fund it." Similarly, they described their sources of information as coming from their SEAs, via webinars, PowerPoint presentations, and regional meetings of LEA Title I directors with state representation. They rarely referenced the federal Department of Education as a source of information about permissible uses of funds.

Administrators consistently described their programming choices as driven by the desire to improve student achievement for their struggling students. We asked administrators whether they had used Title I to support a number of specific activities. For activities they did not support, they often commented that their decisions were based on their expectations about what would improve student achievement. For example, the sampled districts did not use Title I funds to support arts instruction, nor did they have any interest in doing so. They also reported little to no use of funds for class-size reduction, one of the most intuitively obvious options opened up by the schoolwide program designation. Several described class-size reduction as not supported by research as an effective way of increasing achievement;[25] others noted that it would take funds away from existing Title I programs.[26]

Some administrators described these choices as constrained by concerns about supplanting. For example, one administrator explained that she does not use Title I for software because it would be "hard to buy a computer program for a school with Title I one year and then expand to the rest of the district the next year." Those using Title I funds in high schools reported that they did not use funds to support initial enrollment in credit-bearing courses to avoid supplanting, though some used funds to support credit recovery programs. Another noted more generally, "It's hard because we can't add to current programs, or enhance them, because it might not necessarily be viewed as a supplement." Multiple administrators said concerns about supplanting had deterred them from funding school nurses or other health initiatives they would have liked to pursue.

District policies also constrain them: several administrators reported that they would not consider using Title I to upgrade a core curriculum in a school (such as reading) because then the school would not be using the same curriculum as the rest of the district. They also reported that they were encouraged by their state agencies to buy "people" rather than "things" with Title I, and that technology in particular was "very hard to keep track of."

25. Despite some debate in the literature about the effectiveness of class-size reduction, some well-regarded research suggests smaller classes do increase achievement (for a review, see Chingos 2013).

26. In its National Assessment of Title I from 2009, the Department of Education reported that the average Title I school used 90 percent of its allocation on personnel costs; they also reported that "Title I added $408 per low-income student to personnel expenditures" on average. Abstracting away from mandated set-asides such as parental involvement, the typical Title I school's budget could be supplemented by a maximum of $453 per low-income student. For a Title I school with this average allocation and five hundred students, Title I would thus add $113,250 to the school's budget. If a teacher costs about $60,000 in salary and benefits, this funds about 1.9 FTEs. If this school had five grades and operated a schoolwide program, it could use its entire Title I budget to reduce class size from about twenty-five to close to twenty in two grades (Chambers et al. 2009).

One administrator described how in past experience as a school principal, "We were always encouraged to spend it on people for support, and the rationale that was given to us was that that's how the state prefers it, it's easier to get approved that way."

We asked administrators whether federal or state rules prohibited them from doing anything they would otherwise like to do with their Title I money. The answer was almost uniformly no—that is, the administrators did not name any specific activity that fiscal regulations had prevented them from doing.[27] Within this uniformity, however, were two clear camps: those who used their discretion to move around funds creatively within the limits of the law, and those who identified strongly with Title I's compensatory mission and felt that using funds for other (nonsupplemental) activities would dilute the program as experienced by disadvantaged students. Those in the first camp often described themselves as creative and those in the second emphasized transparency and fidelity to the program. Federal and state rules and regulations may both constrain and enable local implementers. Variation in how local implementers interpret and exercise discretion has been documented and studied in many settings (Hill and Lynn 2015). Aside from the standard principal-agent concerns, in this setting we argue that the goals of the (federal) principal historically have been poorly communicated to the (state and local) agent.[28] It will be interesting to observe how very recent clarifications at the federal level affect state and local behavior going forward.

Of the eight districts represented in the administrator interviews, three districts used schoolwide programs in all of their Title I schools, and one large district did so in nearly all of them. Schools in one district operated only targeted assistance programs, despite eligibility for schoolwide status. This interview provided some interesting insights. The Title I director would like the schools to move to schoolwide programs, but resistance due to job security concerns is evident among current Title I staff at the schools. The director also expressed mixed feelings about whether switching to schoolwide programs would benefit the schools: "Tier 1 instruction is the problem, so a schoolwide program might not fix it." This statement suggests that the director may not be aware that Title I can be used to support tier 1 (applied to all students) instruction in a schoolwide context.

In the remaining three districts, schools operated a mix of schoolwide and targeted assistance programs. Conversations with these district grants managers proved particularly useful in contrasting the activities supported with Title I in the two types of programs within a district.[29] Schoolwide programs consistently did the same things as targeted assistance schools but offered some additional services. Key differences between schoolwide and targeted assistance use of funds in these three anonymized districts follow.

- District X described using Title I in all its program schools primarily to provide extra academic support during the school day, via both push-in and pull-out modes. In schoolwide programs, this support comes from certified teacher interventionists. In targeted assistance schools, it is provided by highly trained paraprofessionals.

- District Y reported using funds similarly in each of its Title I schools, for instructional support specialists, including a certified teacher who oversees a team of highly qualified paraprofessionals, and for an instructional coach. This model is followed by both schoolwide and targeted assistance programs; both types of programs identify individual students to be served by Title I

---

27. One administrator described a recent federal change in the rules now prohibiting districts from using funds to buy food for staff while participating in professional development as "a big problem."

28. Jennings (2015) discusses a distinct principal-agent tension between Congress and federal Title I administrators.

29. These interviews came from administrators in districts with two to five Title I schools total, and at least one schoolwide program and at least one targeted assistance school per district.

using state and district assessments. Additional expenditures in schoolwide programs not found in targeted assistance schools included Chromebooks, a social worker for the school, and tutoring (by teachers) before and after school.

- District Z has one SWP and one TAS. In both schools, Title I funds "mostly teachers"—math and literacy supplemental instructors providing Tier 2 (typically small group) interventions. They describe the teachers as serving students who need a "short-term boost of academic support... who function just below proficiency." In the SWP, the specific students served change throughout the year as individual needs evolve, but in the TAS program they "must designate the kids" and do "not have fluidity to move kids in and out of support throughout the year."

Overall, administrators across the three districts attributed most of the additional services in schoolwide programs to their higher funding levels stemming from their eligibility ranking within their districts, rather than to flexibility afforded by the schoolwide model. One administrator noted the flexibility of schoolwide programs has made it easier for them to purchase certain supplies compared to their targeted assistance counterparts, including online licensing for remediation programs.

CONCLUSIONS: FISCAL RULES AND EFFECTIVE SPENDING GOING FORWARD

ESEA is reaching its half-century mark in contentious times. The law is widely recognized as essentially inoperable as a funding mechanism, prompting widespread use of the waiver process under ESEA Flexibility because Congress has been unable to reauthorize a more functional version of the law. The political obstacles to reauthorization are primarily related to the strings attached to Title I funds, particularly resistance to state accountability systems. By comparison, the issues related to Title I's fiscal rules discussed here have received little attention. Yet however the debates about testing and standards are resolved, the questions we raise about how to optimally monitor Title I spending will remain critical. They also apply more broadly to federal education policy, as other programs have their own fiscal rules.[30]

The problem of targeting funds while promoting quality is widely recognized as a thorny one.[31] All parties involved clearly expend a great deal of effort trying to get things right. The federal government tries to develop and enforce appropriate compliance regimes, introducing potential sources of local flexibility via policies such as schoolwide programs and the ability to consolidate federal funds. States and districts try to best serve their students while adhering to those complex and evolving sets of rules, devoting considerable staff time to documenting their compliance and formally associating particular expenditures with permissible titles ("moving money around"). In our interviews with district Title I administrators, several of the more creative told us of their efforts linking costs to pots of money they perceived to be legal and away from Title I, where they feared they would be supplanting; in multiple cases, in fact, the specific expenditures would have been permissible uses of Title I funds.[32] Similarly, more cautious Title I directors often described roads not taken because of concern about supplanting. In both situations, misperceptions about the rules were costly to the district, either in terms of administrative burden or by preventing a perhaps more effective allocation of funds.

States also have developed their own categorical programs, often with compliance requirements similar to the federal ones. This creates a still more complex problem for district administrators needing to show that multiple funding streams each distinctly contrib-

---

30. These rules can vary across programs within one federal agency. For example, supplement not supplant is defined differently in the context of IDEA than in ESEA.

31. Indeed, our recommendations are very similar in spirit to those of past decades (Kirst 1988).

32. We cannot speak to their full problem-solving strategy, however, given the case-specific state and local requirements with which we are not familiar.

ute to educational inputs. At this point, even if districts moved away from justifying the supplemental nature of Title I expenditures in schoolwide programs on a cost-by-cost basis, their discretion over their budgets would still be significantly restricted by the amassed compliance requirements over a variety of federal and state categorical programs (see, for example, Roza 2010; Hanna 2014).

We concur with Duncan and Murnane when they write, "The challenge is to devise organizational structures that provide high-poverty schools with the resources, knowledge, and freedom to choose the collection of supports they need" (2014, 136). To the extent that Title I's fiscal rules—and those of the web of other federal and state categorical programs contributing to district budgets—impinge on that freedom, we have two concrete recommendations. First, replace existing guidance with new, clear, and concise guidance and disseminate it. The dissemination challenge is significant, requiring a concerted effort by the federal government to get word to state education agencies who in turn must get the word out to local districts. Guidance should reach not only Title I personnel in districts and schools, but also others involved in allocating instructional resources. Clear guidance would empower districts to push back against state agencies that require them to remove legally permissible uses of Title I funds from their federal funding applications, and to question their preliminary single-audit findings before the results are finalized and passed on to federal authorities. It would also empower school district staff more closely associated with the work of instruction itself—in offices of teaching and learning, or curriculum and instruction, for example—to question district-level Title I administrators when they deny them access to funds on the basis of supplanting. Finally, it is critical for this guidance to reach auditors. Decisionmakers need to know what they are allowed to do, and that legal uses of funds will not yield inaccurate and damaging audit results.

Our second recommendation relates to the challenge districts face in handling multiple streams of state and federal categorical funding, each with their own compliance requirements. Title I schoolwide programs are permitted to consolidate their Title I funds with other federal, state, and local funds so that they do not have to maintain distinct fiscal trails for each separate program. But a recent survey found only 6 percent of districts operating schoolwide programs took up this option, and found that "state or district accounting rules and fear of potential audit exceptions were major barriers to consolidation of funding" (Chambers et al. 2009, xxvii). Consolidating funding is not the explicit focus in this article, and our recommendation here is correspondingly broad: states and local governments should reconsider the impact of their rules on schools' ability to use funds productively. The U.S. Department of Education requires each state education agency to "eliminate State fiscal and accounting barriers so that these funds can be more easily consolidated" (2015, 8). The federal government and national nongovernmental organizations could potentially play an important role in providing technical assistance in these efforts. We view both these policy recommendations as necessary but not sufficient for addressing the big problem—the lack of instructional capacity in school districts. We do not offer a magic bullet for building this elusive capacity, but instead hope that reducing the complexity of compliance and enhancing flexibility will contribute to creating an environment where efforts to do so have a better chance of flourishing.

APPENDIX A

Current Statutory Language on Supplement, Not Supplant, in No Child Left Behind

SEC. 1120A. FISCAL REQUIREMENTS.
(a) MAINTENANCE OF EFFORT- A local educational agency may receive funds under this part for any fiscal year only if the State educational agency involved finds that the local educational agency has maintained the agency's fiscal effort in accordance with section 9521.
(b) FEDERAL FUNDS TO SUPPLEMENT, NOT SUPPLANT, NON-FEDERAL FUNDS-
   (1) IN GENERAL- A State educational agency or local educational agency shall use Federal funds received under this part only to supplement the funds that would,

in the absence of such Federal funds, be made available from non-Federal sources for the education of pupils participating in programs assisted under this part, and not to supplant such funds.

(2) SPECIAL RULE- No local educational agency shall be required to provide services under this part through a particular instructional method or in a particular instructional setting in order to demonstrate such agency's compliance with paragraph (1).

(No Child Left Behind Act of 2001, Pub. L. No. 107-110, § 115, Stat. 1425 [2002], section 1120A)

APPENDIX B

Excerpt from Department of Education Nonregulatory Guidance on Fiscal Issues in Title I (February 2008 Update)

E-18. How can a schoolwide program demonstrate that it supplements, and does not supplant, State and local funds?

In a schoolwide program, Title I, Part A funds and other Federal education program funds may be used only to supplement the total amount of funds that would, in the absence of Federal funds, be made available from non-Federal sources for that school, including funds needed to provide services that are required by law for children with disabilities and children with limited English proficiency. (Section 1114[a][2][B])

It is generally an LEA's responsibility, and not a school's, to ensure that the "supplement not supplant" requirement is met and that a schoolwide program school receives all the State and local funds it would receive were it not a Title I schoolwide program school. In other words, an LEA may not reduce its allocation of State and local funds and resources to a schoolwide program school because the school receives Federal funds to operate a schoolwide program. An LEA should be able to demonstrate, through its regular procedures for distributing funds and resources, that it distributes State and local funds fairly and equitably to all its schools–including schoolwide program schools–without regard to whether those schools are receiving Federal education funds.

A schoolwide program school is not expected to keep records of the particular services paid for with Federal education funds that are used in the schoolwide program, nor is it required to demonstrate that any particular service supplements the services regularly provided in that school. (Section 1114[a][2][A])

APPENDIX C

Excerpt from A-133 Circular on Presumptions of Supplanting

In the following instances, it is presumed that supplanting has occurred:

    a. The SEA or LEA used Federal funds to provide services that the SEA or LEA was required to make available under other Federal, State or local laws. (See note below, ESEA Flexibility, regarding this presumption and ESEA flexibility).

    b. The SEA or LEA used Federal funds to provide services that the SEA or LEA provided with non-Federal funds in the prior year.

    c. The SEA or LEA used Title I, Part A or MEP funds to provide services for participating children that the SEA or LEA provided with non-Federal funds for non-participating children.

These presumptions are rebuttable if the SEA or LEA can demonstrate that it would not have provided the services in question with non-Federal funds had the Federal funds not been available.

Schoolwide Programs – In a Title I schoolwide program, a school is not required to provide supplemental services to identified children. A school operating a schoolwide program does not have to (1) show that Federal funds used within the school are paying for additional services that would not otherwise be provided; or (2) demonstrate that Federal funds are used only for specific target populations. Such a school, however, is required to use funds available under Title I and any other Federal programs to supplement the total amount of funds that would, in the absence of the Federal funds, be made available from non-Federal sources for that school, including funds needed to provide services that are required by law for children with disabilities and children with limited English proficiency (Title I, Part A, Section 1114(a)(2) of ESEA (20 USC 6314(a)(2)); 34 CFR sections 200.25(c) and (d)). (Executive Office of the President 2014, Section 84.000)

REFERENCES

Bailey, Stephen K., and Edith K. Mosher. 1968. *ESEA: The Office of Education Administers a Law.* Syracuse, N.Y.: Syracuse University Press.

Borman, Geoffrey D., and Jerome V. D'Agostino. 1996. "Title I and Student Achievement: A Meta-Analysis of Federal Evaluation Results." *Educational Evaluation and Policy Analysis* 18(4): 309–26.

Cascio, Elizabeth U., Nora Gordon, and Sarah Reber. 2013. "Local Responses to Federal Grants: Evidence from the Introduction of Title I in the South." *American Economic Journal: Economic Policy* 5(3): 126–59.

Chambers, Jay G., Irene Lam, Kanya Mahitivanichcha, Phil Esra, Larisa Shambaugh, and Stephanie Stullich. 2009. "State and Local Implementation of the No Child Left Behind Act. Volume VI—Targeting and Uses of Federal Education Funds." In *National Longitudinal Study of No Child Left Behind* and *Study of State Implementation of Accountability and Teacher Quality Under No Child Left Behind.* Washington: Education Publications Center for U.S. Department of Education, Office of Planning, Evaluation and Policy Development, Policy and Program Studies Service.

Chingos, Matthew M. 2013. "Class Size and Student Outcomes: Research and Policy Implications." *Journal of Policy Analysis and Management* 32(2): 411–38.

Cohen, David K., and Susan L. Moffitt. 2009. *The Ordeal of Equality: Did Federal Regulation Fix the Schools?* Cambridge, Mass.: Harvard University Press.

Coleman, James S. 1966. "The Concept of Equality of Educational Opportunity." Paper prepared for Equality of Educational Opportunity, a conference sponsored by the U.S. Office of Education. Cambridge, Mass (July 2, 1966).

Duncan, Greg J., and Richard J. Murnane. 2014. *Restoring Opportunity: The Crisis of Inequality and the Challenge for American Education.* Cambridge, Mass.: Harvard Education Press.

Executive Office of the President. 2014. *OMB Circular A-133 Compliance Supplement: 2014*, vol. 1, part 4. Washington: Office of Management and Budget.

Gordon, Nora. 2004. "Do Federal Grants Boost School Spending? Evidence from Title I." *Journal of Public Economics* 88(9–10): 1771–92.

Hanna, Robert. 2014. "Seeing Beyond Silos: How State Education Agencies Spend Federal Education Dollars and Why." Washington, D.C.: Center for American Progress and The Broad Foundation - Education. Available at: https://www.americanprogress.org/issues/education/report/2014/06/13/91216/seeing-beyond-silos (accessed July 29, 2015).

Heuer, Ruth, and Stephanie Stullich. 2011. "Comparability of State and Local Expenditures Among Schools Within Districts: A Report from the Study of School-Level Expenditures." RTI International and U.S. Department of Education. Washington: U.S. Department of Education, Office of Planning, Evaluation and Policy Development, Policy and Program Studies Service.

Hill, Carolyn J., and Laurence E. Lynn Jr. 2015. *Public Management: Thinking and Acting in Three Dimensions*, 2nd ed. Thousand Oaks, Calif.: Sage/CQ Press.

Honig, Meredith I., ed. 2006. *New Directions in Education Policy Implementation: Confronting Complexity.* Albany: State University of New York Press.

Jennings, Jack. 2015. *Presidents, Congress, and the Public Schools: The Politics of Education Reform.* Cambridge, Mass.: Harvard Education Press.

Junge, Melissa, and Sheara Krvaric. 2011. "The Compliance Culture in Education." *Education Week*, October 24. Available at: http://blogs.edweek.org/edweek/rick_hess_straight_up/2011/10/the_compliance_culture_in_education.html (accessed January 17, 2015).

———. 2012. "How the Supplement-Not-Supplant Requirement Can Work Against the Policy Goals of Title I: A Case for Using Title I, Part A, Education Funds More Effectively and Efficiently." Washington, D.C.: Center for American Progress and American Enterprise Institute for Public Policy Research.

Keaton, Patrick. 2012. "Numbers and Types of Public Elementary and Secondary Schools from the Common Core of Data: School Year 2010–11." Washington: National Center for Education Statistics. Available at: https://nces.ed.gov/pubs 2012/2012325rev.pdf (accessed January 17, 2015).

Kirst, Michael W. 1988. "The Federal Role and Chapter 1: Rethinking Some Basic Assumptions." In *Federal Aid to the Disadvantaged: What Future for Chapter 1?*, edited by Denis P. Doyle and Bruce S. Cooper. Philadelphia, Pa.: The Falmer Press.

Martin, Ruby, and Phyllis McClure. 1969. "Title I of ESEA: Is It Helping Poor Children?" Washington, D.C.: Washington Research Project and National Association for the Advancement of Colored People Legal Defense and Educational Fund.

Matsudaira, Jordan D., Adrienne Hosek, and Elias Walsh. 2012. "An Integrated Assessment of the Effects of Title I on School Behavior, Resources, and Student Achievement." *Economics of Education Review* 31(3): 1–14.

Murphy, Patrick. 2014. "Help Wanted Flexibility for Innovative State Education Agencies." Washington, D.C.: Center for American Progress and The Broad Foundation - Education.

President's Council on Integrity and Efficiency. 2007. "Report on National Single Audit Sampling Project." Washington: President's Council on Integrity and Efficiency Audit Committee. Available at: https://www.ignet.gov/sites/default/files/files/NatSamProjRptFINAL2.pdf (accessed July 29, 2015).

Puma, Michael J., Calvin C. Jones, Donald Rock, Roberto Fernandez, Edward C. Bryant, Judith Pollack, James McPartland, and Abt Associates. 1993. *Prospects: the Congressionally Mandated Study of Educational Growth and Opportunity: The Interim Report*. Washington: U.S. Department of Education Planning and Evaluation Service.

Roza, Marguerite. 2008. "What If We Closed the Title I Comparability Loophole?" In *Ensuring Equal Opportunity in Public Education: How Local School District Funding Practices Hurt Disadvantaged Students and What Federal Policy Can Do About It*. Washington, D.C.: Center for American Progress.

———. 2010. *Educational Economics: Where Do School Funds Go?* Washington, D.C.: Urban Institute Press.

Smith, Marshall. 1986. "Selecting Students and Services for Chapter 1." In *Designs for Compensatory Education: Conference Proceedings and Papers*, edited by Barbara I. Williams, Peggy A. Richmond, and Beverly J. Mason. Chapel Hill, N.C.: Research and Evaluation Associates.

Spillane, James P. 2004. *Standards Deviation: How Schools Misunderstand Education Policy*. Cambridge, Mass.: Harvard University Press.

Stanton, Larry and Alison Segal. 2013. "The Bold and the Bureaucrat: The Top Ten State Education Agency Levers for School Turnaround." Washington, D.C., and Boston, Mass.: Federal Education Group for Mass Insight Education and State Development Network for School Turnaround.

Turnbull, Brenda J. 1981. "Promises and Prospects of Education Program Consolidation at the Federal Level." *Educational Evaluation and Policy Analysis* 3(3): 21–32.

U.S. Department of Education. 2006. "Designing Schoolwide Programs Non-Regulatory Guidance." Washington: U.S. Department of Education.

———. 2008. "Non-Regulatory Guidance. Title I Fiscal Issues: Maintenance of Effort; Comparability; Supplement not Supplant; Carryover; Consolidating Funds in Schoolwide Programs; Grantback Requirements." Washington: U.S. Department of Education.

———. 2015. "Supporting School Reform by Leveraging Federal Funds in a Schoolwide Program." Enclosed in a "Dear Colleague" letter from the office of the assistant secretary. Available at: http://www2.ed.gov/policy/elsec/guid/esea titleiswguidance.pdf (accessed September 10, 2015).

U.S. Government Accountability Office (GAO). 2003. "Report to Congressional Requestors: Disadvantaged Students: Fiscal Oversight of Title I Could Be Improved." Washington: Government Printing Office.

Van der Klaauw, Wilbert. 2008. "Breaking the Link Between Poverty and Low Student Achievement: An Evaluation of Title I." *Journal of Econometrics* 142(2): 731–56.

Wong, Kenneth K., and Stephen J. Meyer. 1998. "Title I Schoolwide Programs: A Synthesis of Findings from Recent Evaluation." *Educational Evaluation and Policy Analysis* 20(2): 115–36.

The Shift from Adequacy to Equity in Federal Education Policymaking: A Proposal for How ESEA Could Reshape the State Role in Education Finance

ERIC A. HOUCK AND ELIZABETH DEBRAY

ESEA's original intent was to provide educational assistance to less privileged students. However, ESEA's supplemental funding for students and teachers has often been inadequate in addressing pervasive and systematic disparities in fiscal resources. These disparities exist between states, within states, and within school districts. In the spirit of the original legislation, this article proposes addressing educational fiscal inequities via a new program within ESEA that would reward states for reforming their education finance systems to address inequities between and within states, and within districts. The program would effectively steer federal resources to encourage thoughtful work to reform and recalibrate state- and district-level finance mechanisms. It would be designed as a competitive grant program built upon the framework of Race to the Top. This article articulates a rationale for the program, especially the need for a renewed federal focus on opportunity-to-learn, reviews relevant research, outlines program details, and reviews political considerations.

Keywords: finance, federal policy, politics

Beginning in the 1990s, the field of school finance began to reflect the wider world of education policy by undergoing a conceptual shift from an equity perspective focused on the equalization of educational inputs toward an adequacy perspective focused on the performance of the educational system overall, measured by student performance on systematically aligned assessments. Federal policymaking—best exemplified by the No Child Left Behind Act (NCLB)—also came to reflect this outcomes-oriented approach. No Child Left Behind was the 2001 reauthorization of the Elementary and Secondary Education Act (ESEA), and any subsequent reauthorization will be made within the context of this legislation.

Despite the positive intentions of many members of Congress who supported NCLB's direct school-level, subgroup accountability model, observers of the law have written that its design includes many dis-equalizing incentives. Scholars have decried the pervasiveness of standardized testing, the historical bias of standardized tests for poor and mi-

---

Eric A. Houck is associate professor of educational leadership and policy at the University of North Carolina, Chapel Hill. Elizabeth DeBray is professor of educational administration and policy at the University of Georgia.

The authors wish to thank Dr. Marshall Smith, former undersecretary of education and former dean and professor, Stanford University, Andrew Rotherham of Bellwether Associates, and Jack Jennings, former director of the Center for Education Policy, for their substantial comments on the policy ideas in this paper. Direct correspondence to: Eric A. Houck, eahouck@unc.edu, University of North Carolina at Chapel Hill, School of Education, 121F Peabody Hall, CB 3500, Chapel Hill, NC 27599; Elizabeth DeBray, edebray@uga.edu, University of Georgia, 325 River's Crossing, 850 College Station Rd., Athens, Georgia 30602.

nority students, the subsequent narrowing of the curriculum for students as a result of NCLB's focus on reading and mathematics, the state level system-gaming undertaken to meet NCLB requirements, the potential effect on teacher labor markets, and the chilling effect of accountability sanctions on schools and communities (Burroughs, Groce, and Webeck 2005; Schoen and Fusarelli 2008; Berliner 2011; Cawelti 2006; Grodsky, Warren, and Felts 2008, 385; Reich 2013; Porter, Linn, and Trimble 2005; Bushaw and Calderon 2014). The law has also been criticized for overregulation of local schools (Howe and Meens 2012); and being an unfunded mandate (National Conference of State Legislatures 2005; McColl 2005, 604).

Federal education policy should not continue unchecked in this outcomes-based approach indefinitely, we argue. Unequal funding across states, districts, and schools harms low-income and minority students disproportionately; consider that in 2005, 76 percent of the nation's low-income students attended public schools in districts with a per pupil expenditure below the national average (Southern Education Foundation 2009, 17). Continuing unabated, trends of unequal school funding in the United States have obvious compounded negative effects on equality of opportunity for both individual citizens and the society as a whole, namely, diminishing economic security, citizens' living standards, and democratic participation (Southern Education Foundation 2009; Kenworthy 2014; Mr. Y 2011; Carter and Welner 2013). In response, the federal government should use ESEA to develop an "equality orientation," which does not necessarily revolve solely around inputs to education; it may be just as concerned with equal outputs or equal access to schooling (Reich 2013, 52). State and local governments can foster equality of opportunity by alleviating levels of concentrated poverty in schools, expanding health care and education for very young children, and creating conditions for strengthening the economic and housing opportunities in the communities in which schools are located. Yet after so much focus over the past fourteen years on the NCLB paradigm, those states undeniably require inducements to formulate different kinds of policies.

State-level work on the equitable provision of educational resources has occurred without substantial federal assistance due to a host of legal and political factors. The tenth amendment, and the 1973 Supreme Court decision in *San Antonio ISD v. Rodriguez* (411 U.S. 1), have hampered federal activism in the realm of school financing. We see an opportunity to address such lack of action.

By reaching back into the litigious origins of the concept of adequacy, this paper develops a notion of resource sufficiency closely aligned with the concept of opportunity-to-learn standards advanced by education policymakers in the 1990s. It then proposes a competitive grant program that could be embedded within ESEA, the goal of which is to spur innovation in closing inter- and intradistrict resource gaps, while also offering states the opportunity to develop resource sufficiency to address student academic achievement gaps (*San Antonio ISD v. Rodriguez*). States would compete based on their plans to both reform their finance systems and design innovative interventions in the areas of early childhood education, community supports, and desegregation. This proposal represents a focus different from the often-contentious recent debates over the federal role in supporting charter schools, teacher evaluation plans, and adoption of the Common Core standards.

As observers of developments in education finance and federal education policymaking, we note that these two fields, although sharing goals, aspirations, and values, have developed separate vocabularies to describe the work of resource allocation. We seek to bridge these two nomenclatures by aligning the concept of equal opportunity from the policymaking field with the concept of resource equity from the education finance literature, and by aligning opportunity-to-learn from policy with a specific notion of adequacy—resource sufficiency—from school finance. Although ESEA has provided billions of dollars in supplemental funding to states and districts, and although Congress and the federal Department of Education (ED) have successfully leveraged ESEA dollars to drive educational policy in terms of standards, assessment, governance, and accountability, we believe this proposal provides federal policymakers with the ability to begin to address one systematic component that it has long been restrained from addressing: the inequitable per-pupil funding levels between states, within states, and within districts.

Others have written about the evolution of ESEA from a focus on equality of opportunity to one primarily on adequacy via standards-based reform, and our aim here is not to review that evolution in substantial detail (McDonnell 2005; McGuinn 2006; DeBray 2006; Wells 2009). Our premise is that if state legislatures and federal courts are no longer active arenas for addressing issues of equal educational opportunity, Congress should do so for democratic reasons (see Belfield and Levin 2013). As noted earlier, both national economic security and individual living standards, like democratic participation and educational attainment, are directly affected by funding inequality. Layered over these factors, however, is a growing educational and economic opportunity gap in the United States since 1970 (Duncan and Murnane 2014). Data from the National Assessment of Educational Progress (NAEP) indicate that, though racial and ethnic achievement gaps are narrowing, socioeconomic gaps in achievement remain. These gaps have far-reaching implications: in school completion, lifetime earnings, and the wide range of resulting societal outcomes. Gaps in achievement related to family background, therefore, persist into the school system, and the system itself does little to blunt their impact. Furthermore, returns to education in the labor market have risen dramatically in the past forty years. "Between 1979 and 1987," Greg Duncan and Richard Murnane write, "the inflation-adjusted earnings of male high school graduates plunged by 16 percent, while the earnings of college-educated workers rose by nearly 10 percent" (2014, 15). Upward intergenerational mobility, to which education was the key in the United States for most of the twentieth century, has also witnessed a downward trend since the mid-1990s and a flat long-term trend in addition to widening income gaps (Duncan and Murnane 2014, 20; Chetty et al. 2014).

We do not contend that the federal role in education alone can be tasked with alleviating these problems. Compensatory education has a harder time equalizing outcomes under such conditions. As we will see, other scholars have called for more comprehensive solutions that cut across social service sectors to serve students. However, a federal program that seeks to create the public finance contexts in which a genuine equality of opportunity-to-learn exists is long overdue in U.S. elementary and secondary educational policy. This proposal outlines a mechanism to achieve what plaintiffs sought in Rodriguez and what two generations of litigators have pursued in state courts: a more equitable resource base for students, justifying the existing accountability framework of federal policy.

In the following section, we review first what we believe to be the problems of unequal resource distribution among American schools, and then the concepts of equity and adequacy as they are discussed in the fields of educational policy and education finance.

FUNDING VARIATIONS AMONG AND WITHIN STATES AND DISTRICTS AND POSSIBLE REMEDIES

As a state-led function in a federalist system, interstate variation in school finance has presented federal policymakers with a perennial problem. Measures of fiscal inequality between and within states are not new and have not dramatically changed in recent years; substantial variation in per pupil expenditures is long-standing (U.S. Department of Education 2009). As Bruce Baker and Sean Corcoran report in an analysis of regressive and progressive state funding formulas, state rankings in terms of progressivity are relatively immune to such statistical controls for regional cost and wage variations when examining the differences in mean revenues between districts in the lowest and highest poverty quintiles within a state (2012). This point has been made through school finance litigation—*Serrano v. Priest* (5 Cal.3d 584, 1971) being the earliest and most commonly cited example—and has been enshrined as the field of school finance's Proposition One: "The quality of a child's schooling should not be a function of wealth, other than the wealth of the state as a whole" (Guthrie et al. 2007, 174).

Interstate Variation

Interstate variation in funding is driven by two factors: variation among states in the soundness of school finance systems that raise and distribute educational funds, and state political will and fiscal capacity to raise money. Our proposal seeks to improve the interstate variation in educational funds by focusing more on the former than the latter. To that end, a number of finance system tools serve to decrease both the impact of local wealth and the disproportional underfunding of poor or minority communities. Providing states incentives to adopt and strengthen these policies will help address—but not eliminate—interstate spending variation. Three tools are pupil weighting, power equalization, and full state assumption of educational costs.

Pupil Weights
Pupil weights steer dollars to high needs or high-risk populations. These weights overcount students in these populations—an economically disadvantaged student may count 1.4 times a normal student—and funds are allocated on this adjusted per-pupil basis. Pupil weighting systems add a dimension of vertical equity into a finance system, primarily by steering additional funds to districts with concentrations of high-needs students. More recently, districts have adopted pupil weighting strategies to allocate resources to schools, with notable examples being Oakland, Houston, Cincinnati, and Boston.

Power Equalizing, or Guaranteed Tax Base Plans
Many states require a local district's contribution from local property taxes to ensure local political will and to shift costs to districts. A guaranteed tax base (GTB) structure subsidizes local property so that one tax unit brings in an equal amount of funds across all districts.

Full State Funding
Another strategy for diminishing the impact of local wealth variation is for the state to assume higher proportions of overall funding in a state. Doing so eliminates variations based on property wealth that drive interstate funding disparities. In a sense, experiments with aspects of full state funding are occurring in some of the forty-two states with charter school legislation on the books, since charter schools often receive only the state amount of funding per pupil or reduced contributions from sending LEAs. As of this writing, the National Center for Education Statistics estimates the number of charter school students to be approximately 2.3 million, or approximately 4.6 percent of the public school population. The charter sector, in other words, currently lacks the scale for its school funding and attendance to affect statewide funding systems substantially.

Some have argued that state assumption of the fiscal burdens of public education breaks Tiebout relationships between local communities and their schools—stating that local communities are more supportive of taxation that supports local schools. We acknowledge that how much a jurisdiction chooses to spend on lowering property taxes versus purchasing educational services (a substitution effect) is a question of political will. Stated another way: taxpayers may express preferences for tax savings over enhanced (and price-discounted) educational quality in funding systems that are more centralized and rely less on local effort for school funding. Our sole purpose here is to focus on policy mechanisms that have the potential to reduce within-state inequities. This is a separate problem from the inequity introduced into finance systems by intrastate variations in property wealth (Tiebout 1956; Fischel 1989), and can be addressed by variations to the models themselves, up to and including leaving some districts off-model to enhance equity (Reschovsky 1994; Rothstein 1992).

Another approach would be for the federal government to provide direct federal equalization money to states. However, providing additional funds into antiquated, inefficient school finance systems is akin to throwing good money after bad; we think that instead federal actors should first ensure the quality of school finance systems before dramatically investing in them, and envision a competitive grant program as one way to incentivize these state-level improvements.

Intrastate Variation

This approach of using state-level funding formulas to leverage national equality in student access to resources correlates highly with a state's capacity to improve equity within its borders and across district boundaries. Multiple state-level studies have examined the inequity of intrastate (or interdistrict) resources allocation by examining levels of funding as well as the inequality of resource allocation based on measure such as race and poverty (for examples examining North Carolina and Tennessee, see Rolle, Houck, and McColl 2008; Rolle and Liu 2007). In addition, multiple papers have examined the results of changes in state funding formulas as a result of school finance litigation, generally finding that changes in funding formulas can reduce overall interdistrict levels of inequity and sufficiency (Baker and Welner 2011; Sims 2011; Springer, Liu, and Guthrie 2009; Murray, Evans, and Schwab 1998). Multiple studies confirm the efficacy of successful litigation during this period in both increasing spending and reducing inequality within states (Murray et al. 1998; Jackson et al. 2014). Kirabo Jackson, Rucker Johnson, and Claudia Persico find a correlation between increased per-pupil expenditures for all twelve years of elementary and secondary education for children from poor families and higher earnings and reduction in the annual incidence of adult poverty (2014). Finally, national studies of interdistrict equity include those from the National Center for Education Statistics, *Education Week*, the Education Trust, and the Education Law Center (ELC). The ELC publishes an annual report card analyzing funding fairness across districts within states. Although it is beyond the scope of this article to examine each model in detail, we feel that the preponderance of such analyses indicate that work in this area is available for adoption in assessing state-level equity from a federal perspective. States can be assessed on the level of fairness in their funding system along a number of dimensions. Adopting such measures at the federal level would provide states with a set of resource allocation goals and allow cross-state comparisons. Although states have different school finance systems, they would be able to compete with each other in providing equalized educational opportunities for students from different racial, ethnic, and socioeconomic backgrounds.

Intradistrict Variation

Recent research in school finance has demonstrated that equitably allocating resources to school districts does not necessarily ensure equitable distribution of resources to schools within those districts. The subfield of intradistrict school finance has seen increased attention with the development of more sophisticated data collection systems and a focus on disaggregated student performance (on intradistrict finance, see Berne and Stiefel 1994; Burke 1999; Condron and Roscigno 2003; Hertert 1995; Iatarola and Stiefel 2003; Owens and Maiden 1999; Roza 2005; Rubenstein 1998; Stiefel, Rubenstein, and Berne 1998; Houck 2010). Studies indicate that the interaction of district transfer policies results in migration across schools within districts, the result of which is that schools with higher concentrations of high-needs students end up with aggregately less credentialed, less experienced teachers (Roza and Hill 2004). This, paired with the ubiquity of the single salary schedule, results in real-dollar gaps across schools, with high-needs schools being the most disadvantaged (Freeman, Scafidi, and Sjoquist 2005; Lankford, Loeb, and Wyckoff 2002; Ingersoll 2001; Houck 2010; Baker 2012). Current debate over intradistrict equity has focused on the comparability provisions in Title I, including an ED policy brief that estimated a shift to a dollar-based comparability requirement instead of the current credential-based requirement would result in an additional 18 to 28 percent of districts falling out of compliance, a per pupil expenditure increase estimated at 2 to 15 percent for Title I schools, and a disproportionate (that is, vertically equitable) benefit deriving to the lowest spending schools (Stullich 2011). Members of Congress have advanced proposals to change Title I comparability requirements, but these efforts have so far been resisted by a range of interest groups. Changes in addition to comparability may also help. University of California law professor Goodwin Liu recommends increasing the appropriation for the concentration grants in Title I, because they "provid[e] the most equitable distribution of Title I aid across states" with their 15 percent poverty-eligibility threshold for districts, as well as strengthening maintenance of effort requirements and use of district salary averages in calculating comparability requirements. He also calls for Congress to "build research-based cost factors into Title I formulas" because costs vary between states and districts, noting that Congress could commission new studies to accomplish this (Liu 2008, 973).

Although ED and the federal government have not proposed direct remedies to the problems of finance inequity along these three dimensions, two recent federal policy proposals have sought to address resource equity in other ways. First, the Obama administration's 2015 budget proposal contained a draft of a new Race to the Top (RTT) priority focused on equity and opportunity. Envisioned as a competitive grant, the budget "recognized the harmful impacts of economic segregation in schools, and encourages grantees to identify and carry out strategies that help 'break up and mitigate' the effects of concentrated poverty" (National Coalition on School Diversity 2014, 2). Although Congress appropriated no funds to support this new priority, the proposal indicates some measure of influence of the National Coalition on School Diversity and other civil rights advocates in continuing to press for a federal investment in equity.

Second, in October of 2014, ED's Office for Civil Rights (OCR) issued guidance to school districts regarding what it termed *resource comparability*. This guidance "highlights and explains what Federal law requires regarding the provision of educational resources, how OCR investigates resource disparities, and what States, school districts, and schools can do to meet their constitutional obligations to all their students" (U.S. Department of Education Office for Civil Rights 2014, paragraph 2). Notably, OCR re-circulated a letter from Clinton Secretary of Education Richard Riley about resource disparities by race and ethnicity as constituting potential violations of Title VI of the Civil Rights Act, and called on states to examine whether their provision of educational resources was equitable (Riley 2001).

Clearly, therefore, efforts have been made within the research community and at the federal policymaking level to document and address resource disparities along a conceptual continuum beginning with notions of equity and ending with notions of adequacy. The following section traces the development as well as our conceptual understanding of key terms, specifically those of adequacy and equality of opportunity.

ADEQUACY AND OPPORTUNITY-TO-LEARN

Adequacy does not rest on the principle of equal treatment, and school finance adequacy cases reflect the goal of providing a minimum basic education (Reich 2013), such as the Kentucky Supreme Court's 1989 *Rose v. Council for Basic Education* ruling (90 S.W.2d 186, 60 Ed. Law Rep. 1289). The adequacy orientation in finance and policy also emphasized school outputs. Equality of opportunity, by contrast, pertains to states' "attempt[s] to improve or equalize life chances and opportunities, or to provide an opportunity for each person to flourish" (Reich 2013, 44). "Equality is necessarily comparative or relational; sufficiency is not" (48). Both the 1965 ESEA and the wave of school finance litigation from 1973 through 1989 embodied the equality principle (Reich 2013; Reed 2001). Although the two concepts are easily distinguished, the philosophical arguments for state or federal action to promote either approach are quite complex.

We posit that in the absence of court-mandated actions, the federal government has a future role for providing states with incentives to ameliorate school funding disparities. The range of fiscal factors that make up opportunity-to-learn is wide. NCLB's exclusive focus on adequacy, as measured by test score outcomes, as equity has narrowed the federal role, and future versions of the law need a counterbalance toward other kinds of supports.

OPPORTUNITY-TO-LEARN AND ADEQUACY FROM A SCHOOL FINANCE PERSPECTIVE

In the literature in school finance, the idea of opportunity-to-learn has developed under the umbrella of the value of adequacy. The notion of adequacy, though contested in the school finance literature, has been made quite clear in successive rounds of school finance litigation, through which courts have developed definitions and specific resources necessary for state finance mechanisms to provide students with adequate educational opportunities.

Some saw the development of adequacy standards and methods after 1989 as a new subfield in education finance, others as more an extension of the more venerable concept of equity, referring to work around adequacy as "equity II" (Ladd, Chalk, and Hansen 1999; Guthrie et al. 2007). This definition shifts the focus of the adequacy agenda toward safer ground: ensuring the fair distribution of existing funds (Clune 1994).

In school finance, the term *adequacy* is subject to multiple interpretations. William Clune was the first to formalize it as representing a legal and policy conceptual shift away from equity. Bruce Baker describes it, relative to school finance, as having both an absolute and a relative dimension, where the absolute is concerned with the overall total spending needed for an educational system to meet stated educational outcomes goals, and the relative indicating the expenditure differentials necessary to support different types of students in supporting those goals (2005).

Eric Houck and Moonyoung Eom expanded on this framework by conceptualizing equity and adequacy dimensions along the spectrum of educational productivity by tracing the concept of adequacy through input, throughput, and output phases of production, corresponding to the concepts of sufficiency of funds, purchased inputs, and performance (2012).

Federal action on finance and fiscal equalization was circumvented via Rodriguez (Ryan 2010; Robinson 2015; Reich 2013; Reed 2001). Combined with the scant change in school finance distribution structures and systems since the development of tax base equalization schemes in the 1930s (Springer, Houck, and Guthrie 2007), school finance reform advocates have gravitated away from state houses and into courthouses to adjudicate and seek redress (Hanushek and Lindseth 2009). That is, although additional funds have flowed into schools, the basic mechanisms by which those funds are raised and distributed have perpetuated structural inequality.

Recent adequacy-based policy proposals, such as weighted student funding (WSF) models, have gained limited traction at the LEA level but not engendered any innovation or development at the state level (Ladd 2008). State-level student weights are still more politically than scientifically derived and are not pushed through districts to schools: that is, a state weight to the advantage of economically disadvantaged students that determines how much funding a district receives is not necessarily passed through the district to the school. From a structural perspective, therefore, school finance mechanisms are weak, and there is little incentive to do anything more than marginally affect the amount of dollars flowing into the system.

OPPORTUNITY-TO-LEARN AND ADEQUACY FROM A POLICY PERSPECTIVE

The concept of opportunity-to-learn grew from the recommendations of the National Council on Education Standards and Testing's (NCEST) 1992 report, which held that a new national system of standards and assessments ought to be accompanied by assurances that students had had preparation to learn the material, sometimes called delivery standards. Marshall Smith of Stanford University, chair of the NCEST standards task force, advocated for these service delivery standards, but was strongly opposed by Governor Carroll Campbell (R-SC), who "objected to focusing on inputs rather than outcomes and feared that this would stifle teacher creativity." The compromise Campbell proposed was that "states would develop indicators to assess the quality of the education they offered but would be free to select the data they reported" (Vinovskis 2008, 53).

A year later, Smith and Jennifer O'Day published an article outlining a vision for "standards-based, systemic reform" as a strategy to support educational equity: "It is not legitimate to hold students accountable unless they have been given the opportunity to learn the material on the examination. Similarly, teachers or schools cannot be legitimately held accountable for how well their students do unless they have the preparation and resources to provide the students the opportunity to learn" (1993, 272). In addition, the National Governors Association in 1993, recognizing that the issue might surface in upcoming legislative debates, convened a special task force on how opportunity-to-learn standards might be defined. Numerous scholars wrote papers as background, considering the question "What role should outcomes, processes, and inputs play in monitoring education performance?" (Traiman 1993, 22). As far as Congress was concerned after 1995, the ultimate answer would be that outcomes should play the chief role.

As many have elsewhere elaborated, one version of a national certifying body for state-level opportunity-to-learn standards was authorized as part of the 1994 Goals 2000: Educate America Act (Jennings 1998). This quasi-governmental entity, the National Education Standards and Improvement Council (NESIC), was to be staffed by presidential appointees holding rotating terms of service, and would certify both state-level content and performance standards, as well as opportunity-to-learn standards. NESIC was repealed by the new Republican-majority Congress in 1995. The National Governors Association, in registering its own opposition to NESIC, wrote that it "comes dangerously close to derailing our hard-won emphasis on student achievement" (Schwartz and Robinson 2000, 194).

Over the past decade or so, many observers of the federal role in K–12 education have written in various ways about the need to match NCLB's focus on outcomes with provisions for opportunity-to-learn, whether explicitly termed thus or not. In their 2008 book *Moving Every Child Ahead*, Michael Rebell and Jessica Wolff outline a detailed proposal for reauthorizing ESEA, which they characterize as having been highly inadequate at achieving its stated vision of equality of opportunity, to give greater emphasis to "opportunity" provisions over proficiency provisions (7). They first recommend including in ESEA a statutory provision that states must ensure a "meaningful educational opportunity" in several "designated essential categories" of opportunity, which included both in-school and out-of-school factors (79). Among these essential categories were "effective teachers, principals and other personnel," "adequate school facilities," and "instrumentalities of learning, including, but not limited to, up-to-date textbooks, libraries, laboratories, and computers" among other essential resources (157). Rebell and Wolff also propose that the "practices and conditions" needed to create what they termed "meaningful educational opportunity" be devised on a state-by-state, and perhaps even local, basis (78). We similarly endorse the premise that the federal government can and should provide assurances of capacity and support to states, if the states undertake the reform of their state finance systems.

Also concerned with opportunity-to-learn is legal scholar Kimberly Robinson, who in addressing the failures of NCLB to close the achievement gap has developed a conception of "disruptive federalism" (2015). Robinson advocates for a federal role that would incentivize development of a national common floor of educational opportunity that states must provide; provide necessary research, technical, and financial assistance to accomplish this goal; monitor state progress to achieve this goal through a collaborative enforcement model (984–85); and notably, "distribut[e] financial assistance with the goal of closing the opportunity and achievement gaps" (985). The collaborative enforcement model Robinson envisions would consist of states voluntarily adopting compacts for provision of opportunity-to-learn standards at the state level. The federal government, in turn, would offer technical assistance and a base of research and development, and monitoring of state progress (990–91). She writes that through this collaborative model, which would require new legislative measures and would also include enforcement via sanctions of states when necessary, "the federal government would reestablish itself as the final guarantor of equal access to an excellent education" (1002).

Former Undersecretary of Education Marshall Smith, in a 2011 essay, posited that a competitive grant program situated within Title I could help address state-level intra- and interdistrict funding inequalities. The competition as he envisioned it would address "state inequality in resources by stimulating the use of state finance formulae that take into account the special needs of low-income and other students." Extra federal resources, competitively awarded to states that would agree to change their funding formula to be more sensitive to students with disabilities and English-language learners, for instance, "could make a very important contribution to equal opportunity in many states" (Smith 2011, 241). Although his proposal was not elaborate, Smith's envisioned linkage between Title I and a competitive state-level grant competition is the only one of which we are aware.

Other authors have called for federal incentives to be developed for states to alter districts' or schools' levels of poverty concentration (Suarez 2014; Kahlenberg 2012), to promote interdistrict transfer plans (Holme and Finnigan 2013), to more closely coordinate housing and education policy, and to expand the Promise Neighborhoods program to enhance community-based services in high-poverty areas (DeBray and Frankenberg 2011; Smrekar and Goldring 2011; DeBray and Blankenship 2013). An initiative of the Economic Policy Institute called the Broader Bolder Approach to Education, positioning its comprehensive social-services approach as the decided opposite of No Child Left Behind's narrow focus on test-driven accountability, calls for improved federal policies to support early childhood, health and nutrition, after-school, as well as school reform (2013). Prudence Carter and Kevin Welner's *Closing the Opportunity Gap* is a comprehensive examination of the multiple factors contributing to deficits in opportunity-to-learn, particularly from the standpoint of racial, socioeconomic, linguistic, and geographic barriers. Some of the solutions they propose are improving fair housing enforcement, racial desegregation of schools, and meeting students' need for adequate health care (Carter and Welner 2013).

In a section of its 2013 report, the Commission on Equity and Excellence calls for "bold action by the states—and the federal government—to redesign and reform the funding of our nation's public schools" (U.S. Department of Education 2013, 17). The report delineates general recommendations for both states and the federal government in this area. The commission calls on the federal government to "provide incentives for states to explore and pursue ways to reduce the number of schools with concentrated poverty, because schools without concentrated poverty are less expensive to run than schools with concentrated poverty" (19); as well as to

> direct states, with appropriate incentives, to adopt and implement school finance systems that will (1) provide a meaningful educational opportunity for all students, along with appropriate budgetary and other frameworks to ensure the effective and efficient use of all funds to enable all students to achieve state content and performance standards as outlined above, and (2) demonstrate progress toward implementing such a school finance system. (19)

Further, the report recommends that the federal government "reassess its enforcement regime with respect to issues of school finance equity," noting that "enforcement mechanisms derived from other areas of federal civil rights law" were a viable policy tool (U.S. Department of Education 2014, 20). Thus, the commission recommends that the federal government play a stronger role in leveraging—if not enforcing—state-level finance equity, but did not lay out any specifics for how this ought to be accomplished programmatically (26).

Other scholars have also called for changes to ESEA funding, especially in terms of targeting. Linda Darling-Hammond in her book *The Flat World and Education* sharply criticizes school finance policies in the United States, whereby state aid offsets some of the core inequalities produced by the local property-tax based system, and then federal categorical grants are layered on, "often with extensive strings attached" (2010, 311). She calls on Congress to "equalize allocations of ESEA resources across states," "enforce comparability provisions for ensuring equally qualified teachers to schools," and "require states to report on opportunity indicators along with reports of academic progress for each school" (309). Her recommendations about funding echo many of those of the Equity and Excellence Commission.

To summarize, since the 1990s, many justifications of support have been advanced for the principle of federal and national efforts to foster the many components of "opportunity to learn." Many of these reports call for federal action in alleviating fiscal inequity among and within states; others call for specific changes in how the current ESEA drives funding to districts. With a few exceptions, however, these have generally not laid out how legislative or statutory changes might advance them through the ESEA. Our proposal is a first step in this direction.

GOALS AND DESIGN

We envision a competitive grant program, modeled after the recent Race to the Top grant competition, to bring reform to the three levels of school finance inequity outlined.[1] This program could be a pilot to be subsequently developed into a permanent part of the legislation. We conceptualize it as a competitive grant to provide states with the incentives to undertake the difficult work of school finance reform in exchange for priority consideration in a grant competition designed to provide substantial federal funds for work in developing integrated and successful schools in supportive communities across the P–12 spectrum. This approach privileges finance equity as a value in exchange for providing students with greater opportunities to learn. Our supposition is that states will be willing to do the former in exchange for funding and flexibility to implement the latter.

Structure

Although Race to the Top has been criticized along many dimensions, few have argued that it has not resulted in states adopting meaningful, systemic changes to policies ranging from adoption of the Common Core State Standards (CCSS) to addressing charter schools caps and streamlining data systems policies. An important criticism—and one our proposal also faces—is that states with a greater capacity for reform are advantaged in zero-sum competitions of this nature. Much like RTT, our proposal seeks to yoke this competition to federalist impulses by seeking states willing to address issues of finance equity in the search for scalable solutions.

State Finance Reform

We recommend beginning with roughly one quarter of the states eligible for awards. Although the competition will be open to all states, states will be able to increase their standing by committing to a series of reforms to their school finance systems. These commitments will serve as priorities in the competition. In this way, the federal government can leverage ESEA dollars to support state-level (state-initiated) finance reforms. Although the nature of the reforms will be left up to states, the competition would outline specific target goals for each of the three dimensions of finance inequity.

Measures and Indicators

Operationalizing notions of equity and adequacy will be a critical first step in developing this program. The field of school finance has developed such measures. This section reviews these measures, briefly discusses their applicability, and offers examples of indicators that states and the federal government could use to assess outcomes in the opportunity-to-learn component of the program.

Horizontal Equity

The concept of horizontal equity in school finance is concerned with the equal treatment of equal units. The coefficient of variation is one such measure borrowed from the field of economics; the McLoone index is another measure of horizontal equity specific to the field of school finance and indicates the degree to which variation exists within the bottom half of a distribution. Indexing state levels of horizontal equity and asking for annualized stair-step improvements toward established

---

1. The major difference being that our proposal lives within ESEA, unlike RTT.

thresholds would be one way of ensuring state focus.

Vertical Equity
Vertical equity is expressed as the different treatment of differently situated units. In this case, positive vertical equity in state-level finance systems would steer additional funds toward higher-needs classes of students—such as economically disadvantaged students. The degree of vertical equity is measured via a regression coefficient that shows an association with resources such as dollars or teacher qualities. The federal government could index vertical equity on one dimension or class, or add multiple measures, including racial and ethnic subgroups, such as those identified under NCLB. Similarly, the department could look solely at dollars allocated per pupil as a dependent variable or instead include multiple resource variables. Whatever the decision, indexing vertical equity relationships and requesting maintenance or improvement of these measures is well within ED capacity.

Adequacy
The notion of sufficiency can be operationalized across dollars, throughputs such as teacher and instructional practices, or outcomes. Measures such as adequate yearly progress (AYP) indicators already purport to measure levels of performance adequacy. Another adequacy-based measure is cost functions—econometric models that indicate the amounts of funding that should be necessary for different classes of students to meet established performance standards. These measures will yield insight into how close a state system is to covering these adequate costs. Additional methods exist—the use of professional judgment panels, costing out studies, and others.

Desegregation
The federal government would have multiple measures from which to choose when examining levels of desegregation in states over time. The dissimilarity index has been a bellwether measure in sociological and policy studies for years, but other measures may be more appropriate (Reardon and Firebaugh 2002; Gorard and Taylor 2002).

Housing Density and Distribution
Measures of housing policy outcomes could include the same measures of spatial segregation used to examine segregation in schools or measures of the types of contexts present in neighborhoods (Goldring et al. 2006).

Early Childhood Education
Measures of state provision of early childhood education can be measured with counts of enrolled children as a percentage of the overall age cohort population, credentials and experience of early childhood teachers, and similar distributive measures of administrative data.

Although the nature of the targets would be subject to political debate, we propose the following examples:

- To address interstate finance equity, states could focus on increasing the proportion of educational revenues from state sources, thereby bringing more funding into the equity-producing mechanisms of state finance systems and reducing inequalities in funding based on differential property wealth across districts. ED would support these efforts by indexing state levels of resource provision accounting for regional cost differentials. ED could provide support by further subsidizing existing power-equalizing plans or working to support states in creating power equalizing components within their state finance structures. (For example, the state of Georgia subsidizes districts at the 75th percentile of district wealth up to 14 mills of taxation on property. Georgia could increase the equity of its finance system by requesting federal equalization funds to equalize at a higher percentile of local wealth, and to provide assistance beyond the 14th mill of taxation). To address intrastate finance inequity, states could focus on significant proportional reductions of key equity statistics for key resource variables; a stair-step reduction toward a federal goal in the coefficient of variation across measures would be an ambitious target. Similarly, increases in vertical equity as measured by key regression coefficients would be a place for federal assistance. To address intradistrict finance inequity states would develop policies that redefined comparability for Title I schools within a framework of waivers from ED. Comparability could move to a metric of teacher salaries per pupil in Title I versus non–Title I schools, or some measure of teacher qualification or performance.

- Because education finance analysis builds evidence of inequity through the analysis of multiple variables of interest using multiple statistics (Berne and Stiefel 1994), decisions about which measures and which statistics to assess may therefore best be left to the states. Conversely, allowing states this discretion might also create a bewildering array of analyses for federal administrators. For the sake of simplicity, we recommend straightforward measures such as total per pupil expenditures or the pupil-teacher ratio. In terms of statistics, variation as measured by the coefficient of variation is a traditional approach, as is the comparison of regression coefficients on variables indicating student types. For example, a stair-step reduction toward an established goal over three years of negative coefficients indicating inequitable relationships between race and class variables and resource variables might be an approach. We anticipate that ED would be able to convene school finance researchers and economists to determine what kind of modeling would be acceptable within proposals. Undertaking this work should also build capacity within ED to support states in school finance reform efforts, which we describe in the next section.

Priority will be given to states that undertake this package of policies. Funds through this program will be awarded in two main areas. The primary one is to support state transition to these new funding structures by providing funds for hold-harmless or grandfathering provisions.

State-Initiated Interventions Supporting Opportunity-to-Learn

The mechanisms described so far seek to reduce the inequitable distribution of critical input variables, but do not consider resource sufficiency. A secondary goal would therefore be to provide funding for states to better develop and innovate within an opportunity-to-learn structure. Specifically, competitive priority points will be awarded to states that address developing and supporting an opportunity-to-learn infrastructure. The general areas of focus would be: early childhood education; student assignment and desegregation; and housing and community support policy.

Each of these policy areas has shown promise of reducing resource, opportunity, and outcome gaps across student groups. Early childhood education interventions have been linked to a host of positive school preparedness and life outcomes, but rather than being included in a meaningful way in most federal education policy conversations, they have been almost exclusively relegated to debates over Head Start's often-disputed effectiveness. (President Obama's expansion of early childhood grants into a final round of Race to the Top is an important exception.) Defining early childhood as a focus area builds on established research indicating that schools are less well equipped to narrow achievement gaps than they are at maintaining achievement trajectories, establishes a mechanism that draws ED and the U.S. Department of Health and Human Services (HHS) into closer relationship, and provides openings for school to create opportunities for remediation and acceleration for high needs students before they enter the formal K–12 pipeline (Heckman 2011; Heckman and Masterov 2007; Weiland and Yoshikawa 2013). Expanding access to preschool and providing incentives to improve its quality, in other words, should not be the exclusive domain of Head Start and HHS. Incentives for states to experiment with new structures and emphases should be jointly devised between HHS and ED.

Multiple studies have indicated that resegregation of schools has consequences for students in terms of peer effects, teacher qualities, and qualifications that lead to achievement gaps and unequal and inequitable resource distribution (Lee 2007; Linn and Welner 2007; Schofield 1995). Defining school segregation as a focus area allows states and districts to work on ways to create student populations balanced in terms of race, class, and ethnicity, which some indicate may influence teachers' decisions to work in any given school (Scafidi, Sjoquist, and Stinebrickner 2007; Houck 2011). There is precedent for a federal role in providing this kind of technical assistance to local school districts, first to desegregating schools in the 1970s through the Emergency Schools Assistance Act (Orfield 2011), through the Equity Assistance centers, and more recently, through the Technical Assistance for Student Assignment Plans grant program (McDermott, DeBray, and Frankenberg 2012). Districts could focus on integration by either socioeconomic status or race, as constitutionally permissible, to create schools within relatively balanced student populations, thus disrupting the influence of internal teacher labor market dynamics and providing opportunities for higher-needs students to become more acculturated to the middle-class norms of schools (Frankenberg 2011; Kahlenberg 2003).

Finally, and more ambitiously, this proposal would reach beyond the schoolhouse walls to address an issue raised by many in the Broader Bolder Approach coalition: how community-level preconditions affect attendance zones with high concentrated poverty. Department of Education support for housing and community development would address the legacy of residential segregation left unaddressed by courts that establishes the preconditions of school segregation. David Kirp identified the Promise Neighborhoods initiative that invested $10 million in 2010 as an example of a federally supported incentive program that may strengthen the community schools movement (2011, 139). The program is designed to get communities to identify district-specific problems and develop research supported solutions that incorporate multiple community agencies, including education, health, law, and social services. Promise Neighborhoods' principles could serve as a basis for the technical support to communities within awardee states (Goldring et al. 2006).

State applications should specify the particular interventions (desegregation, community interventions, improving or expanding early childhood education) they seek to develop, in which districts, and should submit relevant documentation of support from district leadership. States, in cooperation with participating districts, should submit quantifiable goals to be achieved over five years (that is, number of additional children to be served, reduction in school-level student poverty rates, or expansion of health services at community schools), with accompanying budgets. Federal officials would then negotiate awards with states.[2]

The legislation should specify that applications need to be reviewed by policy analysts with high levels of technical expertise and a substantive background in school finance—and that those who would administer the program should have the same qualifications. Because the pilot program includes an experimental component, the legislation should also mandate a strong and independent evaluation of all awardee states' activities, during the funding cycle and beyond.

In sum, the principal reason for inducing changes in these state and district contexts is to ensure the presence of nonfinancial inputs (opportunities) that have been shown to produce better student outcomes. The competitive program could be undertaken in concert with other recommended changes in Title I targeting (like altering comparability), as well as other changes to NCLB's present accountability system; at the same time, however, its equity-based principles are a counterbalance to NCLB. We next examine the overall political climate in Congress and how it might affect both the reauthorization and support for an equity agenda.

---

2. One of the criticisms of competitive programs in education, such as Race to the Top, notes that states with greater capacity to undertake reform were advantaged in the competitive process. An analogue in our plan would be that states with progressive school finance structures would have greater capacity—and greater political will—to undertake the reforms, and thus also the unintended consequence of increasing interstate inequities. One way to avoid this potential difficulty would be to include existing measures of fiscal inequity as part of the application package, thereby ensuring that need for reform, as well as capacity, is emphasized.

POLITICAL CONTEXT AND INSTITUTIONAL CONSIDERATIONS

Although the structure we focus on here is a competitive grant program within ESEA, our conversations with observers of the politics of federal education policy lead us to understand why a role for the federal government in supporting state finance reform could be politically feasible in the next reauthorization. Even though the overall composition of Congress is more conservative than at any point in the law's history, the Senate floor debate in 2015 showed that the two parties can agree on greater flexibility for states in holding schools accountable (Rich and Lewin 2015, paragraph 18). We argue that this renewed attention to more equitable state finance systems and granting states broader discretion in interventions in low-performing schools are complementary reforms.

One long-standing political condition that might indicate the potential for such support to grow is the fairly broad bipartisan dissatisfaction with the perceived overregulation of states with respect to school accountability. The Every Child Achieves Act, approved by the full Senate in July 2015, maintains the annual federal testing schedule and the requirement for disaggregation of data, but permits states to decide how tests and data are used (Camera 2015b). On the Senate floor, Senator Richard Burr (R-NC) offered an amendment to change the state Title I funding formula so that 80 percent of aid would be based on poverty rates and 20 percent on population (thereby disadvantaging relatively wealthier states). It was approved by a vote of 59-39 (Camera 2015a; White 2015), an indicator of potential support for other federal policy measures to improve targeting of funds.

A second and related point is that, as we have reviewed here, during the NCLB era, calls for greater equity have been widespread and vocal from both the practitioner and academic communities. If the reauthorization hearings are not structured to offer some of those constituents and experts a voice, or at least more of a voice than they had when NCLB was passed, then members of Congress are likely to pay some political price. Governors, state chiefs, the Council of Great City Schools, and the Committee on Education Funding continue to be powerful actors on Capitol Hill, and all of these groups ought to be in support of greater finance equalization within states.

Current policy controversies may also carry some future seeds for such a political bargain. The halting progress toward national adoption of Common Core State Standards across the states may provide a common metric for state performance comparison. By removing the ability of states to game the NCLB accountability system via a patchwork of state assessments and cut scores, one result of the CCSS may be to encourage states to push for greater finance equity through the provision of baseline student performance comparison data.

Monitoring of State-Level Finance Statistics, Oversight by OCR

Currently, the technical expertise within the Department of Education about state finance systems is located within the National Center for Education Statistics (NCES). NCES would play a vital role in designing reporting requirements for states. Also, we note throughout this article that an important federal function to accompany this grant program would be possible cost and feasibility studies for state finance. The Office of Planning and Evaluation could take the lead, given that it commissions comparable projects, such as a study currently under way that is examining practices of states that are considered leaders in collecting school-level expenditure data (U.S. Department of Education 2014). Staff from both OCR and the Office of Elementary and Secondary Education would also have important roles, particularly in providing capacity and technical support to awardee states. To help oversee the technical support on the early childhood education priority in particular, ED should establish a cross-cutting team with HHS. Staff knowledgeable about Title I from the perspective of community involvement should also be involved. OCR's newly released guidance on resource comparability constitutes a serious policy statement that equity is being defined as a civil rights issue under Title VI. In sum, multiple technical dimensions to how to best assist states are possible, from commissioning studies to providing models for better data collection, to continuing to send clear messages with respect to civil rights. This will not be a straightforward process, and the Department of Education will need to consult with many outside experts and constituents.

Political Sustainability

Any substantial paradigm shift in federal education policy requires the cooperation of numerous actors across many levels of government, as well as the support of a broad and diverse array of constituents—what historian Carl Kaestle has termed "the polity" (2007).

A revived federal role in educational finance is only as viable as the governors and state legislators who ultimately must advocate for and oversee the political changes needed to sustain longer-term changes in state finance systems. The competitive grant funds are designed to provide political cover for governors to ask legislators to make changes they might otherwise not. To sustain longer-term change, the federal government could make changes to state finance systems an explicit condition of aid to K–12 education. Jack Jennings advances the argument that the categorical structure of federal education programs has not been effective because of the inequitable state funding structures in which they have been administered; and that categorical aid (with the exception of special education funds under the Individuals with Disabilities Education Act) ought to be gradually converted to general aid in exchange for assurances from states in the areas of finance equity, as well as pupil and teacher factors related to learning (Jennings 2015; Marshall Smith, personal communication with authors, October 9, 2014).

CONCLUSION

School finance equity is the third rail that has too long gone unaddressed in the politics of U.S. education. Federal court actions have failed to move state-level finance equity forward, and the work of state courts has not been uniform. However, as we argue here, the moment is right to consider how federal resources and authority, through legislation, can demand more from states in terms of equity and the resources that matter most to learning. The long-standing partisan logjam on ESEA will be broken when a bargain is struck between demands for flexibility and easing of regulations for states on the one hand, and support for some targeted opportunity-to-learn measures like early childhood education on the other. Here we have proposed a first step to what could eventually become part of a comprehensive rethinking of ESEA: a variety of incentives that could reduce interstate funding inequality, as well as interdistrict inequities within states, and a deliberately designed federal role in the areas of technical support and capacity-building for states seeking to address aspects of opportunity-to-learn. We also emphasize that there is no single approach to an effective federal role in supporting state-level finance equity in the coming decades. As we began to explore here, increasing the overall federal share of education funding to states, encouraging states to change their funding formulae, and requiring districts to change the way they allocate federal compensatory dollars are not mutually exclusive. We believe that, if carefully planned and accompanied by the requisite capacity and expertise, a number of strategies to bolster an equality orientation to federal education policy are plausible; and we look forward to witnessing that conversation advance.

REFERENCES

Baker, Bruce D. 2005. "The Emerging Shape of Educational Adequacy: From Theoretical Assumptions to Empirical Evidence." *Journal of Education Finance* 30(3): 259–87.

———. 2012. "Rearranging Deck Chairs in Dallas: Contextual Constraints and Within-District Resource Allocation in Urban Texas School Districts." *Journal of Education Finance* 37(3): 287–315.

Baker, Bruce D., and Sean P. Corcoran. 2012. "The Stealth Inequities of School Funding: How State and Local School Finance Systems Perpetuate Inequitable Student Spending." *Center for American Progress*, September 19, 2012. Available at: https://www.americanprogress.org/issues/education/report/2012/09/19/38189/the-stealth-inequities-of-school-funding/ (accessed July 22, 2015).

Baker, Bruce D., and Kevin G. Welner. 2011. "School Finance and Courts: Does Reform Matter, and

How Can We Tell?" *Teachers College Record* 113(11): 2374–414.

Belfield, Clive, and Henry Levin. 2013. "The Cumulative Costs of the Opportunity Gap." In *Closing the Opportunity Gap: What America Must Do to Give Every Child an Even Chance*, edited by Prudence Carter and Kevin Welner. New York: Oxford University Press.

Berliner, David. 2011. "Rational Responses to High Stakes Testing: The Case of Curriculum Narrowing and the Harm That Follows." *Cambridge Journal of Education* 41(3): 287–302. doi: 10.1080/0305764X.2011.607151.

Berne, Robert, and Leanna Stiefel. 1994. "Measuring Equity at the School Level: The Finance Perspective." *Educational Evaluation and Policy Analysis* 16(4): 405–21.

Broader, Bolder Approach to Education. 2013. "Policy Areas." Available at: http://www.bold approach.org (accessed July 22, 2015).

Burke, Sarah M. 1999. "An Analysis of Resource Inequality at the State, District, and School Levels." *Journal of Education Finance* 24(4): 435–58.

Burroughs, Susie, Eric Groce, and Mary Lee Webeck. 2005. "Social Studies Education in the Age of Testing and Accountability." *Educational Measurement: Issues & Practice* 24(3): 13–20. doi: 10.1111/j.1745-3992.2005.00015.x.

Bushaw, William J., and Valerie J. Calderon. 2014. "Americans Put Teacher Quality on Center Stage: The 46th Annual PDK/Gallup Poll of the Public's Attitudes Toward the Public Schools: Part II." *Phi Delta Kappan* 96(2): 49–59. doi: 10.1177/0031721714553411.

Camera, Lauren. 2015a. "Efforts to Change Federal Formulas Prove Tricky." *Education Week*, May 16. Available at: http://www.edweek.org/ew/toc/2015/05/06/ (accessed July 22, 2015).

———. 2015b. "Senate Education Committee Unanimously Passes Bipartisan ESEA Rewrite." *Education Week*, April 16. Available at: http://blogs.edweek.org/edweek/campaign-k-12/2015/04/senate_education_committee_una.html (accessed May 15, 2015).

Carter, Prudence, and Kevin Welner, eds. 2013. *Closing the Opportunity Gap: What America Must Do to Give Every Child an Even Chance*. New York: Oxford University Press

Cawelti, Gordon. 2006. "The Side Effects of NCLB." *Educational Leadership* 64(3): 64–68.

Chetty, Raj, Nathaniel Hendren, Patrick Kline, Emmanuel Saez, and Nicholas Turner. 2014. "Is the United States Still a Land of Opportunity? Recent Trends in Intergenerational Mobility." *American Economic Review* 104(5): 141–47.

Clune, William H. 1994. "The Shift from Equity to Adequacy in School Finance." *Educational Policy* 8(4): 376-94.

Condron, Dennis J., and Vincent J. Roscigno. 2003. "Disparities Within: Unequal Spending and Achievement in an Urban School District." *Sociology of Education* 76(1): 18–36.

Darling-Hammond, Linda. 2010. *The Flat World and Education: How America's Commitment to Equity Will Determine Our Future*. New York: Teachers College Press.

DeBray, Elizabeth 2006. *Politics, Ideology & Education: Federal Policy During the Clinton and Bush Administrations*. New York: Teachers College Press.

DeBray, Elizabeth, and Ann Blankenship. 2013. "Future Policy Directions for Congress in Ensuring Equality of Educational Opportunity: Toward Improved Incentives, Targeting, and Enforcement." *Peabody Journal of Education* 88(1): 21–36.

DeBray, Elizabeth, and Erica Frankenberg. 2011. "Federal Legislation to Promote Metropolitan Approaches to Educational and Housing Opportunity." In *Integrating Schools in a Changing Society: New Policies and Legal Options for a Multiracial Generation*, edited by Erica Frankenberg and Elizabeth DeBray. Chapel Hill: University of North Carolina Press.

Duncan, Greg J., and Richard Murnane. 2014. *Restoring Opportunity: The Crisis of Inequality and the Challenge for American Education*. Cambridge, Mass.: Harvard Education Press.

Fischel, William A. 1989. "Did Serrano Cause Proposition 13?" *National Tax Journal* 42(4): 465–73.

Frankenberg, Erica. 2011. "Integration After 'Parents Involved': What Does Research Suggest About Available Options?" In *Integrating Schools in a Changing Society: New Policies and Legal Options for a Multiracial Generation*, edited by Erica Frankenberg and Elizabeth DeBray. Chapel Hill: University of North Carolina Press.

Freeman, Catherine, Benjamin Scafidi, and David Sjoquist. 2005. "Racial Segregation in Georgia Public Schools 1994–2001: Trends, Causes and Impact on Teacher Quality." In *Resegregation of Southern Schools? A Crucial Moment in the History (and the Future) of Public Schooling in America. Chapel Hill: University of North Carolina Press.

Goldring, Ellen, Lora Cohen-Vogel, Claire Smrekar, and Cynthia Taylor. 2006. "Schooling Closer to Home: Desegregation Policy and Neighborhood Contexts." *American Journal of Education* 112(3): 335–62.

Gorard, Stephen, and Chris Taylor. 2002. "What Is Segregation? A Comparison of Measures in Terms of 'Strong' and 'Weak' Compositional Invariance." *Sociology* 36(4): 875–95.

Grodsky, Eric, John Robert Warren, and Erika Felts. 2008. "Testing and Social Stratification in American Education." *Annual Review of Sociology* 34: 385–404. doi: 10.1146/annurev.soc.34.040507.134711.

Guthrie, James W., Matthew G. Springer, R. Anthony Rolle, and Eric A. Houck. 2007. *Modern Education Finance and Policy*. Chicago: Allyn & Bacon.

Hanushek, Eric A., and Alfred A. Lindseth. 2009. *Schoolhouses, Courthouses, and Statehouses: Solving the Funding-Achievement Puzzle in America's Public Schools*. Princeton, N.J.: Princeton University Press.

Heckman, James 2011. "The Economics of Inequality: The Value of Early Childhood Education." *American Educator* 35(1): 31–35.

Heckman, James, and Dimitriy Masterov. 2007. "The Productivity Argument for Investing in Young Children." *Review of Agricultural Economics Association* 29(3): 446–93.

Hertert, Linda. 1995. "Right Game, Wrong Field? The Pursuit of School Funding Equity." *School Business Affairs* 61(8): 8–12.

Holme, Jennifer Jellison, and Kara S. Finnigan. 2013. "School Diversity, School District Fragmentation and Metropolitan Policy." *Teachers College Record* 115(11): 1–29.

Houck, Eric A. 2010. "Teacher Quality and School Resegregation: A Resource Allocation Case Study." *Leadership and Policy in Schools* 9(1): 49–77.

———. 2011. "Intradistrict Resource Allocation: Key Findings and Policy Implications." *Education and Urban Society* 43(3): 271–95.

Houck, Eric A., and Moonyoung Eom. 2012. "Resource and Output Equity as a Mechanism for Assessing Educational Opportunity in Korean Middle School Education." *Journal of Education Finance* 38(1): 18–51.

Howe, Kenneth, and David Meens. 2012. "Democracy Left Behind: How Recent Education Reforms Undermine Local School Governance and Democratic Education." Boulder: University of Colorado, National Education Policy Center. Available at: http://nepc.colorado.edu/publication/democracy-left-behind (accessed July 22, 2015).

Iatarola, Patrice, and Leanna Stiefel. 2003. "Intradistrict Equity of Public Education Resources and Performance." *Economics of Education Review* 22(1): 69–78.

Ingersoll, Richard 2001. "Teacher Turnover and Teacher Shortages: An Organizational Analysis." *American Educational Research Journal* 38(3): 499–534.

Jackson, Kirabo, Rucker Johnson, and Claudia Persico. 2014. "The Effect of School Finance Reforms on the Distribution of Spending, Academic Achievement, and Adult Outcomes." *NBER* working paper no. 20118. Cambridge, Mass.: National Bureau of Economic Research.

Jennings, Jack. 2015. *Presidents, Congress, and the Public Schools: The Politics of Education Reform*. Cambridge, Mass.: Harvard Education Press.

Jennings, John. 1998. *Why National Standards and Tests? Politics and the Quest for Better Schools*. Thousand Oaks, Calif.: Sage Publications.

Kaestle, Carl. 2007. "Federal Education Policy and the Changing National Polity for Education, 1957–2007." In *To Educate a Nation: Federal and National Strategies of School Reform*, edited by Carl Kaestle and Alyssa Lodewick. Lawrence: University Press of Kansas.

Kahlenberg, Richard D. 2003. *All Together Now: Creating Middle-Class Schools Through Public School Choice*. Washington, D.C.: Brookings Institution Press.

Kahlenberg, Richard. 2012. "Turnaround Schools and Charter Schools that Work: Moving Beyond Separate but Equal." In *The Future of School Integration: Socioeconomic Diversity as an Education Reform Strategy*, edited by R. Kahlenberg. New York: Century Foundation.

Kenworthy, Lane. 2014. *Social Democratic America*. Oxford: Oxford University Press.

Kirp, David. 2011. *Kids First: Five Big Ideas for Transforming Children's Lives and America's Future*. New York: Public Affairs.

Ladd, Helen F. 2008. "Reflections on Equity, Adequacy, and Weighted Student Funding." *Education Finance and Policy* 3(4): 402–23.

Ladd, Helen F., Rosemary Chalk, and Janet S. Hansen. 1999. *Equity and Adequacy in Education Finance: Issues and Perspectives*. Washington, D.C.: National Academy Press.

Lankford, Hamilton, Susanna Loeb, and James Wyckoff. 2002. "Teacher Sorting and the Plight of Urban Schools: A Descriptive Analysis." *Educational Evaluation and Policy Analysis* 24(1): 37–62.

Lee, Jaekyung. 2007. "Can Reducing School Segregation Close the Achievement Gap?" In *Lessons in Integration*, edited by E. Frankenberg and G. Orfield. Charlottesville: University of Virginia Press.

Linn, Robert, and Kevin G. Welner. 2007. *Race-Conscious Policies for Assigning Students to Schools: Social Science Research and the Supreme Court Cases*. Washington, D.C.: National Academy of Education.

Liu, Goodwin. 2008. "Improving Title I Funding Equity Across States, Districts, and Schools." *Iowa Law Review* 93(3): 973–1013.

McColl, Ann. 2005. "Tough Call: Is NCLB Constitutional?" *Phi Delta Kappan* 86(8)(April): 604.

McDermott, Kathryn A., Elizabeth DeBray, and Erica Frankenberg. 2012. "How Does 'Parents Involved in Community Schools' Matter? Legal and Political Influence in Education Politics and Policy." *Teachers College Record* 114(12): 1–39.

McDonnell, Lorraine. 2005. "NCLB and the Federal Role in Education: Evolution or Revolution?" *Peabody Journal of Education* 80(2): 19–38.

McGuinn, Patrick. 2006. *No Child Left Behind and the Transformation of Federal Education Policy, 1965–2005*. Lawrence: University Press of Kansas.

Murray, Sheila, William N. Evans, and Robert Schwab. 1998. "Education Finance Reform and the Distribution of Education Resources." *American Economic Review* 88(4): 789–812.

National Coalition on School Diversity. 2014. Internal staff memo (on file with authors). Washington, D.C.

National Conference of State Legislatures. 2005. "Task Force on No Child Left Behind: Final Report." Washington, D.C.: National Conference of State Legislatures. Available at: http://www.hartfordinfo.org/issues/documents/education/nclb.pdf (accessed July 26, 2015).

O'Day, Jennifer A., and Marshall Smith. 1993. "Systemic Reform and Educational Opportunity." In *Designing Coherent Education Policy: Improving the System*, edited by Susan Fuhrman. San Francisco: Jossey-Bass.

Orfield, Gary. 2011. "Conclusion: Returning to First Principles." In *Integrating Schools in a Changing Society: New Policies and Legal Options for a Multiracial Generation*, edited by Erica Frankenberg and Elizabeth DeBray. Chapel Hill: University of North Carolina Press.

Owens, Tom, and Jeffrey Maiden. 1999. "A Comparison of Interschool and Interdistrict Funding Equity in Florida." *Journal of Education Finance* 24(4): 503–18.

Porter, Andrew C., Robert L. Linn, and C. Scott Trimble. 2005. "The Effects of State Decisions About NCLB Adequate Yearly Progress Targets." *Educational Measurement: Issues & Practice* 24(4): 32–39. doi: 10.1111/j.1745-3992.2005.00021.x.

Reardon, Sean F., and Glenn Firebaugh. 2002. "Measures of Multigroup Segregation." *Sociological Methodology* 32(1): 33–67.

Rebell, Michael, and Jessica Wolff. 2008. *Moving Every Child Ahead: From NCLB Hype to Meaningful Educational Opportunity*. New York: Teachers College Press.

Reed, Douglas. 2001. *On Equal Terms*. Princeton, N.J.: Princeton University Press.

Reich, Rob. 2013. "Equality, Adequacy, and K-12 Education." In *Education, Justice, and Democracy*, edited by Rob Reich and Danielle Allen. Chicago: University of Chicago Press.

Reschovsky, Andrew. 1994. "Fiscal Equalization and School Finance." *National Tax Journal* 47(1): 185–97.

Rich, Motoko, and Tamar Lewin. 2015. "Schools Wait to See What Becomes of No Child Left Behind Law." *New York Times*, March 20, para 18. Available at: http://www.nytimes.com/2015/03/22/us/politics/schools-wait-to-see-what-becomes-of-no-child-left-behind-law.html (accessed July 22, 2015).

Riley, Richard. 2001. "Dear Colleague." Washington: U.S. Department of Education.

Robinson, Kimberly Jenkins. 2015. "Disrupting Education Federalism." *Washington University Law Review* 92(4): 959–1018.

Rolle, Anthony, Eric A. Houck, and Ann McColl. 2008. "And Poor Children Continue to Wait: An Analysis of Horizontal and Vertical Equity Among North Carolina School Districts in the

Face of Judicially Mandated Policy Restraints 1996–2006." *Journal of Education Finance* 34(1): 75–102.

Rolle, Anthony, and Keke Liu. 2007. "An Empirical Analysis of Horizontal and Vertical Equity in the Public Schools of Tennessee, 1994–2003." *Journal of Education Finance* 32(3): 328–51.

Rothstein, Paul. 1992. "The Demand for Education with 'Power Equalization' Aid." *Journal of Public Economics* 49: 135–62.

Roza, Marguerite. 2005. *Strengthening Title I to Help High-Poverty Schools: How Title I Funds Fit into District Allocation Patterns*. Seattle, Wash.: Center on Reinventing Public Education.

Roza, Marguerite, and Paul Thomas Hill. 2004. "How Within-District Spending Inequities Help Some Schools to Fail." *Brookings Papers on Education Policy* 7: 201–27.

Rubenstein, Ross. 1998. "Resource Equity in the Chicago Public Schools: A School-Level Approach." *Journal of Education Finance* 23(4): 468–89.

Ryan, James. 2010. *Five Miles Away, a World Apart: One City, Two Schools, and the Story of Educational Opportunity in Modern America*. New York: Oxford University Press.

Scafidi, Benjamin, David L. Sjoquist, and Todd Stinebrickner. 2007. "Race, Poverty, and Teacher Mobility." *Economics of Education Review* 26(2): 145–59.

Schoen, LaTefy, and Lance D. Fusarelli. 2008. "Innovation, NCLB, and the Fear Factor: The Challenge of Leading 21st-Century Schools in an Era of Accountability." *Educational Policy* 22(1): 181–203.

Schofield, Janet W. 1995. "Review of Research on School Desegregation's Impact on Elementary and Secondary School Students." In *Handbook of Research on Multicultural Education*, edited by James A. Banks and Cherry A. McGee Banks. New York: Simon and Schuster Macmillan.

Schwartz, Robert, and Marian Robinson. 2000. "Goals 2000 and the Standards Movement." *Brookings Papers on Educational Policy* 3: 173–214.

Sims, David P. 2011. "Lifting All Boats? Finance Litigation, Education Resources, and Student Needs in the Post-'Rose' Era." *Education Finance and Policy* 6(4): 455–85.

Smith, Marshall S. 2011. "Rethinking ESEA: A Zero-Base Reauthorization." In *Carrots, Sticks, and the Bully Pulpit: Lessons from a Half Century of Federal Efforts to Improve America's Schools*, edited by Frederick Hess and Andrew Kelly. Cambridge, Mass.: Harvard Education Press.

Smrekar, Claire, and Ellen Goldring. 2011. "Rethinking Magnet School Policies and Practices: A Response to Declining Diversity and Judicial Constraints." In *Integrating Schools in a Changing Society*, edited by Erica Frankenberg and Elizabeth DeBray. Chapel Hill: University of North Carolina Press.

Southern Education Foundation. 2009. *No Time to Lose: Why America Needs an Education Amendment to the U.S. Constitution to Improve Public Education*. Atlanta, Ga.: Southern Education Foundation.

Springer, Matthew G., Eric A. Houck, and James W. Guthrie. 2007. "History and Scholarship of United States Education Finance and Policy." In *Handbook of Research in Education Finance and Policy*, edited by Helen F. Ladd and Edward B. Fiske. New York: Routledge.

Springer, Matthew G., Keke Liu, and James W. Guthrie. 2009. "The Impact of School Finance Litigation on Resource Distribution: A Comparison of Court-Mandated Equity and Adequacy Reforms." *Education Economics* 17(4): 421–44.

Stiefel, Leanna, Ross Rubenstein, and Robert Berne. 1998. "Intra-District Equity in Four Large Cities: Data, Methods, and Results." *Journal of Education Finance* 23(4): 447–67.

Stullich, Stephanie. 2011. *The Potential Impact of Revising the Title I Comparability Requirement to Focus on School-Level Expenditures*. Washington: U.S. Department of Education.

Suarez, Christopher. 2014. "The School District Boundary Problem." Paper presented at the Education and Civil Rights Conference. Penn State University, University Park (June 7, 2014).

Tiebout, Charles M. 1956. "Pure Theory of Local Expenditures." *Journal of Political Economy* 64(5): 416–24. doi: 10.1086/257839.

Traiman, Susan L. 1993. *The Debate on Opportunity-to-Learn Standards*. Washington: National Governors' Association.

U.S. Department of Education. 2009. "National Public Education Financial Survey (NPEFS)," fiscal year 2009, Version 1a. Common Core of Data (CCD). Washington: National Center for Education Statistics.

———. 2013. *For Each and Every Child: A Strategy for Education Equity and Excellence*. Washington:

Commission on Equity and Excellence. Available at: https://www2.ed.gov/about/bdscomm/list/eec/equity-excellence-commission-report.pdf (accessed July 22, 2015).

———. 2014. "Study Description: Feasibility Study on Improving the Quality of School-Level Expenditure Data." Washington: Office of Planning and Evaluation Studies.

———. 2015. "Fiscal Year 2015 Budget Summary and Background Information." Washington: U.S. Department of Education.

U.S. Department of Education. Office for Civil Rights. 2014. *Resource Comparability Materials*. Washington: U.S. Government Printing Office. Available at: http://www2.ed.gov/about/offices/list/ocr/resourcecomparability.html (accessed August 18, 2015).

Vinovskis, Maris. 2008. *From A Nation at Risk to No Child Left Behind*. New York: Teachers College Press.

Weiland, Christina, and Hirokazu Yoshikawa. 2013. "Impacts of a Prekindergarten Program on Children's Mathematics, Language, Literacy, Executive Function, and Emotional Skills." *Child Development* 84(6): 2112–30.

Wells, Amy Stuart. 2009. "'Our Children's Burden': A History of Federal Education Policies that Ask (Now Require) Our Public Schools to Solve Social Inequality." In *NCLB at the Crossroads: Reexamining the Federal Effort to Close the Achievement Gap*, edited by M. Rebell and J. Wolff. New York: Teachers College Press.

White, Herbert L. 2015. "Change Would Aid Title I Funding: Burr Amendment Would Add $99M for NC." *The Charlotte Post* (online edition), July 22, 2015. Available at: http://www.thecharlottepost.com/news/2015/07/22/local/change-would-aid-title-i-funding (accessed August 17, 2015).

Y, Mr. 2011. "A National Strategic Narrative." Princeton, N.J.: Woodrow Wilson School for Public and International Affairs. Available at: http://www.wilsoncenter.org/sites/default/files/A%20National%20Strategic%20Narrative.pdf (accessed July 22, 2015).

PART III
ESEA Policy Instruments and Their Future

Stability and Change in Title I Testing Policy

LORRAINE M. MCDONNELL

This article examines the history of Title I's student testing requirements, focusing on the two purposes they have served as a policy tool and measurement instrument. It argues that these purposes have been defined by a stable core of testing requirements whose specific targeting and technical characteristics have evolved in response to changes in Title I's institutional and interest group environment. In concluding, it considers the form and purpose that the testing requirements are likely to take in the future of the Elementary and Secondary Education Act.

Keywords: Elementary and Secondary Education Act (ESEA), student testing, federal K–12 education policy

As the cornerstone of federal education policy, Title I of the Elementary and Secondary Education Act of 1965 (ESEA) has a multifaceted history spanning five decades and extending from Congress to the classroom (for early histories, see Bailey and Mosher 1968; McLaughlin 1975; Graham 1984; Murphy 1991; and Kirst and Jung 1991; for later analyses, see McDonnell 2005; Manna 2006; McGuinn 2006; DeBray 2006; Cohen and Moffitt 2009; and Rhodes 2012). This article revisits some of that history through the lens of how Title I's student testing provisions have evolved from 1965 to the present. It focuses on the elements that have remained basically the same, those that have changed, and the factors that explain this combination of stability and change.

Program requirements specifying which students should be tested, how they should be assessed, and how the results should be used have served two distinct but related purposes.

First, like most major federal policies, Title I includes provisions designed to act as political and policy instruments. They aim to make targets' behavior consistent with federal policy goals, and typically operate through a combination of incentives, regulations, and bargaining. Although the choice and use of these instruments depend on goals articulated in congressional and executive branch policies, their ultimate effectiveness in a federal system is shaped by a broad array of interests and institutions extending from Washington to local classrooms. Requiring states and school districts to test students and to evaluate local programs as a condition of Title I funding has been, together with financial reporting requirements, the federal government's main tool for promoting its goal of improving the educational opportunities afforded low-income students. As a policy tool, testing can fulfill several functions. It may reduce information asymmetries between the federal government and the street-level where Title I services are delivered by providing information (albeit imperfect) about the program's effectiveness.

Lorraine M. McDonnell is professor of political science at the University of California, Santa Barbara.

Direct correspondence to: Lorraine M. McDonnell, mcdonnell@polsci.ucsb.edu, University of California, Santa Barbara, Department of Political Science 9420, Santa Barbara, CA 93106.

Such information can mobilize program constituents to take action in support or opposition to the status quo, and test results often become evidence used in debates about future program directions.

At the same time, these testing requirements also function as a technical instrument for measuring student outcomes. In this second role, the student assessments are judged by established psychometric standards of reliability, validity, and fairness. Is student achievement—however defined—being measured consistently across students and over time? Is a test actually measuring what it purports to measure, and are the conclusions and inferences drawn from the test results appropriate? Is a test systematically underestimating the skills and knowledge of a particular group (National Research Council 1999a, 71–72)?

Throughout the history of ESEA, these two purposes have rarely operated independently of each other and, in some cases, have posed direct trade-offs among them. For example, the policy uses of testing have often yielded reactive effects because educators have organized their teaching to improve their students' scores on required assessments (Stone 2012, 198). In these instances, policy purposes may preempt educators' professional judgments in using testing to guide their teaching. Similarly, when policymakers have used test results for purposes for which an assessment has not been validated, they compromise it as a measurement instrument. The ways in which these two purposes have interacted with each other over time have depended on how policymakers, educators, and interest groups have applied them. The result has been that though the overall purposes of the testing requirements have remained constant, some aspects of how they have been operationalized have changed but other elements have remained stable. The next three sections examine this pattern of enduring policy purposes combined with changing strategies for pursuing them.

STABILITY IN TITLE I TESTING POLICY

As Title I's testing provisions have been operationalized as a policy tool and measurement instrument, three aspects have remained stable throughout its history: a focus on student assessment as central to an evaluation and accountability strategy, testing as a tool to leverage state and local practice, and a constituency with testing and evaluation as part of its advocacy strategy even though its membership has changed over time.

Evaluation and Accountability Through Student Assessment

At one level, the path to testing as a central component of Title I began with a seemingly small event. Senator Robert Kennedy (D-NY) made clear to the Johnson administration's ESEA architects that he viewed the educational problems of poor children as partly due to the inability and unwillingness of local school districts to address their needs. Kennedy indicated that his support for the ESEA legislation depended on the addition of a reporting requirement that would hold educators responsible for educational achievement as the major criterion in judging ESEA's effectiveness. Part of that accountability strategy was to make information available to parents about how their children were doing. As a result of Kennedy's ultimatum, language was included in the original ESEA legislation requiring that "effective procedures, including provisions for appropriate objective measurements of educational achievement, will be adopted for evaluating at least annually the effectiveness of the programs in meeting the special educational needs of educationally deprived children" (ESEA, Title I, sec. 205 (5)).

As Milbrey McLaughlin notes in her analysis of the early history of evaluation in Title I, Kennedy viewed evaluation as a political accountability strategy (1975, vii). The widespread provision of information as a basis for holding public agencies accountable and as a resource that those affected by a policy can use in making decisions and in taking action was not a common policy instrument at the time of ESEA's passage. However, it has now become a customary element in environmental, consumer finance, and health-care policies as well as in education (Fung, Graham, and Weil 2007; McDonnell 2004). But the effectiveness of these hortatory or transparency policies ultimately depends on the quality of the information provided. Informational quality is where ESEA's evaluation requirement as a policy tool intersects with testing as a measurement instrument. The data available to the U.S. Office of Education (USOE) in the early years of Title I were often spotty and anecdotal. The quality and methodological approaches of local district reports varied considerably and in many cases, districts ignored state requests for student achievement results or provided incomplete data (Borman and D'Agostino 2001, 26).

This failure to provide reliable and valid data stemmed partly from the lack of technical expertise in local school districts. However, as histories of ESEA's early years have documented, much of the low quality and variation were due to ESEA's vague legislative language and the political circumstances surrounding its passage (McLaughlin 1975; Graham 1984; Kirst and Jung 1991; Murphy 1991). Competing expectations on the part of policymakers and interest groups about whether ESEA would be the first step in general federal aid or a program specifically targeted on underachieving, low-income students had been successfully sidestepped in the vague statutory language that aided its quick congressional passage. Inexperience on the part of USOE and state education agencies in managing a large grant program and their political vulnerability unprotected by clear legislative intent meant that Title I's initial implementation was characterized by "compromise and ambiguity" (Kirst and Jung 1991, 46). Even after four successive reauthorizations of ESEA between 1965 and 1980 specified more precisely that Title I should be used to assist educationally disadvantaged students and USOE increased its monitoring, the focus was on fiscal accountability, not programmatic substance. This focus was not surprising, given that Title I remained "more a funding mechanism than a specific program or policy for helping at-risk students" (Vinovskis 1999, 189).

Assessment as a Tool for Leveraging State and Local Practice

Despite the shortcomings of ESEA's testing and evaluation provisions, they have continued on the path begun with the legislation's initial enactment. The primary reason is that these regulations have been the strongest tool available to the federal government for leveraging state and local practice. Given that its limited constitutional authority and funding status in education make it the proverbial junior partner in the federal system, the federal government has few tools available to advance its social policy goals among state and local targets. As Helen Ingram argued more than thirty-five years ago, rather than buying compliance by offering grants-in-aid such as ESEA, the federal government really only purchases the opportunity to bargain with the states (1977). It exerts limited authority over state and local uses of ESEA funds through fiscal targeting requirements and subsequent audits. However, in the federal government's attempts to influence educational programs delivered to Title I students, the testing provisions have been among its strongest bargaining chips. Even if it had known what instructional strategies are most effective in educating low income students, a provision in the original ESEA statute—still applicable today—prevents the federal government from prescribing that level of programmatic detail: "Nothing contained in this Act should be construed to authorize any department, agency, officer, or employee of the United States to exercise any direction, supervision, or control over the curriculum, program of instruction, administration, or personnel of any educational institution or school system" (ESEA, Title VI, sec. 604).

Consequently, the federal government has had to rely primarily on requiring ex post reporting of program results rather than prospectively mandating or even guiding the organization of classroom teaching. The effect has been that the Title I testing requirements have created an enormous system of state and local testing, and they also launched the development of educational evaluation as a research specialization (U.S. Congress 1992; National Research Council 1999b; Shepard 2008). As we see in subsequent sections, Title I's modest effects, documented in several national evaluations, eventually led to changes in ESEA. Nevertheless, the basic principle of requiring that students be regularly tested in reading and mathematics on a standardized assessment has persisted. A major reason has been the extent to which the early statutory language, included to secure ESEA's enactment, precluded alternative forms of federal leverage.

Testing and Evaluation as Part of an Advocacy Strategy

At the same time, a coalition of interest groups has reinforced the continuation of the testing requirements as an accountability mechanism to monitor whether local Title I programs are serving their intended beneficiaries effectively. The membership of this coalition has shifted over time. During ESEA's early years, organizations such as the National Welfare Rights Organization, the NAACP, and the Lawyers Committee for Civil Rights Under Law advocated on behalf of low-income students by pushing for increased federal monitoring to ensure that Title I funds were spent to meet their educational needs (Kirst and Jung 1991). Over time, the groups and the focus of their advocacy changed. Organizations pressing for greater accountability expanded to include the Business Roundtable and the National Alliance of Business as well as newer organizations with an equity agenda such as the Education Trust (DeBray-Pelot 2007; Rhodes 2012). What has been constant throughout ESEA's history is that these groups have supported enforcement of Title I's categorical requirements in counterpoise to traditional education interest groups that, though now supporting Title I's social policy goals, have advocated for greater state and local flexibility in program administration.

The explanation for how testing became a core part of Title I and why it has endured are linked. The original impetus is an example of a seemingly small, contingent event, but the reasons for its continuation are due to historical forces extending beyond just ESEA. Robert Kennedy's amendment established testing and evaluation requirements as a central element of Title I. As states' and local districts' past history of segregation and disregard for poor children had demonstrated, his distrust of their likely use of federal funds and his efforts to institutionalize a partial remedy were well placed. Local districts' expenditures of ESEA funds during its early years further buttressed the view of those advocating on behalf of low-income students that federal monitoring was necessary. Because the primary concern during ESEA's early days was ensuring that funds were spent on appropriate program targets and less on which goods and services were purchased, fiscal monitoring took precedence over testing to measure student outcomes (Jennings 2001, 14). Nevertheless, during ESEA's first fifteen years, eight evaluations of Title I were conducted based on student test data to produce national estimates of the program's effectiveness (Borman and D'Agostino 2001).[1]

Although its original inclusion in Title I can be explained by Kennedy's amendment, the stability of testing as a key policy tool for federal leverage is best explained by the institutional factors that define education policy in the U.S. federal system—namely, the federal government's limited formal authority and an ingrained political culture legitimating state and local autonomy along with the variation it produces. The centrality of testing requirements in Title I is a case of strong path dependency in which institutional characteristics fundamental to the nature of the American state have made the costs of diversion from that path politically and administratively prohibitive. However, as policy ideas, testing technology, and political dynamics have shifted, the configuration and direction of that path have also been altered.

CHANGES IN TITLE I TESTING POLICY

Although Title I has maintained its essential policy goals and basic categorical structure for fifty years, its program rules have been significantly altered. The testing and evaluation requirements have been central to this transfor-

---

1. Carl Kaestle and Marshall Smith, writing in 1982, argue that after massive evaluations had been conducted, policymakers became skeptical of whether such studies could provide useful outcome and cost-benefit data on the overall effects of large educational interventions. At the same time, research conducted between 1965 and 1980 on the implementation of federal programs had yielded useful information about that process as it related to the distribution of program resources and the delivery of services to students. Not surprisingly, given their political implications, these Title I program outputs were the focus of policymakers' attention and expectations.

mation with three developments defining the changes: the focus of accountability has moved from monitoring the distribution of inputs to evaluating the effectiveness of program outcomes; states are now required to incorporate Title I recipients into their standards and assessment systems as they apply to all students; and the technical characteristics of tests have changed and their uses have become more consequential.

A Shift in Focus to Program Outcomes

The major changes in Title I's testing requirements began early in ESEA's third decade with its 1988 reauthorization.[2] States were required for the first time to define the levels of academic achievement that Title I eligible students should attain as a way to identify schools whose students did not show substantial progress in meeting the achievement outcomes (Jennings 2001, 15). This new focus represented a significant shift in Title I's rationale by highlighting the academic achievement of Title I students, and by beginning to identify them not just as recipients of special services but also as participants in a school's general academic program (Manna 2006, 73).[3] Nevertheless, despite emphasizing accountability for program outcomes and articulating an explicit connection between Title I services and the general education program, the 1988 reauthorization still framed Title I recipients as a distinct group. That segregation was further reinforced because the required Title I testing regime functioned as a separate system that affected only those 20 percent of the nation's students who were Title I eligible (Manna 2006, 75).[4]

In 1993, the Advisory Committee on Testing in Chapter 1 [Title I], established by the Department of Education (ED) to review the standardized tests used to evaluate the program, issued its report. The committee, composed primarily of testing experts and other researchers, concluded that "Chapter 1 testing should no longer be an independent system but should be linked with the education reforms that states and school districts are undertaking for all children," and that "national Chapter 1 evaluation should be decoupled from state, local, and classroom assessment functions" (vii). The report also noted that researchers and practitioners were finding that Chapter 1 procedures "may be narrowing Chapter 1 curriculum and instruction by rewarding those practices most likely to produce gains on norm-referenced tests," and that such tests may encourage teachers to spend too much time teaching low-level skills and test preparation (13).

Title I Linked to State Standards and Assessments

In the 1994 ESEA reauthorization, Improving America's Schools Act (IASA), the Clinton administration relied heavily on the testing provisions to cement the connection between Title I and the general education program in states and local districts. As a condition for receiving federal funding, states were required to ensure that the learning goals and standards for Title I students were the same as for all other students. Although Title I students might receive supplemental instruc-

---

2. Between 1981 and 1994, Title I was known as Chapter 1. With the 1994 reauthorization of ESEA (Improving America's Schools Act [IASA]), it was once again called Title I.

3. The Title I program and its students were moved closer to the core instructional program in individual schools with the initiation of school-wide programs. In response to concerns that pull-out services were preventing eligible students from receiving full exposure to the regular curriculum and to findings from the effective schools research showing that successful schools are characterized by comprehensive instructional strategies, the 1988 ESEA reauthorization allowed schools in which 75 percent of the students came from low-income backgrounds to operate school-wide programs without requesting matching funds from the local school district.

4. As states adopted standards-based reforms and enacted accountability systems that focused on student outcomes, state officials—particularly governors—pressed the federal government to move away from its policy that allowed and even encouraged tests of basic skills and to make the Title I testing provisions more consistent with state policy (McDermott 2011, 69).

tion, schools now had to ensure that these students were part of the core instructional program, and schools had to be accountable for the Title I students' academic progress in whatever way states held them accountable for all other students' achievement.

The assumptions underlying IASA and its testing requirements were those articulated in the academic writing of Clinton's undersecretary of education, Marshall Smith, and reflected in the policies of states that had adopted some form of standards-based reform (SBR) (Smith and O'Day 1991; O'Day and Smith 1993).[5] Although the strategy has varied from one jurisdiction to another, four elements have typically characterized it: a focus on student achievement; an emphasis on academic content standards specifying the knowledge and skills that students should acquire and the levels at which they should demonstrate mastery; a desire to extend the standards to all students, including those for whom expectations had traditionally been low; and a heavy reliance on achievement testing to spur the reforms and monitor their impact (National Research Council 1997).

IASA required that state assessments had to be aligned with the content standards, test at three separate grade levels, be based on "multiple, up-to-date ... measures that assess higher order thinking skills and understanding," and "provide individual student interpretive and descriptive reports" as well as disaggregated results at the school level by race, gender, English proficiency, migrant status, disability, and economic status (Improving America's Schools Act, section 1111). States were required to hold schools and districts accountable for making adequate progress toward achieving the standards, and they were to identify districts and schools in need of improvement and to take corrective action in cases of persistent academic failure.

Congress gave the states a long implementation period, allowing them to implement major provisions of IASA over six years with the assessments not required to be aligned with a state's content and performance standards until the 2000-2001 school year. However, by early 2001, only seventeen states were prepared to meet the deadline for aligned assessments that tested all students in reading and mathematics at least once in the elementary, middle, and secondary grade spans.[6] In addition, states varied considerably in how they implemented the required student performance standards. Although all but five had set absolute goals for student performance, they had significantly different expectations about the proportion of students who would need to meet the state's definition of proficiency. Twelve states expected 90 to 100 percent of students in each school to meet the state's proficiency standard, and another ten set a goal of 50 percent. Only fourteen states had specific time lines for meeting performance standards, on average ten years with a range of six to twenty years. States also used different methods for defining adequate yearly progress (AYP). Some required schools to meet an absolute performance target, others expected relative improvement each year or reductions in the achievement gap among subgroups of students, and still others used various combinations of these approaches. States also varied in the proportion of Title I schools they designated as "needing improvement," ranging from a low of 1 percent in Texas and 5 percent in North Carolina to a high of 76 percent in Michigan (Cohen 2002, 5).

---

5. The rationale for what they call systemic reform is that if states set high academic content and performance standards common to all students, the wide gaps in achievement among students of different ethnic and income groups would narrow. Their vision of reform is one where state governments set the standards, but allow individual districts and schools to decide on the instructional strategies to meet them. The systemic notion refers to the close links among curriculum, professional development, and school organization in implementing academic standards.

6. An additional fourteen states had been granted a waiver on the implementation deadline, but were expected to meet the requirements given some additional time. Four other states, Alabama, California, Wisconsin, and West Virginia, were found to have been substantially out of compliance and unlikely to meet the requirements without federal enforcement action (Cohen 2002, 3).

More Consequential Uses of Test Results

A number of scholars have analyzed the legislative history of No Child Left Behind (NCLB), IASA's successor (Rudalevige, 2003; DeBray 2006; Manna 2006; McGuinn 2006). Among the issues that they document as contentious were the testing provisions, stemming mainly from some states' opposition to changing their existing assessment systems. Once again, the federal government faced the dilemma of seeking greater accountability over how its funds are spent, but depending on the states for the necessary information. The challenges associated with the federal government continuing to depend on state assessments but being able only to set general guidelines for their design and administration were compounded by concerns about test use. Because AYP was viewed as both an indicator for reporting student achievement uniformly across all the state testing systems and a tool for leveraging state and local behavior, it was the focus of considerable debate. The requirement that all student subgroups within a school meet the AYP standard and that, for the first time, consequences would be tied to test scores in the form of potential sanctions meant that it had become a high-stakes indicator and policy tool. Before and after NCLB's passage, researchers warned that AYP and the consequences attached to its use compromised its validity as a measurement instrument (Kane and Staiger 2002; Linn, Baker, and Betebenner 2002). While the legislation was in the conference committee, congressional staff scrambled to revise the AYP formula even though researchers warned that it would eventually result in large numbers of failing schools (Manna 2006, 125). Nevertheless, NCLB passed both houses of Congress with large majorities, and with the testing provisions essentially intact from what the Bush administration had originally proposed (Manna 2006, 127).

The NCLB testing mandates represent a more precise and detailed version of the IASA requirements, and they embody stronger regulatory teeth in moving test use from essentially informational, hortatory uses to ones with high-stakes consequences.[7] As a condition for receiving Title I funding, states are required to test all students in grades three through eight annually in mathematics and reading–language arts and once in grades nine through twelve on a statewide standardized assessment aligned with the state content standards.[8] Test scores are to be disaggregated and reported at the school-, district-, and state-levels by race-ethnicity, gender, low income, disability, and students learning English. States must also participate in the fourth- and eighth-grade National Assessment of Educational Progress (NAEP). The high stakes aspect of NCLB's testing regime is represented in an AYP formula that requires states to set annual targets for increasing student achievement and closing gaps among groups so that by the 2013–2014 academic year, all students were to be proficient in mathematics and reading as measured on their state assessments. NCLB sanctions for schools failing to meet AYP include giving parents the option to transfer their children to other schools, using part of their Title I support to provide parents with funds to secure supplemental assistance for their children, and in cases of failing to meet AYP over four consecutive years, undergoing major restructuring with the possibility of the school closing

---

7. Low- and high-stakes tests represent two fundamentally different ways of using testing in service of policy goals. "A low-stakes test has no significant tangible, or direct consequences attached to the results, with information alone assumed to be a sufficient incentive for people to act. The theory behind this policy is that a standardized test can reliably and validly measure student achievement; that politicians, educators, parents, and the public will then act on the information generated by the test; and that actions based on test results will improve educational quality and student achievement. In contrast, high-stakes policies assume that information alone is insufficient to motivate educators to teach well and students to perform to high standards. Hence it is assumed, the promise of rewards or the threat of sanctions is needed to ensure change" (National Research Council 1999a, 35).

8. In addition to testing in mathematics and reading, states are also required to test students in science once in elementary, middle, and high school.

and being reorganized under new management. As a number of evaluations of NCLB have found, the results have been decidedly mixed (for a summary of these studies, see Dee and Jacob 2010). Nevertheless, even when the Obama administration offered waivers in the face of states' inability to meet the 2014 proficiency standard and Congress's failure to address problems with NCLB and reauthorize ESEA, the annual testing and reporting requirements remain in place.[9] The waivers have offered states the opportunity to alter how they use their test scores for accountability purposes, but the frequency of testing and the subjects and grades tested are unchanged.

NCLB's mixed results are reflected in how its requirements have served the two purposes of testing. As policy tools, they have reinforced what was already known from state policies: mandates that students be tested on standardized assessments are the most powerful levers that elected officials and other policymakers have for influencing what happens in schools and classrooms. A growing body of research has found that although the changes may not have the desired or expected effects on student learning, they do in fact change school and classroom practices (National Research Council 1999a, 29). In complying with the testing requirements that NCLB imposed on them as a condition for Title I funding, states made major changes in their assessment systems. At the time of NCLB's enactment, forty-six administered a statewide assessment, and thirty-one reported that the tests were aligned with their state standards. However, because most states tested at just a few grade levels or tested only a sample of students, only five fully met the NCLB requirements. The remainder had to develop at least one new test and thirty-five states had to develop seven or more new tests (U.S. General Accounting Office 2003, 8, 13).

At the same time, the AYP requirements, coupled with the provision that each state could develop its own content and performance standards, created incentives for some states to shirk by setting their standards low and making it easier for schools to reach AYP. As a result, Robert Linn, an expert on state assessments, concludes that "the variability in the stringency of the state standards defining proficient performance is so great that the concept of proficient achievement lacks meaning" (2008, 7). This discrepancy in standards became clear when state assessment results were compared with NAEP scores. In mapping state proficiency standards in mathematics and reading for grades four and eight onto the appropriate NAEP scale, researchers found that state differences in the percentage of students scoring at the proficient level on state assessments did not represent real differences in achievement as measured on NAEP, but instead reflected where a state set its proficiency levels. Most state cut points, moreover, fell below the equivalent of the NAEP proficient standard, and some even fell below the NAEP basic standard (National Center for Education Statistics 2007).[10]

The effects of NCLB's testing provisions in

---

9. The department first offered waivers to states in 2011. To be exempt from having to meet the 2014 proficiency standard and to implement specific interventions in schools that fail to meet AYP for two consecutive years, states could apply for a waiver subject to annual renewal. The waiver includes four requirements. First, they must adopt college- and career-ready standards and administer high-quality assessments based on those standards by the 2014–2015 school year (states were allowed to continue to use their earlier SBR assessments in the interim). Second, they must develop differential accountability systems that include multiple indicators in addition to test scores (for example, graduation rates, student attendance) and that are publicly reported by student subgroup (though the number of groups can be fewer than those required for NCLB if the categories are broader). Third, they must implement teacher and principal evaluation systems that factor in student achievement. Fourth, they must identify three levels of schools based on their performance (*reward, priority,* and *focus*) with interventions required for the lowest performing (priority—equal to at least 5 percent of the state's lowest performing schools) and those with large achievement gaps among subgroups (focus schools). As of the fall of 2014, the department had granted forty-three state waivers and had withdrawn two of these.

10. Comparing NAEP scores for a given state with those on the state's own assessment is not entirely valid. The NAEP tests are not aligned with the standards or curriculum of any particular state and the NAEP proficiency

functioning as a measurement instrument are also mixed. The costs of meeting the requirement to test all students in grades three through eight annually has led states to increase their use of multiple-choice items in their assessments because of the ease of scoring within the time frame specified by NCLB. In 2009, thirty-eight of the forty-eight states responding to a Government Accountability Office (GAO) survey, reported that multiple-choice items made up all or most of the items for their reading and language arts assessments and thirty-nine reported the same format for their mathematics assessments. About 20 percent of the states reported increasing their use of multiple-choice items since NCLB's passage. State officials and their technical advisers acknowledged the significant trade-offs they have faced between validly measuring cognitively complex content and accommodating cost and time constraints. The GAO found that some states have attempted to address these trade-offs by including open-ended, constructed response items on their assessments that are outside the NCLB reporting requirements and used only to provide information for instructional purposes (2009).

However, during this same period, NAEP has become a more visible and credible source of information about student achievement. The NCLB requirement that all states participate in NAEP and the introduction of the Trial Urban District Assessment (TUDA) in 2002 has provided more uniform data about student performance. In addition, it has highlighted the shortcomings of state performance standards and has functioned as the main source of information about differential student outcomes during national policy debates.[11]

From their beginnings in 1965, an overarching function of the Title I testing requirements has been their role in evaluating the effectiveness of the program. That task has not produced clear-cut answers, and in the case of NCLB, has been the subject of considerable contention. However, even researchers who have attributed positive changes to Title I agree that the effects have been modest. In their synthesis of seventeen federally commissioned evaluations of Title I's effectiveness between 1966 and 1992, Geoffrey Borman and Jerome D'Agostino found that the program "has not fulfilled its original expectation: to close the achievement gap between at-risk students and their more advantaged peers.... The results do suggest, however, that without the program, children served since the 1960s would have fallen further behind academically." (Borman and D'Agostino 2001, 49). These authors conclude, as have others, that although Title I has produced a modest effect on students' annual achievement gains, the effect has been highly variable across subject areas, testing cycles, grade levels, and schools. Subsequent studies of the effects of NCLB, using a variety of analytical techniques and primarily relying on NAEP and state assessment data, have reached differing conclusions. Some have found no achievement effects associated with NCLB, and others have found either that growth in student achievement has been flatter since the enactment of NCLB or that it tracks trends that existed prior to NCLB. In contrast, a more recent study by Thomas Dee

---

standards have been set very high so scores on that assessment can systematically overstate the shortcomings of state performance standards and assessments. However, another large data base from tests aligned with individual state standards confirms the NAEP results. The Northwest Evaluation Association (NWEA) maintains a large pool of test items from which it designs diagnostic tests for local districts using items closest to the relevant state assessment. Because all the items are pegged to a common scale, NWEA can make comparisons across the states. Using data from 2003 and 2006, collected on 830,000 students in twenty-six states, NWEA found significant variability in the level of difficulty in state assessments ranging from the 6th percentile (94 percent would pass) to approximately the 77th percentile (23 percent would pass) (National Research Council 2008).

11. Another development, implemented by states independently of the NCLB requirements, has also contributed to the design of more reliable and comprehensive student data systems and more effective use of them. Over the past decade, states have begun to develop longitudinal student-level data systems and to link their student and educator data, pre-K–12 and postsecondary systems, and across education, social service, and employment agencies.

and Brian Jacob that compares test score changes between 1990 and 2007 across states that already had school accountability policies before NCLB and ones that did not finds modest and mixed effects. They report that NCLB has been associated with statistically significant increases in the average mathematics performance of fourth graders with somewhat larger effects among the highest- and lowest-achieving students. The effects on eighth-grade mathematics scores are also positive, especially for low-achieving groups. However, there is no evidence that NCLB has had any effect on either fourth- or eighth-grade reading scores. The researchers note that these achievement gains appear limited when compared with NCLB's goal of 100 percent proficiency and that the program has contributed only modestly to reducing the achievement gap (Dee and Jacob 2011).

EXPLAINING STABILITY AND CHANGE IN TITLE I TESTING POLICY

The history of the Title I testing requirements raises two questions:

- Why in the face of continuing evidence about the limitations of testing as a policy tool and measurement instrument have these provisions endured through multiple ESEA reauthorizations?
- Why have significant changes been adopted even while the core elements of the testing requirements persist?

Perhaps surprisingly, the same two factors explain both the stability and changes: the institutional structures and rules that make federalism a defining feature of government in the United States, and the interest group dynamics that have shaped ESEA.

The Influence of Federalism

More than in some other policy domains, federal authority in education is essentially limited to enforcing constitutional civil rights and civil liberties guarantees. Beyond that, the federal government's major policy tools are categorical programs that seek to change the institutional behavior of state and local agencies by offering financial assistance on the condition that they undertake certain prescribed activities (McDermott and Jensen 2005; McDonnell 2005). This arrangement has two central features. First, because schools are "coping organizations" where neither outputs nor outcomes are truly observable, the federal government must rely on proxy indicators and limited information (Wilson, 1989, 168). Consequently, information about how Title I funds are spent has become the proxy for outputs and test scores the main proxy for outcomes. The fifty-year history of ESEA suggests that a wholly different strategy is not likely to be politically or administratively feasible.

The second feature is that the federal government's enforcement powers in the case of Title I are limited. In theory, a categorical program carries the threat of the withdrawal of funds if recipients fail to comply with the conditions of the grant. However, although the Department of Education has been willing to impose some partial withholding of Title I administrative funds, it has avoided more stringent penalties because of the likely political pushback from Congress and the potential harm to students receiving Title I services.[12] Consequently, the shaming of malefactors through information dissemination and bargaining with states have been the modal enforcement mechanisms.

Although federalism has functioned as an institutional constraint ensuring the stability

---

12. A recent example of the federal government's limits on enforcing its categorical requirements was ED's response to California's decision to suspend accountability testing and reporting required under NCLB for one year as it field-tested new Common Core assessments in 2014. The initial ED response was to threaten to withhold at least $15 million in Title I administrative funds from California with the possibility that the amount would increase as the federal government also withheld ESEA funds spent on testing in the previous year and on turnaround schools. However, six months later after California's governor, legislature, state board of education, and state education agency refused to change their position, ED secretary Arne Duncan granted the state a waiver. California students took the pilot test in 2014, but the results will not be publicly reported by school and subgroup and will not be included in the formula for calculating AYP (Klein 2013; McNeil 2014).

of the testing requirements, it has also provided the federal government with opportunities for changes that have extended and strengthened its programmatic reach over state and local behavior. Several analysts have concluded that NCLB's design, especially the more prescriptive testing requirements, was possible only because of profound changes in the state role beginning in the 1980s (McDonnell 2005; Manna 2006). In the wake of the "Nation at Risk" report and the implementation of standards-based reforms in a number of states, academic content and performance standards along with standardized assessments became an integral part of state policy (McDermott 2011). This major development at the level of the governmental system with constitutional responsibility for education allowed the federal government "to borrow strength." Paul Manna defines this process as occurring "when policy entrepreneurs at one level of government attempt to push their agendas by leveraging the justification and capabilities that other governments in the federal system possess" (2006, 5). Policy entrepreneurs promoting NCLB could mobilize around the license, or arguments that states had already made to justify the involvement of higher levels of government in classroom processes and outcomes, and around the capacity or resources and administrative structures that state reforms had created.[13]

The last point about capacity and structures is particularly important for the Title I testing requirements. One effect of more than twenty years of state SBR policies is that a substantial testing infrastructure has been institutionalized (McDonnell 2008). Networks of state agency staff, testing contractors, vendors of instructional materials, and local testing and evaluation staff are now well developed. Most states had to change their testing policies in response to NCLB, but the institutional infrastructure was already firmly in place. That capability and the policy ideas animating it have allowed substantial changes in Title I testing over the past two decades yet ensured that its core elements remain stable.

The Role of Interest Groups

A number of recent studies have analyzed the changing politics of education through the lens of groups with a stake in this policy domain. Taking somewhat different but complementary perspectives, this research has focused on the growing density and diversity of interest networks and on the altered issue definitions and policy ideas that the groups have embraced (for example, see DeBray-Pelot and McGuinn 2009; Rhodes 2012; Mehta 2013; Wolbrecht and Hartney 2014). These interest group dynamics—their ideological and material interests, how they frame them, and their policy preferences and strategies—are a second factor in explaining Title I's change within stability. This interest-focused explanation also has institutional dimensions that closely connect it to the first explanation. Just as the federal government borrowed strength from the states, groups with an interest in testing as part of a reform strategy have taken advantage of the multiple policy arenas in the federal system in advancing their agenda. Their promotion of SBR at all governmental levels has resulted not only in a range of policies, but also in new institutions to develop and maintain those reforms. The testing infrastructures now operating in states and local districts and used in implementing the NCLB requirements are prime examples.[14]

One of the most noteworthy changes in the politics of education since the 1980s has been

---

13. Although borrowing strength is typically used to explain the emergence of new federal policies that are legitimated through existing state ones, the process can also work in the opposite direction. So, for example, although state policymakers may oppose the strictures imposed by NCLB, the law has allowed them to use the federal mandate as leverage to strengthen their own influence over local districts and schools.

14. Jennifer Hochschild notes that theories of issue expansion identify the creation of new institutions as a strategy that interest groups use to maintain their policy gains even as public attention shifts to other problems and opponents seek to diminish or alter those gains. Once established, institutional rules and incentives are more difficult to change than policies, and Hochschild suggests that this difference helps account for the continuing success of groups pressing for greater educational accountability (2003, 119–20).

a substantial expansion in the array of groups beyond those representing the interests of teachers, administrators, and education governing bodies. Although the traditional education interest groups disagree among themselves on a number of issues such as labor relations, they have historically coalesced in pressing for greater state and local flexibility in administering Title I, and they have opposed the NCLB testing and AYP requirements as overly prescriptive. In contrast, newer entrants into the education policy arena, such as business interests and groups promoting various reform agendas, actively support the NCLB testing requirements as part of a larger accountability strategy. Their support has ensured the continuation of testing as a policy tool central to Title I, but it has also helped promote the changes that have made the requirements more prescriptive.

The reasons for these groups' support can be traced to a combination of revised problem definitions and new policy ideas framed as solutions to those problems. Because different groups have accepted and promoted alternative problem definitions and rationales, their shared agreement on stricter accountability provisions as a solution does not always extend to the reasons for it. Space limitations preclude a thorough discussion of the new problem framings and policy ideas that contributed to changes in the Title I testing requirements. However, several of these are specific to ESEA, and others reflect broader changes in education politics and policy. One factor, directly linked to ESEA's history and reflected in the congressional deliberations over NCLB, was a perception on the part of much of the Republican caucus and many moderate Democrats that federal education policy had not demanded real results for the billions of dollars spent (Rudalevige 2003; DeBray 2006). Consequently, NCLB was seen as a way to deal with the persistent and vexing problem of Title I's modest effects by moving federal regulation away from an emphasis on fiscal audit trails, and trading some increased flexibility in program operations for states and localities in exchange for their greater accountability for student outcomes. Frustration with Title I's shortcomings also motivated some civil rights groups who view SBR with a strong testing and accountability component as a way to focus attention on the underachievement of historically disadvantaged students, and to create political momentum for improving the schools they attend. These groups, like Robert Kennedy decades earlier, believe that states and localities will not adequately serve disadvantaged students without federal pressure to do so.[15]

Title I's own history and how past evaluations have shaped definitions of the policy problem partly explain changes in the testing provisions. However, the selection of a standards-based strategy with high-stakes assessment as a central feature of the solution is best explained by the broader SBR rationale. That rationale is now well known, having been repeated in media commentary and policy deliberations dating back to the publication of "A Nation at Risk" in 1982. Its statement of the problem includes an economic and demographic dimension: to be competitive in a technologically advanced, global economy, the United States needs better-educated workers, and the changing demographics of the U.S. labor force require that schools do a more effective job of educating those students who have historically been poorly served by the public schools. Much has been written about how this problem definition became linked to standards and accountability and school choice as the solutions now dominating education policy (for example, see Manna 2006; Rhodes 2012; Henig 2013). Similarly, numerous researchers and commentators have questioned the underlying assumptions of these policy ideas and the evidence about their effectiveness (for example, see Cohen and Moffitt 2009; Ravitch 2010; Kirp 2013).

What is perhaps most important from the

---

15. In his analysis of what he calls "civil rights [policy] entrepreneurs," Jesse Rhodes makes a distinction between these groups as one faction within the civil rights community and other organizations that do not support SBR. The groups working on behalf of NCLB and related state policies include the Citizens' Commission on Civil Rights, the Education Trust, and the National Council of La Raza.

perspective of Title I is that these policy ideas moved the program and its recipients from the periphery of schooling to the instructional core with its academic standards and accountability requirements. This shift occurred because the dominant policy image of what constitutes educational equity was changed. A problem statement requiring that all students be educated to higher standards shifted the definition of equity away from access to educational resources and compliance with legal mandates to a focus on students' learning opportunities and their achievement. As Kathryn McDermott concludes, "by defining equity in terms of a common educational threshold for all students, the performance-based understanding of educational equity shifts to a universal definition of equity and away from understandings of equity that targeted specific disadvantaged groups such as low-income students, students of color, or girls" (2011, 167). As a result, Title I, in effect, became an example of what Theda Skocpol calls antipoverty programs based on "targeting within universalism" (1991). In this case, the testing requirements have placed Title I within a universal policy framework, and the interests promoting the broader SBR idea have made that shift politically feasible.

CONCLUSION

Three conclusions emerge from the history of the Title I testing and evaluation requirements: their dual policy and educational purposes, the persistence of change within a stable policy core requiring regular student testing, and the institutional and interest-based reasons for how the testing requirements have evolved. Looking ahead to ESEA's future, questions arise about whether the testing requirements will survive and, if so, will they continue to serve the same two purposes. Because a number of groups and commentators are calling attention to problems with the overtesting of students and poor quality assessments, the testing requirements will likely become less prescriptive in a reauthorized Title I. Nevertheless, despite significant disagreements between Democratic and Republican members of Congress on major parts of the legislation, the requirement that students be tested appears in most proposals, the leadership still focused on students continuing to be tested in grades three through eight, and some rank-and-file members pressing for less testing but still requiring it on a regular basis (Camera 2014; Rich 2015a, 2015b).

What is likely to change is which governmental level establishes the rules for state accountability plans and how test results are used in rewarding and sanctioning schools and educators. If states are given greater flexibility in how often they test students, some may decide that with less frequent testing (or testing only samples of students), they can afford to increase the validity of their assessments through improved item design and curriculum coverage. Increased state flexibility in test use may also move assessments back to earlier low-stakes, hortatory uses that depend on transparency and reducing information asymmetries among policymakers, their constituents, and educators. If granting states greater flexibility leads them to administering assessments that more validly measure student performance and using the scores only for purposes for which a test is designed, the result will be higher quality assessment systems more closely aligned with the standards established by the testing profession (American Educational Research Association et al. 2014). However, not all states will use such flexibility to improve their tests as either policy tools or measurement instruments.

Consequently, if the federal government is to maintain its core policy goal of enhanced learning opportunities for low-income students, two key elements of NCLB need to remain in a reauthorized ESEA. The requirement for reporting the distribution of test scores by student subgroups has been one of the most effective examples of the federal bully pulpit in highlighting social problems and in providing a major resource for political mobilization. Similarly, the requirement that states participate in NAEP has generated substantial payoffs for education reformers as comparisons between state assessment results and NAEP scores (as flawed as these comparisons may be) have functioned as powerful rationales for subsequent policies such as the Common Core

State Standards. So a stable core of required testing and public reporting of the results should continue in a reauthorized ESEA even if the level of state discretion over test design and use is increased.

If such changes occur, the issue will be whether testing can continue to function as a policy tool and measurement instrument. Despite continued criticisms and identified flaws, the testing requirements have proven to be among the federal government's most effective strategies for pursuing its ESEA social policy goals. As a tool for leveraging state and local behavior, the requirements have significantly increased the federal government's influence over the allocation of program resources and its ability to reach further down into the education system in shaping decisions about who will be served with Title I funds and how they will be served. The evaluations conducted during Title I's early years led to more precise targeting of program resources, and the SBR orientation reflected in IASA and NCLB integrated Title I recipients into the instructional core with other students. Consequently, the testing requirements will continue to function as a policy tool in providing the information that allows federal policymakers to know whether subnational governments are meeting the categorical conditions for receiving funding, to negotiate with states from a stronger bargaining position, and to provide constituents with a mobilization resource.

The record of Title I testing requirements as a measurement instrument has been mixed. The requirements led to expanded use of student testing and increased capacity of states, local districts, and commercial test developers in designing and using standardized assessments. At the same time, Title I has also created disincentives for developing more reliable and valid tests. Most testing experts would argue that the move from norm-referenced tests to standards-based ones improved the validity of the inferences that could be drawn about student progress because they were measuring knowledge and skills more closely aligned with what was being taught in individual states. However, these advances were halted by the cost and administrative constraints imposed by the NCLB testing requirements and the move to more multiple choice testing. How the testing requirements continue to function as a measurement instrument will depend on the amount of flexibility that states (either individually or in consortia) will have in designing their assessments and on how the federal government will decide to incorporate the use of test results in ESEA program rules and administration. What can be predicted with some certainty, however, is that the status of the measurement function will continue to depend on the demands placed on testing when it is used as a political and policy tool.

The degree to which federalism is embedded in the structure and political culture of the United States has created a symbiotic relationship between the policy and measurement purposes of the Title I testing requirements, but it has also generated some unproductive trade-offs. On the one hand, pursuit of the federal government's policy purposes has politicized Title I testing and its uses in ways that have weakened its quality as a measurement instrument, especially to the extent that it has created incentives for educators to narrow their teaching to the content being measured (National Research Council 2011). At the same time, the federal government has been limited in how it can use testing for policy purposes because it must depend on the states to be its enforcer, information source, and main policy implementer.

Consequently, the Title I testing requirements have never completely fulfilled Robert Kennedy's vision of objective measurement in the service of effective programs for students living in poverty. Yet when we consider the institutional constraints on federal action in education and the competing demands placed on Title I by an expanding range of interests, the testing requirements have been more successful and enduring than what might have been predicted early in ESEA's history. The challenge now is the same one the program has faced for fifty years: ensuring state and local behavior consistent with federal goals while acknowledging the technical limitations of testing and balancing political accountability by elected officials with educators' professional judgment.

REFERENCES

Advisory Committee on Testing in Chapter 1. 1993. *Reinforcing the Promise, Reforming the Paradigm*. Washington: U.S. Department of Education.

American Educational Research Association, American Psychological Association, and National Council on Measurement in Education. 2014. *Standards for Educational and Psychological Testing*. Washington, D.C.: American Educational Research Association.

Bailey, Stephen K., and Edith K. Mosher. 1968. *ESEA: The Office of Education Administers a Law*. Syracuse, N.Y.: Syracuse University Press.

Borman, Geoffrey D., and Jerome V. D'Agostino. 2001. "Title I and Student Achievement: A Quantitative Synthesis." In *Title I: Compensatory Education at the Crossroads*, edited by Geoffrey D. Borman, Samuel C. Stringfield, and Robert E. Slavin. Mahwah, N.J.: Lawrence Erlbaum Associates.

Camera, Lauren. 2014. "AFT Backs Newest Proposal to Reduce Testing." *Education Week*, September. Available at: http://blogs.edweek.org/edweek/campaign-l-12/2014/09/aft_backs_n (accessed October 6, 2014).

Cohen, Michael. 2002. "Implementing Title I Standards, Assessments, and Accountability: Lessons from the Past Challenges for the Future." Paper prepared for the conference Will No Child Be Left Behind? The Challenges of Making This Law Work, Washington (February 13, 2002).

Cohen, David K., and Susan L. Moffitt. 2009. *The Ordeal of Equality*. Cambridge, Mass.: Harvard University Press.

DeBray, Elizabeth H. 2006. *Politics, Ideology, and Education*. New York: Teachers College Press.

DeBray-Pelot, Elizabeth. 2007. "Dismantling Education's 'Iron Triangle.'" In *To Educate a Nation*, edited by Carl F. Kaestle and Alyssa E. Lodewick. Lawrence: University Press of Kansas.

DeBray-Pelot, Elizabeth, and Patrick McGuinn. 2009. "The New Politics of Education: Analyzing the Federal Education Policy Landscape in the Post-NCLB Era." *Educational Policy*, 23(1): 15–42.

Dee, Thomas S., and Brian Jacob. 2010. "The Impact of No Child Left Behind on Students, Teachers, and Schools." *Brookings Papers on Economic Activity* Fall (2010): 149–94.

——— 2011. "The Impact of No Child Left Behind on Student Achievement." *Journal of Policy Analysis and Management* 30(3): 418–46.

Fung, Archon, Mary Graham, and David Weil. 2007. *Full Disclosure*. New York: Cambridge University Press.

Graham, Hugh David. 1984. *The Uncertain Triumph*. Chapel Hill, N.C.: University of North Carolina Press.

Henig, Jeffrey, 2013. *The End of Exceptionalism in American Education*. Cambridge, Mass.: Harvard Education Press.

Hochschild, Jennifer. 2003. "Rethinking Accountability Politics." In *No Child Left Behind*, edited by Paul E. Peterson and Martin R. West. Washington, D.C.: Brookings Institution Press.

Ingram, Helen. 1977. "Policy Implementation Through Bargaining." *Public Policy* 25(4): 499–526.

Jennings, John F. 2001. "Title I: Its Legislative History and Its Promise. In *Title I: Compensatory Education at the Crossroads*, edited by Geoffrey D. Borman, Samuel C. Stringfield, and Robert E. Slavin. Mahwah, N.J.: Lawrence Erlbaum Associates.

Kaestle, Carl F., and Marshall S. Smith. 1982. "The Federal Role in Elementary and Secondary Education, 1940–1980." *Harvard Educational Review* 52(4): 384–408.

Kane, Thomas J., and Douglas O. Staiger. 2002. "Volatility in School Test Scores: Implications for Test-Based Accountability Systems." *Brookings Papers on Education Policy* 5: 235–83.

Kirp, David L. 2013. *Improbable Scholars*. New York: Oxford University Press.

Kirst, Michael, and Richard Jung. 1991. "The Utility of a Longitudinal Approach in Assessing Implementation: A Thirteen-Year View of Title I, ESEA." In *Education Policy Implementation*, edited by Allan R. Odden. Albany: State University of New York Press.

Klein, Alyson. 2013. "Ed. Dept.: Calif. Could Lose at Least $15 Million in Federal Funds Over Testing." *Education Week*, October. Available at: http://blogs.edweek.org/edweek/campaign-k-12/2013/10/education (accessed September 30, 2004).

Linn, Robert L. 2008. "Educational Accountability Systems." In *The Future of Test-Based Educational Accountability*, edited by Katherine E. Ryan and Lorrie A. Shepard. New York: Routledge.

Linn, Robert L., Eva L. Baker, and Damian W. Betebenner. 2002. "Accountability Systems: Implications of Requirements of the No Child Left Behind Act of 2001." *Educational Researcher* 31(6): 3–16.

Manna, Paul. 2006. *School's In*. Washington, D.C.: Georgetown University Press.

McDermott, Kathryn A. 2011. *High-Stakes Reform*. Washington, D.C.: Georgetown University Press.

McDermott, Kathryn A., and Laura S. Jensen. 2005. "Dubious Sovereignty: Federal Conditions of Aid and the No Child Left Behind Act." *Peabody Journal of Education* 80(2): 39–56.

McDonnell, Lorraine M. 2004. *Politics, Persuasion, and Educational Testing*. Cambridge, Mass.: Harvard University Press.

———. 2005. "No Child Left Behind and the Federal Role in Education: Evolution or Revolution?" *Peabody Journal of Education* 80(2): 19–38.

———. 2008. "The Politics of Educational Accountability: Can the Clock Be Turned Back?" In *The Future of Test-Based Educational Accountability*, edited by Katherine E. Ryan and Lorrie A. Shepard. New York: Routledge.

McGuinn, Patrick J. 2006. *No Child Left Behind and the Transformation of Federal Education Policy, 1965–2005*. Lawrence: University Press of Kansas.

McLaughlin, Milbrey Wallin. 1975. *Evaluation and Reform*. Cambridge, Mass.: Ballinger.

McNeil, Michele. 2014. "California Wins Prized NCLB Testing Waiver." *Education Week*, March 7. Available at: http://blogs.edweek.org/edweek/campaign-k-12/2014/03/california (accessed September 30, 2014).

Mehta, Jal. 2013. "How Paradigms Create Politics: The Transformation of American Educational Policy, 1980–2001." *American Educational Research Journal* 50(2): 285–324.

Murphy, Jerome T. 1991. "Title I of ESEA: The Politics of Implementing Federal Education Reform." In *Education Policy Implementation*, edited by Allan R. Odden. Albany, NY: State University of New York Press.

National Center for Education Statistics. 2007. *Mapping 2005 State Proficiency Standards onto the NAEP Scales*. Washington: U.S. Department of Education.

National Research Council. 1997. *Educating One and All*. Committee on Goals 2000 and the Inclusion of Students with Disabilities. Edited by Lorraine M. McDonnell, Margaret J. McLaughlin, and Patricia Morison. Washington, D.C.: National Academies Press.

———. 1999a. *High Stakes*. Committee on Appropriate Test Use. Edited by Jay P. Heubert and Robert M. Hauser. Washington, D.C.: National Academies Press.

———. 1999b. *Testing, Teaching and Learning*. Committee on Title I Testing and Assessment. Edited by Richard F. Elmore and Robert Rothman. Washington, D.C.: National Academies Press.

———. 2008. *Common Standards for K-12 Education? Considering the Evidence*. Summary of a Workshop Series. Alexandria Beatty, rapporteur. Committee on State Standards in Education. Washington, D.C.: National Academies Press.

———. 2011. *Incentives and Test-Based Accountability in Education*. Committee on Incentives and Test-Based Accountability in Public Education. Edited by Michael Hout and Stuart W. Elliott. Washington, D.C.: National Academies Press.

O'Day, Jennifer A., and Marshall S. Smith. 1993. "Systemic Reform and Educational Opportunity." In *Designing Coherent Education Policy*, edited by Susan Fuhrman. San Francisco: Jossey-Bass.

Ravitch, Diane. 2010. *The Death and Life of the Great American School System*. New York: Basic Books.

Rhodes, Jesse H. 2012. *An Education in Politics*. Ithaca, N.Y.: Cornell University Press.

Rich, Motoko. 2015a. "White House Still Backs Annual Testing in Schools." *New York Times*, January 12. Available at: http://www.nytimes.com/2015/01/13/education/arne-duncan-says-administration-is-committed-to-testing.html (accessed July 29, 2015).

———. 2015b. "Reviewing Federal Education Law, Senator Seeks More Local Control." *New York Times*, January 14. Available at: http://www.nytimes.com/2015/01/14/us/reviewing-federal-education-law-senator-seeks-more-local-control.html (accessed July 29, 2015).

Rudalevige, Andrew. 2003. "No Child Left Behind: Forging a Congressional Compromise." In *No Child Left Behind*, edited by Paul E. Peterson and Martin R. West. Washington, D.C.: Brookings Institution Press.

Shepard, Lorrie. 2008. "A Brief History of Accountability Testing." In *The Future of Test-Based Educational Accountability*, edited by Katherine E. Ryan and Lorrie A. Shepard. New York: Routledge.

Skocpol, Theda. 1991. "Targeting Within Universalism: Politically Viable Policies to Combat Poverty in the United States." In *The Urban Underclass*, edited by Christopher Jencks and Paul E. Peterson. Washington, D.C.: Brookings Institution Press.

Smith, Marshall, and Jennifer O'Day. 1991. "Systemic School Reform." In *The Politics of Curriculum and Testing*, edited by Susan Fuhrman and Betty Malen. Philadelphia, Pa.: Falmer.

Stone, Deborah. 2012. *Policy Paradox*. New York: W. W. Norton.

U.S. Congress. Office of Technology Assessment. 1992. *Testing in American Schools*. OTA-SET-519. Washington: Government Printing Office.

U.S. General Accounting Office. 2003. "Title I: Characteristics of Tests Will Influence Expenses; Information Sharing May Help States Realize Efficiencies." GAO-03-389. Washington: Government Printing Office. Available at: http://www.gao.gov/new.items/d03389.pdf (accessed July 30, 2015).

U.S. Government Accountability Office. 2009. "No Child Left Behind: Enhancements in the Department of Education's Review Process Could Improve State Academic Assessments." GAO 09-911. Washington: Government Printing Office. Available at: http://www.gao.gov/assets/300/295827.pdf (accessed July 30, 2015).

Vinovskis, Maris A. 1999. "Do Federal Compensatory Education Programs Really Work? A Brief Historical Analysis of Title I and Head Start." *American Journal of Education* 107: 187–209.

Wilson, James Q. 1989. *Bureaucracy*. New York: Basic Books.

Wolbrecht, Christina, and Michael T. Hartney. 2014. "'Ideas about Interests:' Explaining the Changing Partisan Politics of Education." *Perspectives on Politics* 12(3): 603–30.

The State of Title I: Developing the Capability to Support Instructional Improvement

SUSAN L. MOFFITT AND DAVID K. COHEN

Title I has a mixed legacy. It helped cultivate and sustain the political salience of improving the education of children who live in poverty. It helped sweep schools, regardless of their student population's poverty levels, into the broader national standards-accountability reform effort. It has been a vehicle for liberal, conservative, bipartisan, public, and private reform agendas. It developed durable constituencies and appetites for federal funds. While Title I helped expand governments' administrative capabilities, it did much less to remedy the unevenness in instructional capability on which Title I built. The combination of Title I funds and standards based reform has enabled some interventions, such as Success for All and America's Choice, to demonstrate instructional improvement. Yet the potential for interventions like these to reduce the achievement gap remains profoundly constrained by the persistently unequal allocation of educational resources, rising income inequality, and the lack of assistance from social and economic policy.

Keywords: instructional improvement, accountability, achievement gap

To consider the legacy and future of ESEA Title I, one must understand its past, and especially the past of the governance system in which any conceivable Title I would operate. Title I is situated in a federal system in which federal policies and programs depend for success on the state and local school governments that are responsible for implementation. Those governments have historically devoted relatively few staff and resources to instructional improvement: to support teaching and learning, especially ambitious teaching that treats children like active sense-makers. Those governments have also historically relied heavily on school-based policies to address educational problems that arise in good part outside of the schools, and do so with only modest assistance from social and economic policy. This was not a problem as long as federal policies had modest expectations of what such policies should accomplish and made modest demands on state and local instructional capability. Beginning in the late 1970s, however, federal education officials began efforts to expand ESEA's Title I beyond the modest goal of fiscal transfers to include the much more ambitious goal of instructional improvement with the aim of eliminating the achievement gap, an initiative

---

Susan L. Moffitt is Mary Tefft and John Hazen White Sr. Assistant Professor of Political Science and Public Policy at Brown University. **David K. Cohen** is John Dewey Collegiate Professor at the School of Education and Ford School of Public Policy at the University of Michigan.

The order of authorship was determined by a coin toss: we have enjoyed contributing to this article equally. We are grateful to Kelly Branham and Ferris Lupino for their careful research assistance. All errors are our responsibility. Direct correspondence to: Susan L. Moffitt, susan_moffitt@brown.edu, Brown University, Taubman Center for American Politics and Policy, 67 George St., Box 1977, Providence, RI 02912; David K. Cohen, dkcohen @umich.edu, University of Michigan, School of Education, 610 E. University Ave., Ann Arbor, MI 48109.

that found its way into law a decade later with the Hawkins-Stafford amendments to ESEA. Yet as ESEA Title I began to grow increasingly ambitious, state and local governments did not match the pace; they did not develop the capability to effectively implement those policies and programs to support significant instructional improvement. In other nations, governments support instructional practice through national curricula and examinations keyed to the curricula that are reflected in university-based teacher preparation and in inspectorates that enable school and teacher-level quality-control. The United States does not have such forms of capability to support instruction and relies instead on a congeries of efforts provided through nongovernmental organizations (NGOs) and some state and local governments to encourage instructional improvement.

Limited capability to support instructional improvement has been due in part to the ways in which the governance system developed for education in the United States.[1] By governance, we mean not only government entities at all levels of the U.S. federal system, but also the nongovernmental organizations that participate in policy implementation and service delivery. During the twentieth century, state and local school governments gradually developed more financial and other administrative capabilities; but those grew with more speed and depth than the capability related to the design, management, and improvement of instruction. State and local governments developed few methods to provide teachers with rigorous opportunities to learn or to oversee teaching. That would not have been a problem had federal and state policies continued to focus on the allocation of school resources such as funds and on the regulation of those inputs. But, by the late 1980s, federal education policy began to expand to include efforts to regulate schools' results and to refocus Title I on student achievement outcomes, in addition to regulating and allocating school resources. By the mid-1990s, the Clinton administration incorporated that idea in a larger design for standards-based schooling—the Improving America's Schools Act (IASA), which sought to engineer school improvement nationally by regulating student achievement outcomes tied to academic standards. Seven years later, No Child Left Behind (NCLB) took the core of IASA and added a much more demanding compliance schedule and penalties. Within half a dozen years, schools' success on that compliance schedule began to seem doomed. The states and several state-related agencies then shifted the political and operational center of gravity from Washington to the states and a few nongovernmental organizations with the Common Core, but preserved the frame and key elements of standards-based reform.

This, in brief, is the situation in which we find ESEA Title I: standards-based reform, which was written into Title I by the Clinton and Bush reforms, remains the frame of education policy. But the Clinton and Bush reforms and Obama's administration of those reforms did little to enable state and local school agencies to develop the instructional capability—the knowledge, norms, and communities of practice—to respond constructively to the policies' ambitions. We present our analysis of how this situation developed and conclude with a discussion of the problems it presents and some ideas about how they might be managed. We discuss one possibility for managing the inherited problems Title I faces—using Title I funds to support interventions like several of the Comprehensive School Reform Designs—as well as the problems facing those designs.

IDEAS, AMBITIONS, AND POLICY

The capability to implement policy depends on a policy's ambitions and the gap between the policy's ambitions and current practice (Cohen and Moffitt 2009, chapter 2; Moffitt 2014). Changing ideas about what schools in general and Title I in particular should accomplish created a growing imbalance between the policy aims that defined the scope of federal,

---

1. We approach governance in a way consistent with Theda Skocpol's definition of a state as "any set of relatively differentiated organizations that claims sovereignty and coercive control over a territory and its population" (Skocpol 1992, 43).

state, and local governments' responsibilities and authorities and the capabilities to deliver on those aims. The evolution of these ideas has been discussed elsewhere (Cohen and Moffitt 2009, chapter 4), but we revisit them here to highlight the importance of improving instruction to Title I's legacy, and what might be done to encourage greater capability for instructional improvement and implementing Title I's ambitious aims.

The expansion of education policy in the 1960s is a familiar story. In the context of growing concern with poverty, pressures from the civil rights movement and its allies, and a high tide of liberal ideas in Lyndon Johnson's administration, a stream of quite unprecedented federal and state policies took shape. The passage of the 1964 Civil Rights Act facilitated the passage of other legislation (Cohen and Moffitt 2009, 48–49; Jennings 1985, 55–60), and the federal government and some states devised policies that sought to correct several of the nation's most fundamental social and educational problems. Great weaknesses in the education of disadvantaged children were the focal point of two federal programs: Head Start and Title 1 of the 1965 Elementary and Secondary Education Act. Like many policies, Title I combined multiple aims and purposes, and used legislative enthusiasm for antipoverty programs as a vehicle to create a breakthrough for federal aid to education (Cohen and Moffitt 2009, 49). Title I did not emerge from a rational design to end poverty, nor from a rational design to promote civil rights, nor from a rational design to improve instruction. Instead, it represented a pragmatic approach to funnel federal funds to schools—something some members of Congress had been attempting to accomplish for a decade before the act's passage—that linked federal funding for schools to concurrent ideas about promoting civil rights and addressing poverty. Roughly a decade later Congress passed Public Law 94-142, the Education for All Handicapped Children Act, which aimed to correct the almost complete neglect of education for children with disabilities. Several states had their own programs in these two areas, and all states participated in the three federal programs. Other federal legislation sought to improve schooling for the children of migrant workers, for Native American children, and for homeless children. In addition, the Supreme Court's 1974 *Lau v. Nichols* (414 US 563) decision helped break new ground for educational support for English-language learners. Erika Frankenberg and Kendra Taylor's article in this issue discusses the passage of Title I ESEA further.

These policies began to set a new course for education governance. They asserted a federal priority to help the disadvantaged, and they broke with long resistance to a significant federal role in schooling. They set new ambitions for federal and state policy, involved the federal government more deeply in the management of schooling, and expanded government responsibility. It bears remembering, however, that Title I's principal design feature is a formula grant that distributes funds to state and local education agencies, which then distribute the funds to schools. Title I was explicitly prohibited from getting in the business of federal involvement in specifying curriculum and guiding instruction. Though it is difficult to conceive of Title I as a singular treatment, in that it could be used in many different ways, studies have suggested it purchased about thirty minutes of additional instruction several days per week for children who received Title I services during the late 1970s and 1980s (Cohen and Moffitt 2009, 74). Although these policies, programs, and ideas were path-breaking and significant when we situate them in the longer history of schooling, they brought modest resources to teachers, students, and implementation in schools.

Put differently, Title I began as a way to distribute federal funds to schools and for those funds to support schooling for children in poverty. As Nora Gordon and Sarah Reber discuss elsewhere in this issue, Title I faced problems targeting those funds and ensuring that new federal resources supplemented rather than supplanted local resources. Federal and state governments developed fiscal accountability to manage these problems during the 1970s and 1980s (Cohen and Moffitt 2009, chapter 3).

But soon after federal and state governments began to manage that problem, Title I's original mission came to seem too modest. Expectations mounted for Title I to eliminate the racial and socioeconomic achievement gap. The first major step in that direction followed the publication of a study, mandated under Title IV of the 1964 Civil Rights Act, that was to report on the extent of inequality in education: *Equality of Educational Opportunity Survey* (EEOS), commonly referred to as the Coleman report (Coleman et al. 1966; Coleman 1966, 70–75).[2] It became an instant cause célèbre. It announced that the school inputs that were commonly thought to shape student performance had little or no differential effect on that performance. The chief influence on differences in school-level average student performance was not the educational resources that school funds purchased but school-level average of students' social and economic class.[3] This was thought to raise fundamental questions about the value of investment in schooling, and about the schools' vaunted role as "the balance wheel of the social machinery" (Mann 1891, 251). Few readers understood that the report dealt only with differences among schools, and that most of the differences among students' performance were within, not among schools. The survey could not connect teachers or other resources to students within schools, and so it could not analyze the relations among student background, school resources, and student performance within schools.

A few years later, those questions were given added force as a stream of evaluations reported that government policies and programs seemed not to have the expected effects; federal efforts to repair fundamental problems in U.S. schools and society had few discernable effects. In retrospect, we can see that it would have been astonishing had they reported anything else, for the problems were fundamental, the programs were modest (despite being major departures from past policy), and the programs' chief vehicles were the schools and school systems whose weak capability was one key source of the problems. Less discouraging accounts of effectiveness appeared in studies of Title I such as *Sustaining Effects*, but generated little political or scholarly attention (Carter 1983, 1984). Current analysis from Rucker Johnson in this issue provides further evidence of the positive impact that Title I had in its early years, even though it resided at the margins of the average participating student's school day.

Despite disconfirming evidence, one important effect was the growing sense, in the late 1970s and 1980s, that ESEA Title I was not sufficiently improving students' performance. Another was the quite novel idea of what would be sufficient—that the problem that ESEA Title I should solve was the racial or social class gap in achievement. Moreover, by the late 1980s another idea had begun to gain acceptance, namely, that the source of the problem was the schools' deficiencies, not the students' disadvantage, an idea discussed further in Gloria Ladsen-Billing's article in this issue. It took most of the 1980s for a new policy frame to develop, but with the 1988 Hawkins-Stafford amendments to Title I of the ESEA, a fundamental shift in ideas about the purposes of federal education policy took shape. The aims of federal and state education policy began to shift to regulation of outcomes, thus moving beyond the original emphasis on the allocation and delivery of resources to the achievement of results. The 1988 amendments targeted poor performance in schools as the central problem for ESEA Title I, and made high-poverty elementary schools eligible for whole school grants, which were intended to encourage across the board organizational change to improve instruction.

---

2. This had been intended as a survey of educational resources and racial segregation. But Alexander Mood, the U.S. Commissioner of Educational Statistics selected James Coleman to lead the study; and they designed something quite different.

3. The Coleman report suggested that students' social and economic class was the chief influence on school-to-school differences in their academic performance, and that there were large differences in the average achievement of black and white students. These were things that educators, testing experts and some academics had known since tests began to be administered early in the twentieth century, but school systems had held test results closely and quietly; and problems of race and inequality in education had not been a topic of great scientific, public, or political interest.

The 1994 Clinton administration reforms built on these ideas that Title I should eliminate the achievement gap and that a chief source of the problem resided in schools' deficiencies. The 1994 IASA encouraged states and localities to hold schools responsible for weak student performance and marked a new era in education policy, in which the federal government sought to focus action on group inequality in school outcomes, and to require state and local action that was thought likely to reduce that inequality. Goals 2000 and IASA required that state and local school systems set academic standards, require assessments that were "aligned" with the standards, and hold schools accountable for students' performance on those assessments. These ideas were adopted but framed in much more rigid mandates in NCLB, President George W. Bush's school reform bill. One key idea in both the Clinton and Bush bills was that research reports of weak student performance, coupled with schools' accountability for student performance, would prompt school, school district, or state action to improve performance.

These policies marked major developments. They expanded schools' mission to ensure that there were no intergroup inequalities in achievement and that all groups met specified outcome targets. That in turn greatly expanded the responsibility of governments and school systems, from ensuring the allocation and delivery of resources to achieving results. The expanded responsibility was manifest in many ways, perhaps most strikingly that schools, teachers, and school officials would be accountable for their students' performance.

Yet this expanded responsibility collided, paradoxically, with the legacy of education governance: government grew in size and scope, but that growth was neither consistent across government functions nor did it keep pace with the demands that policies placed on government. That created Title I's current predicament: the gap between the program's great new ambitions and the capability to achieve them.

INHERITED PROBLEMS FACING TITLE I

Several inherited features of the development of governance for education help to explain the gap between the ambitions for Title I and the capability to achieve those ambitions. These inherited features include weak teacher education, disproportionate growth in government administrative capability relative to its capability to support the practice of teaching and learning, reliance on nongovernmental organizations for the capability to support instruction, and local and state control of finances that express deep inequalities. We discuss how each of these inherited problems bears on schools' instructional capability, their capability to learn systematically from their operation and effects, and the implications for Title I. We discuss the historical roots of current predicaments to emphasize how entrenched Title I's problems of instructional improvement are.

Occupation of Teaching

One chief challenge to improved instruction—the capability to engage in rigorous teaching and learning and school, district, and state support for such capability—has arisen from the key occupation in schools: teaching. In the United States, teaching has more resembled an occupation than a profession, because teachers have less control over entry, over standards of quality and performance, and over professional education than do plumbers and electricians, for instance. As American public schooling developed throughout the nineteenth and early twentieth centuries, the job requirements for entry to the occupation were modest. Preservice education was also modest: universities did not invest in demanding programs for intending teachers, state legislatures oversaw this feature of higher education very lightly, and teacher education programs rarely tried to promote deep content knowledge among educators in the subjects they would later teach (for a summary of training requirements, see Bureau of Vocational Information 1924, 309–11; for illustrations of training through summer institutes, see Department of Public Instruction 1903, 1–3; 1900, 38–39.). State and local education agencies invested little or not at all in monitoring or regulating the quality of schools or classrooms, partly in deference to localism and partly for lack of expertise and staff. Hence most decisions about instruction were delegated, actively and passively, to teachers. Federal and state governments followed this pattern, devolving authority and responsibility to agencies below as they added to the agencies' missions. As expressed in the New York State Department of Education's annual report published in 1905: "It is not believed that the good of the school system is to be promoted by too much inspection; on the other hand, it is felt that local officers and teachers will grow in capacity for school work by doing it independently. It is believed that substantial improvement must come through freedom of local initiative and administration, rather than through too much direction on the part of the state" (36).

These weaknesses persisted through the post–World War II decades: most teachers reported that their pre-service education was little help to them in classrooms, few institutions of higher education tried to take teacher education seriously, and few elementary school teachers had deep knowledge of the subjects they taught. Although the technical and professional capability of teaching has generally been weak, it has been assigned a central and lightly regulated role in practice and policy implementation. For Title I, the legacy of weak teacher education has meant that the general education program on which many supplemental Title I services built has been typically weak as well (Lankford, Loeb, and Wyckoff 2002, 37–62). Title I, in other words, layers on top of this uneven and weak occupation.

Disproportion Between Administration and Instruction

A second inherited problem arises from the disproportionate growth of government capability in areas such as finance and administration relative to the capability to guide, inform, and improve instruction. Many state education agencies added staff in finance, assessment, and other areas through the first six decades of the twentieth century, but much less in the core domains of schooling—that is, teaching, curriculum, teacher education, and instruction. States delegated a great deal about these matters to localities. Many localities added capability in finance, assessment, and, later, specialized federal programs, but few had much capability in the realms most closely tied to instruction, including teaching quality and curriculum. School systems often tacitly delegated decisions about these matters to schools. School heads often left them to teachers. Although new authority and responsibility accumulated in states and localities during the twentieth century, the capability to design, organize, and improve instruction did not keep pace with the added authority.

Take, for instance, the case of New York State, which reflects where we most expect to see evidence investment in capabilities to support instruction of any governmental entity—federal, state, or local—from the Progressive era. Unlike other states, for instance, New York began to develop its statewide Regents exams in the 1860s and 1870s, and later developed curricula tied to the exams (Office of State Assessment 1987). Consistent with the standard portrait of Progressive era state expansion, the New York State Department of Education experienced considerable growth in the first four decades of the twentieth century in state administrative staff positions for tasks such as finance, communications, and supervision as well as the expansion of staff for specialized subunits, such as vocational education (State of New York 1905, 35, 56–57; State Department of Education 1912, 311–12; 1924, 321; 1925, 327; 1936, 170–71). Our estimates suggest that, in 1934, more than 25 percent of New York State staff positions were devoted to administration and finance, yet only 2 percent of positions focused on teacher education and certification: only seventeen state officials were employed to work on teacher education and certification in 1934 out of 719 total staff members.[4] These seventeen employees were responsible for a daunting range of tasks, one of which entailed overseeing and evaluating "17,000 teachers' credentials toward teaching certificates" and

---

4. Recall that New York took pride in its approach to teacher education: "In the establishment and maintenance of training classes, state normal institutions, city training schools, teachers institutes, summer schools, and a system of examination and certification of teachers, [New York] has occupied a position second to no state in the Union" (State of New York Education Department 1917, 5).

issuing "more than 7000 teachers' and principals' certificates" over the course of the year (State Department of Education 1936, 176). Even the motion picture bureau had more employees than teacher education and certification.[5]

The disproportionate growth of administrative capability relative to instructional capability in New York leads us to expect even greater differences in other states. New York state officials did oversee the curriculum for state teacher colleges (State Department of Education 1936, 175). Yet it invested very few human resources to such oversight. Most other state agencies had too little capability to actually oversee either university teacher education or local school system operations, and the federal education agency was in most cases even weaker. Few local central offices had the capability to actually oversee either educational programs or leadership in schools. Given the structural limits of U.S. governance and political attachment to Jeffersonian ideas about the virtue of a weak state, it was easier to add to the schools' missions than to strengthen state agencies and school systems in ways that would enable them to deliver on the missions (for challenges to the conventional view of a weak American state, see Balogh 2009; Novak 2008, 752–72). This history should be no surprise. Traditions of limited government restricted the development and oversight of instructional capability.

This legacy, however, has meant that Title I has been implemented in organizations that had more capability and resources devoted to administrative oversight than instruction. Title I's ability to develop fiscal accountability mechanisms in the 1970s were consistent with this tradition that focused on administration as distinct from instructional practice. Moreover, variation in the capabilities to support instruction currently appears across states. Some states such as North Carolina, a Race to the Top (RTTT) state, presently devote an impressive number of staff to school improvement, instruction, and curriculum: ninety-three positions for district and school transformation, fifty-two for teacher effectiveness, and fifty-nine for curriculum in 2013–2014.[6] This pattern of state administration stands in marked contrast to state departments during the Progressive era or during Title I's early years, when state investment in curriculum and instruction was thin, at best. Kansas, in contrast, makes no mention of positions devoted to teacher education or professional development in its 2013–2014 staff directory: only licensure and accreditation.[7] Florida labels forty-one positions devoted to instructional and school improvement out of more than two thousand state positions; it devotes many more positions to accountability and measurement.[8] Our review of organization charts from forty-five states suggests Florida is not alone: thirty-three of the forty-five have divisions devoted to accountability or performance audits.[9] Related research finds that many states devote significantly more resources to student assessment than to capacity-

---

5. The Motion Picture Division consisted of twenty employees in 1934 (State Department of Education 1936).

6. Authors' calculations based on North Carolina Education Directory, 2014–2015. Available at: www.dpi.state.nc.us/docs/nceddirectory/education.pdf (accessed January 18, 2015).

7. Authors' calculations based on Kansas State Department of Education, Kansas Educational Directory, 2013–2014. Available at: http://www.ksde.org/Home/QuickLinks/Directories/2013-2014EducationalDirectory.aspx (accessed January 18, 2015).

8. Authors' calculations based on directory information provided by the Florida Department of Education through an information request in November 2014. Our estimate is based on the number of positions in the Bureau of School Improvement, in the Instructional Support Services Section, and in the Bureau of Standards and Instructional Support, all within Florida's Division of Public Schools. For Florida, as with other states, we relied on the department's organizational classifications and labels and did not conduct a study of what department employees actually did.

9. Authors' calculations based on organization charts retrieved from state departments of education.

building interventions (Jochim and Murphy 2013, 7). States' administrative units devoted to testing, measurement and outcome accountability extend and build on the Progressive administrative architecture devoted to fiscal accountability. Holding others to account reflects an enduring component of the American governance repertoire, though accountability for what, by whom, and to whom has changed. Investments in teaching and learning that appear in Race to the Top states such as North Carolina may be promising, but it is much less clear whether those investments will persist when the stream of federal RTTT funds discontinues and what those investments have meant to the process of instructional improvement.[10]

Nongovernmental Organizations

A third inherited problem arose outside the governmental sector: a good deal of the development of capability related to instruction has occurred in private-sector professional, reform, and education organizations. For instance, early in the twentieth century the school surveys of George Strayer (a professor at Columbia's Teachers College) and his associates were influential in setting standards of school district quality and management; yet they were the creation of a nongovernmental organization (Steffes 2012). Similarly, the commission that produced the *Cardinal Principles* report in the late 1910s was quite influential in efforts to diversify high school curricula and make them more "practical"; yet this also was the work of a nongovernmental organization (Rice 1893; National Education Association 1918). General standards of occupational or educational quality also were devised by nongovernmental organizations. The National Council for the Accreditation of Teacher Education is one case in point, and the six regional agencies that accredit elementary and secondary schools—the North Central Association, the Middle States Association, and so on—are others.

Efforts to create consistency in instruction were also chiefly nongovernmental. The core elements of curriculum have until very recently been created by private publishing firms that seek national markets, and have been pushed in one direction or another by nongovernmental organizations such as the National Council of Teachers of Mathematics. In addition, the technology for assessing students' academic progress has been almost exclusively devised by private testing and publishing firms. The New York Regents examinations and curricula were one of the rare exceptions to that arrangement. Since the beginning of the twentieth century, nearly all research and evaluation related to public education has been carried out by private agencies; government funds for such research, which materialized well after the close of World War II, have been primarily from federal sources and private philanthropy.[11] In sum, the development of several central instructional elements in public education occurred almost completely outside of government. The design of governance meant that much of the core technology of schooling on which Title I layered developed beyond democratic oversight or control.

Financing Public Education

The fourth inherited challenge arises from education financing that has relied heavily on localities, with states taking an increasing share since World War II. Investment in schooling became a function of local and state wealth and elected officials' willingness to tax the citizens who elected them. For most of the history of public schooling, educational quality was tied to local wealth and appetite for schooling: wealthy districts were more likely to spend

---

10. In related parts of our project, we are examining state resources devoted to instructional improvement more systematically. This includes determining what fraction of state positions are devoted to the bureaucratic work of managing the increasing procedural and other administrative requirements that have grown markedly over the past fifty years, compared with the fraction devoted to the support, guidance, and improvement of instruction.

11. One early twentieth-century estimate suggests, "Several state departments of education and some fifty city departments of education have opened research bureaus for the study of current educational problems, chiefly problems of administration, in their respective jurisdictions" (Bureau of Vocational Information 1924, 304).

generously on schools and offer relatively high-quality education, but most others were likely to spend less, often much less, and offer more modest programs (Roza and Hill 2006, 246; Roza 2010; Baker and Welner 2010; Baker and Corcoran 2012; Baker 2014). These fiscal inequalities have had hugely important consequences for ESEA, because that program, which aimed to improve educational opportunity for children from poor families, was overlaid on a pattern of state and local school funding that created enormous inequality in the distribution of educational resources and thus educational opportunity. ESEA Title I has done little to correct those patterns (Cohen and Moffitt 2009, 148–52).

THE PROBLEM OF EDUCATION POLICY AND ESEA

Twenty years after the Clinton standards-based reforms and thirteen years after the Bush administration's extension of those reforms, evidence is scant that standards-based reform expressed through Title I created the deep change in schools' operations and outcomes that they intended. The curriculum students receive has narrowed, and some achievement gaps have narrowed and others have widened (Barton and Coley 2010; Dee and Jacob 2011; Lauen and Gaddis 2012). We are nowhere near NCLB's goal of "ensuring that all children have a fair, equal, and significant opportunity to obtain a high-quality education." The effects of standards-based reform remain uneven. Even though the policies did much to create new authorities and responsibilities for federal, state, district, and nongovernmental entities, the newly expanded scope and responsibility of governance did not build significant new capability to redress the problems Title I inherited: weak teacher education, disproportionate growth in administrative capabilities, a reliance on nongovernmental organizations for key instructional resources, and fundamentally unequal school finance.

One consequence of recent policies has been to tie various parts of the state more closely together and implicate them all in the failure to redress these inherited problems. The success of the recent policies, as with many social policies, depends on what the implementers—the people and agencies with the problems—do (Cohen and Moffitt 2009, 17–44). If many, many schools fail to improve, as happened with NCLB, doubts can bubble up about the policy, its sponsors, and implementers at all levels. Once again, we are in a period of doubt about whether Title I or public education "works." As before, these doubts about Title I pay little if any attention to the first-order condition of whether the program, its governance, and its environment were structured in a way that it could conceivably eliminate the achievement gaps. At no point in history has the governance of U.S. public education been organized to provide capability for serious, sustained instructional improvement that reaches across the expanse of American schooling.

School failure became epidemic in response to NCLB because the uneven development of U.S. schooling left very large areas of weak capability at the heart of the enterprise. IASA and NCLB depended on the capability of schools and systems to respond effectively to pressure for instructional improvement, but the governance arrangements that Title I inherited meant not only that most schools and systems did not have the wherewithal to respond effectively, but also that neither the federal nor state governments could mobilize the resources to build the missing local capability. The new policies drew the layers of the federal system in education closer together, but they did not undo the inherited weaknesses (for more on state level capability problems manifest at the beginning of NCLB's implementation, see Manna 2010). The collision between ambitious policies and the weak instructional capability created something of a crisis in education policy: the ambitious federal initiatives that culminated in NCLB became politically toxic, and something had to be done.

Something was done, and policy did change, in several directions more or less at once. The Common Core State Standards Initiative (CCSSI) shifted much of the action in reform away from the federal government to the states, and the Obama administration's use of waivers to ease several NCLB requirements that cause widespread and contagious failure slowed the bad news about school failure. The Race to the

Top program, funded with monies from the American Recovery and Reinvestment Act of 2009, revised reform relationships from state compliance to contracts in individual states that promised to undertake sweeping reforms in return for unprecedented federal financial assistance. These measures did shift attention away from Washington to the states, and away from a one-size-fits-all federal policy, though aspects of federal policy did encourage states to adopt the Common Core. They also helped ease the crisis of perceived school failures that implicated policy in those failures. These and other changes swirled together over the past decade to produce significant changes in education governance, especially governance connected to accountability. ESEA remains the most important federal K–12 education program because it offers support to so many schools and school systems, and because it expresses a by now long-standing federal commitment to improved schooling for disadvantaged students. Hence it is unlikely to vanish from the scene. At the same time, little evidence suggests that standards-based reform now written into ESEA had much success in dramatically improving student achievement. The chief problems that Title I inherited remain, and others have emerged.

What Might Be Done to Protect and Extend the Legacy of ESEA?

The question is presumptuous, the future being quite uncertain and our ability to forecast being weak. We cannot begin an answer without stipulating several points. One, which seems reasonably likely, is that the formula grant portion of ESEA Title I will remain roughly in its present form. Another, which may be somewhat less likely, depending on the political composition of the federal legislature and the presidency, is that standards-based reform will remain stitched into the ESEA; we assume that it will remain, but it may not. A third, which seems even less likely, is that most states will try to aggressively implement the CCSSI version of standards-based reform.

We also stipulate that four problems will persist. One is that education policy is suspended between the ambitions of standards-based reform and persistently uneven capabilities to develop instructional capability. The Common Core, which attempts to provide some elements of state support for instructional improvement through ambitious standards and assessments, combines political initiative and ingenuity with the most serious work on standards that the United States has yet seen. But the states that signed on to the CCSSI did so without much evidence that they understood how difficult it would be to implement much more demanding academic standards, or the capabilities that doing so would require. What standards-based reform means in practice continues to depend very much on the context in which it is implemented.

A second and related problem also has its roots in the development of educational governance. Both the Common Core and Title I of the ESEA aim to reduce inequality of educational outcomes, yet both are overlaid on patterns of unequal interstate, intrastate, and intra-district allocation of educational resources. We can discern no signs of a serious effort to deal with any of these resource inequalities and related structural problems. Hence another question for the developing egalitarian legacy of ESEA is how the states and the nation deal with the underlying unequal structure of educational resource allocation as they press to make school outcomes more equal.

A third and related problem is the growing income-achievement gap, as more advantaged Americans invest more aggressively in their children's schooling, while investment for most children has not kept commensurate pace (Reardon 2011, 91–115). When, in the 1980s, Title I's goal was shifted toward reducing the achievement gap it expressed the idea that federal policy could enable schools to overcome inequalities that the society and economy visited upon children. The IASA and NCLB have had several constructive effects, including greater attention to inequality in education. But the growing income-achievement gap reveals that the society and economy are making that task much more difficult. Moreover, U.S. social and economic policies do not aggressively attack either poverty in particular or social and economic inequality in general. Compounding problems of income inequality and weak U.S. social and economic policy is the growing racial and ethnic resegregation of schools following districts' release from court-ordered desegregation (Reardon et al. 2012). ESEA Title I seeks to solve educational problems that arise in good part outside the schools (Downey, von Hippel, and Broh 2004, 613–35), and it does so with only modest assistance from social and economic policy.

A fourth problem is that, unlike the civil rights legislation of the mid 1960s, standards-based reform is not the expression of a social and political movement with broad and active popular support that has political clout. This reform is instead supported by government officials, by advocacy groups that lack mobilized mass membership (for more on the education advocacy organizations that lack a membership base, see Manna and Moffitt 2014), and by some elected officials and academics. It has unsteady support and opposition among organized teachers. Because it lacks deep roots, the reform and its possible legacy are politically fragile and vulnerable. Standards-based reform remains the frame of federal and state education policy, but it is not clear how it will fare as the states decide whether to persist with the CCSSI,[12] as those that do persist decide how aggressively to implement the Common Core, or, for that matter, in the newly Republican federal legislature and in the fallout from the soon-to-arrive 2016 elections.

The question, for those who wish to protect and sustain the accumulated legacy of ESEA Title I, is whether there might be a strategy that holds some promise in the circumstances that we stipulate here. As Title I looks to its future, we see some hope in the past. The governance of U.S. public education was not designed to provide serious and sustained support for instructional improvement that reaches across the full expanse of American schooling. However, some smaller-scale systems have managed to navigate the four problems of capability, local, and state funding, growing inequality, and no mass movement; have provided serious and sustained support for instructional improvement; could not have existed without Title I funds and standards based reform ideas and accountability; have posted some noteworthy results; and have done so in traditional public schools in high-poverty areas. These are remarkable accomplishments. Moreover, they have appeared across different organizational forms, in some traditional public schools and in some charter networks.[13] Unlike the ideas expressed in Progressive-era policies and many current reforms, which give primacy to organizational design (hierarchical or site-based) or to mechanisms of accountability (market or government), recent successful approaches to instructional improvement focus on building systems that are designed to improve teaching and learning. Organizational design and accountability mechanisms are secondary to the first-order condition of sustained support for instructional improvement. Put differently, these instructional improvement approaches started with the intention to improve instruction, and sought to build organizations to enable that support, rather than to expect instructional improvement to emerge from organizational design or accountability (Correnti and Rowan 2007, 298–338; Cohen et al. 2014; Peurach 2011).

Our suggestions are far from comprehensive, but we see real promise in efforts to invent and adapt nongovernmental organizations that could pioneer approaches to implementing the Common Core and related state initiatives, and begin to build the capability for broader implementation. This proposal builds on a long tradition in the United States, in which nongovernmental organizations were invented and used to accomplish things that weak and fragmented government could not. Given the capability problems that we have already described, some such action seems essential. Yet, we emphasize that our proposal

---

12. Alaska, Indiana, Nebraska, Oklahoma, Texas, and Virginia have not adopted the Common Core. Minnesota has adopted only the ELA standards. See http://www.corestandards.org/standards-in-your-state/ (accessed November 11, 2014).

13. Two charter networks that have developed capability for instructional improvement are Aspire and Achievement First.

does not imply reducing governmental authority, responsibility, or capability. To the contrary, successful NGO service provision in public education depends on robust governmental engagement to fund, support, and oversee NGO implementation as well as to provide coverage and services that NGOs do not (Brass 2014; for a helpful overview of government and NGO relationships, see Cammett and MacLean 2014). Moreover, recall that such NGOs would not supplant existing governmental responsibilities and services, for chief elements of instructional improvement—common educational practices that are grounded in a common curriculum, sustained teacher education that focuses on helping teachers learn how to teach the curricula that students study, and oversight of the quality of practice (see Cohen and Moffitt 2009; Cohen et al. 2014)—are not presently provided by governments at any level in systematic fashion.

Precedents exist of nongovernmental organizations supporting instructional improvement from recent education policy in which ESEA Title I played a key role. Several cases in point are found in some of the Comprehensive School Reform Designs (CSRDs), especially Success for All (SFA) and America's Choice (AC). These were models of school improvement for high-poverty elementary schools. The designs were invented by private nonprofit organizations, and development and some continuing costs were funded mostly by private philanthropies. The designers contracted with public schools that chose to work with them, and provided extensive services and materials over the course of many years. Those services and materials were paid for chiefly by the schools' ESEA Title I funds, though schools' incentive to adopt also was encouraged by the Obey-Porter Amendment to ESEA Title I. Hence, Title I made it possible for the CSRD organizations to stay in business, and for many of the schools to improve instruction and student outcomes.

The materials included print accounts of the reform designs, examples of lessons, and implementation guides. Services included extensive assistance with implementation, continuing professional development, quality control and troubleshooting, and building networks or communities of practice with the schools. Several studies showed that students in schools that worked with these two design organizations learned much more than otherwise similar students in otherwise similar schools (Correnti and Rowan 2007; Cohen et al. 2014; Peurach 2011; Quint et al. 2014). Success for All and America's Choice were able to help the staff in many hundreds of high-poverty schools develop the capability that enabled them to accomplish things that ordinary Title I schools usually did not accomplish. Moreover, SFA and AC were able to navigate the four problems we identify. Although these designs faced serious implementation challenges, reviewed elsewhere, they nonetheless were able to mobilize the capability to support instructional improvement, despite the unequal distribution of resources facing schools, despite growing income inequality, despite the absence of more comprehensive and supportive U.S. social and economic policy, and despite the lack of a broad social movement supporting its efforts (Cohen et al. 2014; Peurach 2011). It seems likely that these interventions could have accomplished a good deal more had any of these inherited problems been addressed in a significant way.

Although looking to these features of the past gives us hope for the future, several extraordinary circumstances coalesced to enable these two CSRDs. These include the creation of the New American Schools Development Corporation in 1991 that poured $130 million into public-private partnerships to develop comprehensive school reform designs; ESEA's shift toward supporting schoolwide improvement which allowed schools to use their Title I's allotments for comprehensive school reform designs; the emergence of standards based accountability promoted through some state initiatives as well as nationally through IASA and NCLB; and the Obey-Porter amendments from 1997 that provided $50,000 per school competitive grants to support comprehensive school reform designs, to the tune of $150,000,000 overall. Should similarly extraordinary circumstances reappear in the form of federal funding and federal incentives to use CSRDs, states could authorize and regulate CSRD-type systems. States could set standards for such systems, subsidize their operation, regulate the quality of their work, and offer schools and systems incentives to participate. Were they to take such steps, states would expand the public-private boundary space currently occupied by test and text designers and a variety of education related professional associations. With careful attention to design, regulation, and funding, these could help states and localities develop the capability that could enable broader effective implementation of the Common Core and related state initiatives. They would be no panacea, of course, and would open up some significant problems.

One would be the lack of knowledge needed to design such systems, to inform implementation, and to regulate them. Were states to take our proposal seriously, they would need to invent ways to generate knowledge of several sorts: evidence on the learning and unlearning needed for progress toward implementation; document and explain success and failure in the implementation of the Common Core and related initiatives; document the relative effectiveness of a range of systems in creating opportunities for teachers and managers to learn; and organize a program of study that could keep attention focused on patterns of educational inequality.

Sustained political support presents another problem, one that commonly confronts nongovernmental service provision (Cammett and MacLean 2014; Allard 2009, 2014). In this period of fiscal austerity and political deadlock over federal funding, it is difficult to imagine how political support for such funds may emerge. This problem is exacerbated by political ambivalence on both the Left and the Right toward instructional improvement efforts: both sides express preferences for other policy approaches (markets on the Right, or tougher regulation in some regions of the Left, and less regulation in other regions). Related political challenges arise from two very different approaches to improvement: evaluating teachers in terms of their students' test scores, and school turnaround that often requires eliminating a poorly performing school's teaching force and replacing it with a new set of teachers. These actions express the view that schools could be improved by regulating teachers through additional accountability measures or by eliminating poorly performing teachers. These are very different from direct efforts to improve instruction of the sort we described earlier. Time, investment, and opportunities to learn add related political challenges, for instructional improvement does not appear in one test cycle or election cycle. It requires sustained support, commitment to the idea of students as sense-makers and thinkers, substantial resources, and patience. None of these is readily compatible with American politics.

Still other problems emerge at the level of coverage, another common problem for nongovernmental service provision (Cammett and MacLean 2014; Allard 2009, 2014). Success for All, for instance, is in operation in about a thousand schools and focuses primarily on reading. How could such instructional improvement become much more pervasive and extend to other subjects? What will happen in states, districts, and schools that do not choose to invest in instructional improvement? Moreover, as Patricia Gándara's article in this issue points out, serious instructional improvement has largely neglected English-language learners and children with special needs.

CONCLUSION

Title I's legacy is profound. It helped put improving the education of children who live in poverty on the national agenda, where it remains politically salient. Title I helped sweep schools, regardless of their student population's poverty levels, into the broader national standards-accountability movement. It has been a vehicle for liberal, conservative, bipartisan, public, and private reform agendas. Although resistance to some aspects of federal authority remains and may have intensified, Title I has developed durable constituencies and appetites for federal funds. Although Title I helped create a new politics of education and fashioned mechanisms for state development through several forms of accountability, these policies did much less to remedy most state and local systems' weak capability to design, manage, and improve instruction. That weakness is a serious threat to ESEA Title I's revised role as the key federal agent for standards based reform. Moreover, unlike the era that accompanied the passage of the original ESEA, the era of No Child Left Behind has been marked by rising social and economic inequality and a lack of a broad-based mass movement for improved schooling, with social and political clout.

We have focused on instructional capability because it is at the heart of Title I's new mission, and because what schools do matters, as evidence from studies of the CSRDs and studies of summer learning show. The same studies of summer and school year learning also show that inequality in U.S. society means that children from different social classes and racial groups arrive in schools with large achievement gaps already in place, and that when students are not in school, during the summer, those gaps grow. If the United States had more egalitarian social and economic policies, some of these gaps would likely decrease.

Such egalitarian policies seem quite unlikely at the moment, but evidence is persuasive that states and localities could do far more to support instructional improvement with the support of ESEA. Despite the inherited problems, some CSRDs worked with high-poverty schools to use Title I to build instructional capability and improve students' learning. Such creative use of ESEA would not resolve the deep problems that many public schools face, but it could improve schooling for many children and their teachers.

REFERENCES

Allard, Scott W. 2009. *Out of Reach: Place, Poverty, and the New American Welfare State*. New Haven, Conn.: Yale University Press.

———. 2014. "State Dollars, Non-State Provision: Local Nonprofit Welfare Provision in the United States." In *The Politics of Non-State Welfare*, edited by Melani Cammett and Lauren MacLean. Ithaca, N.Y.: Cornell University Press.

Baker, Bruce D. 2014. *America's Most Financially Disadvantaged School Districts and How They Got That Way*. Washington, D.C.: Center for American Progress.

Baker, Bruce D., and Sean Corcoran. 2012. *The Stealth Inequalities of School Funding: How State and Local School Finance Systems Perpetuate Inequitable Student Spending*. Washington, D.C.: Center for American Progress.

Baker, Bruce D., and Kevin G. Welner. 2010. "Premature Celebrations: The Persistence of Inter-District Funding Disparities." *Educational Policy Analysis Archives* 18(9): 1–30.

Balogh, Brian. 2009. *A Government Out of Sight: The Mystery of National Authority in Nineteenth-Century America*. New York: Cambridge University Press.

Barton, Paul E., and Richard J. Coley. 2010. *The Black-White Achievement Gap: When the Progress Stopped*. Princeton, N.J.: Educational Testing Service.

Brass, Jennifer N. 2014. "Blurring the Boundaries: NGO's, the State, and Service Provision in Kenya." In *The Politics of Non-State Welfare*, edited by Melani Cammett and Lauren MacLean. Ithaca, N.Y.: Cornell University Press.

Bureau of Vocational Information. 1924. *Training for the Professions and Allied Occupations*. New York, NY: Bureau of Vocational Information.

Cammett, Melani and Lauren M. MacLean. 2014. *The Politics of Non-State Social Welfare*. Ithaca, N.Y.: Cornell University Press.

Carter, Launor A. 1983. *A Study of Compensatory and Elementary Education: The Sustaining Effects Study*, final report. Santa Monica, Calif: Systems Development Corporation.

———. 1984. "The Sustaining Effects Study of Compensatory and Elementary Education." *Educational Researcher* 13(7)(August–September): 4–13.

Cohen, David K., and Susan L. Moffitt. 2009. *The Ordeal of Equality: Did Federal Regulation Fix the Schools?* Cambridge, Mass.: Harvard University Press.

Cohen, David K., Donald J. Peurach, Joshua L. Glazer, Karen E. Gates, and Simona Goldin. 2014. *Improvement by Design: The Promise of Better Schools*. Chicago: University of Chicago Press.

Coleman, James S. 1966. "Equal Schools or Equal Students." *The Public Interest* 4(1): 70–75.

Coleman, James S., et al. 1966. *Equality of Educational Opportunity*. Washington: Department of Health, Education, and Welfare.

Correnti, Rip, and Brian Rowan. 2007. "Opening Up The Black Box: Literacy Instruction in Schools Participating in Three Comprehensive School Reform Programs." *American Educational Research Journal* 44(2): 298–38.

Dee, Thomas S., and Brian Jacob. 2011. The Impact of No Child Left Behind on Student Achievement. *Journal of Policy Analysis and Management* 30(3): 418–46.

Downey, Douglas B., Paul T. von Hippel, and Beckett A. Broh. 2004. "Are Schools the Great Equalizer? Cognitive Inequality During the Summer Months and the School Year." *American Sociological Review* 79(5): 613–35.

Jennings, John F. 1985. "The Elementary and Secondary Education Act: The 1960s and 1970s." In *A Compilation of Papers on the Twentieth Anniversary of the Elementary and Secondary Education Act of 1965*. Subcommittee on Elementary and Secondary and Vocational Education, House of Representatives. Washington: Government Printing Office.

Jochim, Ashley, and Patrick Murphy. 2013. *The Capacity Challenge: What It Takes for State Education Agencies to Support School Improvement*. Seattle, Wash.: Center on Reinventing Public Education.

Lankford, Hamilton, Susanna Loeb, and James Wyckoff. 2002. "Teacher Sorting and the Plight of Urban Schools: A Descriptive Analysis." *Education Evaluation and Policy Analysis Spring*, 24(1): 37–62.

Lauen, Douglas Lee, and S. Michael Gaddis. 2012. "Shining and Light or Fumbling in the Dark? The Effects of NCLB's Subgroup-Specific Accountability on Student Achievement." *Educational Evaluation and Policy Analysis* 34(2): 185–208.

Mann, Horace. 1891. "Twelfth Annual Report to the Massachusetts State Board of Education, 1848." In *Life and Works of Horace Mann, Vol III*. Boston, Mass.: Lee and Shepard Publishers.

Manna, Paul. 2010. *Collision Course: Federal Education Policy Meets State and Local Realities*. Washington, D.C.: CQ Press.

Manna, Paul, and Susan Moffitt. 2014. "New Education Advocacy Organizations in the U.S. States: National Snapshot and a Case Study of Advance Illinois." Prepared for the Wallace Foundation. Available at: http://www.wallacefoundation.org/knowledge-center/school-leadership/state-policy/Pages/New-Education-Advocacy-Organizations-in-the-U.S.-States-National-Snapshot-and-a-Case-Study-of-Advance-Illinois.aspx (accessed July 31, 2015).

Moffitt, Susan L. 2014. *Making Policy Public: Participatory Bureaucracy in American Democracy*. New York: Cambridge University Press.

National Education Association. Committee on the Reorganization of Secondary Education. 1918. *Cardinal Principles of Secondary Education*, republished, by the Bureau of Education, Department of the Interior, Bulletin no. 35. Washington: Government Printing Office.

Novak, William J. 2008. "The Myth of the Weak American State." *American Historical Review* 113: 752–72.

Office of State Assessment. 1987. "History of Regents Examinations: 1865 to 1987." State of New York Education Department. Last modified August 22, 2012. Available at: http://www.p12.nysed.gov/assessment/hsgen/archive/rehistory.htm (accessed October 27, 2015).

Peurach, Donald J. 2011. *Seeing Complexity in Public Education*. New York: Oxford University Press.

Quint, Janet C., Rekha Balu, Micah DeLaurentis, Shelley Rappaport, Thomas J. Smith, Pei Zhu. 2014. *The Success for All Model of School Reform: Interim Findings from the Investing in Innovation (i3) Scale-Up*. New York: MDRC.

Reardon, Sean F. 2011. "The Widening Academic Achievement Gap Between the Rich and Poor: New Evidence and Possible Explanations." In *Whither Opportunity: Rising Inequality, Schools and Children's Life Chances*, edited by Greg J. Duncan and Richard J. Murnane. New York: Russell Sage Foundation.

Reardon, Sean F., Elena Tej Grewal, Demetra Kalogrides, and Erica Greenberg. 2012. "Brown Fades: The End of Court-Ordered School Desegregation and the Resegregation of America's Schools." *Journal of Policy Analysis and Management* 31(4): 876–904.

Rice, Joseph M. 1893. *The Public School System of the United States*. New York: The Century Co.

Roza, Marguerite. 2010. *Educational Economics: Where Do School Funds Go?* New York: Urban Institute Press.

Roza, Margerite, and Paul T. Hill. 2006. "How Can Anyone Say What's Adequate if Nobody Knows How Money Is Spent?" In *Courting Failure*, edited by Eric Hanushek. Stanford, Calif.: Hoover Press.

Skocpol, Theda. 1992. *Protecting Soldiers and Mothers: The Political Origins of Social Policy in the United States*. Cambridge, Mass.: Belknap/Harvard University Press.

State Department of Education. 1912. *Annual Report of the Education Department for the School Year Ending 1911*. Albany: University of the State of New York.

———. 1924. *Twentieth Annual Report of the Education Department*. Albany: University of the State of New York.

———. 1925. *Twenty-First Annual Report of the Education Department for the School Year Ending July 31, 1924*. Albany: University of the State of New York.

———. 1936. *Thirty-First Annual Report of the Education Department for the School Year Ending June 30, 1934*, vol. 1. Albany: University of the State of New York.

State of New York Department of Public Instruction. 1903. "Announcement of Summer Institutes for 1903." No publication information available. Chautauqua Institution Archives, C.L.S.C. Announcements 1895–1903.

State of New York. 1905. *First Annual Report of the Education Department for the School Year Ending July 31, 1904*. Albany: New York State Education Department.

State of New York Education Department. 1917. *Agencies Employed in Training Teachers for the Public Schools of the State Annual Report 1915*, vol. 2. Albany: University of the State of New York.

Steffes, Tracy L. 2012. *School, Society & State: A New Education to Govern Modern America, 1890–1940*. Chicago: University of Chicago Press.